DISCARDING THE ASYLUM

From Child Rescue to the
Welfare State in
English-Canada
(1800-1950)

Patricia T. Rooke
R.L. Schnell

UNIVERSITY
PRESS OF
AMERICA

LANHAM • NEW YORK • LONDON

Copyright © 1983 by

University Press of America,™ Inc.

4720 Boston Way
Lanham, MD 20706

3 Henrietta Street
London WC2E 8LU England

Library of Congress Cataloging in Publication Data

Rooke, Patricia T.
    Discarding the asylum.

    Includes bibliographical references and index.
    1. Child welfare–Canada–History. 2. Asylums–
Canada–History. 3. Orphanages–Canada–History. 4. Poor–
Canada–History. I. Schnell, Rodolph Leslie. II. Title.
HV875.7.C2R66 1983   362.7'0971   83–10569
ISBN 0–8191–3304–3
ISBN 0–8191–3305–1 (pbk.)

To those who shared our childhoods in the slums of Melbourne and Detroit.

We acknowledge their struggles to keep their children with them and their working-class family life intact through penury, desertion, death, illness, strikes, depression, and unemployment just as we recall those who failed to do so. It is to all these parents and children as well as those who have worked to "make the way more comfortable" for generations of dependent children that we dedicate this book.

iv

acknowledgements

Throughout the five year period during which we conducted research in Canada and Great Britain and tentatively began to present and publish our initial findings, the following granting agencies have been invaluable and the following persons have been helpful, interested and encouraging.

We wish to acknowledge the University of Calgary for a sabbatical leave (1978-79) and the Social Sciences and Humanities Research Council of Canada for a leave fellowship (1979) that made our initial research in Great Britain and Canada possible and a SSHRCC research grant (1979-81) that enabled us to continue our work. The University of Calgary Research Services Office has twice (1979 and 1980) provided funds to complete specific parts of the research. The Rockefeller Foundation, through its generous "Scholars-in-Residence" Program, gave us a month of intensive work at its Bellagio Center on Lake Como in May-June 1982. Finally, the award of a Killam Resident Fellowship, January-April 1983, by the University of Calgary has provided the uninterrupted time needed for the final revisions.

Madame Francoise Houle, Public Archives Canada, who encouraged us to request the processing of the Charlotte Whitton Papers, a source that has given an entirely different perspective to our work, deserves our warmest appreciation. Doug Whyte, also of the PAC, is thanked for his generous assistance in sharing his own work connected with the Immigration Branch Records and sources for the British juvenile immigration movement with us.

We have enjoyed the assistance of archivists and librarians in Great Britain and Canada. Some, such as Mr. F. Burnham Gill of the United Church Archives, St. John's, rescued us in moments of despair by making available the records essential to this study. Our debt to them and the individuals, institutions, and agencies that created the records and papers are amply demonstrated in our notes.

We owe a special debt to Neil Sutherland, not only because of his pioneering work in Canadian childhood history and generosity of his friendship and collegiality, but because of his recognition as early as 1977 at the Learned Societies meeting in Fredericton that our work was worthwhile.

We extend our warm gratitude for the assistance given in the completion of the first papers that formed the basis for the present study and of the first draft and the final preparation of this manuscript:

Noreen Monroe Guzie's careful calligraphy and artistic sense turned two scholars' work of love into a work of aesthetic pleasure.

Anne Marie Main, who has been our typist from the beginning of this study as well as earlier ones on American student organizations and British West Indian slavery and who has seen a book grown out of many papers, patiently bore with difficult handwriting and impossibly messy drafts, with numerous alterations and inserts, to produce the first draft.

Janis Dawson, who helpfully dropped in from her doctoral program at the University of Alberta, served as our copy editor and indexer. She undertook the most tedious of tasks associated with turning a manuscript into a book and met impossible deadlines with scrupulousness, cheerfulness, and critical acumen.

Finally, Shaun Lawson worked long and often hectic hours on the final draft. Her efforts - well beyond the call of duty - and meticulous typing gave our manuscript its final form. Shaun's generosity with her time and genuine support of our work will not be forgotten.

contents

illustrations

Although concerned about the use of photographs, that new version of "whig" history with its emphasis on the recent and an assumption of progress, we concluded that a proper selection of institutions would demonstrate two aspects emphasized in the book. First, as most orphanages no longer exist, their architecture as with any other historical source can be examined and interpreted. Second, the fact that institutional records contain surprisingly few pictures of the inmates themselves is an eloquent statement of the major concern of institution builders - that children may come and go but that the moral and spatial manifestation of the "asylum" and "child-rescue" remained. Unfortunately for the founders of these institutions, they were never able to embody their visions in grand edifices such as established by their counterparts in Great Britain.

Childhood as Ideology   1

> But the children began
> To be sorely weary
> And cried unto Him
> That loveth pilgrims
> To make the Way more Comfortable.
>
> <u>The Pilgrims' Progress.</u>

For those born and reared in 'regular' family life, the empathetic imagination required to identify with the thousands of past orphaned, abandoned, neglected and dependent children, must fall short at the enormity of such a task. Recent psychological theory suggests that even the most impoverished and unsupportive family life is better than institutional life or the caprices of constant fostering experiences. To imagine the trials, the pains, the lonelinesses of those youthful past lives we classify and objectify as "dependent children," to understand either their environmental or psychosociological deficits is sobering.

Unavoidably we feel compassion for such children and profound admiration for those who somehow transcended the hardships and grew into wholesome, productive, and even loving individuals. Once again we see in them testimony to the resilience of the human spirit. It is impossible not to feel the tragedy of those past lives, snuffed out in infancy in foundling homes or wasted away with that which we now realize was "maternal deprivation" despite the best will in the world of their caretakers to keep them alive; or not to feel for the thousands of youngsters who succumbed to the impartial onslaughts of "serial contamination" that raged through their institutions; or to fail to blush for shame at the cynicism of adults who "adopted" children out and into families, using this means as a shoddy pretext for their exploitation while simultaneously denying them the usual familial guarantees of inheritance or identification. We must also feel discomfort at the practices of blatantly indenturing dependent youths and growing girls into menial tasks which would keep them forever part of the "lower orders." Moreover it would be a grave injustice to overlook the desperation of parents, unable to cope emotionally and economically with their numerous offspring or the compulsion that led them to abandon, foster or give over into custodial care, the children they may have loved much or those they were unable to love at all. The wasting away and the indifferent discarding of young human lives due to poverty and other socio-psychological constraints must cast a pall over our history.

In his bold and creative Centuries of Childhood, Philippe Ariès was the first to illumine the tenuousness and fragility of past childhoods and scrupulously trace the significance of the shift in sensibility that had occurred within bourgeois families toward their children by the end of the eighteenth century. It is necessary, however, to remember that by that time the transition of sensibility was neither universal nor uniform in Western society and nowhere is this discrepancy more glaring than in the case of dependent and neglected children. The precariousness of their existences had scarcely lessened in British North America until well into the nineteenth century. Some salutary reminders of this fact immediately come to mind as in the case of a young girl immigrant, just one of the 80,000 or so like her who constituted the juvenile immigration movement from Britain to Canada from 1869 to 1930. In later life she remained bitterly disconsolate believing that "no one" had ever wanted her. Again we recall the sad comment in the daily journal of the Halifax Orphan Asylum that "our little Stewy," the "pet of the household," had silently passed away during the night. We also remember the incident of several tiny infants wrapped in their cheap cotton shrouds, victims of a measles epidemic in a Nova Scotia Infants' Home, being inconspicuously carried to their burial in the city hearse especially borrowed for the occasion, unmourned and anonymous.[1]

This book cannot recreate the flesh and blood of these young lives with all the tenderness, empathy, and quickening they deserve, for the mass of dependent children are destined to remain mute and faceless - Malthusian ghosts crying in a wasteland of destitution - the sports of social and natural caprice. William Wordsworth's words in "The Excursion" (Pt. VI) still plead their cause:

> Can hope look forward to a manhood raised
>   On such foundations?
> "Hope is none for him!"
>   The pale recluse indignantly exclaimed,
> "And tens of thousands suffer wrongs as deep."

> At this day
>   Who shall enumerate the crazy huts
> And tottering hovels, whence do issue forth,
>   A Ragged Offspring?

Given the impossibility of the task to "enumerate" the desperate biographies of British North America's and then Canada's "ragged offspring," what then can this book do even as it attempts to recreate a fragment of their life history for a century and a half? Four points are worth stressing in relation to our own attempt at doing just this.

First, in our attempt to cover a broad historical period to establish a national perspective we shall examine dependent child life and not that of the general population. Throughout, our understanding of "dependent" children as distinct from the psychological or conceptual dimensions of the term will include those children living outside their natural family setting, and excluding those generally identified as "delinquent." This study does not emphasize this latter category except by way of contrast and in instances when the two categories were often confused. Given the scope of such a topic as juvenile delinquency in Canada, this exclusion has been deliberate for it deserves a study of its own and as part of an already massive topic could not have been subjected to the appropriate rigorous analysis. There awaits for some enterprising scholar an abundance of data and a variety of approaches to this particular aspect of childhood history. A score or so of American books reminds us

3

that it is a topic that can tolerate a variety of approaches and which raises a multitude of critical questions regarding attitudes to "deviant" youngsters and the organization of western society itself.2

Second, there are several points of disagreement with the existing work that has been done on Canadian child life. A major problem is the tendency to narrowly define the topic or to limit it chronologically. For example Joy Parr, by not examining the juvenile immigration movement in the 1920s, failed to understand the role played by the Canadian Council on Child Welfare and Charlotte Whitton or to appreciate the significance of that campaign in Canadian social welfare reform. Terrence Morrison's study of late nineteenth century Ontario had such a narrow time frame and regional focus that it seems dropped into the middle of a series of events without being tied to earlier and later reforms. The study of J. J. Kelso by Andrew Jones and Leonard Rutman suffers from a failure to deal adequately with the materials from Scott or Whitton and others who viewed Kelso and his role in child and family welfare in Ontario and in Canada with some dismay. Finally, the invaluable work of Neil Sutherland who first posited the idea of a twentieth century "consensus" on childhood - an argument which helped us focus our own study - was not extended far enough to establish the institutional and political base for that consensus which had not occurred until the 1940s. There is also a tendency in those studies which cover the period of the establishment and growth of the Children's Aid Society model in Ontario and elsewhere to assume that the theory and discussion around the idea of the CAS were in fact reflected in actual practice. Our own work and the current controversy surrounding the CAS suggest that a thorough study of the operation of the CAS model would contribute greatly to an understanding of social reform and social welfare in Canada.3

With regard to matters of historical interpretation it should be noted that there have been two major traditions - that is, whig and social control. The tendency of whig historians is to identify every change and innovation as a sign of human progress and social uplift and to see social

4

reformers as fundamentally heroes and their opponents as villains. But in the long run the whole story is one of success and betterment. The social control theorists on the other hand have viewed change and innovation as primarily the coercive actions of dominant classes to retain spheres of power and expand them. Unlike the whigs the social control theorists see history as a story of self interest and class betrayal. We cannot accept either one of these views as an adequate interpretation of historical action and actors. In a general sense social control refers to the ability of a society to educate and train its members so that they may participate in a human community without the necessity of force being exerted on them; in a more limited sense, social control also means the efforts of society to regulate what are perceived to be deviant members, for example, delinquents. It is obvious that in our study the first meaning of social control pertains. The more limited meaning is only partially applicable since most of the children concerned were not identified as deviant and one of the outcomes of child rescue was to separate dependent children from delinquent or feebleminded ones. Not being whigs we have not found the history of charity organizations, professionalism and scientific social work as having unequivocal beneficial results. It is clear to us that those developments have created problems as well as solving some. In some cases the new problems seem more difficult to resolve than the ones put to rest. Even those cases in which positive benefits accrued to children and youth we notice the self-interest and righteousness of many of the reformers.4

It is difficult for us to assume either interpretative stance since history is simply too complex for such reductionist perspectives. Consequently, the readers will find that the dilemmas and paradoxes of child rescue and social reform are reflected in our interpretation of these events and that many of the conflicts and contradictions are not readily resolved. The case that readily comes to mind as demonstrating these problems is the British Juvenile Immigration Movement, fully discussed in chapters five and six. Without going into the particulars of the movement one aspect involving the developing Canadian child

welfare network tells us much about the
contradictions in human nature. The newly organized
Canadian Council on Child Welfare under Charlotte
Whitton's leadership opposed the movement on grounds
that it violated the principles of child welfare in
that it did not provide for the adequate protection,
supervision and welfare of the young immigrants.
Such a claim obviously was meant to imply a
sensitivity about child life as against the
calloused disregard for it by the British societies
and their Canadian supporters. However, in their
efforts to protect the children from exploitation
and separation from their families and homeland,
Whitton and her colleagues engaged in a campaign of
vilification not simply against the societies but
against the children themselves. It is difficult to
understand how such a campaign which went against
the sentiment and logic of child rescue could be
justified by contemporaries or by historians
studying those events. It is a case like this in
which one sees the web of motives, rationalizations
and ambiguities of human life. The real losers in
the campaign had to be the children because they
were the ones who bore the stigma of being
unacceptable immigrants. On another level, the
campaign was a crucial element in the professionalization of Canadian child welfare in that the
immigration societies served as proxies for Canadian
societies and institutions whose standards of
performance were no better.

At this point, we should say something about
juvenile delinquency in relation to the two major
interpretations. It is clear to us that delinquency
in whatever form society deals with it is in fact an
exercise of social control whether we are talking
about prevention, treatment, or incarceration, for
the object is to change behavior and to force
individuals to conform to social norms expressed by
legal codes. However, with dependent children the
interest is in socializing and training them so that
they acquire those particular attitudes and values
that will enable them to function in their society.
In that sense it is, relatively speaking, the same
kind of initiation into society and its ways that
ordinary parents extend to their children. The work
with dependent children is offered not as a matter
of reformation as with delinquents or as a matter of

repression and control as with defective children but as a formation of character and social behavior.

Third, our sources have been taken from predominantly Protestant or public institutions, agencies, and orphanages. Although a thorough examination of Catholic institutions, like juvenile delinquency, is imperative, for similar reasons it cannot be taken up in this volume. The Catholic contribution to child welfare in English-Canada, necessary to provide a comprehensive sequel and a balance to this volume, has not yet been attempted.

Fourth, we must provide a framework to focus, organize, and interpret the variety and quantity of sources and data encountered during our research into dependent child life. The data base is taken from a score or so of children's homes across the country in the form of minutes, correspondence, annual reports and miscellaneous items, several substantial collections of individuals involved in Canadian child welfare such as J. J. Kelso, W. L. Scott, and Charlotte Whitton, and of agencies such as the Canadian Welfare Council or the Montreal Society for the Protection of Women and Children. The records of child rescue societies, juvenile emigration homes, charity organization societies, and poor law unions at the Public Record Office, all in Great Britain, have been examined as well as many tracts, treatises and pamphlets from the British Library and city libraries or archives of London, Birmingham, Bristol, Liverpool, Manchester, and Glasgow, and the National Library of Ireland, Dublin. Finally the Immigration Branch records relating to juvenile immigration at the Public Archives of Canada along with specific and relevant collection from provincial and private archives in all provinces have been used. Since it was virtually impossible to provide a detailed history of developments in individual colonies or provinces, we have written an analytic and interpretive history of dependent child life. Much of our data simply represents illustrative case studies of particular aspects that we have emphasized and in no sense are comprehensive in scope.

Without a conceptual framework this variety of sources threatened to remain unmanageable, discrete, fragmented and nebulous. Our framework must go back once again to its source - the original exploration of Philippe Ariès into unchartered territory; therefore, it is with his history of childhood that we begin. It is his interpretation that we will analyze and extend beyond the early nineteenth century European middle class experience where he prematurely finished his study, and into the late nineteenth century British North American context.

Ariès posited a relationship between the "discovery" of childhood and institutional developments in western society, a position he supports with various kinds of evidence and which carries with it a certain degree of plausibility. By terminating his study with the bourgeois family of the early nineteenth century he in effect challenged other historians to continue the exploration and the explication of this relationship to different classes and into the nineteenth and twentieth centuries. Although not explicitly or mechanistically stated, the "concept of childhood," which evolved out of the medieval milieu to become a depository of sentiment in the bourgeois family of later centuries, can be defined according to the four major criteria of dependence, protection, segregation and delayed responsibilities. Moreover it becomes clear through a closer examination of the criteria that childhood is synonymous with "child rescue." This analytical breakdown has been carefully explicated by one of the authors.5

The endeavors to protect children from both physical dangers and moral contamination, along with the concomitant urge to segregate them from these perceived vicious influences and the rigors of adult life, led to the necessity of extending their period of dependence. The occurrence of such separation and protection along with dependence resulted logically in an increasing delayal of responsibilities. As such, solicitude toward children transformed from the unusual to the usual and from the extraordinary to the common-place with social perception shaping social reality. The objects of such solicitude, primarily middle class children, were assiduously cultivated and deliberately trained. In turn they became categorized as a special class with special needs. This psychological insight created particular precepts, attitudes, and techniques of child rearing which in effect increased the segregation of children as a special class from adult members of society and alienated them from their milieu. Thus child rearing and the socialization of the young members of society became more self-conscious, more systematic and consequently created new and special needs. The systemization of the psychology of childhood in the literary rather than the oral tradition in the West can be traced back to the humanist thinkers who both reflected the shifts that were already occurring in relation to the changing social structures and helped shape new perceptions.

It is essential to recall that organization of concepts such as "childhood" are the means by which our social world is constructed. To borrow from Erik Erikson, such concepts constitute an ideology. They provide us with a world image that makes our lives and actions reasonable and have point. Concepts define our world, our reality, and our morality. The concept of childhood has defined for us our perceptions and consequently, treatment of children.6

Until we grasp the nature of the triumph of the "discovery" of childhood, we will underestimate its explanatory power. What Ariès described in great detail is not merely a social transformation in all its complexity but more importantly the victory of a concept that radically changed the mentality of Western society. Childhood and adolescence made progress slowly and found the most rapid assimilation among the middle classes in western nations. Once the concept of childhood has been assimilated, the socially conscious among the middle classes saw their social reality as including childhood. With childhood as a normal part of society, with childhood as a moral requirement, social reformers were confronted with an anomaly within their social world, namely that some children either rejected or were denied a childhood.

We can, thus, understand the campaigns of "child saving" as the working out of the middle class mentality that had come to see childhood as an essential and normative aspect of its world image. The world of the middle class reformers demanded that every child have a "childhood." The social groups still without a childhood were variously identified as the poor, the lower orders, the

"dangerous and perishing" classes, the common
people, and the dependent. Their children were
still largely independent, not segregated, exposed
to drink, crime, neglect, and hard labor, and made
to assume responsibilities early. If these children
were to be made "normal," that is, to conform to a
true position of childhood, then their conditions of
life had to be radically altered. For those
children without parents or with unfit parents, the
reformers created refuges, asylums, and orphanages
and later on adoption and fostering. For those
children deemed guilty of or prone to activities
seen as unfit for children they established
reformatories, the term "delinquent," and juvenile
courts and laws. For normal children with parents,
the common schools became the means of including ALL
children in the middle class concept of childhood.
In this way did the middle class mentality manifest
itself in social reality.

Thus, in rescuing children from adult society
and in ensuring that children have a childhood, the
proponents of childhood effected a series of
revolutions in Western society. Dependence meant
that children must not only be withdrawn from adult
society, from an early participation into meaningful
labour, but that the weaknesses of children must be
emphasized and made into absolute, although
temporary, disabilities. In brief, dependence
demanded the notion of childish incompetence. The
duties and responsibilities of life had to be
portrayed as particularly onerous and damaging to
children - the final separation of children from the
socially useful. Since children were to be rescued
from the evils of adult society, they must be the
objects of special legislation and regulations and
specialized institutions that would protect them.
This protection required that children be segregated
in order both to control the contacts between them
and unauthorized, therefore undesirable, adults and
to allow for the guarded discipline so essential to
ensure their ultimate "rescue."

We have found that the analytical breakdown of
the concept of childhood into the criteria of
dependence, separation, protection and delayed
responsibilities has considerable heuristic value.
The criteria might be seen as the heuristic mortar
that gives form to the convolutions and lateral

10

detours of a sophisticated and demanding interpretation. Just as the conceptual mortar aids students of childhood history in putting together all the pieces of Ariès interpretation, it will assist us in the following chapters to organize the evidence, the ideas, and the institutional expressions we shall discuss. Because of the subtlety and complexity involved in coming to grips with a century and a half of evolving attitudes and transforming institutional patterns, a strictly chronological ordering of phenomena or events would prove limiting and mechanistic, as well as leading readers and authors into the seductive terrains of whig history - of heroes and villains, of progress and inevitability. To avoid this our endeavor will be chronological inasmuch as it will begin at the early part of the nineteenth century and end at the mid-twentieth. Between these two points we shall weave in and out, back and forth, to fill in a tapestry whose richness cannot be described in unilinear fashion.

The shaping of Canada's dependent childhood experience was neither vertical nor one dimensional. New forms, shifting patterns, transforming sentiments, fresh experiments occurred simultaneously and unfolded alongside with old ones; some had early but short lived starts, others appeared gradually or rapidly as the case may be. For example, although charity organization was being discussed and tried in Halifax as early as 1830, it was not really until 1890 that its strength began to be felt; and while fostering was becoming popular, congregate systems were being founded. In other words, different forms co-existed, some of which conflicted while others did not.

The criteria of childhood are not, of course, inflexible categories artificially imposed on historical data. Notions of protection, segrega-tion, and dependence, for example, vary both tempor-ally and socially. Shifting psychological and theological views have significantly altered the understanding of what was desirable and possible in human reformation. Sociological and psychological studies have raised questions about the efficacy of conventional means of treating dependency, pauperism, and delinquency. Consequently, the four

11

criteria will be examined as transforming and
transformed aspects of child life.

Once the four criteria are grasped and their
interdependence established then it becomes clear
that rescue which is synonymous with childhood, has
a dual and opposite component - that of restraint.
In short, while rescuing children psychologically
from the trials of adult preoccupations and while
rescuing children physically from the most strenuous
of social conditions - labor and subsistence - the
concept of childhood simultaneously has fostered a
control over them. A new social category (that is,
class of people) was created and as an aggregate
group it is less difficult to socialize systematically so that expectations regarding children as
adult members of their society were more realizable.
During the nineteenth and twentieth centuries
childhood and citizenship became inexorably linked
as the criteria were gradually imbedded into the
legal and political structures of western industrial
nations.

The typology of childhood, consisting of rescue
and restraint, liberation and control, solicitude
and surveillance, included the obvious advantages
and humanitarian aspects of protection and delayed
responsibilities with the constraints of separation
and dependence. For very young children, the
constraints were less problematic than in the case
of adolescents, for whom they have produced unhappy
side effects. We witness these in the atmosphere of
disaffection generated in groups of adolescent
cohorts, the sense of social uselessness that seems
to pervade their activities and the anomie that
represents so much to their lives and is almost
palpable in their schools.

Historians of family and child life have often
argued that the modern concept of childhood has
grown out of the bourgeois family. Indeed, one of
the authors postulated in 1979 that it was the
middle classes that were the first to accept these
concepts of childhood and adolescence as functional
in their lives and to later campaign for a universal
application of the concepts to all children. It was
also argued that childhood became an ideology as it
was assimilated by all socially respectable classes.
Consequently, childhood no longer depended on

bourgeois values or sentiment. This transformation is amply demonstrated by the central place of child welfare and sentiment in the planning and activities of states such as China, Cuba, and the Soviet Union whose political ideas are quite dissimilar from those of the United States and France. The universal nature of childhood sentiment and services suggests that it no longer depends on a version of the middle class family. Nations that greatly restrict or even work against the bourgeois family ideal have most of the rhetoric and services.7

Like formal education, childhood is a perceived good that cuts across ideology and politics. Good capitalists and communists alike agree on the values of childhood and many programs are universally desired. Although the roots of childhood are probably distinctive within the history of each nation, the consequences are remarkably and depressingly uniform. Despite different economic systems and aims, despite the multiplication of services and programs specifically addressing the needs of children and youth, despite the same glowing optimism in the natural goodness of children, and despite the input into the making of good citizens for whatever state, a lack of innovation and creativity regarding problems of child life and youth culture cannot help but continue given the similarity of assumptions and practices. This is depressing because these problems provoke uncertainty and even anxiety. If we are correct in concluding the relative sameness of approach and attitude (only the amount of money and organized adult effort put in the endeavor differ) then childhood within modern industrial states is independent of political and economic systems and truly does function as, and have the power of, an ideology.

The ideology of the nineteenth century child savers, whose roots can be discerned in the humanist tradition and the emerging class consciousness of the post-reformation, was made possible by two major shifts in western sensibility. The first is the shift that represents the discovery of childhood itself - the belief that "a redeemed childhood means a redeemed generation" as a Canadian child saver, the Reverend W. H. Sedgewick of the London Children's Aid Society in Ontario would say. He was merely reiterating the belief that had evolved over several centuries and had become common wisdom when applied to the mass of children by the nineteenth century.

> The work of childsaving is one of the
> grandest movements of our time - caring
> for little ones, who through stress of
> circumstances, misfortune or vice, are
> thrown into the streets. It is not
> charity but simply a matter of common
> justice to those, who through no fault
> of their own, are the victims of a bad
> environment, example, and training.
> Childhood is a compact of untold
> possibilities. A neglected childhood
> is almost a sure prophecy of a miserable
> or hurtful life. A redeemed childhood
> means a redeemed generation.8

By the nineteenth century, childhood, as with society generally, was viewed optimistically, and a society of adult members who had been raised carefully and "progressively" would be perceived as the realization of, if not utopian fancies, then reasonable expectations and rational experiments in child rearing and citizen-making.

The second major shift in Western sensibility which contributed much to the ideology of the child savers was also born out of the remarkable optimism of the intellectual and theological ferment of the preceding century so ably analyzed by Peter Gay. The belief in progress and in man's improvability, if not perfectability, put to rest the Calvinistically grounded assumptions of a society resistant to "cure." Enlightenment thought and the breakthrough facilitated by the adoption of Arminian theological beliefs resulted in an urge to "rescue" individuals and whole societies. Reformers, evangelical and, later, progressive, fairly bulldozed their way with unflagging zeal into "useful" activities and a multitude of "good works." If all men now could be saved, then whole societies would be transformed in consequence. And if all men could be saved then certainly little children could be completely and efficiently rescued - even before they had fallen. Prevention became the keyword rather than cure in relation to children with the term "child at risk" having a historical precedent much longer than the mid-twentieth century. Child saving literature abounded in such examples of effusion and sentiment combined with practical measures to ameliorate the worst aspects of child neglect as demonstrated in works such as Charles Loring Brace, The Dangerous and Perishing Class of New York (1872), Enoch C. Wines, State of Prisons and of Child Saving Institutions (1880), William Mitchell, Rescue the Children; or Twelve Years Dealing With Neglected Girls and Boys (1886), and M. A. Spielman, The Romance of Child Saving (1920).9

Earnest and enthusiastic believers in the possibility of human and societal redemption either individually or as philanthropic societies expressed the "rescue motive" by opposing lotteries, drunkenness, obscenity, bullbaiting, atheists, brothel keepers, dance halls, radicals, fairs and Sabbath breakers with equal zest and equal discrimination. They endowed, subscribed to, and founded anti-slavery campaigns, Bible societies, missionary societies to convert the heathen and the Jews, climbing boys asylums, lunatic asylums, fever institutions, penitentiaries, Sunday schools, foundling homes and orphan asylums. They helped infirm gentlewomen, distressed widows, juvenile medicants, fallen women, and neglected children. They passionately rescued the laborer from his gin, the prostitute from her earnings, the cleric from his nominalism, the rake from his stews and the street arab from his trades. The rescue motive was as apparent in politics as it was in the pulpit and was as crucial to nineteenth century social reform in British North America as it was to Britain and the United States.

David Rothman describes both the ferment surrounding and the results of the rescue motive and the belief in the improvability of man by discussing the unlimited faith in the institutional arrangements that proliferated as a result in the United States. Ford K. Brown and Bernard Semmel best describe both the extent and the expressions of the Arminian breakthrough in British society. Although English-Canada has not produced similar social histories, Richard Allen's work allows us to draw useful parallels. Anglophone social reforms of British North America, although greatly influenced by American events and ideas, remained aloof from its republican sentiments and sought to transplant working models of reform from the British experience.10

Fundamentally committed to the belief that all men might be saved, the child savers saw the recalcitrance of adults (especially from the lower orders) as being obvious, while the improvement of their social condition under an economic philosophy of laissez-faire being less obvious. Unwilling to support economic dislocation and radical redistribution of the means of production, exchange, and wealth, the remedy to any perceived threat of disorder seemed more obvious through the "rescue" and inculcation of the children from the lower orders. Thus institutions, child rescue societies, boys' brigades, girls' friendly societies, schools and Sunday schools appeared like so many mushrooms on the landscape.

It is at this juncture that the relationship between the work of Ariès and our own becomes clearer. While Ariès demonstrated the triumph of the concept of childhood (and also adolescence) among the bourgeoisie, he failed to extend his argument or his time period into the century of popular schooling for working class children. This failure missed an opportunity to comprehend the full significance of the concept of childhood. The establishment of systematic schooling was initially an imposition, which, with astonishing smoothness (in the historically relative sense) became assimilated even by the working classes. Although we recognize the conflicts that ensued over matters of schooling, it is interesting to note that most of these reflected concerns over the kinds of schools and who should control them rather than over the principal of universal schooling itself. A century and a half is a remarkably short time for implementing a distinctly new social experiment with all its continuing deficiencies. That is why we claim the relative "smoothness" of the process and the relative thoroughness of the assimilation.11

The networks of schooling that occurred during this century and a half, without a doubt, succeeded in institutionalizing "normal" children, that is, children with a family support structure, and this institutionalization was assured a modicum of success because the powerful legal support system legitimated the concept of childhood through the schools. This we shall take up again in the concluding pages of the study.

Ariès also failed to consider the extension of the concept of childhood into other institutional forms especially devoted to children and which manifestly articulated the four criteria in physical arrangements and moral dimensions. It is this second aspect which this book predominantly examines. The various institutions for dependent and deviant children which arose in British North America in the second half of the nineteenth century succeeded in creating total environments in which to implement the four criteria in policy and practice. Nowhere is the dual nature of the concept, that is, rescue and restraint, more visible than in the rhetoric and the institutional arrangement of children's homes and in schools. Nowhere either are the constantly changing criteria of the concept of childhood adapting to new social norms and shifting social conditions more apparent than in the transforming institutional patterns of children's institutions.

Many books are criticized because they have not done what they never intended to do in the first place; thus we see an institutional history criticized for not being a social history, or a history of a student movement being criticized because it did not focus on women's role in the movement, or as Professor Sutherland experienced, a book whose title clearly delineated its scope as dealing with English-Canadian society criticized because it failed to include French-Canadian society. Likewise Andrew Jones and Leonard Rutman have been subjected to similar strictures. We wish to anticipate such criticism by stipulating from the outset what the book is not attempting and which groups it does not examine. We have already mentioned Catholic child care and juvenile delinquency as not coming under the mandate we have set for ourselves. Neither is this a book that examines child rearing literature, advice manuals, how children were "physiked," how children lived their lives in the average Canadian household, or how the native, ethnic or French-Canadian experience

17

differed from that of English-Canadian dependent children. This is not because we are unaware of the challenge or the richness of such topics but because we believe arranging a history around such concepts as "childhood," "charity" and "dependency," offers possibilities for interpreting the significant shifts in sensibility and philosophy which in turn contribute to social transformation and organization.

Another major criticism of books on the history of childhood is the general failure to write history from the bottom up, that is, to write it from the experiences of the children themselves. This has been a major weakness to the area's credibility and the better attempts to overcome the fault are those which use psychological, or preferably psychoanalytical tools and frameworks. This is not to suggest that there are not significant problems related to this approach as the lively debate and profound suspicions aroused by the uses and abuses of psychohistory demonstrate. The application of theory whose origins and functions come out of a particular set of norms and socio-cultural conditions must be utilized cautiously. We are not presuming to use psychohistorical tools and this is not a psychohistorical study of any sort. As for "bottoms up" history (not to be facetious when speaking of childhood history), there are problems that, quite frankly, seem insurmountable at this stage in this development of the area.

Since subject-centred history assumes the existence of personal data generated by the "mute of history," the problems of retrieving or constructing historical evidence from the personal lives of children seem impossible. First, whatever evidence available comes from the pens and lives of children belonging to a very minute segment of society. Second, more general views of child life, either in terms of direct observation or reminiscences, are the products of adult perceptions of childhood experiences. The filtering of experiences through the prism of adult understanding raises immense problems as to what was originally undergone and what has been created out of it. The debates over contemporary events and their meaning within both public and private spheres should alert us to the

18

pitfalls in seeking to impose a standardized adult perception on childish experiences.12

On the other hand, we do have good evidence regarding the establishment, structure, and operation of the children's homes. We have a wide array of documents relating to what the founders, managers, and employees of these institutions said and did in admitting, caring for, and demitting their charges. This evidence permits us to understand the assumptions and attitudes that the adults associated with these institutions brought to bear on the children under control. What the children thought about their institutions and what they suffered, we can only speculate; however, if as most historians and others assume, we are not too different from them in human sensitivity, then we can deduce from the objective conditions a reasonable estimate of their pain and joy or indifference.

The following study will establish how the institutional arrangements for dependent children in British North America faithfully reflect the four criteria of the concept of childhood and, thus, by discussing its implications in nineteenth and twentieth century English-Canada giving a further dimension to Ariès' compelling argument. The study will address itself to a separate and specific category of child - the "dependent child" in a different geo-cultural setting and chronological period to Aries. This, then, is the broad terrain that we will chart. The particulars of that exploration will include questions regarding the British North American transition from generalized poor relief to child-rescue, the transfer of British philanthropic models to match the changing sentiments concerning dependent child life, and the shifting sensibilities of philanthropy and charity organization. We shall demonstrate that the first consequence of these attitudinal transformations and shifts was the idea of the "orphan asylum," viewed as a place of refuge and a place of order by its advocates but which in turn was discarded as its function came into question. Its total life span, however, covered a century of seemingly inflexible assumptions which led to practices which proved unsuitable to new ideas of social order and of family organization. The orphan asylum's custodial function in a time without modern forms of "outdoor relief," for example, family allowances, will be elaborated. The sociological dimension of this aspect will be discussed alongside the psychological dimensions concerning the women who controlled the orphanages.

To demonstrate the relatively slow assimilation of the criteria of delayed responsibilities and protection in the case of dependent children, the practices of indenture and fostering will be examined. The British Juvenile Immigration Movement to Canada, which contributed to the debate over indenturing practices common to Britain and Canada, will be analyzed both in terms of the "rescue motive" and the extension of the "boarding-out principle." The spillover effects of the controversy surrounding this movement will be stressed with regard to the child welfare concerns of a new and influential body of reformers, the social work profession.

The study will describe and analyze three major organizational modes - from philanthropy to scientific charity, from voluntarism to professionalization, and from professionalization to state welfarism - that demonstrate the extension of the concept of childhood as it came to influence more and more areas of individual, family, and child life. The most remarkable figure representing these shifts is Charlotte Whitton while head of that influential social agency, the Canadian Welfare Council in the 1920s and 1930s. The final synthesis of the data, arguments, major themes and sub-themes will constitute the concluding chapter and present the case that the combination of the common school and the welfare state represents the "most ordered" of rescues by fully incorporating, supporting, promoting and supplementing all public aspects of Canadian child life, or as Whitton observed, resulting in "the nationalization of children."

Finally, the authors wish to assert that given the "rescue and restraint" elements of the concept of childhood the study cannot be described as an eulogy to progress. As childhood has embraced more groups of young members of Western societies it has also produced a distinct rhetoric of its own and an insidious tendency to infantalize these groups for

20

longer periods of time. It has created repressive norms and social problems alongside its liberalizing aspects. The increasing incursion of the state into the privacies of everyday life and domestic affairs of average families represents an obtrusiveness with tendencies that are both humanistic and paternalistic. Thoughtful action based on rigorous social analysis is required in determining how much state assistance is needed and how much state control should be allowed. These and many more issues will be raised throughout the following discussion. Meanwhile let it suffice to say that the following pages, while not necessarily a story of "progress," are nevertheless ones of hope.

establishing the asylum

1

2

Bruce County House of Refuge, Walkerton, Ont.

3

25

4

5

PROTESTANT ORPHANS' HOME,
LONDON, ONT.

8

9

10

11

12

31

13

14

Poor Relief 2
and Religious Benevolence in
British North America

> From six in a bed in those mansions of woe,
> Where nothing but beards, nails and vermin
> do grow,
> And picking of oakum cellars below,
>   Good Lord, deliver us!
>
>   Joseph Howe

If there was little social differentiation in British North America between the adults and the children of the "lower orders," then it was virtually non-existent among the pauper classes that rapidly appeared in the colonial societies which were themselves subject to the usual rigors of pioneering life, climatic extremities and irregular social organization.

At the turn of the century adult and "infant paupers" alike begged along the muddy causeways of thriving commercial towns such as Montreal and Halifax, engaged in sordid and penurious transactions along the wharves of St. John's or Kingston, and sought alms in Toronto and Fredericton from the local benevolent societies, which were somewhat sickly and straggling models of the more robust British philanthropies. The early nineteenth century - a time when neither gentleman nor working man could depend on remaining prosperous all his life - was also a time of sporadic private benevolence and limited outdoor relief to aid those affected by capricious trade policies, new waves of immigration, and unstable market conditions. It was not assured, although always hoped for, that one would enjoy the support structures of a thriving family group, an adequate table, or a guaranteed "nest egg" put aside for old age.

The colonial experience often exaggerated the insecurities of urban migration that forced individuals and families to leave kinfolk to seek employment in the conditions of industrial capitalism and urban squalor in Great Britain. The trans-Atlantic migratory experience by separating whole family groups and dislocating communal support systems left in its wake spectres of illness, misfortune, bereavement and economic distress. In those colonies that maintained them, the poorhouse and house of industry were, as in England, sombre reminders to all of the uncertainties of human expectations and, as in England, the poor houses and houses of industry were frequently the "nurseries" of pauper child life with the parish or municipality that administered poor relief serving as "foster parent."1

As this study traces the transformations that occurred in English-Canadian childhood sentiment and practice it must begin at a time when the majority of children were, in effect, a "non-specialized" social group. That is, they were not perceived as children per se but as a dependent category with some potential for social usefulness. Their needs were seen as basic - food, shelter, and employment when old enough - but they were a non-individualized although a physically vulnerable class. Indeed, by mid-century it was children who were first to receive individualized attention as a social group and then as individuals within that social group during the next century.

PUBLIC RELIEF FOR THE DEPENDENT POOR

The two major classifications of the Elizabethan Poor Laws - deserving and undeserving poor - were found in both law and custom in British North America. The potent poor consisted of the "sturdy" or "lusty" vagabond, or the "valiant" beggar and were identified as part of the undeserving whereas the impotent poor consisted of the aged, infirm, and the properly unemployed were part of the deserving. The former, being seen as transients or imposters, were viewed as a source of social mischief as well as a financial burden while the latter were seen as a rather tiresome but nonetheless inescapable cross that the rate paying citizenry was obliged to bear. Dependent children

34

were included in the category "deserving" and definitely worthy of reclamation and relief. By the eighteenth century these children, as well as the offspring of the undeserving poor, were worthy, not only in themselves, but inasmuch as they were proper subjects for sympathy and rescue. Always part of the poor law "worthies" they became identified by excited enthusiasts as deserving of systemized relief and philanthropic schemes. Although public relief was neither uniform in custom nor even in statute, prevailing attitudes in the various colonies reflected a similarity of practice despite confusion of legal procedure.2

As in Britain the settled and prospering citizenry objected that anyone should "go openly begging" or that recipients of poor relief should gather together to be given "common and open doles." The clergy were enjoined "to exhort their flocks to show charity" and much of the founding of benevolent societies was the consequence of such exhortation. In Upper Canada, parish responsibility for its own poor transformed into municipal obligation. Difficulties regarding residence were as perplexing to those colonies operating under poor laws or to those that administered other systems of relief, as they were in England under the Acts of Settlement.3

While payments in support of orphan or bastard children were frequently authorized, their inclusion in the legislation regarding indoor relief meant that such children were seen as part of the general pauper population and, except in the case of early Halifax, provided no specialized treatment. Therefore, to understand the treatment accorded past dependent English-Canadian child life we must first understand the conditions pertaining to its adult counterpart.

The introduction into Upper Canada of the main body of English civil law in 1792 specifically forbad inclusion of the equivalent British poor laws. There were several possible explanations for this deliberate exclusion. Perhaps Governor Simcoe believed that to maintain the perceived "pristine" nature of Upper Canada it was necessary to exclude the possibilities of the introduction of poverty, abuse, or degeneracy, familiar to the Old World and to the colonies to the south the Loyalists had fled.

35

The perception, too, that poor law enactments strengthened local government at the expense of centralized government could not have eluded him. Two practical matters possibly shaped the decision as well, that is, the absence of any developed parish system to effectively administer poor relief and the obvious reluctance of settlers to agree to the necessary local taxes that would be burdensome and prohibit further immigration.4

Despite this official policy, support for the poor on a family, individual, parish, philanthropic or municipal basis, was given. Payments for orphan children, the children or persons in gaol, and unmarried mothers, as well as burial fees and maintenance of the destitute ill were assumed by public authorities. Nevertheless, until the passing of the Charity Aid Act of 1867, the general "piecemeal assumption" of public responsibility led to practical effects which were deplorable in the extreme. The dependent poor found themselves incarcerated in common gaols along with the incorrigible, the idle, and the disorderly. The public institutions provided for under the 1837 House of Industry Act and supervised by a board of five inspectors proved to be poor houses since little employment took place in them. Moreover, despite institutional regulation governing their behavior, inmates were generally free to come and go at will due to the practical difficulties of enforcing rules in most institutions.5

The Houses of Industry in Kingston and Toronto, the Toronto Almshouse (approved at the same time as the Bridewell in 1834), and the Industrial Farm approved in 1846, and the Hamilton House of Refuge were all impoverished and quasi-punitive congregate systems which housed the indigent, the able-bodied "potent" poor, the able-bodied unemployed, the "impotent" poor, the lewd, the dissolute, the lunatic, and the vagrant. They frequently housed the children of the poor or the young unprotected street arabs who were deemed better off in these appalling places than exercising the freedom of the streets or plying their trades. Orphans and deserted children had come under the first significant piece of legislation for child protection in Upper Canada, enacted in 1799, which provided that town wardens might place out orphans and children as apprentices. Houses of Industry were established in Kingston and Toronto in addition to the Houses of Providence in these two centres as well as those in Dundas and Guelph. Houses of Refuge were founded in Hamilton, London, and St. Catharine's. Despite a repugnance for the provision of municipal indoor relief, it became imperative in the long run to provide shelter for the indigent, the infirm, the aged, the lunatic, and the chronic cases of need.

Nevertheless, similarities can be seen between the Ontario municipal structures and the British parish system in that the basic responsibility to provide for its own was placed on a local unit of government. Centralizing administrative tendencies were apparent as early as 1786 when, in Kingston for example, overseers of the poor were appointed to provide for persons "who, from age or accident, may be rendered helpless." The overseers were required to make regular reports of the state of their district to the courts and public taxation supported the poor although, unlike Nova Scotia, local assumption was not obligatory.6

Voluntary philanthropic societies were aided by public grants and worked side by side with the systems of municipal relief. Without recourse to legislation, Ontario adapted British poor law precedents by gradually emphasizing municipal or local responsibility, thus developing a system "half way between the preponderant reliance on private charitable and religious effort by New France and the out-and-out public relief of the poor law system of Nova Scotia, New Brunswick and the New England States and the English Parish." Both New Brunswick and Nova Scotia, however, saw a transplantation of the English poor laws, the vestiges of which in New Brunswick remained up to the 1960s. A Nova Scotian "poor tax" (which was not repealed until 1956) plus township revenues supported needy supplicants.7

In the case of New Brunswick, the records of the Poor House in the late eighteenth century deal with the aged, infirm, and widows with children, that they might not suffer from "hunger and privation," as well as the "idle and the disorderly." The first Poor Law Act of 1786 stipulated that if such persons had children "in a suffering condition, the said overseers with the consent of the said justices, are hereby empowered to bind such poor children apprentices," males until they were twenty-one and females until they were eighteen or married.8

The English speaking community of Montreal consciously developed measures based on British philanthropic models, which had grown out of joint stock company principles of financial support, voluntary subscriptions, and donations and a presumption of the necessity of religious benevolence and private charity. By 1819, however, a committee for the Relief of the Poor was set up by Sir Peregrine Maitland in response to a petition which saw existing provision as inadequate. As a result a House of Recovery consisting of only two rooms was rented as a refuge and hospital in the Recollet suburbs.9

Nineteenth century Prince Edward Island, which seemed to operate as a large rural parish dominated by absentee landlords, maintained a casual system of relief well into the twentieth century. The municipality made no provision for the relief of its poor and expected private charity to alleviate distress, although a "pauper's fee" of $5 per month for the destitute and indigent could be made by order-in-council, after an application for assistance supported by a recommendation from a citizen, clergyman, or social agency. It certainly cannot be construed, however, that the lack of formal relief was the result of prosperity since in 1852 the Ladies' Benevolent Society of Charlottetown, after only fifteen years harried service, was compelled to dissolve because it could not keep up with the amount of relief required. Apart from isolated examples, the evidence concerning dependent children is so scarce that it can only be assumed that informal arrangements and binding-out practices dealt with nineteenth century problems of dependent, orphaned, and neglected child life. These ad hoc arrangements prevailed until the founding of the Children's Aid Society (CAS) in 1909 and the passage of the Neglected Children's Act the following year. The minutes of the PEI Poor Home, Charlottetown, for 1869-1899 tell us that children taken off the streets for begging were temporarily housed there

before they were apprenticed out to whomsoever
required such services.10

Established in 1759, the Halifax Poor's Asylum,
formerly the Workhouse, was also an early example of
organized indoor relief in British North America.
From its beginnings, the institution was regulated
by the overseers of the poor and sanctioned by
justices of the peace with the inmates' earnings,
which were supposedly to defray the costs, to be
supplemented by the Treasury. Orphans and poor
children were admitted from the indigent population
as well as from the faltering Orphan House. Once
again the optimism regarding inmates defraying costs
proved illusory for there was very little profit
involved in making brooms, rakes, bowls and ladles,
occupations which were still being encouraged in
1802.11

These activities were in keeping with an
advertisement placed in the Gazette by the keeper of
the asylum, John Woodin, in 1774.

> This is to give notice that any number of
> persons, whether women, boys or girls, that
> are willing to pick oakum or spin, shall
> have employment, good usage, good victuals
> and drink, and a good warm stove room to
> work and lodge in if required, without
> confinement, by applying to the said house.

Eighty-three years after the original workhouse was
appropriated and three rooms set aside for the poor,
it was converted into an even more melancholy place
- a Bridewell. In the meanwhile, it accommodated
transient paupers, dependent children, and lunatics,
and, in an additional wing, hospital cases. In
1802, the overseers were replaced by commissioners
of the poor, and its funding included provincial
grants, rarely exceeding $600 per annum plus $25 for
a school house on the premises, assessment of
townspeople, and the imposition of a ten per cent
duty on imported "goods, wares, and merchandise."12

Legislative grants for similar forms of indoor
relief were extended to poor houses in Annapolis,
Horton, Yarmouth, Pictou, Amherst, Cornwallis and
other townships. However, not even an Act of 1823,
which commissioned townships to support their own

39

poor, resolved the perennial problem of residence requirements (that is, the matter of "settlement") for admission into the poorhouses, and the subject as to what precisely constituted eligibility continued to be debated acrimonously. Even children in a suffering condition were required to seek settlement where their parents, alive or dead, were presumed to reside or have resided.

A committee before the House of Assembly in 1832, in response to a petition exposing the intolerable conditions of the poor of Halifax, examined the condition and comfort of the Poor's Asylum. It commented on the absence of "comfort and cleanliness" and observed that a great number of the seventy-four children slept with male or female adults "without any regard to fitness of health or morals" for these "tender creatures." The petition stated that the building had no ventilation or cross windows and that "cellar to garret [it] was filled to excess and very unhealthy." Two of the three rooms, thirty feet by twenty feet, had twenty beds and twice the occupants, while the lunatic ward had eighteen beds and forty-seven occupants. Debility, tuberculosis, senility, and typhus were the constant companions of the children, most of whom were under ten years of age. Two years later the cholera victims sent to the poorhouse were inadequately interred at death in burial grounds close by which had become "a seat of dangerous infection" due to the improper drainage and disrepair. Such was the atmosphere in which young children lived and breathed.13

Although the House of Assembly was inclined to disagree with the claims of the petition, in the same year an outraged citizen of Halifax, Mr. Crabtree, wrote to Joseph Howe, the editor of the Nova Scotian, protesting the state of affairs in the Poor's Asylum. He described that sorry establishment as a place that was familiar with the

> drivelings of the idiot, the ravings of
> the maniac, the profanity of the wicked,
> the obscenity of the lewd, the curses of
> despair, the lamentations of grief, the
> prayers of repentance, the jeers of the
> depraved, the thoughtlessness of child-
> hood, the signs of a broken heart, the

screams of pain, the pestilence of
disease, the groans of amputation, the
pangs of parturition, and the agonies of
death; all, all, are blended together.14

In 1834 the cases representing the "thoughtlessness
of childhood" included 115 transient children and
175 child inmates. Obviously classification of any
sort in 1832 did not exist in this particular poor
house, nor in any others in British North America,
apart from the obviously dangerous cases of
contagion: indeed, "all, all [were] blended
together." The poorhouse generally was a grim place
of death and dying, as can be seen in the 1828
<u>Journal of Assembly</u> recommendation regarding the
exercise of economy in the costs of coffins and
space in burial grounds, since there had been 247
deaths out of 899 admissions for that year. These
were not deemed particularly unusual numbers.15

Newfoundland, not being recognized as an
official settlement, had no official poor relief
legislation. Although the British government
discouraged permanent settlement in favor of a
migratory fishery, yet from the beginning emergency
efforts by government were applied to relieve
starvation of the wintering-over population which
consisted of Irish migrants and fishing servants.
Officially though, these settlers did not exist.
Instead they were classified as the "surplus
population" and their relief consisted of cash and
kind appeals, imperial funds, food from the military
and transportation, particularly of the Irish
"surplus," to England, Ireland, Nova Scotia and
Prince Edward Island. Not surprisingly, in 1821
Governor Hamilton of Nova Scotia objected to such
transportation policy. Nevertheless, as early as
1791 John Reeves had been appointed the first Chief
Justice which was "a tacit acknowledgement of the
existence of a permanent society in Newfoundland."16

Workhouse, almshouse, and stocks were missing
from early Newfoundland society but paupers were
auctioned off by public authorities to the lowest
bidder to provide domestic and agricultural service.
By 1825 Governor Cochrane was extracting work from
the able-bodied in return for relief and part wages.
Children were also auctioned in a similar fashion,
with boys being bound until they were twenty-four,

and girls until they were twenty-one or married. Up until eight years of age pauper children were boarded in private homes at government expense.17

It was not until 1846 that the question of poor relief was urgently debated as a result of the Great Fire of that year which razed St. John's. The homeless victims of this event were sheltered in camps at Fort Townshend. Six years later we see that these temporary accommodations had developed a permanent nature because forty official paupers remained there and were receiving government supplies and shelter. The forty and their children were allowed half a pound of soap, kiln dried tea without molasses, and received a pound of beef on Sundays. They slept on canvas cases filled with straw. The camps, therefore, were crude precursers of the Poor House. It was not until 1861 that the Poor House was completed "for persons wholly friendless having no property" and their offspring.18

In the early twentieth century this same poor house was described by a Grand Jury as being "the saddest place in Newfoundland." It was no less sad in 1861 when it was spanking new. Even then it was scarcely an edifying environment for either adult or infant pauper. A forbidding structure, it was only in 1911 that it boasted of a "liberal plan" that included baths, a laundry for a "foul wash house," and a mortuary for those who were admitted to die. Therefore, we might assume that none of these amenities were enjoyed by previous generations of paupers or their children. The building of the St. John's Poor House had been motivated by the debate that surrounded the failure of the seal and cod industry and potato crops for almost a decade although its plan had been presented before the Crown earlier in 1846.19

The general consensus in Newfoundland to promote industry rather than resort to outdoor relief had proven consistent. Thus in St. John's, continuing the precedents begun in 1787 by the Humane and Charitable Society and the 1808 Society for Improving the Condition of the Poor, a Factory Committee set up as its first efforts in 1836 by establishing industrial schools for poor women and girls. The appointment of a Commissioner of

Distribution (of relief) in 1861 was intended to discourage, through severe superintendence, "wilful pauperism," as The Standard, in 12 December 1860 observed in its editorial comment. Part of the Poor House policy included the delusion that inmates, through industrial occupations, would help contribute to their own maintenance. Given the tender ages of many occupants and the decrepitude of many of the other ones, this was an unlikely prospect.20

Undoubtedly the Nova Scotian concern for its pauper population and dependent children was exacerbated by the rapid growth of the colony due to immigration. Its members swelled at various times when ex-soldiers, and ex-seamen, refugee blacks from the United States, and immigrants, not only from the Old World but from the flagging settlement of Newfoundland remained. The population of the poor house was representative of all of these groups, many of whom found themselves in great distress. For example, between 1827 and 1838 Nova Scotia's population grew from 123,630 to 202,575 and within thirteen years this rose again to 276,834. Consequently, during this period, public concern reflected anxiety that the colony's socio-economic conditions, continually beset by periodical economic crises, were unable to absorb such immigration.21

Similar public concern is observable in previous decades. In 1834, the Nova Scotian reported that "the trade of the capital has been in great languor and disarrangement, and at times, of almost total stagnation," a statement applicable to the situation on and off for several decades. For instance the distribution of public outdoor relief both in cash and in kind was put into motion in 1818 when the Governor provided funds to remove families to the outskirts of the city of Halifax with two eminent gentlemen, Samuel Cunard and Michael Tobin, distributing the funds. This philosophy of "out of sight out of mind" pandered to the sensibilities of those comfortable citizens who found begging and importunity discomforting reminders of their duty towards the victims of economic circumstance.22

Similarly, at the beginning of the nineteenth century St. John's consisted of scattered buildings and crooked and dirty thoroughfares "with scarcely any regard to order or management." The policy of non-colonization prevented works and the town was a very irregular inauspicious kind of place. In 1807 the 5000 inhabitants and 700 troops championed cockfighting under "rules to be in every respect comparable to those practised at the Royal Pit and Newmarket" while roaming rowdies found "vent in mischievous horse play" such as tearing down knockers from doors or carrying off gates. Merchants and mariners alike enjoyed a rough but convivial social life in the thirty taverns, with fishing monopolized by the merchants who gave out supplies in return for fish at fixed prices. There was no cash exchanged at all and the poor were driven to extremities. The court of sessions in that year was involved in promulgating the bettering of social conditions by debating the muzzling of dogs and the removal of hogs, both of which clogged up the narrow paths. Anxious about "crime, disquiet, and unrest," the court of sessions implored the Government a year later to enforce laws "against blasphemy, polygamy, profaneness, adultery, fornication, profanation of the Lord's Day, swearing, drunkenness and immorality." The court of sessions, it must be noted, expressed little interest in the hardships of the destitute, the unemployed, or the new immigrants who so often lived a daily routine of quiet desperation.23

The Nova Scotian, 3 July 1834, lamented the "unpropitious seasons" but castigated its population by noting:

> We must declare our honest conviction that
> a large amount of the distress, both in town
> and country, has arisen from the indulgence,
> of foolish pride, and extravagance, and the
> want of those habits of self denial, economy,
> and industry, which are the surest foundations
> of individual and national independence.

Nevertheless, although the press reprimanded the affluent's "improvidence and folly," it was not remiss in pointing a finger of blame at its worst victims - the unemployed and the pauperized - by insisting that their employment "in useful labour" was "the very best mode of administering to their wants." Thus the able-bodied poor found themselves breaking stone for footpaths at thruppence a bushel, with the town, as observed by the <u>Nova Scotian</u>, 2 April 1835, improved both in appearance and in "its moral organization." Apparently the notion of work for its own sake, no matter how unrenumerative or unsatisfying the task, was intended to pacify the poor and tend to their daily needs.

Newfoundland too insisted on labor in return for public relief. The duties of the Commissioner of Distribution were spelled out in a circular from the Colonial Secretary regarding "the regulation of poor relief" on 26 July 1861. He was to check potential abuses regarding the appropriation of poor funds, to restrict the supply of casual relief, and to carefully classify the poor into two categories - casual and permanent. The casual poor were refused relief unless proven "destitute" and "deserving" and then only in return for their labour."[24]

A public notice of 1863 referred to the growing and wide extent of both categories in the colony due to economic distress. It continued in the spirit of "strongest condemnation" to berate the "gross imposition" on government coffers as a consequent of the distress and noted that

> . . . the pernicious consequences shown to
> have been produced by a periodical and
> gratuitous distribution of food, in the
> destruction of every feeling of self
> reliance and of all motive for industrious
> effort, and in the creation of habits of
> helpless indolence on the part of the poor.

Subsequently it was resolved that relief would only be distributed to the sick, infirm, destitute, widows and orphans while in Labrador stricken fishermen were given relief if they agreed to engage in road works and then only for a six week period before the commencement of the seal fishing.[25]

The comment found in the <u>Times and Courier</u>, 22 March 1849, that "Halifax is . . . the very headquarters of poverty" could have been as easily applied for almost any decade before the mid-century. The paper further noted that "the exceedingly precarious nature of industrial pursuits with the hopelessness of looking elsewhere for employment naturally creates a vast amount of poverty in our city." Even the Irish immigrants who had fled or were transported from Newfoundland found it difficult to remove themselves elsewhere for sustenance or employment. Prince Edward Island and New Brunswick scarcely offered a lugibrious economic alternative for those not already comfortably ensconced in these unproductive colonies. Nevertheless, it must not be forgotten that Halifax was in fact the most prosperous city in early nineteenth century British North America and, while harboring hopelessness and deprivation in its meanest quarters, it also cultivated through its mercantile trade and commerce a thriving class of some substance. It is not surprising, therefore, that in addition to indoor poor relief and some outdoor public relief this comfortable middle class responded to the poverty and subsequent perceived disorder in customary ways that expressed humanitarian impulses and religious benevolence. These customary ways, which have already been observed in Newfoundland in the St. John's charitable societies, revealed the transplantation of the British philanthropic spirit and models of charity organization to its colonies.

PRIVATE PHILANTHROPY

Not all societies were strictly religiously motivated, for some, such as the St. George's and the St. Andrew's benevolent societies, specifically gave relief to Scots or English needy, although they frequently operated out of Anglican or Presbyterian congregations. Theirs, however, was more "nationally" motivated than sectarian. The membership of a Society for Improving the Condition of the Poor of St. John's, founded in 1808, consisted of town merchants with the governor as patron; whereas, a similar society formed four years previously had organized charity schools supported by donations received from the sumptuous annual breakfasts it gave in the Courthouse and the London Tavern. This society lamented four years later about the want of cleanliness on the part of its school children, most of whom were under twelve years of age, and the irresponsibility of poor parents who did not compell their offspring to attend school where the girls engaged in carding, spinning and knitting and the boys in the making and mending of nets.26

46

Some societies, such as the Nova Scotia Philanthropic Society, insisted that both their membership and recipients be natives of the province and described their categories of deserving and undeserving in rather stark terms. As a mutual benefit society, the Nova Scotia organization only gave allowances to those subjected to sudden misfortune rather than to the "settled poor," that is, those on the poor rates.27

The St. John's Benevolent Irish Society (BIS), which can be found today in Charlottetown and St. John's, began as a non-denominational enterprise catering for the Irish population of whatever creed whose privation was fearfully visible due to their relative lack of earning power. The original 1806 committee, whose first vice-president was Lieutenant Colonel John Murray, was predominantly Irish-Protestant although Bishop Dr. O'Donel was a major advisor. The BIS gradually took upon itself a sectarian identification because it mainly dealt with the Irish Catholic immigrants. The BIS flourished during the War of 1812 because of military construction and the presence of troops who spent lavishly, as well as the inevitable boom in war trade, but at the same time it received fresh influxes of immigrants seeking refuge from the events of war. By 1816-18 the economy was in a post-war crisis, the fisheries were failing and severe winters increased destitution in the city and the outposts. The BIS flagged also during this period and by 1823 was forced to find a solution regarding their depleting resources. A resolution stated that relief would be provided only to those "who showed industry and economy in their efforts to support themselves." The categories of deserving and undeserving were thus hardened into the organization of relief, and seed potatoes were provided to those who had a genuine desire "to rescue themselves from poverty by honest industry." Orphans were designated clearly at this time as deserving for an Orphan Asylum was included as a priority of the society.28

A committee of charity from the outset had observed that it must "attend carefully to the claims of children of parents whose vices and misfortunes prevented their supporting their offspring" and it agreed that such children must be placed out "to good masters." By 1823, however, the BIS had realized that in a colony so distressed as Newfoundland even this was easier said than done and suggested that an orphan asylum be erected to alleviate their "unhappy condition." The society, which never received crown aid nor was granted incorporation because of its exclusive Irish membership, lacked the necessary funds to support such an institution. Therefore, a curious situation arose. The BIS had an orphan asylum but no orphans, although approximately four hundred children attended day schools in the building. The cellars of the St. John's orphan asylum were used to store general relief supplies and its rooms used for meetings. The asylum was used in 1902 for charity balls but not for orphans! The Patriot and Terra Nova Herald in 1859 stated that "for forty years the Society has pledged to open an orphan asylum." A similar situation occurred in Prince Edward Island in 1856 when an orphan school consisting of a room for daily instruction, but not the asylum, was approved by the legislature. Whereas in 1838 in New Brunswick as in Nova Scotia a school was equipped in the almshouse.29

A predominately Anglican "Society for Promoting Education and Industry Among the Indians and Destitute Settlers in Canada" founded in 1827, under the patronage of the Duchess of Dalhousie and Sir James Kempt, conducted industrial schools and infant schools in Lower and Upper Canada. It was not only modelled on its parent society in London but its major impetus came from the fact that this parent society refused to support it financially. Like their parents, poor children were engaged in some "useful labour" in return for bread and clothing. Indeed, according to a School of Industry report dated April 8, 1829, "on seeing a number of orphans and poor children out of employment, destitute of bread and the means of instruction," the Superintendent was compelled by compassion to take in a number as residents.30

The immigrant poor, upwards of fifty a day, partook of a cheap repast at noon and carried "to their lodgings at the close of the day, their little earnings, in bread, clothing, and fuel for their families." In addition to this, the women of the society assisted "many poor orphans and destitute

48

children" with clothing and bread so that they "were enabled to appear with decency in their different schools and places of worship." The objects of the School of Industry in Montreal stipulated that in addition to reading, a useful branch of work would be taught to those who had none and that the helpless poor would be relieved "at their own habitation." The work done was paid for in clothing.31

The School of Industry itself consisted of two large work rooms, also used for Sabbath school instructions, a storage room and a sales room where the manufactured goods were sold. Men did some outdoor work such as chopping and sawing of fire wood and snow removal, which offices were paid for in the form of a shovel, axe, pick axe, and saw, obviously a gentle reminder that they should continue to work, now having no excuse because they could not purchase implements. Indoor work for men involved mat and basket making and the production of leather mittens and winter shoes; whereas the females sewed, knitted, made bonnets, cut out patterns for clothes, and engaged in other similar occupations. Although the work could be done at the School, it was preferred that it be done at home so that women could care for their children. The blind and lame were engaged in sawing and boring stone while a number of the poor were involved in the manufacture of articles "calculated to unite amusement with instruction for nursery and infant schools." Given the monotony of the other occupations, these were the lucky ones.32

While the gentlemen were organizing themselves into societies such as the Poor Man's Friend Society in Nova Scotia and the Benevolent Irish Society in Newfoundland, women were not remiss in fulfilling their charitable obligations either, and eagerly dispensed charity, some useful articles such as food and clothing, and many platitudes. Like their male counterparts, money was given rarely for it offered temptations to gambling, drink, and extravagance that the poor apparently could not withstand. One of Ontario's first effective petitions to gain government funding for its philanthropic efforts, because "the voluntary contributions of individuals" were nearly exhausted, was submitted by the Kingston

Female Benevolent Society in 1830, nine years after it was organized.33

The Montreal Ladies' Benevolent Society, founded in 1832, engaged a committee of volunteer visitors whose main intent was "to rescue the widows and the fatherless." This society began an industrial school for women and children which became predominantly concerned with the care of the young inmates. The St. George's Parish Ladies' Benevolent Society of Halifax, while seeking to "mitigate the sufferings of the mother in her hour of confinement" in 1843 also sought to provide "the industrious poor with employments." Fifty women received cloth each Saturday at ten o'clock as well as 7s ½d. for each shirt they had produced. They were given the option to purchase clothing and shoes at a cut price. Between Saturdays the lot of these poor women must have been painstaking, difficult, tedious and unrewarding. In Ottawa at the same time, the Female Poor Relief and Tract Distributing Committee of the St. Andrew's Kirk was visiting the poor environs of this inauspicious little town, and later in 1873 was to reorganize as the Ladies Aid Society. Female societies inevitably paid a great deal of attention to mothers and children, and such attention would in several instances lead to a specialized facility dealing with the reclamation of "fallen" women and unwed mothers in houses of refuge or for deserted and orphaned children in orphan asylums.34

Dorcas societies were organized by women in many areas. The Newfoundland one, begun in 1824, stated its object was "to provide clothing for the honest and industrious poor" and it noted that it would not dispense charity to those "well known recipients" who followed collections around to "snap up the tickets before those more deserving have a chance to ask for the much needed aid." Ticket systems were a popular form of distributing charity and in this case tickets cost a dollar apiece for whomsoever wanted to support a charity case who could in turn purchase soup at three cents a quart. The above remark is illustrative of a preoccupation among the philanthropists of both Britain and English-Canada about "imposturing" by "valiant beggars," those professional paupers who purportedly received alms from various sources simultaneously.

As there was little or no coordination of charity efforts and impulsive benevolence was not uncommon, the risk of duplication of services was a constant concern.35

METHOD VERSUS MUDDLE

The nineteenth century proved to be a good time when the debate between advocates of outright charity-giving and of "scientific" charity (that is, coordination of services and distribution of relief through a central fund to avoid duplication and prevent imposture) was to become very lively indeed. Charity Organization Societies were to prove as pursuasive to the English-Canadian public as to the British public. The Newfoundland Dorcas Society, however, is only one example of the staying power of more spontaneous forms of benevolence. For in 1877, it was still receiving "wincy, shawls, blankets' and "hose, boots and shirts" while giving money in return for such articles. In turn the profits on re-sale were circulated again to new and needy clients.36

One district visiting society in Halifax, while piously asserting that "benevolence is the gift of God to man, . . . one of the finest affections of the human heart, and a source of purest enjoyment on earth," also insisted that the function of benevolence nevertheless included "the suppression of imposition and fraud alongside the improvement of the moral character of the poor." Thirty years previously the insistence upon the suppression of imposition was less obvious as is demonstrated in the seventh annual report of the Methodist Female Benevolent Society. Finding the growing belief in "scientific charity" essentially unchristian, the report said that

> . . . promiscuous liberality has never been indulged . . . it has not, however, been forgotten that misery itself has a claim for relief and that the cry of distress on its own account should be heard independent of the deserts of the sufferer. . . .37

Misery certainly abounded around the dock areas of Halifax's thriving harbour. In the same year,

1823, a much needed soup kitchen, consciously organized on Count Rumford's Model establishment for the poor of Munich in 1795 and which provided 100 gallons of soup a day, caused controversy and dissention among charity givers. On 24 January 1824, "Mercator" wrote to the Acadian Recorder that the operations were "in the end highly and dangerously prejudicial to those very persons who are the objects of its bounty." Furthermore "charity and co. pays him [the Irish laborer] for keeping his back straight and his hands clean." The deserving poor needed and wanted labor and not doles or soup which were the indulgences given to the undeserving.

The emphasis on relief in return for labor continued although some societies were more willing to give cash and not payment in "kind." The Halifax Association for Improving the Condition of the Poor argued that stone-breaking prevented crime and actually kept people out of the poor house "by providing honest labour at a fair price." The objections of the Board of City Works to an enterprise that undercut its stonebreaking endeavours were denounced as shortsighted. The argument that such provision was wise economy in the long run by keeping recipients off the relief lists was always a compelling one. This society operated, as did many similar ones including its St. John's counterpart founded in 1797, on a "visiting" system. The Association had one hundred visitors who, according to the Nova Scotian, 28 January 1867, searched out "hidden destitution which may fall outside the cognizance of other similar associations." Despite the duplication of this and similar efforts, however, many destitute remained outside their purview for private and uncoordinated charitable efforts could not stay the overwhelming tide of poverty. This society alone had relieved 1097 individuals in 1867, its first year of operation.38

An interesting, although short lived, experiment in non-sectarian philanthropy is seen in the Halifax Poor Man's Friend Society (PMFS) whose origins can be found three years previously in the Association for the Relief of the Labouring Poor. Its significance lies in its organization which reflected quite early the shift from spontaneous benevolence to a form of organized charity. Its methods were clearly misunderstood by much of the middle class public and it became, unjustly, the centre of controversy. Yet this controversy itself reflects the changing sensibilities toward charity and relief which were to become more articulated and made visible in the next century in English Canada. The debate not only reflected changing views of social organization, socio-political shifts from mercantilism to laissez faire, and population theories such as Malthusianism, but the conflicts between Old and New World assumptions about the role of individuals and society.

The society, which first met in February, 1820, to adopt such measures "as would effectively relieve the wants of the numerous poor and destroy the system of begging," stipulated that it would prevent "the imposition" on charitable persons by beggars. The methods it put into practice predated the ideas developed fully in 1835 by the Liverpool philanthropist, William Rathbone, whose pamphlet "Social Duties Considered in Reference to the Organization of Effort in Works of Benevolence and Public Utility" by a "Man of Business" was circulated with great interest. This is not to say that such ideas had not been about before, but this was the first serious attempt to expound them carefully and methodically. Rathbone himself merely explained the principles which had been first put into practice by the Reverend Thomas Chalmers of Glasgow, the acknowledged pioneer of organizing charity between 1815 and 1820, and then in 1831 by two Unitarian ministers of Liverpool, James Martineau and John Hamilton Thom. Rathbone believed that relief should not be given without "sufficient knowledge" of the true status of the recipients. He described this organized charity as "method versus muddle" and argued that business application would overcome the present lack of "system," the obvious maladministration of funds by sincere but less than competent persons, and disestablish well-known charities, thus taking them out of the hands of wealthy cliques who sometimes even disdained the notion of including lowly shopkeepers on their committees.39

Rathbone's plans for giving relief involved the end to enthusiastic and sentimental responses to individual cases of poverty. His advocacy of a judicious budgeting of the wealthy's donations and subscriptions to replace a multitude of rescue societies (so far sporadically supported and often in response to a "fashion"), the amalgamation of funds, the cooperation of like interests, and a central relief bureau to coordinate activities, represented a radicalization of philanthropic thought and practice. Almsgiving became seen as "old," "indiscriminate" and "conservative" charity; whereas, the organization of charity to prevent overlapping has been variously described as "wise," "systematic," "preventative," "discriminate" and "scientific." The main purpose of all this system, however, was as much to <u>detect</u> as to relieve.40

Yet here was a group of gentlemen in the city of Halifax including such eminent citizens as the shipping magnate Samuel Cunard, whose commitments to organized charity were taking on similar direction to those of Rathbone. Cunard's Liverpool connections probably made him aware of the new ideas that were being discussed in the chapels and coffee houses of England's substantial mercantile centre. The original PMFS committee consisted of twenty members who carefully divided a map of the city of Halifax up into seventeen "wards" and who appointed thirty-four visitors to investigate any cases drawn to the society's attention. The visitations were on a regular fortnightly basis. Only after they reported their findings was a decision reached as to which families would be relieved. Committed equally to the ideas of "cure" as to relief, the society set up a rudimentary employment bureau.41

An aim of the society was to destroy the system of juvenile begging so apparent on the streets, and its regulations stipulated that relief would not be given to those parents who brought their children up "to be a fruitful source of crime and villainy" by encouraging begging. In 1820 alone, 4213 individuals received any one or all of the following through a ticket system: molasses, wood, meal, bread, tea, sugar, saltfish, clothing, bedsteads and blankets. Cash relief was strictly forbidden. In addition the colored settlers of Hammonds Plains and Preston were given 150 bushels of seed potatoes. Suitable "objects" were sent to the poor house and if they refused to go were denied aid - a terrible alternative, for most recognized the poor house as a last desperate resort. The PMFS originally intended its recipients to be only the deserving poor, that is, "those who are prevented by sickness or delicacy of feeling from soliciting and consequently remain unnoticed and unrelieved."42

Initially, the views of the Halifax Free Press, 5 March 1822, were representative of the citizenry's sympathy for the project and particularly toward what was perceived of as the utility of an employment bureau. But within a year or so, and after a severe winter had caused great distress and unemployment, the public began accusing the society itself of increasing pauperism rather than decreasing it by discouraging the poor to find their own sustenance. The society, incensed by the criticism, pointed out that the increases in its numbers were due not only to the deplorable objective economic conditions but the fact that nonsubscribers were referring charity cases to the committee and burdening it beyond its capacities. Then, when the PMFS introduced a soup kitchen on Marchington's Wharf, the outcry was predictable, for soup kitchens smacked of indiscriminate almsgiving with the previously clear distinction between undeserving and deserving becoming blurred. A soup kitchen was actually a radical attempt at economy, for then, as today, it was realized that this was the cheapest and most efficient means of immediately satisfying mass hunger. The plan was based on the model of Count Rumford's Institution for the Poor which became a model in systematic indoor relief after it was popularized in 1795.

After it was forced to abandon the soup kitchen experiment, the PMFS was subsequently attacked in a series of letters to the Nova Scotian by the writer "Malthus" beginning 11 January 1825. These scathing criticisms of the society and all aspects of indiscriminate charity succeeded in further under- mining enthusiasm for its efforts, and even the support given to its work by the Philanthropist, on January 27 or the Nova Scotia Royal Gazette on January 26, could not restore its credibility. So much for the original appeal that one's affluence was bestowed "not for your own exclusive gratification but for the purpose of benevolent diffusion."

The third annual report of 1822 asked the reluctant public whether the poor were to be reduced again to scanty pittances from the "uncertain hand of charity." It insisted that, if given a chance of reorganizing present charitable endeavours and of serving as a model of the new ideas of relief and investigation, not only would the destitute population be assisted but pauperism itself would diminish in consequence. Nevertheless, the 1822 report used the florid sentimental appeals of the day.

> Is it not the object of this Society to
> clothe the naked, feed the hungry, to
> enliven the gloom, cheer the sorrow, and
> ease the pain of the afflicted; and to
> soften the pillows of the dying? You
> know it is. And are not the object of
> the Society's solicitude men? Are they
> not human beings, partakers of our
> common nature? They are: and as such
> susceptible of the kindness of our
> sympathy, as well as the bitterness of
> our neglect?

But the soup kitchen finally alienated many who had been pursuaded by the new rhetoric about indiscriminate relief and scientific charity; it had never been destined to appeal to those, who, by the meanness of their characters consistently objected to any form of almsgiving.

In 1825 the legislature gave a minimal support to the PMFS to the extent of £50 despite a petition from the committee which stressed the plight of the children it reclaimed from immoral and drunken parents who could not adequately support them or who willingly abandoned them. It had spent much time seeking employment for adult men and boys between eleven and fourteen years of age in the manufacture of nails which were in short supply in the province. By February 1827, however, the committee of the society met at the Exchange Coffee House for the last time and similar experiments in "method versus muddle" were abandoned until the climate was more receptive to them.

NON-SPECIALIZED CHILDREN

From the previous pages and illustrations, it becomes apparent that the characteristics of childhood as we have come to understand them, including those of innocence and vulnerability, were a middle class luxury and not applicable to all children in British North America in the first half of the nineteenth century. For this period the majority of dependent children can be described as "non-specialized" young people and, because of the absence of special treatment, facilities, and even special childish attributes, not really part of the concept of childhood.

While middle class children were being carefully protected from the ugliness and importunity of the adult world, segregated and carefully trained into appropriate attitudes and occupations in the bosom of their families or in private schools, and kept dependent upon their parents and tutors in both a physical and psychological sense, with responsibilities being apportioned as suitable for various age groups and stages of childishness, dependent children often found themselves outside all four conditions of a "normal" childhood. The first decades of the century saw only the fumbling beginnings of such specialization. The workhouse, the poorhouse, the house of industry, still saw the children of the dependent poor and dependent children within their walls even into the twentieth century. Sometimes, even after the 1850s, common gaols retained children such as is recorded in the Journal of Assembly for New Brunswick in 1857. The penitentiary register showed many young boys and, "In one instance, we find the name of a boy who was committed by the Police Court in Saint John, for some trifling offence, whose age is put down at nine years." This boy died "before the expiration of his sentence."43

In February of the same year, Thomas McGinn, Gaoler and Superintendent of Works, wrote a blistering report on the conditions in the common gaol of Montreal and recommended segregated facilities within the prison itself. He deplored the incarceration of destitute and homeless juveniles among drunkards, prostitutes and diseased persons and claimed that classification of prisoners

57

was necessary, the exclusion of youth and vagrants was imperative, and the separation of cells to prevent "unnatural crimes" urgent. "Our prisons and houses of correction," he grimly asserted, "are little else than houses of corruption and nurseries of crime." This caused the "corrupting of youth" who could not be separated from the "old and hardened offender."44

Neither were pauper and dependent youngsters considered to require the same decorous solicitude as other children (many of whom now were of the working classes) whose sensitivities were strictly protected in the common schools. It is, for instance, ironical that at the same time as ordinary children were being carefully segregated according to sex in Newfoundland schools in the 1830s, the children of the indigent and desperate poor had no separate facilities provided them in public refuges. Dr. Michael Fleming, the Roman Catholic primate, insisted on "withdrawing female children from the tutelage of men, from the dangerous associations which ordinary school intercourse with the other sex naturally exhibited." He therefore supported the Presentation Convent in 1833 which provided education for girls, so that they might not lose "that delicacy of feeling and refinement of sentiment which forms the ornament and grace of their sex." The sisters were to train them into "virtue and innocence" and "integrity and morality." As for the boys, he expressed grave anxiety that they were demonstrating a total independence of their parents once they were trained into the fishing trades at a young age. He further observed that being "free from every domestic restraint" each was accustomed to drinking "a yellow belly" (of rum) from his own "brown jug" three times a day.45

In Halifax, with an appeal for an Orphan Asylum being mounted, the Nova Scotian, 23 March 1839, once again pointed to the conditions in the congested Poor's Asylum and the degraded lives of the pauper population of Halifax. It observed that an orphan asylum was necessary "to furnish means for bringing up the now ill-furnished who are in the Asylum, as healthy persons with industrious habits and improved morals." However, even in 1869 when the Victoria General Hospital had been completed for ten years and the Nova Scotia Hospital for the Insane

58

completed for eleven, thus providing separate specialized facilities for two classes of needy - the mentally and physically ill - the Poor's Asylum was still lamentably overcrowded and its children attended a school house still provided for at the original £25 per annum. This lack of classification between adults and children in public institutions continued even into the twentieth century.46

By 1894, however, a report from the Prisoners' Aid Association of Canada studying conditions in county houses of industry observed that some classification of inmates was occurring, whereas formerly "both old and young, the debased and respectable, those suffering from repulsive and communicable diseases, were indiscriminately mingled." No children over two were to be admitted and infants born in the county poorhouses were to be boarded out or committed to an orphan asylum.47

The records demonstrate that all dependent children were not considered worthy recipients of both public and private relief. Children of the indigent or the fringe elements of society, whose proclivities bordered on the "nefarious" or criminal, as well as those children of the desperately destitute classes became the inmates of poorhouses and workhouses in both Britain and British North America, whereas the children of the "respectable" poor were frequently the ones who were received into the relatively "select" orphan asylums. Subsequently, when child savers boasted of success rates of their inmates in terms of later employment in servile occupations and correct attitudes towards law, authority, morality and work, the claims must be understood in light of the built-in premises used for admission. The success rates probably had little to do with the child savers' talents to either reclaim or reform children. David Rothman's observation of a later phenomenon, the probation system in the United States, seems apropos at this juncture for the Canadian experience with dependent child-life.

> The very existence of a system designed
> to transform "them" into "us" meant that
> those already more like "us" were bound
> to be favored.48

59

An absence of differentiated facilities for dependent children is, in the nineteenth century, most observable in their general inclusion in poorhouses, houses of refuge and industry, penitentiaries and asylums. Although the poorhouses varied in size and in design, general public apathy prevailed concerning their upkeep. Halifax was not exceptional in sheltering transient persons and whole families on relief in the municipal refuge at only a cost of twenty-four cents per diem in 1898. The pittance itself reflects the public's attitude toward the whole affair. As one inspector noted in as late as 1900, "rigid economy is practicably discreditable parsimony."49

Various descriptions compel us to see municipal institutions as disconsolate environments for the most insensitive adults let alone children. Some, such as in Nova Scotia, were so verminous that it was noted of a poor farm in that province that despite "eternal vigilance, the bedsteads [were] occupied by other than sleepers"; while others like the Pictou Poor's House were so decrepit and rudimentary that the inmates wre compelled to haul water for their use in puncheons from the town some distance away.50

Again in 1900 the Halifax Poor Farm included inmates who were "destructively inclined," "uncleanly," and "epileptic," while the Poor House, a two storied ramshackle farm house, was quite without bolts, locks, and handles in its twenty rooms. Subsequently the fifty-seven lunatics among its inmates could roam at will and children, who were included among the others, were not separated according to sex, sanity, social or age distinctions. One patient was reported to be subject to violent outbursts and was, therefore, immobilized by handcuffs and lay exposed without a shirt. In short, almshouses made little or no attempt to classify adults in a rigorous manner and the governors saw nothing inappropriate in having young children promiscuously mixing with the disorderly and incontinent.51

The irony is further compounded when one realizes that in Nova Scotia (as well as Newfoundland) sexual and age distinctions were not exercised in the case of the poor asylum in Halifax even in 1900, while governors of the Annapolis Poor Asylum made separate provision for "colored" inmates in a most precipitious manner. At the same time, insane women in the Yarmouth County Asylum were reputedly in charge of young children. The report of the Inspector of Public Charities observed in a remarkable understatement that this practice was "a very risky business." Fourteen years later, William Hattie, the Inspector of Humane Institutions, was able to comment that

> . . . under the most favourable circumstances, institutional life is not ideal for the child, and the building which houses a considerable number of inefficients, and degenerates, most of them well advanced in years, must surely be a most undesirable environment for the rearing of children.

Already "handicapped by heredity," he continued that they spent day and night "in the company of irritable and complaining old people, of mischievous and profane lunatics, and of drivelling and unclean imbeciles." He noted that children were in the Home for the Poor, Truro, and the Yarmouth Poor Asylum, Arcadia.[52]

The Toronto House of Industry, first organized in 1836 to prevent "an increase in pauperism," provided a house of refuge for women and children from the beginning, until the children were removed to the orphan asylum during the 1850s. Those remaining were apprenticed and subjected in 1858 to the inspection of a committee from the Widows' and Orphan Asylum. The House of Industry was reputed to be overcrowded with many imbeciles, idiots and lunatics.[53]

Nova Scotia presents a distinct contrast to some of the other colonies regarding both the crown's responsibility toward its poor in the administering of poor relief as well as its response to pauper children. However, it cannot be overlooked that one particular experiment with pauper children was out of the ordinary since it preceded the proliferation of similar specialized facilities in English-Canada by almost a century. Its organization, funding, management and philosophical assumptions were directly related to

British institutional arrangements for this was a colonial transplant.

In 1752, seven years before the Poor's Asylum, an "orphan" house, probably English-Canada's first child rescue endeavor involving specialized facilities for children, was established. The Lords of Trade at Whitehall bemoaned the expense of such an endeavor but Governor Hopson pointed out that among the emigrants recently arrived there were thirty who were "useless" after the voyage and that fourteen children, being in great need, were accommodated in the Orphan House. Its accommodations were for fifty orphans although only nineteen were cared for and educated by a representative of the Society for the Propagation of the Gospel, Mr. Breynton, and the schoolmaster, Mr. Sharrock. The children's diet consisted of pork, bread, molasses, and spruce beer," the latter being substituted for rum because it was "so conducive to health." Fifteen of these nineteen children were under sixteen years of age. By 1758 the majority of the orphan house's inmates were removed to the newly erected workhouse and in 1787 the orphan house itself, being in a very "ruinous state" was closed altogether.

This colonial institution, which bound out children "so very young as to be unable to do any serviceable work," employed older girls in the carding and spinning of wool or the knitting of stockings, while the boys picked oakum in the winter and "gathered stones" or performed "other little offices" in the gardens and at Crown hospital in the summer. Correspondence from Jonathan Belcher to the Lords of Trade in 1761 indicates that during a nine year period 275 children, mostly orphans, had been cared for by this Royal Charity, and if they were between eight and twelve years of age, they had been indentured from it.54

That the Halifax Orphan House was an interesting but nevertheless anomalous experiment can be seen in the shortness of its history. A "German" orphan house was erected shortly after the colonial institution but apparently enjoyed an even briefer life. Once the Poor's Asylum was built, colonial authorities and rate payers alike, saw the specialized facility as redundant and dependent children were promptly transferred into surroundings usually accorded their status. In short, once a generalized institution was established, children were clearly identified as suitable objects for its care along with the adult pauper population.

It was to be many years before similarly specialized facilities as the Halifax Orphan House were to be viewed as reasonable and acceptable means for dealing with dependent child life, and then only on a private basis; but many of the attitudes towards children as a special category and which were reflected in the original experiment remained in the colony. For example the House of Assembly on 12 March 1838 voted £25 "for the benefit of orphan and poor children" in the Poor's Asylum and £50 for the Ladies who managed an Infant School for poor children. It had already given grants since 1803 to the Acadian School which provided education for poor children. By 1818 the Acadian School and the National School (run on the Madras system) between them saw a daily attendance of 510 poor children. Moreover, a petition to the Lieutenant Governor in 1839 requested that a threepenny duty be placed on imported wine per gallon in support of the children and the aged infirm in the Poor's Asylum as it was the case in raising a salary for the grammar school master.55

In that same year the legislature promised £600 to match double that amount from public funds to build a new orphan asylum on land set aside for the purpose so long as the project cojointly included "a plan for the employment of the poor," that is, a house of industry. This last condition reflected both the popular belief that such industry would reduce maintenance costs and relieve the ratepayers of some financial burden, and the commonplace assumption that it was quite suitable to have children mixing with the adult poor.56

The emphasis in this chapter on early modern forms of public relief has been necessary due to the limited nature of systematic assistance available to families and individuals in distress and to the deserving and undeserving categories. Children were seen as more hopeful elements of the deserving, that is, those who with proper training and placement would outgrow their deficiencies. Indoor relief

maintained by parish or municipality provided for
the earliest years when children were clearly
incapable of even beginning to earn their keep;
while apprenticeship or binding out were traditional
modes of initiating even young children into useful
employment and hopefully, self-sufficiency. As in
the cases of women with children and the seasonally
unemployed, children were perceived as acute rather
than chronic objects of relief such as the aged and
impaired. In all this, the categories of deserving
and undeserving and of acute and chronic dependence
were the determining factors, not the specific
qualities or needs of classifications of people.
Children were not recognized as a special class
requiring its own unique facilities. Indeed, where
such specialized provisions were made, as in the
1750s in Nova Scotia these were soon replaced by a
more general institution.

The general relief institution represented the
dominance of the need to deal with society's concern
with dependence - to relieve those unable to care
for themselves and to force those able to work to
undertake whatever employment that was available -
and not with any need for considering the
psychological or emotional state of the individual.
The inclusion of children - often infants - in these
institutions and the lack of any specialized care
for them tells us much about the conditions of child
life in early British North America. Moreover, when
compared with the debates, legislation, and
institutional founding of the second half of the
nineteenth century, a discussion of the early
provisions demonstrates the enormous shift in
sentiment and perception of child life that occurred
in less than a century. This transformation would,
of course, be only the first in a series of shifts
that would revolutionize western child and family
life.

Childhood Sentiment and Specialized Children   3

> . . . send these little social pests to
> an institution that would at once protect
> society from their depredations, detach
> them from their evil companions and from
> careless and vicious parents; that would
> keep them under proper restraint and impart
> to them moral and industrial training; and
> so enable them to become useful members
> of society.
>
> Montreal 1857

The 1822 plan of Captain Robert Parker Pelly, the Governor of Assiniboia, for the care of "half breed" children whose parents had died or deserted them was part of the general concern for safety of the trading posts if men with large families were discharged and left in "an uneducated and savage position" to "collect across the country" without "proper superintendence." Pelly observed that while Roman Catholics would be served by their mission Protestants would be "maintained and clothed by the Company" under the care of the Reverend Mr. West of the Church Missionary Society. Pelly concluded that "it will therefore be both prudent and economical to incur some expense in placing these people where they may maintain themselves and be civilized [and] instructed in religion." The expense was only temporary since, once the boys had been trained for agriculture and the girls for industry, they could be apprenticed. Seen as part of a larger problem of an unsettled population, children were not accorded any special treatment.1

If Assiniboia represented the pioneering ethos devoid of sentimental indulgences, Montreal witnessed a significant shift in both sensibility toward and treatment of dependent child life. This was not an unexpected phenomenon for compared with Assiniboia, Montreal was a stable and prosperous community and easily the most important commercial city in British North America in the first decades of the nineteenth century. A substantial English speaking middle class which controlled all aspects of financial and commercial life was well placed to engage in charitable organization and activity. The tracing of philanthropic patterns tells us that the forms of social organization in Halifax, Montreal, Hamilton, and Toronto were not particularly idiosyncratic just as the demographic trends of transiency, migration, and urban drift were common to all. It was from the configurations of commercial enterprise that the impact of organized charity and institutional expressions were most felt in the British North American nineteenth century city.2

A softening of attitude towards dependent children, already evident in Montreal by the 1820s, would soon appear in similar towns and cities throughout the century. Although such growing solicitude would not become institutionalized until mid-century, the first hesitant steps towards specialization were now taking place. For example, although a Montreal Female Benevolent Society is recorded to have been dissolved in February, 1822, with the orphans under its care consigned to various congregations, plans to help both sick and destitute immigrants and some "helpless orphans" soon led to the creation of a Protestant Orphan Asylum by the December of that year with the women actively involved. Cloying euphemisms such as the "launching of the infant bark" for "these little wanderers" represent a sensibility vastly different to Pelly's somewhat offhand remarks. Childhood sentiment was not yet dominant, however, as can be seen in the Ladies Benevolent Society, which while establishing a committee of visitors especially commissioned to visit the "fatherless," nevertheless gave equal attention to "the widow."3

The urge to "child rescue" was as much a process as a sensibility whose origins can be detected in the seventeenth century, whose growth occurred in earnest in the eighteenth, and whose most exotic fruits were harvested in the nineteenth. The process consisted of the assiduous inculcation of the values of the child rescuers and their class interests, the removal of children wherever possible from the contaminations of their environments and

66

the noxious influences of their adult models, and the training of these protected and segregated youngsters into honest, servile, and industrious habits. Miss Monflathers in the Old Curiousity Shop aptly expressed the assumptions behind such an emphasis on training when she remarked that the children of "the hewers of wood and drawers of water class are not made for ornament."

The removal of children from environments which were described more often in terms of being vice-ridden, profane, irreligious, and turgid, rather than brutalized and impoverished, frequently consisted of "snatching" them away from relatives, friends, and even parents. The people involved believed that the more extreme the removal the more effective the rescue. Moreover, effective rescue implied restraining those common and base elements that were all too obvious in the coarsened lives of the restless poor or the totally destitute. Thus order could be imposed on the disorder apparent in the vermin infested hovels, the meanest streets, the drunken licentious of the wharves and the surly looks of the masses.4

As effective rescue could be best supervised and controlled in physical settings, many children's institutions - charity schools, Sunday schools, ragged schools and schools of industry - emerged. Variants of these models were soon transplanted to British North America. Even when the active models were not transplanted the ideology of child rescue and the assumptions on which institutional arrangements were based were and these would be used to justify similar experiments in the colonies.

BRITISH MODELS OF CHILD RESCUE

Although scholars customarily acknowledge the influence of Victorian evangelicals on social action in the slums of Great Britain, the United States, and Canada, they less frequently note the institutional development of the seventeenth and eighteenth centuries that provided the base for Victorian activism. An understanding of these early orphan asylums, schools and houses of industry, and other charitable institutions and societies, is necessary in order to comprehend the first Canadian efforts at relief and rescue. These British institutions also provide the context for the debate over congregate institutions and boarding out and over general policies of relief, intervention, and prevention in trans-Atlantic Anglophone communities during the nineteenth century. A cursory examination of some British precursors to the Canadian experiments of classifying, separating, and subsequently specializing poor and dependent children, will assist in understanding similar Canadian phenomena and models.5

The eighteenth century charity school movement was a major extension of ideas concerning character development to the children of a class deemed a potential threat to the civil and religious stability of British society. As children's institutions, charity schools were the first substantial "modern" attempt to use formal education to instruct children in a protective environment, and as instruments of child rescue, they were the prototypes of nineteenth century pedagogical experimentation that culminated in the common schools.6

The charity schools with their concern for children were supplemented by older forms of mixed relief such as houses and schools of industry that included adults and children and the worthy and unworthy poor. Aware that indiscriminate association of inmates was "destructive of industry, order, and decency," the acting governors of the Dublin House of Industry in 1798 sought to classify them according to age, qualities, conduct, and abilities so that a "class of merit" - based on superior industry, moral conduct, and obedience to House rules - would be lodged and fed separately from their less worthy fellows. The belief in the value of employment and the danger of idleness was succinctly put in 1756 by the founder of the Ladies' Charity School (Bristol), who observed that when "youth, idleness and poverty meet together, they become fatal temptations to many unhappy creatures." Although the Bristol institution claimed to teach poor girls to read and spin, there is nothing in the tract to indicate that reading was actually taught while there is much about spinning.7

Isaac Watts' An Essay Toward the Encouragement of Charity Schools (1728) described in great detail both the regimen of many schools and the destiny of their students. Claiming it to "be a great and unspeakable advantage to these Schools . . ., if . . . some methods whereby all the children of the poor might be employed in some useful labours one part of the day" could be contrived, Watts recommended that children sufficiently instructed and improved should "be placed out, and fixed either in country-labours, in domestic services, in some inferior post in a shop, or in mechanic trades, that so they may not run loose and wild in the World, and forget all that you have taught them and lie exposed to temptation and misery." Robert Parker Pelly would express similar sentiments a century later in the Assiniboia.8

The insistence on useful employment and religious training as fundamental elements in the rescue of children and adults is a major theme in the reports of societies. In 1813, the Edinburgh Society for the Suppression of Beggars argued that its object required that "a great portion of their attention must be devoted to the education of the children of the poor in habits of morality and industry. . . ." Using the "new system of education" [monitorialism], the schools could provide cheap instruction, careful moral and religious training, and such employments as to render their pupils useful members of society. In an early discussion of separating children from their parents, the Edinburgh Society cited the expense of residential care and the hope that, given a proper day school, "the injury they will sustain from the society of their parents will not be so great as is apprehended."9

While much of eighteenth century interest in schools and houses of industry was aroused by the presence of sturdy beggars and other undeserving objects of charity, tract writers and philanthropists were equally attracted by the "educational cure" for pauperism by institutionalizing and instructing children. In a 1728 treatise on indiscriminate or "old" charity, Andrew Gairdner had taken more than a hundred pages and a torturous explication of scripture to conclude that an orphans' hospital was a most worthy object of Christian charity.10

In most cases, very limited schooling was provided children lodged in houses of industry. The 1759 rules of a house of industry in Suffolk required a school "where all children above three years of age shall be kept till they shall be five years old, and then set to spinning and such other proper and beneficial work as they are able to perform." As indicated earlier, the report of the Ladies Charity School in Bristol indicated a similar concentration on spinning as against instruction. Indeed, since the Suffolk institution makes no mention of what might be occurring in its school, one can only infer that the curriculum was the most elementary portion of an English school.11

The parish school of industry, St. James, London, probably typified Church of England activities on behalf of the urban poor. The 1792 regulations limited attendance to between six and twelve years, stressed the need for cleanliness, a slender diet, a mixture of the 3Rs, simple trades and domestic service, and household work. The four servants were to wash the children's hands and faces, comb their hair, clean their shoes and buckles, mend their clothes, and teach them early in life "a habit of cleanliness about their persons." Visits of parents, relatives, and friends were limited to Sundays.12

The Shrewsbury House of Industry sought to prevent children of depraved families from "inevitably imbib[ing] the contagion." The House, "by a total and complete separation of [children and youth] from the abandoned and depraved [would] place them out of the way of temptation, and prevent the fatal contagion of profligate discourse, and vicious examples." Girls at the age "in which their passions require the strictest guard and the strongest control" demanded special facilities, including at least separate working rooms and dormitories, if not a detached building.13

It is not until the nineteenth century that the more subtle possibilities of education are recognized by those seeking to promote a spirit of independence or self-reliance among the poor. An

70

1812 pamphlet, after demonstrating the pernicious results of public charities and parochial relief, concluded that "as education is necessarily the first step towards enlightening the mind, active benevolence can never employ itself more usefully than in the establishment and superintendence of schools." Such institutions were to be an essential means of convincing the poor that "it is upon their own exertions, habits of economy, and prudent foresight alone, that they and their families, must depend for their comforts, as well as their daily bread." That such "self-dependence" was not far from the minds of the poor was demonstrated in the complaint of the Bath Society with its 180 inmates that when "the children can earn something for themselves exclusive of clothing, and contribute towards defraying the expenses [of the school], they are taken away by their parents."14

The conditions that had given rise to the eighteenth century efforts at child-saving continued into the nineteenth century. In 1846, a Manchester committee formed at a public meeting to found a Ragged School, substantially modified their original plans by establishing the Manchester Juvenile Refuge and School of Industry. The society aimed at the rescue of "a large class of destitute and neglected children from the paths of vice, misery, and degradation, and to train them up to honesty, industry, and virtue." Rejecting confinement as inadequate means of reformation, the committee stressed prevention through an education that would "render them better fitted to endure and overcome the necessary hardships and temptations of a poor man's lot." The required education included three elements: first, reading, writing, and arithmetic, which were both useful and an excellent means of keeping the mind engaged; second, moral and religious training which were pre-eminently suited to exercise a "purifying, restraining and elevating influence" on children; and finally, industrial training to prepare the boys for a self-supporting occupation.15

The Society accepted the need to feed - even at its expense - all children during the day. As with the earlier Edinburgh Society for the Suppression of Beggars, children spent nights in their own homes. Minimizing the danger of evil example, the Society argued that "it would be unwise to attempt entirely to break off their family ties. The domestic affections ought rather to be cultivated. In many instances, the influence of an instructed child upon the mind and habits of the parent has been most happy; and its tendency will be almost always good." In support of their efforts to eradicate juvenile vagrancy and delinquency, the Manchester Society cited the success of the Aberdeen Schools of Industry.16

The Aberdeen Industrial Schools were first organized in 1841 as an instrument of reclamation and correction rather than punishment for juvenile offenders. Intended to serve the poorest children of Aberdeen, the founding committee judged that the essential elements of an industrial school were, in order of importance, food, training for industry, and instruction. The day included four hours of instruction, five of work, and three meals. The products made by the children reduced the expenses of the school and fostered in them "a sound principle of self-dependence." In contrast, the common day schools for the lower classes and the educational hospitals were cited as having failed miserably. The day schools failed to demonstrate to their students the importance themselves of what they were learning and stressed the need for uniform good behavior and propriety in the school-room with little application outside the school. The hospital system, after separating the children from their families, gave their inmates a standard of living and education that rendered them unfit "to struggle against hardship and privation."17

In addition to private philanthropic ventures, the poor laws provided a wide variety of indoor and outdoor relief. With the 1834 Poor Law Act Amendment, the process of unionization and rationalization of public charity created the reformed workhouse as the central institution of relief, and promoted the classification of inmates and the provision of special facilities for various classes, including children. These new services for children were hardly in place before the controversy over the results of institutionalization and the effectiveness of workhouse schooling erupted in the 1850s. Advocates of boarding-out, drawing on Irish and Scottish experience, argued for the superiority of rearing poor law children in surrogate families over the stultifying atmosphere of the workhouse.18

The debate brought into focus many of the perennial themes that would dominate thinking about dependent children. Although the new workhouse schools were designed to train and educate poor law children in specialized settings, it represented an older view of the effectiveness of institutional care. Building on principles of Lockean psychology and the organizational efforts such as the monitorial schools, the supporter of the great district schools believed that order, discipline, and a protected setting were the stuff that produced sturdy worthy poor. The opponents generally pushed the need to separate children from the models of pauperism and crime - usually parents and friends - to its logical conclusion, stressed the power of family life in resocializing pauper children, and noted the economy of boarding-out over institution-alization. Psychologically, boarding-out supporters reflected the more sentimental and sophisticated views of Rousseau and the early pedagogical theorists of the nineteenth century. Metaphors of growth and development pointed to the need for careful personal nurture and guidance of children and their inmate capacity to respond to significant primary human relations.19

Thus, with these precedents, sentiments and attitudes toward dependent children clearly established in Great Britain by the early nineteenth century, mature institutional models and ideas were available for transplantation by Canadian reformers involved in child rescue efforts. Given the culture lag generally manifested by colonial societies the nineteenth century efforts in British North America often included a mixture of conflicting organizational patterns and ideologies derived from British experience.

PHILANTHROPIC CHILD RESCUE IN BRITISH NORTH AMERICA

British industrial schools did not separate boys from girls or children from adult society. For children from "debased families," the preferred treatment was to bind them out so that they might have the advantages of family life. In the

73

colonies, this emphasis on labor, usefulness, and
family surveillance, accompanied a seeming absence
of differentiation in schools of industry. In the
1820s, the Montreal Society for Promoting Education
and Industry, like its parent society in London,
freely mixed the objects of its charity by providing
specialized attention for children who were
"destitute of bread" while including them in a
school of industry where they were expected to work
alongside the adult poor. In St. John's,
Newfoundland, a school of industry in 1808 engaged
female children in carding, spinning and knitting
while the boys were set to net making and mending or
otherwise bound out to local mariners. Less concern
was given to childhood sentiment than to imprinting
indelibly upon the lower classes the necessity for
all members of society to labor in order to be fed
and to dissuade the hungry from expecting charity.[20]

Apart from the provision of specialized
facilities in the form of a Protestant Orphan Asylum
in Montreal between 1822 and 1832, the impetus in
this direction was not properly felt until the
1850s. The rapid emergence within thirty years of
orphan asylums suggests a crucial shift in sentiment
and ideas about the care of dependent children. In
the final analysis, the existence of such
specialized facilities is more telling than the
immediate reasons for their creation. After
Montreal, Hamilton (1846), Toronto (1851), Saint
John (1854), St. John's (1855), Kingston and Halifax
(1857), Ottawa (1864) and Brantford (1869) boasted
an orphan asylum. Later in the century, these
models were imitated in Victoria (1873), Winnipeg
(1885) and Vancouver (1892). The provision of
specialized care demonstrates the power of a new
sensibility towards unprotected child life and the
urge to create a specific class of dependents with
specific needs. Institutionalized arrangements for
the new class of dependent children represents the
physical dimensions of the new sensibility.

The specific reasons behind the founding of
such physical arrangements, that is, orphan and
infant asylums, are less important than the changing
sensibilities they reflect, for it was this shift in
sentiment which gave birth to the transplantation of
models and the attitudes which made such
institutions possible. The creation of the orphan

asylum meant the possibility of a completely controlled environment, thus successfully implementing the dual conditions of "rescue" and "restraint" and facilitating the total segregation and protection of dependent children. The asylum, in short, was the logical extension of assumptions regarding the vulnerability, malleability, and ultimately the "educability" of children. The institutions themselves did not provide merely the physical aspects of child rescue - sheltering, feeding, and caring for an unprotected and deserving class - but they also facilitated the psychological aspect of child rescue through a deliberate and systematic training of their inmates into specific social expectations and social attitudes.

The Institution, therefore, was seen as the most efficient and effective means of training. Incarceration in institutions that were not solely custodial in function (orphan asylums) as well as those whose function was more identifiably repressive in management and origins (industrial schools and reformatories) was not to be "looked upon as punishment for crime but as giving the opportunity for the development, strengthening and training of the better qualities of the child. . . ." Both elements of caring and of controlling were woven into the assumptions behind institutions as refuges and as places of training and instruction. The seventh annual report of the Board of Inspectors of Asylums in Ontario delineated carefully the conditions that were requisite for the successful re-socialization to occur. The first was self evident, that is, the physical removal of the child from want and neglect. Second, the child was to be trained into industry. This was not to be confused with being "driven to tasks" but "apportioned according to his strength and capacity" with "due regard being given to his predelictions," a condition which reflects a commitment to Lockean forms of habit formation. Third, daily instruction of a religious and secular nature was imperative. Fourth, the classification of inmates and particularly the removal of dependents from incorrigibles was crucial. As most Ontario institutions housed the "homeless and destitute," the "neglected and abandoned," "orphans and vagabonds," as well as "incorrigibles," these circumstances caused some concern since it was feared that "the infant in years and in crime [was] exposed to the contaminating influence of the youth hardened in iniquity." Removal from unsatisfactory family life and unsavoury environments was destined to fail without a similar vigilance regarding separation of various classes of inmate and their varying degrees of offence. Finally, the report stressed the purposeful encouragement of a "home like" atmosphere to modify the risks of institutional indifference.21

These conditions faithfully depict the institutional model whether in Britain or in the colonies. Such a model was intended to create a new world of childhood for children otherwise denied either its privileges or its burdens. If separation were ensured by removal from "dissolute" relatives, then its psychological dimensions would be achieved through education, that is, training, instruction, and socialization. Such reformed children, would identify with a new social world and reject their former abodes, attitudes, habits and associations. Protection would be ensured through their removal from undesirable peers and a subsequent classification of inmates. The psychological elements of an artificially induced family life would in turn neutralize the more coercive elements of institutional life, although even in the best circumstances was this ideal rarely achieved. In 1859 according to the Kingston Orphan Asylum, the children were "put into so pleasant and comfortable a home, where as one family they [were] preserved from evil influences without, instructed in the fear of the Lord and trained into habits of virtue and regularity." Ten years later the report of the Board of the Inspectors of Asylums for Ontario agreed that the Institution allowed for "a healthy surveillance" which in turn resulted in habits of "regularity and industry."22

Rescue and restraint, care and control, and surveillance and solicitude were essential to successful child rescue. All were present in the concept of childhood just as all were essential to the rationales for and the management of British North American children's institutions.

The consequences of immigration and urbaniza-tion are the historical accidents of a phenomenon occurring simultaneously in Western societies and which manifested different sociological and demographic patterns. That "problems" of dependent child life were dealt with in specific ways, namely through institutional arrangements, is the crux of the issue and the evidence of a filtering down of the four criteria of childhood to new classes of children. This filtering process is evident in the protestant orphan homes (POHs) that emerged out of the urgent need to deal with immigrant children in the fever sheds or abandoned and orphaned children in the houses of industry and in the attitudes articulated in the philanthropic societies that founded the asylums.

In Montreal, St. John's, Hamilton, Kingston, Halifax and Saint John it was the dreadful consequences of the arrival of "ships laden with disease and death" that provided the impetus for rescuing the orphaned. The dead and dying in the fever sheds at Point St. Charles, Montreal, in the primitive shelters on Hamilton's bayshore, or in the typhus and cholera wards of the Toronto King Street General Hospital, left children entirely friendless in a strange land. Their situation resulted in a quickening of sympathy with the practical culmination of this sympathy resulting in the assumption of a social responsibility toward them and an urge to meliorate their obvious plight. In other words, the embryonic asylums, which grew out of this sympathy and which in turn became permanent institutions, were a pragmatic outcome of the combination of tenderer feelings towards dependent children as well as a response to the social problems that their condition presented.23

Margaret Freeman Campbell recreates the conditions which decimated Hamilton's early populations but such descriptions can equally apply to any other commercial centre last century. In stark language and Breughelian imagery she discusses smallpox in 1847 and cholera in 1849 and 1854, with the town crier chanting his requiem "Bring Out Your Dead" and the city's ruthless motto which was short and to the point - "Bread! Quicklime! And transportation out of town!" Her relentless documentation of the stench of "pale voiceless corpses begging burial" reminds us again the tenuous lives our ancestors lived. In the maritime colony

77

of Nova Scotia, Miss Charlotte Creighton wrote on 3 December 1834 to her relations in Scotland of the six hundred deaths from cholera in six weeks in Halifax "with the tar pots burning night and day." Over thirty years later the Toronto Daily Globe, 4 January 1866, observed the filthiness of the streets and recommended the cleansing of the thousands of open cesspools in the city so that "the mass of offensive rubbish and garbage," presently rendered harmless by the winter frost, would not prove fatal again in the warm season by aggravating cholera.24

Thus, in 1832, the consequences of an equally "awful visitation of Asiatic cholera" in Montreal encouraged the building of a permanent asylum for the orphans left in its wake; while, again in 1847, typhus and ship fever led to ninety-five children being admitted into the new building. Although the Ladies Benevolent Society originally attempted placing orphans of the epidemic, it found this an impossible task and was forced to open a permanent refuge for full orphans. In the winter of 1832, the Society had supported between forty and seventy children "on a plan, at once frugal, healthful and abundant."25

In 1854, "a deadly pestilence had been for four long and anxious months" raging in Newfoundland and the first annual report of the St. John's orphan asylum noted that the cholera bequeathed to the island "the widow and the orphan" with the formation of the Church of England Widows and Orphan Asylum accepting "the legacy." On November 10th of the same year, a public meeting was called by the Protestant clergy of Saint John to establish an asylum to shelter orphans left by cholera that ravaged New Brunswick.26

In Kingston, the immigrant sheds on Princess Street housed orphans and widows left from the fever that had been introduced into the city by ship loads of famished and desperate Irish immigrants. Orphaned children were received regularly into houses of industry, and in Kingston and Toronto, their situation in these public institutions generated active sympthy and partially contributed to the founding of orphan asylums. Both societies responded to the growing criticism of the conditions within their respective houses of industry and found

78

the treatment of children in these institutions to be both callous and cheerless.27

Founded by a private committee in 1836, the Toronto establishment aimed at "the total abolition of street begging, the putting down of wandering vagrants, the securing of an asylum at the least possible expense for the industrious and distressed poor" as well as preventing "an increase in pauperism." Supported in part by a parliamentary grant and the City Council, the house in its first year had relieved 857 of whom 638 were children and had forty-six inmates of whom twenty-six were children. By 1853, the House of Industry was giving its "most anxious attention . . . to making permanent provision for orphans, deserted children, and those whose parents have rendered themselves liable to legal punishment." A system of apprenticeship was devised by which a "large number of children were placed out with respectable persons in the country" whereby they were removed "from the temptations and vices to which they are exposed in a large city." To encourage training of children in habits of industry and sobriety that would "prepare them for usefulness and competency through life," the house of industry received children whose parents and friends were unable to support them, placed them at school, and cared for and protected their morals and persons, until suitable country homes could be found.28

In Kingston, the House of Industry, founded in 1814, did not close until 1916. The details of this institution, which are well preserved, give much of the appearance of the workhouses under the English Poor Law. Children, abandoned, orphaned, or destitute, were received by the House which acted in loco parentis with regard to placing them out or employing them in household chores. Children remained part of the House of Industry until the Orphans' Home and Widows' Friend Society opened its first building in 1857. Citing the degraded habits, predisposition to idleness, and the dubious health and morality of inmates as an undesirable environment for the young, the Society charged that the children were not "cared for, supervised [or] protected from the vice and degradation" in an institution that offered "no humanizing influences." The 1859 annual report noted that the Orphans' Home

79

had been established by members of the society who "in their visits to the House of Refuge continually witnessed the suffering and neglected state of destitute orphans and homeless children from whence they were too often consigned to those who desired them only as household drudges and care nothing for their temporal or eternal welfare."29

If benevolent ladies' societies reflected a growing refinement with regard to the concept of childhood by recognizing children as a special class with particular needs such as protection and segregation, there is less evidence that the general population was responding similarly to the shift in the concept. A memorial from the Orphans' Home committee to the House of Industry is recorded in the 1859 report as "representing the want of proper supervision over them [the children], the need of greater circumspection in putting them out, and of maintaining some subsequent control" after they had been bound. The House of Industry was managed by a gentleman's committee with a Ladies' Benevolent Society committee supervising the female wing and the school. It was the female committee which concentrated its efforts on the child inmates and recognized the fundamental problem involved, that is, if it could not approve of the House of Industry as an appropriate guardian, neither could it approve of street life and juvenile begging.30

The records of both Houses of Industry in Toronto and Kingston reveal a sometimes drunken, violent and quarrelsome environment where adult men and women were treated like intransigent and naughty children. Moreover, the Kingston Hospital, often transferred its terminal cases, its degenerates, and even the patients with "the itch" to the other public institution. In Kingston, alcoholics were probably a prevalent class of inmate because the records do not indicate severe chastisement or expulsion for drunkeness as one might have expected, given the regular exercise of the denial of privileges and threat of expulsion that resulted from minor misdemeanours or infractions of the house rules. Although not legally restrained to remain in a house of industry, which meant that it was not a place of punishment or incarceration like a penitentiary, the social and economic circumstances that had compelled inmates to either voluntarily enter or be admitted into the establishment usually constrained them to remain. Women and children, separated from husbands and fathers or from each other, sought temporary refuge until reunited. Children of immigrant mothers were cared for inside the house while the women worked outside during the day to return to the institution in the evening. If, however, the mother "misbehaved" in any way then all family members were summarily discharged. There were frequently far fewer beds than inmates and the majority of inmates were female, over forty, or under ten years with two females to every married man. The first Inspector for Prisons, Asylums and Public Charities, Mr. Langmuir, noted in 1859 that the Houses of Industry in Kingston and Toronto were virtually used as "poor houses" for little industry was conducted in them.31

It must not be thought that with the founding of orphan asylums in Kingston, Toronto or the Atlantic provinces the problems of children in houses of industry or poor houses were automatically resolved. Orphan asylums were overcrowded institutions operating on limited funds and, which, as shall be seen later, were selective in their admission policies. Bastard children were frequently prohibited from them just as were infants, epileptics, defectives, and delinquents. "Childhood" may have been the criterion for the asylum's existence but it was only a limited childhood. Often the children of the least socially acceptable poor - paupers, criminals, or prostitutes - were denied admission. Certain children, therefore, along with certain adults, were labelled as part of the "lumpen proletariat" by the patrons of the poor or the managers of municipal houses well before such a term had become popularized. The orphan asylums exercised considerable discretion as to whom they would admit and considerable arbitrariness regarding whom they identified as the "worthy or industrious poor."

The respectable poor were usually those who would be normally in a position to "help themselves" were it not for the extremities of their situations. In keeping with the attitudes regarding indiscriminate charity, the editor of the Kingston Chronical and News, 6 January 1860, typified the attitudes by observing "the truest and highest manifestation of charity is not made through

81

almsgiving. It is that which teaches and helps the destitute to help themselves." Six years later, the Toronto Daily Globe noted that a transfer of the English Poor Laws in toto or even in principle would "dry up the springs of private benevolence, whose gifts are blessed both to the receiver and the giver." Nevertheless, such rigid stands of economy and sentiment were modified in the case of most children and especially those of the industrious poor.32

The asylum represented a case of "discriminate charity," for although children received an institutional version of almsgiving, their training insisted upon their eventually helping themselves by attending willingly to their work and by preparing themselves for their future stations in life. The asylum consciously took children out of relatively open environments (for example, the streets, the poor houses, the house of industry) with their promiscuous mixing of people, and placed them into the hot-house environment of the institution. In the asylum, they were automatically made dependent while being assiduously protected and segregated from their former associations, friends, and sometimes, families. As the third report of the Toronto asylum explained, they were rescued from undesirable backgrounds and circumstances and placed into "the order and decorum of a well regulated family" where discipline was to be "strictly parental in character." The managers were convinced of "the necessity of a separate institution, such as this, wherein undivided care can be bestowed on the physical, moral, and religious training of its helpless inmates. . . ."33

Originally a Church of England asylum, the Toronto orphanage was organized in 1851 by three businessmen, the Reverend Stephen Lett of St. George's Parish and the mayor, George Gurnett. Its motto was TAUGHT BY THE POWER THAT PITIES ME I LEARN TO PITY THEM. During the first year the committee requested the House of Industry to continue receiving orphans until its building was completed. A ladies' committee appointed seven years previously continued to visit the women and children in the House of Industry. The Home, following the precedents set by the Montreal, Hamilton, and Albany orphanages, charged a fee of five shillings a month to parents or relatives who gave their children over into temporary custody. Not all homes were fee paying institutions and some such as the Halifax POH, for example, took great pride in operating solely on subscriptions after the model of Mr. Muller's orphan asylum in Bristol, England.34

In the case of Toronto, subscriptions for its building fund were received from fire companies, Orangemen, Free Masons, artisans and mechanics who all "cheerfully responded to an appeal by each contributing the produce of half a day's labour." Butchers, market gardeners, and bakers continued to give donations "in kind" to the Home in the following decades. The organizational and domestic management of the Home itself was consciously modelled on the structures and principles behind several British counterparts such as the London Orphan Asylum (although the Toronto POH was never to become so grand an edifice nor ambitious a philanthropy), the Wandstead Infant Asylum, the Female Aid Society of Inslington, and the Soho House of Charity.35

In 1856, an entertainment was given under Lady Head's patronage and the sum of £178.15.9d. was seen as "gratifying proof[d] how very deeply the people of Toronto sympathize[d] with the sorrows of the Protestant orphan." It was firmly believed that the children who came under the Home's "fostering care" would have been "the prey to ignorance, destitution and evil" had it not been for the "interference of the society."36

The importance of the Home's contribution to the rescue of Toronto's abandoned and orphaned children was reported in the Daily Colonist, 4 June 1858, which printed its annual report for that year.

. . . what would have been the probable fate of these sixty children were it not for the place of refuge so opportunely provided for them? . . . What would have been their fate not merely in time but in eternity? Those who walk the streets of this rapidly increasing city can readily answer this momentous question. How often on such occasions are we shocked to hear the lisping lips of infancy uttering their

Maker's name . . . Suppose then these
sixty children again let loose upon
society and what a frightful increase
of crime would be the result?

As their names suggest, the Protestant Orphans'
Home and Widow's Friend Society of Kingston and the
Orphans' Home and Female Aid Society of Toronto
originally included mixed categories in their homes
but soon restricted their interests to children.
Many institutions operated on a presumption of
economy that children could be cared for in the same
premises as other dependents. Indeed, as the
following examples illustrate, this curious mixture
of categories continued in some cases until the
twentieth century. The Montreal Home for the Aged
and Infirm, which always included children, still
retained seven old ladies along with its
ninety-seven youngsters in 1914. Earlier in its
history, the Home had received children from the
City into its industrial school as did the Hervey
Institute, an industrial school for female children,
founded in 1847. These children had been rescued
from ill treatment from their parents, and it was
apparently seen as eminently reasonable that
battered children should be trained into industrial
occupations to keep them from getting into future
trouble.37

In St. John's, an Anglican Widows' and Orphans'
Asylum, representing the interest of the cathedral
and the parishes of Saint Thomas and Saint Mary's,
conducted a modest institution, which, despite its
nomenclature, rarely cared for more than one or two
elderly ladies at a given time. The Asylum's first
report in 1856 stated that it would take in orphans
who had either lost both parents "or whose mother is
incapable of providing for them" as well as "the
destitute" which was understood to mean those
gentlewomen "without friends or means to support
them." The Ottawa POH, organized in 1864 by the
Ladies Protestant Benevolent Association and modeled
on the Montreal POH because one of its founding
members, Mrs. W. F. Coffin, had been associated with
the Quebec institution, originally included a refuge
branch for aged "friendless gentlewomen,"
respectable widows, girls "out of place" and
destitute children. Work with the first class was
not transferred to the Bronson Home for Protestant

Women until 1929, and then only after the strongest urging by provincial authorities.38

A decade after the founding of the Ottawa Home, a POH at St. Catherine's included aged persons with destitute children. In the same year, 1874, the Women's Christian Association (WCA) of London, Ontario, laid the basis for a Protestant Home for Orphans, Aged and Friendless. Initially these women had engaged in city visits "to cheer the sick and the desponding" but on finding many uncared for orphans and aged poor, and having "no extended means of supplying their wants, resolved to cast [themselves] upon a generous public and procure for them a home." The result was a house on Ridout Street, managed by a general female committee, that cared for "rheumatic and crotchety old men," orphans, widows, and fallen women. The permanent home on Richmond Street had inmates ranging from two and one-half to ninety-two years and whole families who were given shelter if their tale was "a pitiful one to which the ladies could not turn a deaf ear." Having a "wretched husband in jail" it seems constituted such a tale in the case of a woman with four children. In the 1880s the Home was restricted to young children.39

An unusual institution in that it did not follow the common pattern of increasing specialization of children to the eventual exclusion of adults is found in the Hamilton Orphan Asylum, which moved in the opposite direction by gradually excluding young inmates and transforming the charity into a Home for the Aged. Yet, in 1846, when the interdenominational Ladies' Benevolent Society organized a district visiting committee, it was noted that the greatest evil in the city was "the number of children half-starved, half-clothed, ill treated and uneducated, brought up in vice and crime." This observation was, however, less natural to this particular group of women than seemed the case, for it is apparent that the provision of outdoor relief, the visiting of their district wards, and the distribution of little benevolences was the work they felt most comfortable in performing. The Home for the Aged provided a permanent form of benevolence and relief whereas the temporary custody of children did not. Only in light of this can the ladies' sustained reluctance

85

to receive non-orphans and their stubborn insistence on the eligibility of full orphans be understood. Twenty-six years after its founding, while most other POHs were thriving this asylum, which could boast of only thirty-one inmates, lamented that the limited supply of children was due to their employment in Hamilton's factories and workshops. There are more likely explanations than this, however, including the Home's abhorrence of non-orphans (a rule which was reaffirmed in 1881); the existence of two other protestant homes, the Girls' Home founded in 1863 and the Boys' Home founded nine years later, and a rival Catholic institution, St. Mary's, which must have received many of the desperate poor's offspring as Hamilton's poorest were Catholic and Irish; and finally the Ladies' Benevolent Society's continued provision of outdoor in preference to indoor poor relief whenever this was possible. Nonetheless, by 1877, the institution was referred to as the "Home for the Aged," and by 1899, only seven children remained with thirty women. A year later this number was further reduced to three boys only. On the occasion of its golden anniversary, the home had sheltered only 829 children in fifty years and at no time did the home have more than fifty children at once. By the turn of the century, the ladies' committee, many of whom were members of the Women's Christian Association, publicly asserted that "as women, no work interests us more than that for women." Be this as it may, the gradual exclusion of children that had occurred well before the Hamilton CAS became involved in child care is an anomalous case in the rise and fall of the Canadian POHs.40

In 1876, another London institution, The Women's Refuge and Children's Home, whose aim was to "shelter helpless infancy and almost helpless womanhood," was operated by the WCA. It also included infants for in 1880 thirty-two inmates were recorded as under two years of age. The Home obviously met a need since this class of child was refused admission to the first London institution. In the same year, the Home for Orphans, Aged and Friendless recorded fourteen women, nineteen men, seventeen girls, thirty-three boys, one matron and five employees, and already 605 inmates had passed through its doors. By 1896 the WCA had three institutions meeting distinct needs - the original

Home, a Home for Incurables and a Home for Aged Men and Women.41

Even after the Toronto POH was organized, the need to separate and categorize children from adults was not general in that city. An interesting example of mixed categories occurred in 1856 when the City of Toronto purchased a tract of land to be used as an industrial farm "where offenders (particularly juveniles) may be classified and reformed, while punished, but also where many of the infirm and maimed might be made to assist, in some way, to their support." The plan as originally suggested to the governors of the House of Industry was intended for both juvenile offenders and "women of ill fame." So much for the separation of children. By 1860, Toronto met the needs of dependent children in the POH (1851), the Girls' Home and Public Nursery (1856) and the Boys' Home (1860), but the problem of "street arabs" and delinquent youngsters still was not resolved. Six years later the Toronto Daily Globe, 4 January 1866 and 10 January 1866, writing about "The Arabs of the Street," rejected the British models of Ragged Schools and heartily endorsed instead a house of industry or reformatory for them. If this could not be effected, then laws must be passed similar to those incorporated in the POH that allowed for them to be bound out. Parental cooperation seemed beside the point. Ragged schools, such as the one that operated in the same decade in Saint John, did not allow for complete separation from unsavory family and friends whereas reformatories or rural indentures did.42

Similar views expressed nine years earlier in Montreal advocated an "agricultural" reformatory because "mechanical" training drew the children to the cities on their release. Realizing that there might be some questions about taking non-convicted children from parents, the pamphlet insisted that the character of the parents and not the activities of the children should be the deciding factor. Similarly, in 1865, the first report of the Halifax Industrial and Ragged School insisted that child-rescue must be effected with or without parental consent.

Few are aware of the misery, the cruel

neglect, the brutal usage to which these
outcast children are subjected. To
leave them to the care of their parents
is to condemn them to certain ruin . . . .
Political economists may preach on the
natural rights of parents, and the
dangerous abuse of charity, but are they
to allow parents to sacrifice their
offspring to their vices, to offer them
in the fire of Moloch? They cannot
stand by without attempting to rescue
them.43

CHILD RESCUE AS PREVENTION

Undoubtedly, fear of societal disorder and
crime as well as a new sensibility towards children
combined in assumptions behind the founding of the
orphan asylum. The Halifax POH was a small and
totally specialized facility with accommodations for
thirty-five orphans between four and ten years. It
rescued young children "exposed to every temptation
and sin, fatherless and friendless in a cold and
infectious world." The belief in contagion, the
infection of the ordinary world, was paramount to
the founding of the asylum. The tenements, the grog
shops, and even the workplace were morally
contaminating places where children "caught" vice
just as they caught disease and were initiated into
loose language and loose living by profligate
adults. Surrounded by lewdness, slovenliness,
dishonesty and disrespect, they succumbed to moral
defects. Like the five boys rescued from the common
jail in 1865, such children, whose education had
been received in the streets, the brothels, the rum
shops and the Rockhead, the Halifax POH noted,
quickly grew "old in ways of deceit and hardened in
depravity." It was imperative that they should be
saved from such a fate, for unlike Dorian Gray,
these youngsters were unwilling but corruptible
victims, who if not "naturally" innocent could be
effectively trained into virtue and morality if
completely segregated from the vice haunts of the
city. From this perspective, boys were seen as
potential criminals and girls as potential
prostitutes.44

A Montreal pamphlet, Philanthropy: Care of Our Destitute and Criminal Population (1857), lumped together unconvicted waifs and strays with juvenile offenders as that class "who, from the circumstances in which they are placed, must of necessity become criminals as soon as they are capable." It recommended that since "the noxious weed must be nipped in the bud," separation from parents was imperative. For "As we pull down a worthless shed or stable to stay the conflageration, so must the family tie, sacred though it be, be snapped asunder when it becomes manifest that it could only be tolerated for evil to all concerned." Thus the children of the streets were perceived as the "dangerous classes" and "social pests," who caught moral contagions and whose very presence might cause a conflagration. Here we see the emergence of a call not just to rescue but also to restraint.45

Thus institutions, whether for neglected and dependent children or for "pre-delinquent" and "delinquent" children, may be understood as physical manifestations of the concept of childhood which either rescued dependent children from unsuitable conditions or reclaimed children from unsavoury environments and occupations. Ironically, reformatories and industrial schools rendered previously independent children dependent by categorizing many who were neither destitute nor orphaned as in need of rescue. Such children were effectively isolated and protected in institutional settings. Indeed, these children's very independence was perceived as an affront to those citizens who were determined to give even street arabs an appropriate "childhood" by imposing protection, separation, and dependency on them. The difficulty with such a task was understood for the street arabs "from infancy" cared for themselves and were ignorant of what was meant by the word "risk." In short "they [were] independent; they resist[ed] the very gentlest restraint, and their first impulse [was] to escape from it."46

A similar observation was made in Great Britain by Lord Houghton, who in reporting on the Leeds Ragged and Certified Industrial School, astutely noted that street children had the benefits of a "very curious education." He continued that

> I have no doubt those who have attended
> to them and see them closer than I have
> done, will confirm the fact of the pre-
> ternatural susceptibility of their
> senses, and the half-manliness, half
> womanliness of their relations to the
> men and women about them.

He optimistically added that once such children came
to appreciate the benefits of schooling and
custodial care in ragged and industrial schools
"they will be on the whole, very much above the
average of the ordinary children of those classes
who are committed to the care of charitable
institutions." The insistence on education and
training which took place under institutional, and
preferably residential, arrangements testified to
the nineteenth century belief in the power of the
well ordered asylum to reform society's deviants.
The externalization of such criteria of childhood in
institutional forms would subsequently lead to an
internalization of its norms by their innmates.47

There is, however, a further explanation for
the enthusiasm expressed in Britain for institutions
of a strictly reforming nature, which received
children who were neither criminal nor yet totally
abandoned. Ideas of prevention and protection were
only one side to a darker reality based on a new and
hard objective economic condition that was justified
and supported by an insidious class ideology that
regarded the lower orders as societal burdens and as
morally and intellectually inferior beings. In
Britain, Mary Carpenter succinctly exposed this
darker side by observing that compulsory and
universal schooling included the "wildest" street
children and the "lowest stratum" of child life, who
were urgently in need of improvement and
civilization because hitherto they had remained
untouched by any refining aspects of society.

In 1875, Carpenter ruefully pointed out that
even if such children were to "present themselves"
before the school authorities, frequently they would
not be included in the ordinary classroom, being
physically debilitated, clothed in tatters, having
skin diseases or head lice or scrofula, and being
not only filthy but quite ignorant of any sense of
order, concentration, or discipline. The social

perception towards such children was one of abhorrence, the school perception was one of fear for the contamination of other children, and the teacher perception was one of dismay. The first two perceptions are scarcely original but the last one is more interesting.48

Carpenter noted that such children, without any saving culture and also coming from circumstances that could not assist their academic progress, were among the most consistent failures in the elementary schools. Their movement from grade to grade was slow as they were the most difficult to teach and the least likely to learn. There seems no evidence at all to support Lord Houghton's optimistic claim that such children would learn faster and more thoroughly than others. Although many such children were not admitted into the regular day schools because of the problems mentioned which created seemingly insurmountable practical and pedagogical difficulties, others were not admitted because teachers prevented them. Payment by results meant that those who did enter were deprived of instruction while "brighter," that is, more socially acceptable, children were taught thoroughly. The wild and untouched street children "could not pass through grades and attain educational results entitling their teachers and managers to receive payment on their account from the Council of Education." This, of course, is not a statement of fact regarding their intelligence quotients but of their achievement. The combination of such a class of children and a system of payment by results was one that would have daunted even the most sincere and zealous pedagogues. Subsequently, many such children were the ones that found themselves in certified industrial or truants' schools in Britain or who busied themselves by avoiding school laws altogether. Due to this system, it must be assumed that not only did the ideas about rescuing street children by institutionalizing them flourish, so did the institutions themselves.49

In British North America the system of payment-by-results could not have been an impetus to the establishment of reforming institutions and industrial schools because there is next to no evidence of the practice; however, the similarity of the ideas and the rhetoric associated with such institutions abounded. Even without such a system, it is not difficult to transfer the principles of the British case to the common school teacher attempting to school the rude and raw material that was born and bred into the dangers and contaminations of street life in colonial societies.50

The Toronto Boys' Home for the Training and Maintenance of Destitute Boys Not Convicted of Crime stated in its 1861 report that one of its principal objects was the prevention of juvenile crime. It enthused that

> . . . many friendless little creatures, some the children of drunkards, some orphans, and others deserted by their parents have been rescued from want and misery, which in a few years would have rendered them almost irreclaimable, and sent them forth among us, vagabonds, thieves, and burglars, the pests and curse of the city.

Most of the 103 boys so far received were so young as to be "almost incapable of doing any sort of work"; however, being between five and fourteen years of age, the inculcation of correct attitudes and habits was possible and their reclamation probable. Significantly, however, perhaps even ominously, only nine of these 103 lads had been full orphans. Although not orphaned, the boys were either utterly friendless, or the children of "dissolute parents." Since a monthly fee was paid by the surviving parent, relatives, or those responsible for placing the boy in the Home, it seemed that many were not utterly friendless after all. The institution also offered a temporary lodging house for homeless employed lads to discourage them from spending their earnings gaming and drinking in "low taverns" or pursuing other "debasing habits."51

In Kingston, the Reverend K. M. Fenwick, fourteen years after the POH's faltering beginnings, understood that where appeals to charity might fail to elicit funds, those that combined both charity and the putting down of "street roughs" and "juvenile rowdyism" would probably succeed. The asylum, he claimed, trained potential criminals into habits of industry and order so that the children rescued from "the intemperance and carelessness of their wretched parents" would not grow up into "ignorance and vice." The natural consequences of an unrescued life would be a "career of degradation and crime, with most injurious consequences for the peace and good order of the city." Moreover, he pleaded eloquently for the cause of the asylum by asking whether no hand would be stretched to save the children on the streets.

> If they were in danger of drowning in
> our lake strenuous efforts would be made
> to save them. But the destruction that
> awaited them in present circumstances
> was more terrible. Should they be
> allowed to fall into it without earnest
> efforts being put forth to rescue them?52

There is considerable duplication of the rhetoric, the sentiments, and the institutional consequences surrounding the confusion of street arabs with criminals, of rowdyism with immorality and of poverty with viciousness. From Ontario to Newfoundland the similarity of sensibility is unmistakeable. A writer to The Standard and Conception Bay Advertiser at Harbor Grace, 30 May 1860, articulated the concern of the middle classes regarding children roaming "lawless" about the towns. The writer, under the pseudonym of "Humanity," deplored the numbers of "guttersnipes" in the streets who were, it seems, "expressing their extreme felicity in a language made up of most extraordinary noises very like a bad street organ." The belief that such guttersnipes were destined to become the criminals of the future was as pervasive as it was compelling. Ideas that related criminality with pauperism spread the assumptions of child rescue which were grounded on the belief that children could be reclaimed from paths of vice, or better yet, prevented from walking them. By mid-nineteenth century, "the hulks, the prison, and the lash," no longer were seen as appropriate means of dealing with young and old alike. The rhetoric that prevention was better than cure was imbedded in child rescue sentiment which said that not only was reclamation wiser and more humane, but, as the Halifax Industrial School report asserted, it was economical too. Reformatories were cheaper in the long run than Bridewells.53

Identical views can be traced in New Brunswick when one examines an inquiry of 1857 into the inmates and operations of provincial institutions. The first session of the New Brunswick House of Assembly in 1857 duly noted that these boy prisoners were "without parents or friends to instruct and guide them, and without homes to attract and improve them." Consequently, they "were thrown into circumstances" of exposure and temptation and thus "became an easy prey to vice." Previously in 1845, the _Journal_ of the House of Assembly had publicized at length the provisions in Great Britain accorded the special treatment of juvenile offenders and suggested similar action be taken. Again in 1857, it was urgently recommended that immediate arrangements be made to provide "for the improvement of this class of offender." Segregation for boys was to be ensured by a special building with a school and special keeper, and for young girls by segregated quarters in the almshouse. Nevertheless, the New Brunswick Boys Industrial Home was not established until 1895, and then on the premises of the former Saint John penitentiary. Meanwhile, vagrant and delinquent children were bound-out, usually in the country, under the appropriate clauses of the Poor Acts.54

To prevent girls from growing up in Halifax in the midst of "baneful influences," a ladies' visiting committee established the St. Paul's Almshouse of Industry in 1867. The girls were trained into household tasks with "systematic regularity" and taught the three Rs. Miss Isobella Binney Cogswell, a Halifax philanthropist, was involved in this endeavor as she was with the establishment of the Industrial school which had emerged from a Ragged school. The girls, rescued by this almshouse committee, were the abandoned, the daughters of widows, or girls reputedly caught begging and buying liquor for their parents with the alms they received. Certain that such girls would one day come under the worst influences of city life and resort to prostitution, the aim of the small establishment was

To preserve young girls, whose position,

94

whether through the fault or only the
misfortune of their guardians, is one
of proximity to vice, from being ruined
by the noxious influences around them.
It is not a house of refuge for those
who have already fallen but a home for
such as in early life are in the midst
of temptation . . .55

The Saint John Haven and Rescue Work Home
established in 1888 operated under a committee of
less than a dozen ladies who superintended the lives
of girls after they left the refuge. The girls were
committed to the Home by police instead of
incarcerating them in the jail as vagrants. Thus,
"unfortunate and despairing" girls and women were
maintained in this Home alongside children who were
taken from the "most appalling conditions." One
case, that of little Ethel Vanbuskirk, "a child
rescued through their means from a life of
wretchedness and vice," was placed carefully and
watched over for some years after she had been taken
from the almshouse in 1890. The ladies committee
tried in vain to get Ethel's mother to surrender the
eight year old girl to the orphan asylum. To
finally separate her from the influence of her
parent, Ethel was placed as far away as Kingston.
At no time did these ladies nor many of their
counterparts elsewhere question their right to take
children away from parents nor would they have
agreed with the rights of parents to retain their
children.56

Disreputable family settings and the freedom of
the streets were both antithetical to the changing
ideas of child savers. Such concern had been
expressed since 1820 as the case of the Poor Man's
Friend Society in Halifax demonstrates. Its second
annual report pleaded that the juvenile poor be
given special attention because of "the abominable
practices associated with street begging such as
theft and seduction." The first annual report of
the Halifax Industrial and Ragged School insisted
that unsupervised "street arabs" be "snatched from
certain ruin." It further noted that

In all large cities there is a number of
boys and girls growing up under influences
that mould and shape them for evil and not

for good. . . . These are the heathen at
our own doors, and worse than heathen;
Arabs in the city; the standing reproach
to our Christianity. These form the
dangerous class in every community.

Between 1840 and 1860 the "climbing boys" of Halifax
received much sympathy and attention from
philanthropists and the press. An argument
fulminated in 1862 as to the public's preference for
chimney sweeps over machines which were
"inconvenient and dirty."57

The "street boy" problem was undoubtedly the
reason behind the establishment of the Industrial
school in Halifax in 1864. The street boys' lot was
seen as "a sad and melancholy" one because,
according to their critics, they came from drunken
parentage and earned their living by "begging and
stealing or playing tambourine at some low public
house." It was also observed that they lived in
sewers, outhouses, dog kennels, or wherever they
might find shelter. It is less obvious that the
street boys themselves, despite their precarious
existences, agreed to their reclamation into "the
paths of industry and virtue." Paper bag making and
the manufacture of nails must have been confining
activities when compared with their previous
independent careers. The 1866 report of the school
observed that the boys seemed less than enthusiastic
about their incarceration for they were
insubordinate and discontented and "the whole place
looked comfortless." Nevertheless, later in the
century the Society for the Prevention of Cruelty to
Animals continued to "snatch" such lads and force
them into the paths of rectitude.58

The Halifax school had combined two efforts in
1864 - the ragged school on Albermarle Street and an
industrial school on Madra Hill; however, within the
year the Christian Messenger, 24 May 1865, requested
that the name "ragged" be removed from its title.
Its prime aim had been the prevention of crime "by
cutting off the supply" because its founders firmly
believed that paupers and criminals were "two
terrible cancers eating into the very heart of the
body politic and if not eradicated, or at least
checked - threatening to its very life." The
Industrial School freely mixing boys convicted of

crime with waifs and strays, treated them identically. Waifs, strays, or criminal lads, these were the DANGEROUS CLASSES.59

Childhood innocence, if it even existed, was all too quickly tarnished with the class of children known as street arabs. The 1867 report of the Halifax Industrial School stressed that

> Here are boys young in years, but old
> in ways of deceit and hardened in
> depravity. Details as to thought,
> speech and behaviour we cannot give.
> He that knows what effects on the
> whole nature, habit, and associations,
> connected almost wholly with dirt,
> discomfort, rudeness, blasphemy,
> lewdness . . . he only can do justice
> to the difficulty of the work that
> has to be done, before such natures
> can be redeemed from the power of evil.

Under the circumstances, Mrs. Grierson, the matron, deserved the public's utmost sympathy for "what mother would cast her lot and that of her children with such a crowd of grown up boys from the worst parts of our city unless renewed by the love of God and man?"60

It must be noted that these comments support the argument that "childhood" was a protected, segregated and dependent state, and that its members were rescued on one hand while restrained on the other. Childhood implied an aura of childish innocence. These "grown up boys" from Halifax did not meet these criteria at all and Mr. Grierson, the superintendent, himself felt bound to resign his position in 1875 because he felt that the school did not succeed in cutting off the supply at its source. Childhood and innocence were luxuries in the streets where so many street arabs still remained enjoying the liberties and enduring the penalties of their unprotected state.61

The confusion of categories of dependent and delinquent children remained even after various pieces of legislation, notably the 1893 Ontario Children Protection Act and the later Dominion Juvenile Delinquents Act of 1908, clearly separated the two. The 1893 act, which was used as the model for subsequent provincial legislation, provided for the protection, care, and control of neglected and dependent children with such mandates particularly given to the Children's Aid Societies. Moreover, after the delinquency act, the juvenile court "in action" was frequently remiss in not clearly delineating the categories despite the strictures "in law" to do so. Discussion regarding age categories in public institutions occurred in Ontario at least since the passage of the 1857 "Act to Provide Gaols for Young Offenders" designated as providing for all "infants" - those under twenty-one years of age. The consequent broad range of offence and age of offenders rendered reclamation practicably impossible.

Older children were viewed as risks to satisfactorily maintaining the order of the institution. In the case of the Mercer Reformatory for Girls, the Inspector of Asylums and Prisons reported in 1884 that girls under twelve offered more satisfactory material for reform "before they [had] constructed habits of sin" which were likely "to contaminate the young and innocent children" in the same institution. Older girls, it was feared, might come to the institution addicted to "the solitary vice." It was generally feared that once the presence of masturbatory habits was felt, it would spread like a disease whose insidious influence debilitated the whole reform and rescue program.62

Not only did the mixing of older and young chidren come to be viewed askance, but sentences come to be seen as far too short to effect reclamation. Thus, in 1866, William Moore Kelly, the warden of Penetanguishine Reformatory for boys, recommended longer sentences generally, and the report of the Inspector of Asylums stressed a fixed minimum sentence of three to five years depending on the child's age. The report said that two year sentences for children under sixteen were too short to "make any solid impression on minds so young and thoughtless." Not only was an absence of classification unsatisfactory on grounds of undesirable moral influences, but the officials involved in the discipline of the public institutions saw as alarming the propensity of older children to return "to former abodes of depravity and crime," as J. P. Kennedy, the Catholic chaplain to Penetanguishine, observed with the result that children over sixteen did not "requite the labor and pains bestowed upon" them.63

The day book of the Church of England orphan asylum in St. John's warned against the evil influences surrounding street children. It advised the rescue of "those human waifs who are scattered over the country" and encouraged their protection in orphanages lest they be "snatched into error and ignorance and into a most dangerous future." By the second half of the century, children were clearly seen as in dire need of protection from adult society and if not in the bosom of their own homes, whether middle class or respectable labouring class, then segregated into artificially created surroundings. The "child institutionalized" was synonymous with the "child rescued." Families, schools, or orphan asylums - these were deemed appropriate settings for children. The Institution generally represents the rationalization and categorization of treatments for deviant and specialized social groups, and as children became increasingly differentiated from the general population, they were accorded their own facilities. Dependent children promised the child savers the most potential for rescue since they could be absolutely protected and segregated from those influences identified as unsuitable for their proper nurture, successful training, and effective resocialization.64

The growing socio-psychological consciousness of the "true nature of childhood" expressed itself in physical facilities. Like the common school, the orphan asylum became an experiment in the modern concept of childhood - a crucible in which the sometimes confused and groping sensibilities depicted in this chapter were transformed into norms that no longer required total institutional surveillance.

Charity Givers and the "Child-Institutionalized" 4

> There is power in sympathy and
> kindness and persevering and
> disinterested efforts for the good
> of others which has proved effective
> in cases of the most hopeless nature.
> We read of much that has been
> accomplished by female agency.
> Let us seek to imitate the examples
> set by our sisters in other lands,
> and 'haste to the rescue'. . . .
>
> Kingston POH, 1860

In 1854, the Reverend Mr. William Bond preached an edifying sermon before the Ladies' Committee of the Protestant Asylum for the Aged and Infirm. Pointing out that the Home was the only Protestant institution in Montreal that accepted children who had not lost both parents, the future Anglican bishop warmed to his subject by praising womankind's "softening, elevating, purifying, gladdening influence; her fond companionship in the seasons of joy, her devoted tenderness in the hours of sickness." His remarks were a salutary reminder that those ladies who had organized themselves into benevolent societies to found houses of refuge and orphan asylums were gentlewomen of means and respectability with virtues peculiar to their sex and entirely suited to such philanthropic endeavors.1

Some two decades earlier, a Ladies' Benevolent Society, activated into charity giving by the fearful cholera epidemic of 1832, had expressed hope "that a Female Society, whatever may be their deficiency in other qualifications will be enabled to devote more time, while they bring no less zeal and affection to the work than one composed of the other sex. . . ." In this case the work referred to was that of a permanent refuge for orphans.2

Largely through the efforts of such

101

organizations the segregation of children was
affected in specialized asylums. Even in cases
where gentlemen's committees founded the institutions or retained official governance, it was
through the ladies' committees that actual management and control were directed. The activities of
these committees represented one of the earliest and
most remarkable demonstrations of female philanthropic genius in British North America. Taking the
sphere of "child rescue" as women's domain, these
ladies were active from Newfoundland to Victoria in
the Protestant Orphans Homes (POHs) and later in
Infants' Homes. The founding era represented the
convergence of sentiment, economic change, and
middle class social conscience. From the records of
these pioneering institutions and their descendents,
it is possible to construct a model orphan asylum
and to examine its founding, institutional
development, policy formation, daily operations, and
its accommodation with external forces. As with
other agencies, the asylums found themselves from
their beginnings victims of changing social values,
scientific knowledge, and economic and demographic
transformations.

THE RISE OF THE ORPHAN ASYLUM

     Being in close contact with the realities of
poverty through their personal ministrations in the
houses of industry or through visiting the poor, it
was not uncommon for the women to seek more radical
means of the amelioration of children's
circumstances through the establishment of
specialized institutions. While the majority of the
institutions grew out of a gentlemen's steering
committee which elicited funds and support by
calling of a public meeting, the steering committee
itself frequently had been formed from interests
expressed through ladies' aid or female benevolent
societies. For example, in the mid-nineteenth
century in Toronto and Kingston, it was their first
hand contact with the wretchedness of conditions in
the public institutions and houses of industry that
prompted female "visiting" committees to first
articulate the necessity of taking children out of
these squalid surroundings and sheltering them in
institutions specifically devoted to their care.
Because of these origins, the same families were

102

often represented on the male committees of the House of Industry and the female committees of the offspring institutions, the Protestant Orphans' Home. For example, Thomas Chown, a prominent Kingston citizen and a proprietor of a flourishing building supplies business, was on the House of Industry board and tendered building contracts to the institution while his wife was actively involved in the Orphans' Home.[3]

The movement to separate the relief of children from adults coincided with the growth of Ladies' Aid Societies in several colonial cities such as Halifax, Ottawa, Toronto, Hamilton and Montreal and later with the Women's Christian Association in London, The Women's Christian Union of Winnipeg, The Local Council of Women in Vancouver, and the Lady True Blues of the Orange Orders in Fredericton, British Columbia and Saskatchewan all of which imitated these earlier female efforts. Consequently the orphan asylums and related institutions offered socially prominent middle class women one of their few opportunities to establish, make policy for, and manage a socially significant agency. The houses of industry and the poorhouses were established in response to poverty and misfortune that left a human residue beyond the capabilities of families and friends to alleviate. As general relief agencies, these institutions relied on organized private benevolence or periodic and often erratic public grants to ease the misery of all classes and ages. As generalized extensions of private and public charity, houses of industry and poorhouses were dominated by men. In contrast, the orphan asylums were specialized institutions that excluded men and served children and restricted categories of women.[4]

Just as the London Refuge was intended to prevent widows and unwed mothers from descending "the path of degradation and become an easy prey for the enemies of souls," the Halifax Ladies' Benevolent Society, a committee of twelve women, reported that the St. Paul's Almshouse of Industry for Girls, founded in 1867, was intended to withstand the awful possibilities of procuring and prostitution. This committee quickly took over the organizational details of the Almshouse of Industry from the founding gentlemen's committee and enthusiastically embraced a supervised and systematic training program for its inmates.5

The Toronto POH's committee, expressing concern equally for widows and girls out of service and for orphans, established an employment registry for seamstresses and servants to prevent the former group from being drawn into "the vortex of iniquity and irrevocable degradation." By concerning itself with such groups, the Toronto POH, served as a rudimentary, although quite insufficient, "advocacy organization for poor women." The ladies committee of the Montreal POH not only provided a soup kitchen in its first years but quickly recognizing that domestic servants were "a class so important to every community" (and certainly not excluding themselves) - maintained a "Register for Domestic Service" for widows for some years.6

Given the inmates of the asylums - even in those cases where a men's committee had organized the home, a "ladies" committee was immediately needed to supervise the domestic economy and management of the institution. Such immediate management soon relegated men to such limited if essential tasks as the audit of incomes and expenses, the preparation of legal instruments, the investment of the societies' endowments, and the provision of honourary services as physicians and solicitors. Many of the medical, auditing and legal officers, as spouses or relatives of the women, were paid only nominal fees for advice on land purchase and the subsequent intricacies of building, architectural and like problems. Sometimes prominent citizens such as Sheriff Glass of London were retained as nominal governors to provide the necessary liaison between the home and the city in the distribution of municipal grants and to assist in the currying of favors regarding civic regulations or the acquisition of suitable land sites.

That such pragmatic use of male involvement cannot be construed in any way as relegating the ladies' committees to a secondary status can be seen from the founding meeting of the Ottawa home. Mrs. Thorburn, an Ottawa gentlewoman and one of the original members, observed in her memoirs that, "It was not customary for ladies to occupy platforms in 1864 and they modestly sat on the side benches" and the gentlemen drew up the bylaws and the constitution. She wryly suggested, however, that in this case such modesty was quickly overcome once the official business arrangements of the fledgling project were completed. In Halifax, too, it might be noted that William Cunard, the powerful shipping magnate, was nominated President of the POH in its first years of formation, but it was his wife who largely contributed to the actual organization of the institution. Cunard, however, was an invaluable member of the male board of governors because of the fund raising endeavors he organized successfully just as were Mr. Bronson's efforts and financial support in Ottawa.7

As committed but genteel Christians, the ladies practised a conventional religious benevolence that distinguished between the worthy and unworthy poor, noted the advantages of careful guidance of dependent and destitute children, understood the differences between middle class family life and the situation of most children of the poor, and recognized the limits of reformation without personal service. A description of Mrs. Thorburn, wife of an eminent Ottawa businessman, and influential member of the Ottawa POH committee for over sixty years, could well be used in summary of her generation of women who founded similar asylums. When she died in 1927, it was said of her that she had been "the last of that group of women who were God-chosen over sixty years ago to be the founders of the POH in Ottawa. She was a woman of stalwart piety, unflinching determination, and great courage." Actually Mrs. Thorburn's "piety" was less noticeable than her singular loyalty to the home (she had missed but one annual meeting in those six decades) and her hard-nosed, pragmatic organizational acumen during this impressive period of service.8

If women such as Maria Thorburn and Mrs. Bronson represented the faithful vanguard in Ottawa, Mrs. G. A. Sargison, founder of the Victoria home and an actual member of thirty years until her death in 1905, and Mrs. E. C. Thomas of the Hamilton Orphan Asylum, whose presence was felt from 1846 for the next thirty years, demonstrated identical fidelity. Frequently generations of the same families, such as the Bronsons of Ottawa, Mucklestons of Kingston, and Haywards of Victoria,

105

held court and monopolized the rules and domestic management of the institutions for decades. Even in 1942 a Mrs. Edward Cridge still sat on the Board of the Victoria Home, a lasting reminder of its faltering beginnings under the patronage of Bishop Cridge in 1873.

The Infants' Home and Infirmary of Toronto enjoyed the unceasing devotion of two women covering a period of seventy years after its establishment in 1875. Mrs. John Ridout, who had been previously engaged in the affairs of the Burnside Lying-in Hospital, became president and a forceful influence until 1918 when Miss J. Vera Moberley took over the Home's management and direction, changing its policy and practices for the next twenty-six years. When such members of the "old guard" of the institutions either died or resigned, the result was usually a feeling of deep loss, a lack of direction, and a vacuum in leadership which frequently led to a major reorganization. Miss Moberley, by replacing the institutionalization of infants and mothers with boarding out care for both infants and mothers thus radically transformed the Home.9

Although much has been made of the POH committees' evangelical proclivities, it is inaccurate to attach common religious characteristics to either the founders or the succeeding generations of women. Most of the women were associated with religious societies and were the wives and daughters of clergymen. In some cases the asylums were fairly direct extensions of individual denominational activities, e.g., the Anglican sympathies of the Victoria and Toronto Homes; however, more frequently, as with the Kingston, Ottawa and Alexandra Homes, women from several churches came together to form non-sectarian societies. In both the denominational and non-sectarian institutions, the brand of religious training and indoctrination offered hardly represented oppressive evangelical fervor. Moreover, aside from a selectivity regarding suitable objects of their benevolence, the ladies rarely promoted religious instruction in excess of that available in most churches and Sunday schools apart from a sometimes perfunctory attention to mealtime and "family" prayers under the supervision of the Matron, who was more often than not too harried by her responsibilities to engage in excessive religious inculcation.10

Curiously, then, the records contain few indications of an obsession to proselytize more than the commoner pious platitudes of their day with religious earnestness definitely subsumed under the simpler practical suggestion to ensure the "spirit of docility and subordination [that] testifies to good management." The assumptions underlying the foundation and policies of the asylum, therefore, reflected broad Christian values relating to social order and individual behavior and not the views of doctrinaire religious enthusiasts. As questionable as these conservative viewpoints may appear to twentieth century secularists, they do not have the heat and intensity of religious revivalism or the dedication commonly associated with evangelical social work in Britain and America.11

Believing implicitly in the peculiar malleability of child life in a quasi-family setting, if a natural one were not possible, the ladies rejected the idea that dependent children ought to be included as part of a pauper class which automatically represented a residual category of outcasts within an economic system that primarily judged its members according to their production. Although the founding of many POHs was a pragmatic response to the orphans left behind after diseases had taken the lives of their guardians or a sentimental response to the presence of children in public institutions, elsewhere the philanthropic urge to rescue children through institutionalized means was a reflection on "noblesse oblige."

In Ottawa, for example, the "relief of destitute children and other kindred objects" had been "long and ardently desired by the charitable and philanthropic part of the community" when Thomas McDowell, the brother of Copper Johnie, a familiar Ottawa beggar, became the first boy orphan admitted for the "cure" of the institution in 1864. Having observed that the Toronto Ladies Aid Society had imaginatively brought the singer Jenny Lind some fourteen years previously to raise the first public subscriptions for an Orphans' Asylum, thirty lady subscribers - representing several Protestant denominations - displayed their social accomplishments before an excited public at literary and musical evenings as well as a Grand Promenade Concert at the British Hotel. A local newspaper speculated "the commodious salon of the British will doubtless be crowded by the beauty and fashion of the city," although it predicted that social intercourse and parading would be impeded in the crowded rooms in these days of "crinoline and amplitude."[12]

The Homes competed for eminent patronesses such as Lady Head, the Countess of Elgin and Kincardine, and the Marchioness of Lansdowne, who featured prominently in the annual reports. Lady MacDonald, the wife of Canada's first Prime Minister was Ottawa's first directress. Not to be outdone, the ladies of the Toronto Infants' Home gained the patronage of Princess Louise. Most POHs, however, began less auspiciously and with a more modest and prosaic awareness of a scheme's utility and urgency. In Victoria, a ladies' committee of twelve members first accommodated neglected and orphaned children in private homes using private subscriptions to pay for their support until a more commodious congregate shelter was obtained.[13]

The institutional arrangements under the Maritime poor laws or under the modified legislation of Ontario, as well as the orphan asylums and infants' homes that sprang up throughout the second half of the century in commercial centres across the country, were dissimilar in several ways from those of Britain. While using much the same rhetoric and seemingly transplanting institutional models, the house of industry and of refuge, even before the segregation of their child inmates, never became the huge, impersonal, and architecturally pretentious buildings of the new 1834 British Poor Law Act. These buildings were mainly show-pieces while certainly older buildings like Westminister Asylum for Female Orphans, or the London Orphans' Asylum, could not have been designed with the needs of either children or adults in mind. As bleak as life must have been for the Canadian dependent poor compelled to remain in their parish and municipal "almshouses," they retained more the appearance and organizational patterns of earlier models and bear a striking resemblance to the American colonial buildings discussed by David Rothman. While being

parsimoniously governed and sorry places, the
Canadian poorhouses were frequently ordinary
(although decrepit and cheerless) "homes" or
farmhouses, and did not exude quite the forbidding
aspect of Britain's "pauper palaces" and vast
congregate systems. The POHs and the Protestant
Infants' Homes were also inauspicious undertak-
ings.14

Although initially the charity-givers affected
grandiose schemes and ambitious architectural plans
for a pretentious asylum so they might boast of it
as an "ornament of the city," no institution
sufficiently captured the public's imagination so as
to secure the necessary funds. Indeed, such plans
were seen as extravagant, if not folly, by a
Canadian public not distinguished for endowments to
philanthropy or education.

Apart from the absence of large benefactors,
the cheapness of individual contributors was
sometimes striking. Lists of "donations in kind"
rather than money expose the inevitable problem
resulting from this kind of charity, although it is
equally obvious that people generally remain more
willing to "donate" worn and often soiled clothing
than dollars. Even wearable clothing rarely fitted
and had to be cut down to the children's size. Food
donations were particularly problematic. Unless dry
goods, they quickly became stale or rotten - if they
had not come to the institutions in that state.
After a generous food donation, the inmates of the
Home had a feast, whereas normally they were
subjected to scarcity. Neither were local merchants
and tradesmen reluctant to donate inferior goods,
merchandise, building supplies, furnishings or
repairs. Dripping, neckties, broken dishes,
cordial, stale buns, hair cuts, pickles, figs, wood,
candy, wool, chicken pies, worn boots, gloves -
these and a thousand other knick-knacks and
miscellanea of dubious permanent usefulness or
monetary value poured in from both ordinary
households and eminent citizens.15

Concerts, teas, bazaars, vocal entertainments,
an "Evening with Dickens," tag days, kirmesses,
auctions, and outright begging letters were some of
the devices eliciting funds for the institutions.
The Toronto Infants' Home advertised cots and

cradles at $1000 for a permanent endowment; and in 1856, the Little Maids Club of the city raised sufficient funds to endow the "Maurice Mason" cradle, permanently set aside for deserted baby boys. The Ottawa ladies were quite agitated in 1868 after they had made arrangements for what they perceived was a coup to elicit funds, a lecture by Honourable D'Arcy McGee on the 18th of April. Unfortunately, it was cancelled when the gentleman was assassinated only eleven days before.16

The annual public meeting with the presentation of the annual report was always used as a fund raising occasion. The printed report, which was frequently published in the local press and freely distributed for publicity, always caused either consternation or gratification with its lists of contributors and their contribution. At one stage, the expense of the report almost convinced the Winnipeg ladies to cut down on the number of pages of names, but it was decided that it might lose donations if the donors did not see their names in print. Good works, it seems, were not to be hidden under a bushel. The public meeting was an occasion of great excitement and preparation. If the orphans were not performing a "Japanese" or "military" drill, they were "evincing careful tuition" in their renditions of hymns specifically chosen for the solemnity of the occasion and the pathos of their situation. They were paraded in their Sunday best with their condition visible to all.17

In Victoria, "What A Friend We Have In Jesus" was certain to move sentimentalists into shedding a tear or two and perhaps even into putting an extra dollar into the collection plate. At Kingston, it was "Rescue the Perishing" that was plaintively sung by the children, spotless in their black dresses and white pinafores or white coats and black trousers. Toronto boasted its own "Orphan's Prayer," set to music, whose words included a plea to "Make Our Orphanhood Thy Care."

> Touch all Christian hearts today
> Till Thy deathless Kingdom come,
> Bless, oh bless, the Orphan's Home!18

In 1882, sitting on the platform with the dignitaries, the orphans of St. John's were smartly

110

dressed in red cloaks or sailor suits, affording "a delightful contrast between charity children of today and those of olden time in England, with their curious and sad coloured dresses, and also between themselves and what they might have been, but for the saving culture of this noble institution."19

Generally speaking, the finances continued in "a languishing state" throughout the history of most POHs. An example of the "genteel" poverty occurred in Winnipeg in 1910 when the ladies' committee received one dollar in the daily post returned by the health inspector who described it as "a bribe." The "criminal" proved to be the matron who was summarily dismissed within three weeks. While there is no reason for her futile moral lapse, one might suppose that perhaps the sewage was not up to standard, her kitchen facilities below par, or she had not quarantined a contagious infection. There are, of course, any number of possibilities but most come back to the basic problem - the lack of money to support proper standards in the institutions. Deficient sanitation and hygiene were common because most buildings were deteriorated and sub-standard accommodations. It was not only in London in 1876 that the boys could have been observed in the depths of winter pursuing "their morning ablutions on the stoop at the back door" due to lack of indoor plumbing or bathroom facilities.20

While unable to fully create the domestic atmosphere and family spirit their directors idealized, nevertheless, the POHs were able to approximate it more closely than their British counterparts. Because most orphan asylums in Canada were modest undertakings with populations ranging from merely a score or so, as in Victoria to several hundred at their height in Toronto, Winnipeg, and Saint John, there was more possibility of "familializing" the institution. Moreover, the Canadian institutions exercised remarkable control over the selection of their clients by careful admission procedures which articulated the ladies' committees implicit assumptions regarding who were the "worthy" and "unworthy" poor. Sometimes children were refused admittance into, or taken out of, the POHs and sent to the houses of industry, which, in light of the anxiety the founding members had expressed about the conditions in these

111

institutions being unsuitable for children, seems rather incongruous unless one keeps in mind the nuances and subtleties between the various categories of the poor. In fact, since the institutions largely received custodial cases for nominal fees rather than full orphans, they did not admit the most alarming or desperate cases or the chronic poor as did the large British institutions, e.g., Ashley Down in Bristol, the National Children's Homes, and the Barnardo Homes, or even the North American Roman Catholic ones.

The British debates over the psychological consequences of institutional life - the lack of spontaneity and initiative on the part of the children - did not apply in the same degree to Canada although in the twentieth century such arguments would be used to advocate fostering practices. True, a matron and superintendent might be harrassed by too many children and tasks, too little money, and too small a domestic staff, but there is little sense of barracks-like discipline and the anonymity of a militaristic atmosphere that later critics suggested was prevalent. Statements in some annual reports that "regular methodical habits" and "cleanliness, order the good management" were enforced, and that "a spirit of docility and subordination testified to good management," must be interpreted cautiously, since the minutes of many asylums testify that such management was not as mechanistically induced or as impersonally imposed as the rhetoric suggests. Indeed, some homes seem to be better examples of confusion and nonchalance than of orderliness and inflexibility, and more the reflections of the temperaments of the matrons themselves than of any institutional plans.

Unfortunately, one of the results of public parsimony regarding the support of orphan asylums was that, despite the smaller establishment and the fewer children, staffing crises frequently occurred and there were too few permanent caretakers to attend to the children. Frequently, the domestic management was handled by either a matron and nurse with a cook and housemaids or a resident married couple, sometimes with a child of their own. With salaries so meagre and working conditions so strenuous, it is unlikely that the most capable candidates applied for the positions as house parents or were employed as domestic staff. In London in its first years, the steward and matron were dismissed from their position, which earned them only $300 per annum, when it was revealed that the man had abused his authority with a young female inmate. Mrs. Hughes, who took care of the nursery earned only $4 with one day off a month. In 1875, the cook and an assistant were reprimanded for "having inbibed too freely" causing a "slight confusion" among the inmates. The "penitent" cook would be fired a year later for her drinking habits.21

In the same decade, however, the kindly Mrs. Harold of the Kingston POH was greatly missed after her resignation, having cared for the children for fourteen years "with all the solicitude of a parent's heart." Great respect must be accorded those houseparents who continually demonstrated good humour, warmth, concern, and even love toward the children, for they could only have retained those characteristics from a generosity of spirit and a genuineness of interest; they could never have been expressed for remuneration or for status.22

The authors suspect that a study of Catholic children's institutions should elicit different findings regarding some of these aspects. Although they were usually much larger Homes, the children within them may have received more attention because whole "orders" of brothers and sisters ran these homes and full time staffs could exceed two dozen or more. Devoted solely to the care of their children, these religious caretakers were able to give more attention because they were in the institution on twenty-four hour call. Moreover, their institutions did not suffer from the same turn over of discontented and overworked staff as in the POHs. Permanent superintendence of the domestic management of homes may have been more satisfactory than the POH practice of having women taking turns on weekly visiting committees and presenting reports. Not even a committee of forty-five women with daily visits of two members, as was the custom for the Toronto Girls' Home, could have provided the psychological sustenance young children are known to need.23

Finally, as already noted, repressive religious fervor and the excesses sometimes associated with evangelical enthusiasm as a means to disciplining young and suggestive minds are surprisingly missing in the Canadian records of these Homes despite their Protestant origins. It seems that interdenominationalism, even if promoted by pragmatic and economic reasons, had some neutralizing effect on such fervor. In sum, there appears to be a dissonance between the rhetoric (which was almost identical to British sentiments) expressed at annual meetings and fund raising functions or in annual reports, and the actual conduct, the physical arrangements, and the clienteles of the POHs.

If these were the differences between the British congregate systems and the Canadian POHs, then what were the similarities? Four aspects seem worth noting: (1) the application of the new awareness for the peculiar needs of children that resulted in actual institutional environments which rendered the child objectively and psychologically dependent upon those maintaining him while assuring the inmate maximum protection and segregation; (2) the segregation of various classes of children from each other, that is, the classification of "dependent" from "delinquent"; (3) the ultimate segregation of children from undesirable adult influences by the Homes claiming the rights of in loco parentis, even to the point of interfering with parental access by binding children out if maintenance fees were not forthcoming; and (4) the training of children into menial occupations through the regimens of the homes and indentures. The latter two points will be elaborated in the next chapter. Although spiritual rescue was seen as crucial for "dependent children, nevertheless, training for "immortal glory in that [life] which is to come" never received quite the same emphasis as training "these little ones" for usefulness in the present life.24

INFANTS, BASTARDS AND FOUNDLINGS

Throughout its history, the Ottawa POH reflected more faithfully than most institutions the "philanthropic mode." Women such as Lady MacDonald and the wealthy Mrs. Bronson, first and second directresses respectively, seemed impervious to the visible demands of public poverty. Founded in 1865 by the Ladies' Protestant Benevolent Association, the Home received widows and women out of place, although full and part orphans quickly came to dominate the population. In the first months of its mandate eleven ladies were elected to "search for destitute children," which suggest careful selection. Indeed, a year later, only twelve orphans were enjoying the ladies' attentions. The exclusive admission policies of the Ottawa institution did not alter until the late 1890s when it began to receive children from the newly organized Children's Aid Society. The Montreal Ladies' Benevolent Society operated on the popular cautionary advice about investigation preventing "imposture" and the necessity of "detecting fraud." Consequently, during their visitations in the early years among the "abodes of wretchedness," they not only exposed mendacity and idleness but they carefully selected the most worthy objects for their charity. Without a doubt, orphans and particularly suitable ones, fell into this class.25

Like most POHs, Winnipeg and Hamilton being notable exceptions, the Ottawa establishment did not receive illegitimate children as Mrs. Armstrong discovered in 1866 when she was obliged to produce her marriage certification for a suspicious ladies' committee before they would admit her three children from Brockville. It became a matter of necessity as well as an imperative of charity that specialized facilities should be encouraged for this class of infant as well as abandoned babies and children of tender years. The founding of infants' homes caused scandal similar to that associated with the foundling hospitals in Britain, Europe, and French Canada - namely that such institutions encouraged women to escape the punishments their fallen condition deserved.26

The problems attached to illegitimacy, foundlings, abandoned infants, infanticide, and nineteenth century back street abortion, are still awaiting sustained and serious quantitative and qualitative study in this country. Without such documentation we can only speculate on the fates of pregnant unwed or deserted women who found themselves without employment or shelter, or who after confinement were either forced to surrender or abandon their babies or to commit infanticide.27

The Canadian case was probably not dissimilar to the English evidence that extensive infanticide still existed. For example, in Bristol in 1869, a public meeting heard discussions and papers on a variety of social problems relating to such women as well as baby farms and "Refuges of Compassion" for mothers and their infants. The coroner for Central Middlesex referred to the appalling number of inquests passed on children under one year "found dead" and to the problems of collecting accurate statistics because of public abhorrence and apathy as well as the absence of birth registration. It was agreed by others that most infanticides were new-born children of servants or young women engaged in light employments.28

Because they could not find employment while nursing their infants, such women were frequently forced into prostitution to prevent starvation. Obviously there was an urgent need of shelter and assistance in finding employment after confinement. As for the objections that these steps would "encourage immorality," it was observed that this had little worth as an argument.

> A poor girl is restored to her occupation;
> a child is rescued from death, and the
> mother has to pay a weekly penalty for
> her sin. Is this an encouragement to
> immorality? Even then do you prefer
> 'murder or unchastity'?29

Nevertheless, despite Victorian rhetoric whose tenor was both censorious and moralizing, it was often the most socially conscious women in Britain and in her colonies who responded to the plight of the unwed mother by organizing lying-in hospitals, female rescue homes, foundling homes, and, in Canada, Protestant Infants' Homes for that unforgiven class of women who received little psychological or physical support during their confinements. The POHs and the Protestant Infants' Homes kept close liaison with each other, and those children who were too young to be received into the former establishment found themselves transferred

116

into the latter ones. Sometimes the children's homes emerged from a specific concern for such infants and their mothers as in the case of the Children's Home of Winnipeg, which was founded by the Christian Women's Union in 1885. Originally "an adjunct of the maternity hospital," afterwards "its doors were opened to any destitute child." The Home finally became of so much importance as to require a board of management and a charter of its own. This Protestant Home, the first in the west, was officially separated from the CWU in 1887 although these women retained a special interest in its affairs and management. Initially it included fourteen mothers and children, but within four years it housed forty-eight children with a few adults.30

Sometimes too, Protestant groups, often working in conjunction with the POHs, not only established lying-in wards but also after-care for unmarried mothers and their infants as well as job placement bureaus with some training for domestic service. This can be seen in London, Ontario, where the Women's Refuge and Children's Home, required a twelve month stay during which a mother might in addition to caring for her own child, be trained "into a gainful situation, or at least be religiously improved." It is improbable that either aims were successfully achieved.31

The Halifax Infants' Home is another example of an institution whose function was as useful as it was benevolent. Although infants were received free of charge due to parental inability to pay for a child's board, many were actually boarded by mothers who visited and nursed their babies, or in cases of weaned children, visited and clothed them, paying for their maintenance and thus using the Home as a residential custodial institution. In 1884, the new physician, Dr. Oliver, recommended that it would be preferable for the child if the mother were actually boarded with it and that in order to ensure the character of the Home and preserve the privacy of the infants, the Home ought not to accommodate by the day the children of women who were in daily service.32

Among the numerous infants' homes, the Toronto institution founded in 1875 offers a lucid overview of the problems and the transforming patterns of infant care. Although its beginnings were uncertain and faltering, within its first twelve years the Toronto Home had already cared for 1,679 infants and 820 mothers. With the Hamilton Infants' Home, it was one of the first to systematically board out infants and mothers by 1920 rather than continue institutionalizing them. In 1855, the ladies of the Burnside Lying-In Hospital had requested a nursery be built in connection with the hospital "for the two-fold benefit of preserving the life of the infant and keeping the mother's mind in a state of comfortable assurance, that, while she was nursing another child her own would be kindly treated." Moreover, the death rates of children discharged from Burnside originated the idea of "thus saving them." Nevertheless, it was almost two decades later before Mrs. Fenton Campbell, who had worked at the Nursery and Child's Hospital in New York, along with Mrs. Ridout of Burnside organized a ladies committee to found the Infants' Home.33

From its first years, in an attempt to counteract the devastating effects of infant mortality and morbidity, the Toronto Infants' Home encouraged mothers, on physician's permit as to a clean bill of health, to enter with their infants under a system of "mother nurses." This system required the woman to remain four months and agree to suckle one other infant at a time in addition to her own. In the first year she was expected to suckle four infants. For this service, the Home received a government grant per mother per diem in addition to the annual city grant of $500. The remaining revenues were collected from subscriptions or from sponsors and parents at $4 and $5 a month for walking babies and infants respectively. The mother nurses provided their services in return for care, food, lodging, training, and the promise of a situation as a domestic afterwards. Although the City urged a reduction in population due to the risks of serial contamination, the suggestion was ignored because such a reduction while not decreasing overhead costs substantially, would, however, reduce government and city grants per mother and per child.34

As with Toronto's Infants' Home, many institutions hired women to live in as wet-nurses which, while guaranteeing temporary relief for

118

herself and her children, was nevertheless a sign of the desperation and poverty that forced women into homes to engage in an occupation, which traditionally had been relegated to the meanest classes and one which was no longer a common practice. Being no exception, the Halifax Infants' Home required wet-nurses wishing to have their own infants with them to pay $3.00 a month for the privilege in 1875. Its first wet-nurse was a girl taken from the Poor Asylum.35

The humiliation and social disgrace such women endured cannot be minimized for wet-nursing cannot be construed as anything but a last resort for most women in desperate socio-economic straits. The fees, although often meagre, were a hardship on those women who tried to retain some semblance of the ordering of their own lives. With wages barely covering their own subsistence, widows, unmarried women, and deserted wives paid nominal fees to keep their children clothed, sheltered, and fed in the homes. The fees usually ranged from one to five dollars a month, depending upon the number of children admitted or the actual financial circumstances of parent or guardian. Domestic service often required women to live-in, and other occupations took up long hours during which children were unsupervised. While the fees were not exhorbitant, the Homes found them essential for their survival due to the parsimony and slowness of provincial and municipal grants and unreliable private funding.

No woman who was judged "low" or "fallen," that is, undergoing her second illegitimate pregnancy, was admitted into the Home but was expected instead to attend the Mercer Woman's Reformatory or one of the several Ontario Magdalen Asylums such as the Good Shepherd Asylum in Ottawa, the Home for the Friendless in Hamilton, the good Shepherd Refuge for Fallen Women and the Magdalen Asylum, both of Toronto, or the Women's Refuge and Infants Home in London. An amicable arrangement was reached with the Inspector of Prisons and Public Charities in 1882 whereby the Home's services were made available to the "babies at the breast" of certified women from Mercer Reformatory at $2 a week. Suckling mothers who were either willing, or desperate enough to agree, were always a scarce commodity.

119

No woman was permitted to leave the home to take up a situation as a wet-nurse.36

There were occasions when the babies of wet nurses were admitted into the Home by their mistresses who paid for their care so that their mothers would be free to care for their employers' children. Thus while money could pay for the thriving of middle class infants without inconvenience to their mothers, many a lower class child wasted away or spent a childhood separated from its own mother if she were employed as a live-in domestic and forced to pay for the custodial service of an infants' home.

Committees of infant homes did not normally approve of such exchanges and sometimes, as in the case of the wife of a Reverend gentleman in 1885, the Toronto Infants' Home refused to cooperate as they thought the arrangement was a screen to save the household from scandal. She claimed that the girl was not strong enough to nurse her child, but as the ladies shrewdly perceived, this apparently did not mean that she was not strong enough to endure the rigors of domestic work.37

Only five years after the beginnings of the Toronto Home, sixty-five mothers attended to 120 infants; however, during the oppressive summer of that year, the Home suffered an epidemic of malarial fever, a situation which was to reoccur in various guises throughout its history. In the first forty years of the institution, there had been thirty-five visitations of contagious diseases and epidemics, a pattern which was in no way untypical. Epidemics had compelled a Cottage Hospital Annex to be built for isolation purposes in 1888. The campaign for its erection had been initiated two years before by a rash of deaths from measles in April and May, which had caused quite a stir in the city. The Mayor, alarmed by the growing criticism of the Home, encouraged the ladies' committee to present a petition before Council for permission to raise funds for a separate infirmary. To detract from the scandal, the annual meeting for that year agitated against the deplorable conditions common to Ontario's baby farms and demanded that they must be licensed and subjected to inspection. As with the earlier British agencies, there were critics who insisted that institutions which took care of "natural" children were in fact "putting a premium on vice." In sentiments that were similar to those expressed at the 1869 Bristol meeting, Mr. Townsend, a supporter of such charities, pointed out that the logical conclusion of such views was that these children should die and that it would then become the "duty of the State to legalize the killing of such children, because by the very abstention from saving they would in effect kill." The Mail, 28 October 1886, continued the campaign against baby farming which eventually led to the passing of the Act for the Protection of Infant Children on the 18 April 1887. This in turn led to the Ontario Maternity Boarding Act some twenty-seven years later.38

That such legislation did not soften public opinion against institutions that cared for unmarried mothers and their children is seen in the 1932 Cooke versus the Kingston Infants' Home Case. The Home was sued for nuisance "as it was distasteful to them [the neighbours] to have an institution which cared for illegitimate children in close proximity to their homes." The plea, which curiously was put forward on "sentimental grounds," was rejected in a rousing court decision which justified the courage and effort of the twenty women of all faiths who not only saw their institution's usefulness in terms of "salvaging" young women but also in directing them and their babies to health and social services. The decision read:

> . . . there must be an inconvenience
> materially interfering with the ordinary
> comfort physically of human existence,
> not merely according to the elegant or
> dainty modes and habits of living but
> according to the plain and sober and
> simple notions among English people.39

Appalling figures of death, disease, unsanitary conditions, lack of funds, overcrowding and abandonment also did little to alter public attitudes. The mortality figures at the Toronto Home continued to be discouraging despite the system of "mother nurses" which was intended to reduce them. Babies succumbed to general debility and wasting away (marasmus) as well as syphilis,

121

scrofula, cholera infantum, dentition, meningitis and lung congestion. Six years after the founding of the Infants' Home, it was reported that there had been in that year a 22.52% death rate which was an improvement, however, on the 39.73% in its first two years of operation when 60 out of the 151 infants admitted died. The report of 1879 publicized figures that were staggering even to the supporters of projects meeting the needs of such women and their infants.40

Similar health problems plagued other Canadian infants' homes. In the first year of the Halifax Infants' Home, the managing committee brought "cheap thin cotton" to be made into shrouds. Several months later with scarlet fever in the home, the committee requested the Commissioners of the Poor Asylum for the use of their hearse in order to save the expense of cab-hire for funerals. In the three summer months of 1875, thirteen babies died. The Home averaged twenty-two boarded children during the time. In 1875, the death rate was 35% and as late as 1890 it was 26%.41

Despite the discouragements of death and sickness, overcrowding and lack of funds, and condemnation and cynicism, the women involved in this particular kind of child rescue remained compassionate and surprisingly generous - given the climate of opinion in which they worked and with which they contended on a daily basis - in their treatment and defence of the women and girls who flocked to their doors.

The popularity of the institution decreased in proportion to the reluctance of even formerly hopeless women to provide wet-nursing services which coincided with a rise in wages, the legislation which improved other facilities for the boarding of infants, and undoubtedly, a rising consciousness of women who rejected the socio-political implications of such a task and the onerous restrictions attached to it. The protests of the Infants' Home in 1886 had in a small way contributed to such a change occurring, and although it had always claimed that its insistence upon mothers nursing their own infants wherever possible saved infant lives as well as bound the mother more to her baby, the practice of nursing other infants could rarely have been enthusiastically performed. As fewer women volunteered such services, the ladies frantically attempted to overcome the lack in supply by insisting in 1899 and reaffirming eight years later that the four month residential requirement be raised to six months "or as much longer as the Board may determine." By 1903, however, the Home's attraction for such women was at its lowest ebb and vacancies were filled by paid assistants and the preparation of special infant diets. Despairing of the situation, Mrs. Ridout stated that "much of this refusal to accept the responsibilities of motherhood is attributable to the spirit of the age," which apparently was a restless "insubordination" that permeated all public institutions.42

The POHs were reluctant to receive infants and most stipulated ages of admission over two years because of the vulnerability of very young children to even the mildest contagion. Because of inadequate nursing staff, many infants' and female rescue homes insisted that mothers who came to them before confinement, or those who wanted their newborn infants admitted, were to remain with the child for some months, or if in service or working, then to visit the child daily. The committee of the Winnipeg Female Refuge was concerned that so many of their mothers objected to the rule of remaining nine months and saw it as an attempt at avoiding "the responsibility and consequences of their sin." The Friendly Home for Young Women founded in 1913 in Montreal set similar conditions by insisting that a girl attend her child during nursing and not "add to one's sin by casting the baby off." In Toronto two religious services were held on Sunday with Bible reading, but this attempt at spiritual reform was offset by a more practical scheme in the form of a night school for nursing mothers in 1886.43

The reluctance of most homes to receive illegitimate children might be understood as more than punitive moralizing when it is recalled that most of these were infants. Such consideration did not answer the questions of where an unmarried mother could go during pregnancy and labor and where her child could be placed once she sought employment. The Toronto Home wanted to provide a creche for mothers who left it in order to "prevent pauperizing those whom they relieve[d]." Most women

123

who required help were out-of-service domestics, and to assure space for women in desperate need, mothers with husbands were not permitted to board their infants. After their confinement in an infants' home, mothers could pay a monthly fee while they sought employment and a suitable home for themselves and their child. Abandoned or surrendered children were frequently transferred from infants' to orphans' home if the age for admission was appropriate. Problems arose, however, if there was an age lag between demission and admission policies between homes in the same city.44

A deputation of the Christian Women's Union of Winnipeg to the Manitoba legislature in 1890 articulated the problem which was endemic to all infants' homes when they pleaded for funds for what they firmly believed to be one of the most essential social services - a female refuge. The refuge was to enable unmarried or recently widowed women "to keep their infants with them until they [were] old enough to do without a mother's care when . . . admitted into the Children's Home or otherwise provided for." The deputation pointed out that infant mortality in institutions was high and the use of wet-nurses unsatisfactory. In the first decade of the following century, the Home, because there was still no infants' home, demanded a twenty-five dollar deposit for illegitimate babies hoping that this would deter irresponsible abandonment.45

Attempts at keeping nursing mothers and unweaned infants together can be seen also in the ninth Annual Report of the Protestant Infants' Home in Montreal. This establishment employed mothers to nurse their own babies (and probably other infants) "to encourage and strengthen the tie that binds them together." With seventeen deaths in 1879, the Report was quite self-congratulatory in observing that the rate was "unusually low, this the more surprising when we take into consideration the deplorable condition of some of the children when we receive them." The Montreal Home, which maintained relations with the Lying-In Hospital, was modelled on the London Rescue Society and aimed at sheltering fallen women and restoring them to respectable employments. It expressed regret that the Infants' Home engaged women as wet nurses even before their children were born. These women were hired by ladies outside the Home. Although such a system was no longer in vogue and was even viewed with growing repugnance, nonetheless such ladies, aided by the appeals of their doctors, succeeded in perpetuating the practice. This society contemplated erecting a separate building for infants so that mothers could continue to care for them once they were hired as domestics or succumbed to the higher wages of wet-nurses, but funds proved too limited.46

The inevitability of infant mortality induced the POHs to refuse admission of not only illegitimate but all children under two and sometimes up to four years of age. On its opening in 1915, the Ottawa Infants' Home quickly discovered that many of the babies it received were really "hospital cases" with government and city grants inadequate to subsidize their care. A certain proportion of abandoned infants were probably mentally or physically defective. If such infants are seen today as an onerous burden on affluent parents who institutionalize them, how much more so in the past in the case of impoverished parents already caring for several children.47

Physical debilitation, the lack of wet-nursing substitutes such as formulae, pasteurized milk and sanitary bottles, and the symptoms of psychological deprivation common to institutional life, meant a dismal prognosis for such children. A matron of the Winnipeg Home observed that many of the infants in the overcrowded nursery were "doomed from the start," having "no backbone or stamina, and simply came to the Home to die in comfort." She added that the babies languished and pined for that which they "did not know." She went on to diagnose this lack as mother love and constant human contact, despite the best will in the world of staff to provide it. The numbers of sickly infants admitted into the Home induced the committee of management to meet with the Hospital Board and arrange that babies should be treated there first until they "got their health back."48

Unfortunately, since many such infants never had "their health" in the first place, they required extensive care. Some infants admitted had barely survived infanticidal attempts. In 1911, Dr. Harvey

125

Smith recommended a trained nurse for the nursery, that no infants be admitted under six years and then no more than four at a given time, and the exclusion of certain skin infections, T. B. related cases, symptoms of congenital syphilitic conditions, ear discharges, and nervous afflictions. Visitors "from poor quarters of the city" were to be given a disinfecting bath and isolated in a reception centre for further observation because such infants were vulnerable to the slightest infections.49

To comprehend the reluctance of the POHs in receiving infants, it is essential to understand that even those institutions especially set up to meet the needs of very young children have high mortality and morbidity rates. Many infants homes, besides those in Hamilton and Toronto, were founded partly to counteract the pernicious practice of baby farming whose adherence to the profit motive resulted in appalling mortality. Semblances of these establishments in British Columbia were detected by the 1927 Social Services survey, which observed that the lives of infants were endangered in "licensed boarding homes" such as that of Ivy Lodge which handled thirty babies. Despite the licence required, such homes were still subject to the most minimal standards of Health Department supervision due to their private status in the province.50

When in 1869 Philip S. Carpenter, Secretary of the Montreal Sanitary Association, wrote on excessive child mortality in Montreal, the Association was involved in raising a dog tax, such as existed in Boston, to fund baths and wash-houses designed on the British model. Montreal was reputed to be not only the largest but also "the most unhealthful city in the Dominion," with infant mortality figures more grim than those of Bristol or Manchester, due to "filth and pollutions," "foetid" and "effete" matter oozing from sewers, its "putrid wood," "daily slops" and "manure heaps" in public places. With two of every five infants dying in the year of birth, Carpenter brooded that "the infantile death rate is therefore the readiest thermometer by which we estimate the virulence of poisonous emanations."51

Carpenter did not preclude this formula from applying to the foundling homes in the city which he suspected of doing more harm than good "in the cure of the foresaken. . . in the facility afforded to escape the shame of unlawful parentage." If the children of the city were generally in a "moribund condition" neither could their survival be guaranteed if they perchance had the added misfortune of being born illegitimate and placed in a "carpet bag or hamper" on the steps of the Foundling Hospital of Montreal (or, for that matter, in a basket on the front door of St. Joseph's Home in Ottawa, also run by the Grey Nuns).52

Frequently debilitated before abandoment or surrender and sometimes even the victims of attempted infanticide, many infants were not strong enough to survive. The Echo, 19 June 1867, had circulated rumours regarding the Montreal Foundling Hospital, and though denied by the Grey Nuns, the actual facts were still "appalling in the extreme." For example, unable to find the necessary wet-nurses in the city or in the country to do "this most loathsome of work," or to provide appropriate nourishment for older babies, some 3,724 children had died between 1863 and 1868. Even as late as 1878, the Lancet stated that 40% of children died before their first birthday in the general population, but that foundlings in Montreal three years previously had exceeded 87% when "farmed out." It was generally agreed that an abandoned waif would have less than a 25% chance of survival even if rescued by a foundling or infants' home. The mortality rates in such homes with all the care given only just succeeded in being lower than the general average of infants outside the home.53

Since the Grey Nuns' establishment was Catholic, and principally served the French-Canadian population of the city and its environs, it is not technically within the boundary of our discussion; however, it cannot be overlooked that its existence and services motivated similar though much smaller institutions to serve Protestants. The Montreal Infants' Home was founded in 1870 for "orphans and those of indigent widows or those whose parents by sickness, poverty or other causes are without means of supporting them - also for illegitimate children of Protestant mothers for whom there is no refuge but the Grey nunnery." Child rescue consisted not only of physical and moral concerns but also evangelical Protestant fears that their own people or the vast 'unchurched' should fall into the embrace of Romanism.54

Ironically, the refusal of many POHs to admit illegitimate children certainly put pressure on the more receptive Catholic institutions. An open door policy was seen, however, as encouraging abandonment and even promiscuity, and led to criticism of Catholic institutions on both counts. Due to their open door policies, the Catholic institutions were destined to suffer greater criticism because of greater infant mortality.

If the conditions for survival were unpropitious in establishments especially meant to care for very young children and babies, it is no surprise that the poorhouses fared even worse. Many of these infants were sent out to wet-nurse at the municipality's expense, a practice that did not guarantee them either long life or adoption. Two year old Lilla M. Martan's case must not have been uncommon. This toddler died in the same year that she had been returned to Cornwallis Poorhouse, although she had apparently thrived at wet-nurse before her return. One cannot tell what happened to tiny Blanch Doorstep who was delivered to a wet-nurse, a Mrs. Best, in 1903. "Doorstep" babies were usually illegitimate and were not destined to survive their first weeks unless wet-nursed or placed out to board. If they survived their initial tenuous origins, the records for infant mortality rates in the poorhouses indicate that a majority of them failed to withstand the physical and psychological deprivations of the experience. The Saint John Almshouse recorded many "bastards" and their deaths on its rolls.55

Frequently unmarried mothers who were unable to keep their babies, husbands whose wives were in asylums, deserted wives or those with husbands in prison, were forced to surrender their children to the overseers for nominal monthly fees. Due to penurious circumstances, overseers of the poor were reluctant to receive infants; however, baby farming was costlier and equally deadly to infant life. The Halifax Protestant Infants' Home (1875) and the Home

128

of the Friendless and Infants' Home in Hamilton
(1869) were established partly to counteract the
pernicious consequences of the practice. Because of
negative comment on the problem of baby farming, the
Home opened a nursery in 1881 to aid working mothers
and, several years later, a day crèche with a
training and employment bureau which were to provide
further assistance. Curiously however, the Halifax
Home declined to admit colored infants, who were
consigned to the county poorhouses until the
founding of the Halifax Home for Coloured Children
in the twentieth century.56

The Halifax Infants' Home committee found
itself in a quandary when it hired its first
wet-nurse because of a rule that "no woman [mother
of inmates] that is not of respectable character"
was to be admitted into the home. Yet it seemed
tautological, given nineteenth century strictures on
morality, that women forced into wet-nursing would
be unwed or deserted therefore not "respectable."
After lively discussion, the dilemma was resolved
that a second-timer at wet-nursing would not be
admitted. Similarly in 1886, the Toronto Infants'
Home committee stipulated that no unmarried mother
could be admitted "except with her first born."
This rule was deemed necessary because of the
disapproving public opinion which had been leveled
at the Home for the eleven years since its
inception, because of the service it provided and
the clientele who received it.57

Unmarried mothers were normally driven to the
poor houses to deliver their babies and the
registers of the institutions had an inordinate
number of "bastards" recorded as inmates. At the
end of the century, James Dowe, Superintendent of
the Halifax Asylum, commented on the ease with which
unmarried women could "hide their shame" at
provincial expense.58

Some poorhouses attempted to discourage unwed
mothers and their "bastard" children. In 1843, the
Board of the Halifax Asylum returned an illegitimate
child to the doctor who had admitted it with the
observation "that whilst the Commissioners deem it
their duty to extend the charity of the House to
foundlings. . . they are anxious in no degree to
cloak vice, or diminish natural affection." Two

129

years previously, Mary Rogers had been summarily expelled from Toronto's House of Industry, presumably her last resort, for becoming pregnant during her stay there. Where this desperate young woman went is anyone's guess, as was the outcome of her condition.59

Such cases had few alternatives in a society that provided no cash relief to carry them over their predicament. Unwed mothers and their infants, therefore, were quickly identified as suitable objects of female philanthropic rescue in both the actual and the moral sense. The Foundling Homes and Infants' Homes that developed out of Women's refuges were melancholy places that received the most wretched and ostracized of the poor - the unwed mother and her unwanted child.

WOMAN'S DOMAIN

Although as noted earlier not all POHs were governed by women, nevertheless, the domestic economies of all institutions were controlled by ladies' committees and their views on policy and practice clearly took precedence over any male input. Moreover, since nearly all the infants and foundlings homes were governed entirely by female interests, children's institutions can be described as a "woman's domain." Consequently, the work of the ladies of the POHs and Protestant Foundling and Infant Homes marked the first major thrust of middle class women in British North America into significant forms of social reform and personal service. As more general and non-religious organizations such as the National Council of Women (NCW) appeared, the descendents of the founders of the original asylums took an active role in restating the social concerns that had attracted the attention of their mothers and aunts. Indeed, after 1893 when the NCW commenced its task, many of the ladies' committees of the orphanages quickly affiliated with the Local Councils. Women of the Winnipeg, Kingston, Ottawa, Toronto and Victoria Homes quickly assimilated broader social concerns and took an active part in sharing the interest in the wider problems of female social concerns and conditions of child life.60

That women should pioneer in the establishment
of child welfare was related to several social and
intellectual developments. First, by the 1830s
there existed in several colonial centres sufficient
population and wealth to make philanthropy possible,
with thriving commercial towns such as Montreal and
Halifax offering the first attempts at female
societies aimed at widows and orphans. Second, the
stirrings of educational reform in the form of more
efficient schools and of pedagogical theories that
argued an analogous relationship between
mother-child and teacher-pupil focused attention on
the psychology of child life. Even those
pedagogical innovations which did not use a familial
model, emphasized the need for careful organization
in relation to psychological knowledge.
Consequently, the pedagogical ferment of the early
nineteenth century pointed to the significance of
careful control of education, particularly in
childhood and youth, and the need to separate that
education from the interference of adults, family
and friends alike. To comprehend this crucial point
more fully, it is necessary to have some
understanding of the preceding centuries' evolution
of the pedagogical principles that came to
assimilate the psychological aspects of family life.

Concern for poverty and pauperization of
destitute children could, of course, take many
forms. Christian charities had sought to relieve
children as part of the general impulse to temporal
works of mercy. Views expressed by men of property
and business in the late eighteenth century were
taken to heart by politicians faced with mounting
costs of financing the old poor laws. Political
economists speculated grimly on the inevitable
outcome of growing populations and the slow advance
in agricultural productivity. These dire
predictions also fed the nineteenth century drive to
control and uplift the poor for reasons of social
stability and economic drag. There was, however,
another stream of social thought, which while
decrying the effects of poverty, saw the results in
terms of psychological development.61

Interestingly, the work of the Renaissance
humanists that re-emphasized much of the ancient
concern for civic and ethical development failed to
touch much of the thought about the education of the

131

masses. Committed to a restricted view of citizenship and a belief in a top down development of social well-being, the humanists saved their concern for princes and the gentry. The beginnings of interest in the commonalty are found in the literature and advice on self-improvement and on vernacular schooling. This economic stress was joined by seventeenth century authors who saw social and individual development as a problem for all. Seventeenth century religious and pedagogical theorists such as Comenius marked the first attempt to unite developmental concerns with general individual uplift. It remained, however, for Pestalozzi to effectively combine the more general notions of citizenship as human development with the education of the poor. Bringing together the two major streams of early modern European thought, Enlightenment belief in rationality and the Romantic belief in the power of the unconscious forces inherent in the folk, pedagogical theorists argued that cultural and political regeneration depended not on the education of the prince and his circle but on the uplift of the people.

Caught up in the tides of national rebirth and military devestation of the late eighteenth century, Pestalozzi first turned his hand to the reclamation of orphaned and displaced children. His efforts at restoring to full humanity the children brought under his care, demonstrated the transformation of an ethos previously identified with the classic exposition of education for the citizen/prince, into a new discourse on human development for ALL children. Moreover, his practices and writings were imbued with a new psychological sensitivity that borrowed greatly from the work of Rousseau. During the course of a long career, Pestalozzi moved away from the regeneration of war victims to the great question of education of the children of the common folk in order that they might fully realize their humanity. His work with the general theory and practice of common schooling marked the final union of two great streams of western social thought and action, that is, the classical educational theories dating from the ancient Greeks with the Christian tradition of temporal and spiritual works of mercy. Despite the imperatives of class stratification, European societies moved towards educational decisions that included compulsory schooling,

132

psychological awareness of human development, a belief in the potential inherent in all citizens, and a faith in the power of rational systematic intervention in the lives of its children.

Early children's institutions represented attempts to implement the general view personified by Pestalozzi and to incorporate the family ideal for which he so carefully argued. Additionally, theorists such as Pestalozzi, and later medical practitioners and popular writers, emphasized the mother's role in the full development of children. The charge that the well-ordered school should be like the well-ordered family, led to the conclusion that the proper teacher, and indeed nurturer of children, was a woman. Just as the common schools of the nineteenth century came to embody these views so did the institutions for orphaned, abandoned, and destitute children. Thus it was not merely that girls should be protected from male abuse that determined the leading role of women in these movements, but a more positive perception that only women were capable of realizing the full potential of the institutions, their quasi-family ideal, and their inmates.

A third social development that influenced the founding of the POHs was that Protestant men and women were aware of the substantial effort made by Roman Catholic religious orders to provide for the destitute and dependent. In particular, various orders of nuns were active, especially in French-speaking areas, in the establishment of orphan asylums, foundling homes, and other institutions for women and children. This was explicit to the founding of Protestant Homes in Montreal, Victoria, St. John's, and London. Fourth, the women who organized the first societies represented Protestant evangelicalism and middle class social ethics, and although it was common that societies were the outgrowth of denominational religious experience, some recruited their members from several Protestant churches and thus served as an early instance of "non-sectarian" organizations for women.

Finally, the most publicized campaigns of the nineteenth century were those aiming at the establishment of systems of state schooling.

Although women came to dominate the classrooms of the common school, they had little to say about the overall operation of the school since policy and administrative positions were open only to men. The significance of the asylums rested first in the policies on admission and demissions, the training and education schemes, and the placing out and apprenticeship practices, which were common almost to the point of uniformity, in the POHs from Newfoundland to Victoria. It was precisely in these areas that women, through their ladies' committees, exercised maximum control. The women performed two significant functions by insuring that the asylum would display the proper home-like characteristics and that unlike the common school, it would indeed provide the "institutionalized" equivalent of a child-centred family permeated by maternal love.

Although it has frequently been observed of children's institutions that any resemblance to an actual "family like" situation was distorted or dislocated, Canadian POHs in some ways offer a curious anomaly to this perception. Without unduly exaggerating the pervasiveness of either mother love or family sentiment, nevertheless, it must be confessed that the POHs did more closely approximate the ideal than some of their huge and impersonal counterparts in the rapidly industrializing centres in the United State or in the great urban centres of Britain.

In 1914, W. H. Hattie, Inspector of Humane and Penal Institutions in Nova Scotia, made the following observation:

> In the small institutions particularly,
> a degree of friendly intimacy is often
> noted which even suggests a family
> spirit, and which assures one that
> institutional life may be happy and
> not devoid of pleasure.62

The institutions in Victoria, Halifax, Fredericton, London and Ottawa, Wood's Christian Home in Calgary and the Alexandra Home in Vancouver, immediately come to mind because of their relatively small populations. Rarely did any POH in Canada exceed three hundred residents at a given time, with those of Winnipeg, and Toronto representing the larger clienteles at their height. If matters of staffing and finances always reigned supreme, problems of the "ins and outs" (those non-orphans provided for by temporary custodial care and who were always in the majority) along with the erratic nature of nursery and domestic help frustrated the possibility of realizing the family ideal.

In conclusion, the Institution proved to be an effective means of imposing the first three criteria of the concept of childhood. It assured segregation and protection, and it created a physical and even legal dependence in an environment that consciously worked towards a measure of psychological dependence. The fourth criterion of delayed responsibility was far less obvious. Indeed, the institution insisted that dependent children be made aware of their social and moral responsibilities, both within and without the POH. Far from having their responsibilities delayed, dependent children were made aware of both their surrendered or orphaned status and their inferior class position.

The Institution was in no way like the family it idealized unless one strains the point to absurdity. Few biological families had the numbers of children even the smallest institutions sheltered or the lack of parental oversight. No family was identified by uniform and cropped hair cuts. Most children who attended the common schools mixed freely with other children. Nor were families, even in the labouring classes, sending their children some distance away to apprenticeships under indentures whose mutual duties could not be guaranteed. "Binding-out" for dependent institutionalized children had connotations other than being apprenticed into a trade or a calling. Finally, no family had so many members coming and going - where affections, bonding, and loyalties could as suddenly and as arbitrarily be severed by disruptive demission polcies, and few families would have remained so indifferent to the treatment their children received from one year to the next in some distant town or farm.

It is necessary to discuss the manner in which children were controlled, trained, socialized and placed out in service. Moreover, the psychological implications of institutional separation and family

135

separation require explication, as do the
relationships between institutionalization and
binding-out practices.

In Service of Their Betters: Custody, Resocialization & Binding Out

5

> Seventy years ago [children] would
> have been scattered like chaff, the
> sport of disease, death, crime and
> infamy.

<u>Winnipeg Tribune</u>, 22 October 1938

The Protestant Orphans' Homes were the most representative children's institution established in the colonial societies of British North America. Beginning with Montreal in 1832, benevolent Protestant societies arose in all major centres to provide for children who were "the sport of disease, death, crime and infamy." The appearance of the POHs by the 1850s in Upper and Lower Canada, Nova Scotia, New Brunswick, and Newfoundland represented the acme of founding and enthusiasm. Later institutions in British Columbia and Manitoba, and finally the new provinces of Alberta and Saskatchewan were modelled on these mid-nineteenth century Homes.1

The POHs were distinct from other nineteenth century institutions established for children and young people. Unlike reformatories and industrial schools or mental asylulms, orphanages were not intended for the delinquent or the defective; unlike the newsboys' lodging homes, they did not house self-supporting adolescents, who, given their social class might have been expected to be gainfully employed even if with their families, and finally, the POHs had not been established to receive illegitimate or abandoned babies. Such children were given to infant or foundling homes or municipal and county poorhouses. As a matter of policy, orphan asylums generally refused to accept children under three years of age. In the very broadest sense, the orphan asylums dealt with "normal" children who lacked, at least as far as the managing committees of the homes were concerned, proper care and supervision.

The establishment of the orphan asylum marked a significant shift in sentiment and practices with regard to dependent children in the colonies; however, as with any social transformation, the new institution mixed emerging and old values. The judgment that casual outdoor relief under the colonial poor laws or the inclusion of children in general purpose relief agencies such as houses of industry and poorhouses were unsuitable for dealing with dependent children was a major transformation in the perception of the vulnerability of child life. The founders of the POHs were determined to separate and protect certain classes of children from the contamination and dangers of adult life.

At the same time, the Protestant ladies and gentlemen of the Homes manifested many of the dominant attitudes towards the "dangerous and perishing classes" exhibited by the patrons of the more general institutions. Their understanding of lower class life included the conventional distinction between worthy and unworthy poor and the firm resolution that their "children" were to be trained and socialized into the ranks of the worthy poor who were to earn their living by domestic service and manual or agricultural labor. This determination to protect and to initiate their inmates into useful work led the managers to exercise a legal authority quite beyond that normally claimed by unspecialized relief institutions. In particular, the POHs asserted a new form of guardianship over children that allowed them to place their inmates without hindrance from families or friends, and to establish an institutional regime that would resocialize and train the children effectively prior to their leaving the Homes.

The following chapter examines the manner in which the POHs sought to establish their control over the custody of chidren placed in the Homes, the legal status of inmates and of children placed out of the Homes, and the ways in which children were resocialized and trained prior to their placement. If the history of the POHs illustrates the transformation of nineteenth-century conventions and customary practices regarding dependent children into the legal and bureaucratic rules and regulations of the twentieth century, then an understanding of an active part played by POH managers in reconciling new and old values and practices is crucial to a proper history of Canadian child welfare. It is both as elements in larger societal change and as historical actors that the POHs provide an insight into social values of British North America.

CUSTODY AND CONTROL

The historical study of nineteenth century institutional development has benefitted from social science studies of how contemporary "total institutions," namely prisons and mental hospitals, function. Indeed, Erving Goffman, the popularizer of the term, defined "asylum" as an institution in which the inmates enter with a "presenting culture," that is, "a way of life and a round of activities taken for granted until the point of admission to the institution." Consequently, Goffman concluded that "there is reason . . . to exclude orphanages and foundling homes from the list of total institutions."2

An examination of the records of Canadian children's homes established by Protestant child savers demonstrates that most homes rarely included a majority of orphans - much less foundlings, that most inmates had both a "presenting culture" and a network of family and friends who frequently probed institutional defenses, and that inmates did not come "to be socialized into the outside world by some process of cultural osmosis even while this world [was] being systematically denied [them]."3

Because most children were not orphans, the POHs had to deal with parents and friends who challenged the asylums' legal right to socialize and bind out their inmates. The attempt to separate children from unworthy parents and associates was modified further by the necessity of preparing inmates to become self supporting at an early age, and by an increasingly hostile rhetoric on the part of child savers who rejected institutionalization of

children as ineffectual if not psychologically
damaging.4

The vague and ambiguous use of terms such as
"adoption," "placing," "binding," "indenture," and
"apprenticeship" by the asylum managers was
partially a result of a claim of control not
formerly acknowledged. The confusion also
demonstrated a striking difference between past
attitudes towards childhood and contemporary
attention to a carefully articulated legal basis for
adoption and foster care that followed the
controversy over the legality of such claims. Less
than fifty years ago, adoption and placing (which
was somewhat equivalent to fostering) were used
interchangeably. In some cases, adoption simply
meant that very young children had been placed with
families. Such children had few if any legal claims
on their "families" in later years. They could be,
and frequently were, returned to the Home at will.
Others at equally tender ages were "indentured,"
which implied that not even the most cursory papers
had been drawn up or signed. Sometimes families
deposited money with the Home as evidence of their
good faith. It was generally understood in such
cases that indentures would be drawn up when the
children were old enough to begin an apprenticeship.
During apprenticeship, children received minimal
wages which were paid to the Homes who held them in
trust until the expiration of their service.

Under such arrangements, the Homes, claiming to
be acting in loco parentis with regard to indentured
or bound out children, retained guardianship.
Despite this putative guardianship, it was not
unusual for Homes to have no knowledge of a
particular child's whereabouts when the time for
formal indenture papers arrived or during
apprenticeship if the family had moved. It is also
clear that not all Homes had statutory authority to
adopt children. At the risk of suggesting more
uniformity than existed, the period before the
signing of the official indenture might be described
being informally "placed-out" and the period
following as being formally "bound-out."

In cases of parental objection or late
admission to the Homes, older children were often
indentured under formal agreements that were as ill

140

supervised as the care provided younger children. In either circumstances, the wages and conditions stipulated in the indentures were usually outmoded and well below apprenticeship conditions elsewhere. Since such antiquated provisions were not in the children's favor, households receiving them had the advantages of relatively unprotected cheap labor. Finally, no matter how described, applications for adoption and placing or binding-out were accepted carelessly and rarely investigated. In most instances, a single recommendation from a local clergyman or prominent citizen was sufficient grounds for approving an application.

Confusions of terminology and practice were further compounded by mixed categories of children within the POHs. Although intended to receive only orphaned children, most Homes quickly admitted such a variety of cases that within a short time, the majority of inmates were either "half orphans" or children placed in temporary custody for a minimal fee while parents or guardians re-established themselves.

The committees were quick to note that surviving parents often unexpectedly took their children out of the institutions and consequently both disrupted the internal management of the Homes and prevented effective resocialization. To forestall such interference, the Kingston Home required that parents of part orphans or children placed in custody agree to relinquish "all claims for the child for two years," since anything less than a two year residence was too short a time for the proper training of children. Most insitutions, however, preferred to require an indefinite commitment, and their demand for an adequate training period agreed with the managers of reformatories and training schools who campaigned for indefinite sentences in order to reform incorrigible children.5

Despite the universal and absolute denunciation of the removal of children by parents or guardians, few institutions could safely refuse such requests. The Kingston Home, for example, proposed to forgive the overdue fees for a girl if her new step-father, a Roman Catholic, would agree not to remove her from the Home. The family's failing in this instance was obviously religious. Fathers reclaiming their children sometimes ran afoul of committees who were convinced that institutional training was preferable to that provided by working men. Mothers who inquired about the whereabouts of daughters were often refused for reasons as varied as disapproval or distrust of a mother, ignorance of a child's location, fear that a girl would be enticed from her place and thus inconvenience her mistress, or, especially if fees were owing, the desire to keep a particularly useful child in the Home.6

Most refusals were justified on the grounds of protecting children from the "demoralizing influences of ungodly homes" and the "downward course" resulting from neglect by "wretched and degraded" parents. In contrast, the POHs saw themselves as providing children with "a fair start in life and the prospect of a comfortable maintenance." Some Homes approached the question of retention on more pragmatic grounds. The Methodist Orphanage of St. John's customarily returned girls to their mothers if they remarried; however, in cases where return was not possible, the children remained in the institution which continued to receive the orphan grant allowed by the Commissioners of the Poor.7

The Church of England POH of St. John's had been compelled early in its history to receive many fatherless children whose mothers were "incapable of providing for them." Similarly, the Toronto POH assisted mothers in domestic service by caring for their children for a nominal fee. Such temporary custodial service was available both to the respectable poor and the widowed and orphaned. Unlike orphans or part-orphans, fee paying children were usually returned to their living parent or relatives rather than being adopted or indentured.8

Since not all homes had statutory authority to adopt children, admission agreements were used to create the color of legality. The agreements usually included a non-interference clause that gave the institutions full control over their inmates and often prohibited parents from interfering with the indenturing of children. These admission requirements also reflected the original intention

142

of the founders of the Homes to provide permanent
refuge for clear cases of dependence such as
orphans.

The problems connected with non-orphans were
clearly put by the Kingston POH when it observed
that "the condition is often more desolate than that
of children left wholly orphans for the very
circumstances of their having a parent living
prevents their adoption into families that would
gladly receive an orphan." Families were reluctant
to "adopt" or to receive children under indentures
with surviving parents or guardians. Their
reluctance was partially prudential given the
potential for embarrassing ethical questions, and
partially cynical given the vulnerable status of
orphan children once outside the Home. The lack of
aftercare meant that orphans were largely
unprotected and that violations of the indentures
rarely were protested. The vulnerability of
Canadian dependent children helps us understand the
preference expressed by many English-Canadians for
British immigrant waifs and strays who began to
appear in Canada during the last three decades of
the nineteenth century. In addition to the same
inadequate supervision, British juvenile immigrants
were thousands of miles from families, friends and
the emigration societies.9

Contemporary social conditions quickly altered
the clientele of the children's homes. In times
without public income supplements and with few means
of relief outside municipal poorhouses and houses of
industry, facilities for children of deserted or
widowed mothers were urgently required. Children of
unwed mothers, or who were "diseased, of physical
blemish, or of unsound mind," were normally excluded
from POHs if not from Catholic institutions.
Children of the unworthy poor, the defective, the
epileptic, the bastard, and the immigrant, joined
the families from the marginal sectors of colonial
societies in the almshouses and lunatic asylums
where they became neglected public charges.10

Privately maintained orphanages by requiring
nominal monthly payments became custodial residences
for children whose admissions were approved by the
ladies' committees. Since such approval was often
made not on grounds of destitution but with regard

to the respectability of the families and their probable ability to pay the fees on a regular basis, the POHs were relatively "elite" institutions catering primarily to the "worthy poor." The municipal almshouses and Catholic institutions were truly the last resort for the less worthy. The Hamilton Orphan Asylum with its civic grant, atypically acted as a municipal shelter for destitute children from the beginning.11

A profound suspicion of lower class family life that produced even temporary custodial cases permeated the management committees. Their conviction that moral flaws were the prime cause of family breakdown was untouched by the starkest examples of socio-economic deprivation. Destitution, unemployment, bereavement and illness paled before countless tales of drunkenness, violence, and desertion. Even in cases without obvious moral fault, the committees were reluctant to encourage parental irresponsibility by lax admission regulations.

It was with a heavy heart that most people chose to admit themselves into a house of industry and it was recognition of this fact that induced Dr. Bovell to inform the board of management of the Toronto House of Industry that many inmates wanted the institution renamed "Hospital for Invalids" because the present name was so "distasteful to many of the poor persons who are forced to resort there." Comparisons between the populations of the Protestant and Catholic institutions in Ontario are representative of situations in other parts of British North America. For example, in 1883, whereas the London POH had a population of seventy-seven, the Roman Catholic Orphan Asylum had 139. Ottawa POH had a mere seventy-one inmates compared with 114 at St. Patrick's Orphan Asylum and 162 at St. Joseph's. The Kingston Hotel Dieu Orphan Asylum had 117 children and the POH thirty-five less while St. Mary's of Hamilton boasted of 216 compared with the POH's mere forty-one. Finally, the Toronto POH, one of Canada's larger ones, had only 157 children in contrast to the Roman Catholic Orphan Asylum's 418 occupants.12

Children of deserted or widowed mothers were institutionalized for longer periods than children of similarly circumstanced fathers who often remarried or took in a spinster relative as housekeeper. This rapid turnover was not welcomed by the POHs since it seriously compromised discipline and domestic economy. Committed to the family ideal within the Homes, the founders and the managers perceived the "ins and outs" as obstacles to the achievement of the well ordered asylums. Since even the worthy poor were classified as more or less respectable, with widows being more so than deserted women, some Homes established priorities for admission which were selectively enforced to insure the reception of the right classes of children. Generally, preference was given to orphans without either parents, children with one living parent (usually the mother), and those "who may, by some unfortunate contingency, be deprived of all care and support from their parents, though living." Respectable Roman Catholic children - which excluded those in public institutions - might be received and, of course, protected from the contamination of their religion and kinfolk.13

Some institutions such as the Victoria POH, supported by voluntary subscriptions, were able to refuse children from families with "serious social problems" along with delinquents and defectives. Others such as the Saint John POH, despite a clear preference for orphans, were forced to take in deserted and destitute children as well as those whose parents were insane, inebriate, helpless, or confined in a penitentiary. Although delinquents and children with contagious diseases were excluded, all Homes admitted boarders and voluntarily surrendered children.14

In the founding years, most POHs were the expressions of self-indulgent benevolence and comparatively modest schemes. Anomalies in admissions merely reflected the preferences and prejudices of the ladies' committees. In the face of increasing social problems of Canadian cities, admission policies became standardized and impersonal. Moreover, financial restraints seriously influenced admission policy. Even nominal fees were important to institutions that operated on shoe string budgets. Boarding fees and the meagre and uncertain municipal and provincial grants often meant the difference between solvency and bankruptcy. Fees and grants represented the failure of a private charity to maintain itself on philanthropy and posed a continuing threat to institutional autonomy regarding management, admisssion, and training. Alternatively, even nominal fees provided a lever by which asylums could coerce parents if they owed money.15

The POHs agreed generally that older children, that is, those over seven years, were not to be given in adoption without the nominal protection of indentures since this was frequently a cloak for using them as cheap labour. Moreover, such children were frequently returned after several years for irresponsible reasons. Adopted children had no claims, of course, regarding family property or support. As indicated earlier, terms such as adoption and apprentice were used so loosely that families could both "apprentice" and "adopt" a child. Even as late as 1904 a Winnipeg girl was "adopted" by a Reverend gentleman to serve as a nurse maid. A six month infant was adopted in 1897 and payments amounting to $110 were made to the Home prior to her death. Since "payments" represented money being set aside for a child in apprenticeship, the status of even infants was unclear.16

The family who had "adopted" Alice Smith out of the Winnipeg Childen's Home in 1904 eight years later wanted to be "relieved" of her. Although the Board declined, the prospects for the girl in such rejecting and depreciating circumstances were certainly not propitious. In the same year, a little adopted boy, Jackie W., was returned, but only after he had already been subjected to circumcision, apparently due to his masturbatory habits. At age two "Minnie" was surrendered for adoption by her mother to the Winnipeg orphanage which cared for her until she was adopted at age seven. At the death of her adoptive mother in 1900, this thirteen-year-old experienced an emotional collapse for two months and was returned to the Home. 17

Since institutions rarely employed their own inspectors to supervise aftercare, they were compelled to rely on informants and local citizens who were reluctant to meddle in the affairs of their neighbours. Lacking even the rudiments of inspectional service, most Homes acted only in cases of gross public misbehavior. One farm family, which had already adopted five children, received yet another girl. Only the tardy completion of the requisite papers attracted the attention of the Home.18

The sentimental novel by L. M. Montgomery, Anne of Green Gables, reflected typical attitudes and practices of the day in Prince Edward Island. Even the upright adoptive parents of the tale, Marilla and Matthew, had reasons beyond a love of children for receiving Anne into their household - reasons that made their disappointment at the discovery that this "adopted" orphan sent over from a Nova Scotia asylum was a girl and not a "smart, likely boy of about ten or eleven" quite understandable.

Marilla informed a neighbour that

We thought we'd get a boy. Matthew is
getting up in years, you know - he's
sixty - and he isn't so spry as he once
was. His heart troubles him a good
deal. And you know how desperate hard
it's got to be to get hired help. There's
never anybody to be had but those stupid,
half-grown little French boys; and as
soon as you do get one broke into your
ways and taught something he's up and off
to the lobster canneries or the States.

Marilla further expounded her views by remarking that they had "decided that ten or eleven would be the best age - old enough to be of some use in doing chores right off and young enough to be trained up proper."19

Since all Homes set ages for demission, they were faced with the problem of placing over-age children. Many institutions refused to return children to their families on the grounds that renewed family interest was evidence of greed and self-interest. Parents requesting the return of their children were usually identified as part of an unscrupulous class of dependent poor willing to fob off their parental responsibilities onto charity during the time of their child's economic dependence. In 1873, the secretary of the Montreal

Ladies' Benevolent Society claimed that twenty-two girls had been reclaimed by parents or guardians that year because "the scarcity of servants made them valuable acquisitions to some who had entirely neglected them in their helpless infancy." In 1894, the corresponding secretary of the Toronto Girls' Home decried the common occurrence of girls absconding from their places to join their mothers and expressed profound suspicion of "maternal tendencies" that were so "suddenly revived" after several years of "neglect." The Home cited "the maintenance of the family circle, the non-separation of parents and children in so far as the child's welfare is involved" as a major aim but in fact families were viewed with a singular lack of sympathy.20

There can be no doubt that some parents did reclaim their children at the age of indenture when they had rarely visited or paid the slightest attention to them previously. The literature of rescue societies, boy brigades, and asylums, all mention the problem. The English child emigration societies claimed that emigration was the most satisfactory means of separating children from the disreputable claims of kinship. The problem, however, becomes acute when one realizes that as a result, children rescued from their potential exploitation by parents or relatives were often subject to actual exploitation by strangers without the emotional ties and feelings of contributing to the family survival.

The "fee" requirement was often used as a threat, for it was implied that after a certain period of non-payment either desertion had occurred or rights over the child had been automatically forfeited. Likewise parents and relatives who did not visit a child, usually over a three month period, were also written off as having abandoned the child to the Home to do with it what it thought best. In some cases such as the Methodist Orphanage of St. John's, the full agreement to bind the child over to the institution had to be signed on admission.21

Not all parents willingly signed over their children for either indenture or adoption, and many objected strenuously to the automatic abdication of parental authority as a result of merely handing their children over to the Homes or by failing to pay maintenance fees. Usually such protests were ignored, and few incidents ended in litigation. If poverty resulted in children being placed in institutions, it was unlikely that the same parents would have adequate finances to fight a court case. An incident involving the Winnipeg Home that illustrates the arbitrary nature of "adoption" procedures as late as 1902 occurred when a Mrs. Morrison demanded to meet with the board members and discuss her "adopted" child Dorothy Bell. Apparently Mrs. Bell recognized her daughter being proudly paraded on the main street and followed her to her adoptive home to reclaim her. As she had never signed any papers giving her up for adoption the Morrisons, who felt "very badly" about this affair, agreed that Mrs. Bell's rights had to be considered and returned little Dorothy to her.22

A widely publicized case, Robinson vs. Pieper, occurred when Mrs. Robinson, who having placed her infant daughter Alice in the Toronto Girls' Home in 1883, sought to have her returned to her when she was apprenticed to Mrs. Pieper of Owen Sound in 1892. The verdict, upheld in 1896, in the Divisional Court, did not recognize parental rights:

> The learned judge can find no reason
> whatever for holding that the mother
> is entitled to have this indenture set
> at naught and the child returned to
> her. She was clearly a child having
> the protection of the Home, when she
> was apprenticed; her mother was, and
> had been for years an assenting party
> to her being at the Home, and under its
> protection and made no application for
> her return until she ceased to be helpless.23

The Pieper/Robinson decision was described as having put the Home's rights to indenture children "on a firm basis" by over-riding an Ontario Act which required that "the parents must sign away their right to the child" before the child could be bound out from the home. The victory, however, was brief, for within two decades, tighter legislation over guardianship and a greater activity on the part of the Children's Aid Societies in Ontario weakened

the principle. Josephine Fletcher's appeal as
Secretary of the Home to consider the rights of
those "who having taken children from this Home
whilst young and useless have fed, clothed and
taught them through years of helplessness," would
finally be resolved by twentieth century legislation
that defined the rights of parents, adoptive parents
and child.24

In brief, the POHs preferred full orphans
because their claims to wardship were clearer and
problems of family interference less likely. In
addition, orphans, particularly if entered at a
young age, had more exposure to the Home's regimen,
were more likely to be successfully resocialized,
and probably were more psychologically inclined to
fully participate in the asylum's programs and to
identify with its norms. Orphan children were,
therefore, the most "appropriate objects for the
cure of the institution."25

SEPARATION, SOLICITUDE AND SURVEILLANCE

In the conduct of the POHs, the charity-givers
attempted a kind of cultural quarantine that not
only sought to prevent any contaminating intrusions
entering their morally antiseptic environments but
also to ensure a change in cultural or class
identification. Working class urchins were to
undergo a metamorphosis thus leaving the institution
with middle class values but with social expectations not exceeding the reality of their hereditary
status.

Most acts of incorporation recognized the
Homes' rights over both the persons of their inmates
and their eventual placement after a period of
training in the Home. Completely dependent upon
their patrons, such orphans could be readily
adopted, indentured, or trained within the Home
itself, whereas temporary cases had dubious ties of
kinship and loyalties which militated against
successful resocialization. The problem of runaways
indicates how strong the ties of kin sometimes
proved to be. Such children caused frustration on
another account for it was a more complicated
process and sometimes impossible to have them

150

"adopted" or even indentured without cooperation from parents.

The POHs quickly came to be identified by the indigent and labouring poor as places of temporary custodial care. If some children, notably street children, were "snatched" by philanthropists for placement in the Homes, the majority were frequently deprived of family life by the decisions made for them by surviving parents or relatives. This was no less applicable to the Canadian experience than it was to the British child rescue movement which emigrated many non-orphan children to Canada.26

Although whole families sometimes admitted to institutional care, the usual pattern was for one or more children to be surrendered while the others remained with a surviving parent or with relatives. Consequently, the breaking up of families was not only a middle class preference but also a lower class solution for handling the worse effects of economic or psychological dislocation. Very often the older and stronger children were retained as homeworkers or child minders or were placed in dead-end but temporarily well paid jobs while useless, young, or weak children were given up. As compulsory school laws became more universal and child labor laws more commonplace in the latter decades of the nineteenth century, more older children were also surrendered. While disinterested observers might sympathize with the grinding poverty that induced parents to surrender their children or pragmatically to use them to supplement the meagre incomes of working class households, young children were not emotionally capable of appreciating the compulsions of their socio-economic circumstances although they might in adult years be capable of accepting rationally or even resolving emotionally the conflicts that surrender precipitated.27

If the personal psychological and socio-psycho-logical experiences of the orphan and the surrendered child were different, so too were the potentials for successful resocialization, which the POH managers quickly came to realize. The trauma of family break up, the bewildering expectations of an institutional setting, and the frightening sense of abandonment or bereavement for orphaned and deserted children were similar to those experienced by

151

surrendered ones. But in the case of those who had kin outside the Homes, there was always the waiting for and the dreaming of the parent to appear and take him or her "home."

In the struggle to control the children, the institutions had to impose a "stronger reality" on them and to deny the possiblity of the parents reasserting their claims on the loyalty of their offspring. By defining the families who surrendered them as morally endangering, the POHs sought to bind the children closer to themselves and to use them to discredit the values and behaviour of the pauperized segments of society. Therefore, the POHs acted upon a set of norms that was an essential part of the middle class mentality and in several aspects in conflict with lower working class life. Naturally, they hoped these norms would continue to operate when the children were placed outside the Home.

The Toronto Girls' Home found the loyalties between girls and their mothers particularly difficult to counteract and these tensions usually erupted when the girl was placed outside the Home. There seems to have been a stronger tendency of daughters to run away from their places of indenture and return to mothers than boys, who normally sought alternative employment. The restrictions of domestic service explain much of the female discontent. The oppressive and confining work conditions, the long hours, the tense relationships between senior and junior servants and between mistresses and servants, the low status, the restrictions on conduct and social intercourse are too well known to require elaboration. As N. Murray observed, "some mistresses not only have the servants do their work but they also undertake to make rules for the servants in matters that do not concern them."28

The Home girls who found themselves "down-stairs" were generally appointed "maids of all work" and assigned the grubbiest and most servile tasks. They were probably much younger than most of the other servants, and if they were not in a multiple-servant household, they were little girls who waited on their mistresses, became companions, nursemaids, or scullery maids, and were treated not as foster children but as menials. Viewed with more suspicion

152

than girls who entered service from regular laboring families and generally left without supervision, theirs was a vulnerable and bitter lot. Moreover, it must be assumed that many home girls, like "Bella" of St. John's, were not temperamentally suited for domestic service. Bella's "abhorrence was so intense that she ran away and her mother protested that this girl who did very well at school should be trained into kitchen work."29

Actually, this orphanage had more interest than most in placing some girls in department stores and offices. The argument proferred by the anxious matron in 1928 was that she was concerned for the girls who were employed out of service because their salaries in stores, offices or factories were usually so low that they found it difficult to subsist in lodgings. The Home agreed to board some of these girls over the age of sixteen to assist them in maintaining themselves. The matron reflected that in service they had food, shelter and supervision which were not guaranteed them otherwise. If wages were so low in this year those received in previous decades must have been alarming indeed. In many ways the lack of regular home life reinforced the Home girl's value as a menial.30

The corresponding secretary of Toronto Girls' Home, Josephine Fletcher, found the problem of girls running away before they had served their apprenticeships frustrating enough to make the following comment about a particular runaway.

> . . . we have been criticized for not
> allowing the relatives of a girl
> indentured out, to know where she is
> residing, but this case proves the
> wisdom of our rule. The girl was in
> a good place, well cared for and
> contented. By persistent application
> and promises of non-interference the
> lady with whom the girl was indentured
> at last gave permission for the mother
> to know where she was. The consequence
> has been that the mother has induced
> the girl to run away.

She insisted that when relatives gained access to their children they rendered them "unhappy and discontented." Moreover, "to hear them talk you would suppose we were separating a devoted mother and her child." She further noted that one mother, who was "distracted" about her daughter's indenture, had surrendered the child ten years previously when she was three years old.

> For years she was quite satisfied to
> have her brought up on charity, but
> now that the girl can earn money and
> is a desirable acquisition, she is
> determined to gain possession of her
> . . . and has been a perfect thorn in
> my side for the last two years.31

A letter written to Mrs. Fletcher in 1893 from a girl patiently serving out her indenture provides another view of parent-child relationships.

> I have been writing to my father.
> I received a letter from him not
> long ago, saying my dear mother was
> very sick. Then I wrote again to
> know how she was. He answered and
> said she was in her grave. It seems
> hard for me to have to write that
> to you. To think I shall never see
> my dear mother again. . . .32

In Winnipeg, Meta Burger, reputedly a "good little worker," was reported as "impertinent and sulky" which is not to be wondered at considering she received no wages from her employers. After she had run away for the fifth time from as many situations and "a terrible account" of her was given by her last employer, Meta was sent to the Industrial School at Portage La Prairie. A friend, Ruby Ayris, stole a horse to make good her escape from the rectory in which she had been placed.33

The loyalty that attached dependent children to the POHs was tenuous at best and was intended to reinforce a commitment to the social and moral values they represented. The Homes sought, therefore, to convince their children that they were particularly indebted to the Homes and the benefactors who supported the work; however, the loyalty extracted from the children did not demand that they sacrifice for and serve their benefactors but that they should cheerfully bear the hardships of their new lives by understanding the sacrifices made on their behalf. Moreover, any attempt to separate them from their placements or new found champions or indeed even the desire of parents and friends to visit them was not seen as the natural urging of parental solicitude but the manifestation of human selfishness and final confirmation of familial depravity.34

As indicated by the many cases of runaways from the Homes or of apprentices who absconded from their placements, the process of binding children to the Homes and their values was a difficult task given the limited time spent in even the best managed institutions and the resources available for binding on an affective, cognitive or loyalty level. If some children defended and cherished their connection with the Homes, others seized the first opportunity to rejoin their parents. The crucial point for reunion occurred when children became potentially self-supporting and the Homes began to place them out.

Modern psychological research can provide a more complete understanding of the psychological stresses to which home children might have been subject. Michael Rutter has provided a synthesis of modern studies on "privation" and "deprivation," which were the psychological problems crucial to the "Home" child. The subject of bond formation and attachment sheds light on the variety of possibilities regarding the child's psychological state. Whereas privation means the lack of opportunity for bond formation in some necessary experience (in this case an attachment figure) or a distortion of care, deprivation suggests having had this necessary experience but then losing it in a disruption of bonds. It is now thought that those children with the least to lose are the most affected when they lose even the little, whereas the loss of an attachment figure "although a major factor in the causation of short-term effects seems only of minor importance with respect to long-term consequences." Moreover, it is likely that the "affectionless character," an extreme pathological personality, results from privation rather than deprivation.35

John Stierlin, using a psycho-analytical approach, reached similar conclusions about adolescents reared by expelling mode parents. As casual runaways, these youths leave home without regret and often form exploitive relationships with their peers. Since a number of Home children were street children, the offspring of negligent parents, or children surrendered by family and friends, they must have sensed that they were burdensome and expendable to their parents. Stierlin's observations that true expelling mode relationships even lacked "the ongoing, though often conflicted and exploitative, investment in the child which gives the [child] a sense of being important to his parents," enables us to understand the loyalty displayed by those children who struggled to rejoin their parents. The dynamics of relationship were not economic or physical well-being, since many children had suffered at the hands of their parents, but psychological since such parents were still able to bind their children. In short, the effects of bond disruption are less damaging than the failure to form bonds.36

There are other findings that add to our appreciation of the Home child's predicament. Prolonged institutional care in early life, and particularly if a child has been reared there from infancy to three years, is an environment least conducive to bond formation. Children in these circumstances often display a lack of guilt, an inability to keep rules, and a craving for affection, all of which are complicated by an incapacity to sustain relationships. It has been suggested that the old style congregate systems impaired bond formation but that children who entered into them with the necessary prior experience were less likely to be subject to permanent psychological impairment. Even institutional care, however, could offer some redeeming qualities if a child formed persisting bonds with several caretakers even if one had to leave the Home. Finally, irrevocable bond disruption as a consequence of death probably leads to fewer psychological problems than disharmony and discord in a home before bond disruption due to desertion by parents. Likewise bereavement in the years before a child is two and has not formed viable attachments is more damaging than bereavement after that age.37

Significantly, conclusions regarding bond formation and emotional deprivation suggest that the most confusion and pain of separation occurs for those children separated from mother <u>and</u> father <u>and</u> siblings <u>and</u> home environment. A syndrome <u>of</u> distress <u>is</u> shown in a sequence of protest, despair and detachment and is due more to a loss than a lack of previous attachment behaviours. In 1876 "little Robbie" was surrendered to the London POH and subsequently "caused much anxiety by his melancholy air and apparent inability to letter a syllable." Apparently Robbie had previous positive bond formation experiences, for when he was adopted some time later he was reported to have become "quite a chatter box" by his adoptive parents. Many Homes had similar cases and concerns about the initiation of surrendered children into Home life. The ubiquitousness of enuresis in children's homes is itself a telling phenomenon and suggests a residue of psychological distance and distress.38

Several of the Homes tried to avoid their children mixing with the more worldly juveniles on the "outside." Such mixing presented a perplexing dilemma, but its allowance would possibly undermine their own regimen of training. Auto drives, picnics and garden parties on patrons' country estates, Valentine Day skating parties, Eaton's picture shows, Elks Reviews, Masonic Lodge Hallowe'en parties, excursions to the various exhibitions, ice-creams in summer, the Stanley Minstrels, the Plowright Mandolins, magic lantern shows and trips to the circus sponsored by the patrons provided adequate diversions in the children's lives as far as the managements of the POHs were concerned.

"Treats" provided by citizens and social agencies were approved of if given solely for their children, but Christmas Trees and Sunday School picnics offered by neighbouring churches were viewed with suspicion. Some anxiety was expressed that the children might be "over indulged" by the duplication of such events which were usually part of the recreation program provided by the Home itself, and it was believed, for example, that a single Christmas Tree was "quite sufficient for children of their situation" because "any more excitement would be injurious."39

The superintendent of St. George's Sunday School of Kingston in 1866 was annoyed because the gifts provided by the parishioners were destined to remain at the foot of the Christmas tree and undistributed because the ladies had originally refused to allow their children to attend the festivities. On this occasion the ladies relented, but only after great soul searching and a determination that it must not happen again. Apart from the fear of overindulgence, the committees were primarily concerned about the results of the social intercourse between their children and neighbourhood children, fully realizing that the ability to maintain constant surveillance over the children's manners and morals would be strained and that some child might quietly disappear midst all the excitement and festivities.40

Two other ingredients, solicitude and surveillance, were required to make resocialization a viable process. Since it implied restraint, rescue contained coercive elements that had be to balanced by such positive qualities as vigilant love which proclaimed that everything done was in the best interest of the children. The illustrations that demonstrate the attention given to the classification of children within the Homes are numerous. Some institutions such as the Ottawa POH not only locked the girls' dormitory each night but also built a high broad fence from the house to the water closets thus dividing the playgound into sections for boys and girls. A separate room was advised to be set aside for "transients," in this case Children's Aid Society children, who were deemed unfit "to associate with our children."41

To limit the unwelcome intrusion of families and friends, visiting hours were stipulated and firmly controlled. Friends and families were often so scrutinized during these times, that some preferred to relinquish visiting "privileges." Others found the hours, which frequently were mid-week and in the afternoons, impossible to meet unless work time was sacrificed. The Kingston POH attached a board to the outside gate stating in bold characters that visiting hours were between four and

158

seven on Tuesdays and Fridays with, "positively none" set aside on Sundays. Long hours of work, especially for women in service, meant that early evening was also a hardship. The visiting hour boards firmly attached outside the Homes said in effect that visitors were unwelcome trespassers on the sacred precincts of the institution.42

When outbreaks of disease occurred either within the Home or in the community, these limited privileges were withdrawn so that the children were further isolated, sometimes for months at a time in cases of extended or serial quarantine. In 1860, for example, the Church of England Orphan Asylum in St. John's was quarantined on and off for a half year due to whooping cough, scarlet fever, and measles. Such extreme efforts to protect and segregate must have aggravated the sense of abandonment, rejection, or bereavement already experienced by the children. As previously observed, young minds cannot be expected to comprehend the social and economic constraints which forced many parents and relatives to seek out institutional custody for their children on either a temporary or permanent basis. Moreover, to be isolated on admission until a clean bill of health was granted, or to be treated in isolation for head lice, pink-eye, ringworm, or the "itch," must have deepened the trauma of separation from familiar surroundings or kinfolk and exaggerated a child's sense of loss and bewilderment.43

The reluctance of most Homes to allow their children to mix freely with the outside world was based on more than the dire consequences of introducing actual contagions into their close confines. The ladies' committees that supervised the domestic economy and decided on admission and demission believed that their institutions were superior to uncontrolled working class family life. To permit indiscriminate association at school and in play was to negate their efforts to separate "their children" from undesirable families and associates. Not only were the Homes selective in whom they admitted, but they sought to create the well ordered asylum within a disordered world as a special moral environment for the proper rescue of the children selected.

This unnatural protection was compounded by the fact that most Homes, at the outset at least, and in some cases, such as the Saint John POH, for several decades further segregated the children by providing their own classrooms. In-house schooling took several different directions. Some Homes had their own classroom or schoolhouse and hired their own teachers, while others received funding from the common school trustees and accepted a common school teacher paid for by the government. Some, such as Kingston and St. John's, used educational societies such as the Lancasterian Midland District School Society Trustees fund or the Colonial and Continental School Society to provide teachers, funds, and books, while some institutions permitted their children to attend common schools. Saint John POH did not integrate its population into the mainstream school system until the 1970s.44

One exception to the general rule that POHs provided only a rudimentary schooling in the "three Rs" and vocational subjects (even these were poorly done) was the Wiggins Home in Saint John. This male governed Home was incorporated in 1867 "for the benefit of destitute male orphans and destitute male fatherless children" [of mariners]. Despite its modest size, the Home was described as "an ornament to the city" with its bathrooms, water closets, basins with hot and cold running water, and central heating system. The boys were not bound-out until fifteen years of age, later than was the custom in other institutions, with this limit raised in 1884 to seventeen years so that the boys would not "lose the good effects of their training." The boys' education consisted of a curriculum that included grammar, geography, history, arithmetic, quadratic equations, writing, and the study of the first six books of Euclid. In keeping with the philosophy of all child rescue institutions, however, the boys were trained into useful occupations and spent two days a week at soldering, telegraphy, carpentry, sewing and patching, wood splitting, knitting, and mattress and pillow picking. Generously endowed under the conditions of Stephen Wiggins' will, the Home was a singularly congenial setting representing the family model under house parents.45

With its own schoolroom ensuring complete segregation from the outside world and the rules on visiting strictly limiting the undesirable influence of family and friends, the orphan asylum established a cordon sanitaire between its children and the general pauper and criminal populations as well as unsavory lower-class family life. For those involved in child rescue there seemed little doubt that the institution which offered surrogate family life was infinitely better than that of lower class upbringing. The 1867 Saint John annual report observed that the Home, with only nineteen children (seventeen had been "adopted" or placed that year) operated "in the routine of a large family [and] there is not much interest beyond its own walls." In-house schooling ensured that the outside world of family and peer groups would not interfere with the internal domestic arrangements of the Homes. Consequently, the Homes turned in on themselves and, using the analogy of the "family," saw their regimen as the most desirable of environments, notwithstanding the inevitable distortion of family values despite the best will in the world on the part of the caretakers.46

At the same time they rescued dependent children by protecting and separating them from adult society and thus ensuring them a "true childhood," the managers of the institutions were compelled to make them socially useful, that is, to teach them to work and to contribute to their upkeep. The work that the children did in and out of the Homes confirmed their inferior social and economic status. On one hand they were ensured a partial childhood, and on the other they were prepared to be exploited on entry into the outside work world. The "noble institution" rescued them as chidren for exploitation as youths and adults. At this point, it is pertinent to examine the emphasis within the Homes on industry and application, as well as the binding-out practices which makes the last remark creditable.

INITIATION INTO USEFULNESS

The Ottawa committee took great pride in the fact that its children had neither the "institutional look" nor the feelings of being "charity bred." Uniforms were frowned upon and the children were seen as one "happy family domiciled

under the friendly roof of the Orphan's Home."
Nonetheless, these same happy family members were
usefully employed. The girls assisted with the
housework of the Home and the older boys worked in
Mr. Bronson's mill with one half of their wages
going to the Home for their upkeep and the other
half put aside for the boys' future benefit. When
children were bound out, the first choice always
went to the subscribers of the society, the ladies'
committee, or to others recommended by them. This
first choice policy was not inconsistent with the
practices of other POHs.47

It has been observed that the admission and
selection policies of the various Homes assured them
a relatively elite character, yet it would be
mistaken to assume, therefore, that the public or
the managements perceived the inmates as other than
"charity children." It would also be mistaken to
overlook the fine gradations of class consciousness
that could quickly delineate the various degrees of
worth and respectability of public charges versus
private institutional cases. The refusal of
undesirables did not lead to an automatic acceptance
of those admitted into institutions as equals.
Indeed nothing further could have been in the minds
of the charity-givers than such democratic notions.
Private philanthropy ameliorated not equalized.

One case in particular illustrates the
situation of the children admitted. In 1891, a
Reverend William Wilkins of Toronto wrote to the
Girls' Home on behalf of the widow of Captain
Cuthbert, yacht builder. She wished to place her
two girls of nine and thirteen at $8 a month in the
insitition, but queried the wisdom of such a step.
Would such an action cause them "to be the subject
of reproach in future years for having been there?"
The decision was unanimous that "this would not be a
suitable place for these children."48

In like vein, a brother of a girl admitted by
their mother into the London Home summarily took her
out because he "did not want to have it said he had
a sister in the home." Apparently some children
were too respectable to mix with those respectable
enough to be selected by the Home. The ladies
committee fully comprehended that despite their
eloquent pleas regarding the rescue of children, the

162

taint of being a charity child, even from a respesctable orphanage, clung like mildew. Occasionally children who had been apprenticed originally, but who later were assimilated into a family, refused wages due them to prevent drawing attention to their previous status.49

To indicate how pervasive and lasting such views were, we have only to take cognizance of the opinion of Frank N. Stapleford, the general secretary of the Neighbourhood Workers' Association of Toronto in the 1920s. He observed that "dependent children who have been separated from their parents do not as a rule represent the best life of the community," and added that children from "high type" family life usually had relatives who were willing to assist them rather than have them admitted into an institution, whereas surrendered children reflected a "lack of family solidarity" if not outright "character weakness." He hastened to assert that not all such children were from "low type families" but "taken as a general class, they [did] not represent the fresh and cleanest blood of the nation."50

Within the Home itself, the ladies sometimes found it impossible to protect children from indignities and demeaning attitudes. An example of the compromising positions in which the institutions found themselves is provided by Dr. Wishart's demand in 1891 that he be provided with a "perpetual grant of children" from the Toronto Girls' Home for medical demonstrations every Saturday morning. These children, he argued, were "callous both morally and physically and therefore not to be compared with other children." The ladies committee reluctantly agreed when the good doctor threatened to withdraw his medical services, given gratis to the Home and worth $400 per annum. A month later, an irate mother objected to her children being used in this manner, and forced the Home not to refuse the doctor's demands, but to decide instead that only orphans would be used.51

In 1919, the thirty-six ladies on the committee of the Winnipeg Children's Home felt constrained to answer public accusations that their children "turn[ed] out badly." Instead of protesting such comments, they foolishly fed the fires of bigotry by virtually agreeing with the criticisms. They replied that "Home babies are gathered from all sources, chief among which are naturally the squalid places of the cities; and it is therefore no wonder that a large proportion are of low intellectual level and perhaps in ripening, provide poor citizenship material." Moreover, "any child that, under the systematic, physical, mental and moral care of a Home, turns out badly, would without the Home have turned out worse."[52]

In addition to such attitudes, the values represented by the institution and instilled through its regimen would quickly disimbue any children who hoped for an improved status in life or who may have been naive enough to affect any social expectations. In Winnipeg, after some agitated discussion on the ladies' committee as to the appropriateness of participating in the entertainments offered by St. Augustine's Sunday School, the problem led to the following entry in the minutes of 2 July 1908:

> This caused a discussion upon the wisdom of so much entertainment and some ladies spoke very forcibly and to the point, that though it was nice for the public to give them treats, yet in the long run, it tended to spoil them for their future life, and it was decided that the children be taught to work, and to understand that they have to look forward to work, and that they be made to do it - places to be found for the big girls Meta Burger and Dolly Ayris, that they be sent to them and given to understand that they must keep them, and not expect to come back to the Home.

This best summarizes the over-riding attitude toward home children - that they must "look forward to work, and that they be made to do it," which was scarcely noteworthy were it not for the assumption regarding the kind of work they must do.[53]

Rarely were home children apprenticed into trades or permitted the comparative freedom of the shop and market place. In 1854, the Hamilton Orphan Asylum, responding to a request for a boy to be trained as a shoemaker, resolved "that Robert Hewitt should be only placed to a trade in the country."

The case of a very bright boy from the St. John's POH being placed as a pupil teacher at a central school in 1874 as a recognition of his "quickness of learning" and aptitudes, although not solitary, nevertheless was so rare as to be insignificant. The Knowles Home for Boys in Winnipeg, which at the turn of the century apprenticed boys to townspeople and trades, required the lads to "repay" their previous upkeep in the Home by contributing a percentage of their earnings, which proved to be a great financial hardship.54

Uniformly, the work that they were trained into and encouraged to do was to serve their betters on farm or in household. Boys invariably became agricultural labourers and girls domestic servants. The preparation for these occupations began early with the care of livestock or gardens and household chores being the most common initiation. The Halifax Home was more blatant than most in using the labor of its inmates. This establishment had no staff, apart from the matron and manager, from its founding in 1857 to 1871, when a permanent servant was hired. In 1861, a washerwoman was brought in twice a week, and three years later "extra labour" was occasionally hired to help with the gardening and the heavy cleaning in the stable. The Home claimed that the children were "trained to habits of order, cleanliness and industry, and taught all kinds of household work, and whatever may fit and prepare them for useful stations in life." A year later the purpose of these activities was more explicitly spelled out as training the children "to be useful servants and good members of society." In the minds of the charity-givers, both were, naturally, synonymous, for they came from the class accustomed to the hiring of servants. No girl in the Halifax or Saint John Homes was to be bound out into service until she was fifteen years of age but since many were "adopted" before this age the regulation sounded more advanced than it actually was.55

The eighth rule of the constitution of the Victoria POH stated that its children were to be taught "to wash clothes, scrub floors, wash dishes and attend younger children and all domestic work as a most important part of their education." The Girls Home of Toronto, in its new rules of 1900, generously agreed that girls under fourteen were not to wash and scrub floors in the institution for more than three hours a day. The Home conducted industrial and serving classes in sewing, laundry, ironing, turning and folding of clothes, and cooking.56

In Kingston, due to the problems attached in the keeping of household help, it was believed that it was of

> . . . essential benefit to them to be thus employed in alternate and regular duties, in which they feel excited to emulate one another as well as desirous of the approval of their superintendents. . . . Even little girls of ten and eleven are pleased at being admitted to the circle of useful- ness, and are exerting themselves to please.

The Reverend T. G. Smith, who was involved in the instruction given at this institution, agreed that

> . . . recognizing the fact that the future welfare of these children must mainly depend on their own exertions it is desirable to exercise them in all useful occupations, both in household matters and in outdoor work, and to give encouragement to their efforts by all suitable means.57

Many years after the above comment, the 1916 annual report of the St. John's POH recorded the following change of attitude:

> Our orphans do not learn to earn, save, spend, or give money, and manual training is non-existent. . . . In every group of children such as we have here, there are many who, through natural limitations are destined to become merely 'hewers of wood and drawers of water.' But there are always some few with larger gifts, capable at any rate of higher industrial efficiency.

Despite the shift in sentiment, however, most home children did remain in occupations that were set aside for the "hewers of wood and drawers of water," which had less to do with their natural limitations, although these were rarely improved given the low standards of formal education found in most Homes, and more to do with the assumed aptitudes associated with social status.58

In spite of their low status, home children were encouraged to be grateful for their rescue and instructed that theirs was a more privileged position than that of many outside the walls of the institution. In Toronto, the children knitted socks and stockings "for the poor" so that "while their fingers [were] taught to work their hearts have been taught to feel for others." Moreover, it was hoped that the self denial of the children "for the comfort of others [would] induce many to deny themselves, if need be, to sustain efficiently an institution which implants such principles in the human heart." These same hapless children in 1869 were rewarded for all their tedious efforts by a "kind gentleman" who presented them with a further large quantity of yarn to continue with their good works, which affirmed the suspicion that menial labor rarely had any end.59

Always an exceptional institution, Wiggins Home for Male Orphans not only provided a challenging curriculum within the Home, but it also insisted on more robust vocational activities "best adapted to their capacities and inclinations." In 1893 a letter to the principal from seven boys complained about the amount of outdoor work and sawing as well as the lack of holidays. Although the letter demonstrated the unusual candor and trusting relationship between staff and boys that prevailed in this asylum, the committee's swift retort was pointed. The boys themselves "should be disabused very decidedly of any idea that they [were] to be brought up in indolence or any kind of self assertion. . . ."60

From these evidences it becomes clear that while exercising the important elements surrounding the first three criteria of childhood - separation, protection, and dependence, the fourth criterion of delayed responsibilities was not recognized as a desirable condition in children's institutions. The initiation into usefulness severely constrained these children from enjoying the full advantages of childhood. The POHs offer a curious reversal of the argument they all too readily used against parents who abandoned young and useless family members to the care of an institution. Besides being a financial burden on a family already suffering from various kinds of material deficits, young children made it especially difficult for a single parent to work full-time to alleviate the family crisis. Consequently, if young children were surrendered, there were often pragmatic reasons behind the decision. Older children could add to the family income because their jobs, despite the absence of future prospects, usually paid more than their subsistence in the household. Older children, who were not employed but could help out at home, did not require the same attention as young ones.

The POHs operated in a reverse manner since older children and adolescents constituted a burden and not an economic advantage. Therefore, part of the initiation into usefulness was to convince the children that on reaching a certain age they had "to look forward to work, and that they be made to do it." The age depended on the particular institution, but usually by age twelve to fourteen the relative securities of the Home were left behind for indenture into domestic work or agricultural labor.

It should be noted that the apprenticeship of children from poorhouses and similar establishments was the common manner in which to deal with such problems of dependence in the nineteenth century. Pauper children's services were advertised routinely on the doors of almshouses or in the local press. As late as 1883, the Charlottetown Daily Examiner advertised a ten year old boy "for adoption" to "any respectable farmer" on application to the Poor House. Commissioners of the Poor reserved the right to reclaim children if the conditions of their indenture were not met. These conditions usually included board, religious instruction, and some education, although there is little indication that any particular vigilance was given to such conditions.61

When Bridget Cody's case of mistreatment was reviewed by the governors of a Cornwallis poorhouse in 1845, they expressed "perfect abhorrence and disgust" at the inhumane treatment the child had received at the hand of her master. Nevertheless, Bridget was summarily indentured again into another household. It was common for poorhouses to indenture children without parental consent as happened in 1855 to Alfred Rooks. In this case, the parental protest was so vigorous that the boy was hastily returned to the asylum. Between 1832 and 1847 in Halifax, 301 had been bound-out as apprentices.62

The custom of binding-out into the care of private families had a long history; however, in the nineteenth century, it became reserved increasingly for dependent children. Respectable families became less inclined to indenture their own children into service, which required they live in another household, and replaced such service with schooling or day-time apprenticeships. Institutions, benevolent societies, child savers and poor law commissioners continued to replenish these households with servile juvenile labor drawn from the ranks of dependent and neglected children. Since they were uniformly placed as domestic servants and farm labourers, these young servants were not even trained into occupations according to the indenture arrangements for ordinary children of previous decades.63

The difference between former agreements and those made by guardians of pauper and home children was the difference between a legal contact and a very loose arrangement hardly worth the paper upon which it was written. There was, moreover, little surveillance of the household to which the apprenticed child would be put either before or after the agreement. In New Brunswick in 1814, the conditions of service for a seven year old colored boy named Dick, who was apprenticed to Joseph Clark to be trained "in the business of husbandry" and of "house servant," bore some similarity with the loose forms for pauper children. Like Dick, most pauper children were put out to agricultural or domestic service and rarely apprenticed into trade, business, or other occupations.64

Young Henry Forrester, at only five years four months, was apprenticed into the household of a printer in 1837 under indentures that clearly stipulated mutual duties. During his service, Henry was to serve faithfully "his master and his secrets faithfully keep, his lawful commands everywhere readily obey."

> He shall do no damage to his Master,
> nor see it done by others without letting
> or giving notice thereof to his said
> Master. He shall not waste his Master's
> goods, nor lend them unlawfully to any;
> he shall not commit Fornication nor
> contract Matrimony within the said Term:
> At cards, dice, or any other unlawful
> Game he shall not play, . . .

Neither was young Henry allowed to "haunt the ale houses, taverns, or playhouses" until his apprenticeship expired at age twenty-one years.65

Similarly in 1815, a yeoman of New Brunswick put out and bound his daughter Jane to "serve him [the Master] from the day of the date hereof and during the term of ten years from the seventh day of February lastpast or untill she arrives at the full age of eighteen years." Like Henry, Jane was allowed to neither fornicate nor marry, nor absent herself day or night from the household without leave. While Henry was to be trained in the art, trade or mystery of a printer, to be provided meat, apparel and board, as well as a complete set of clothing over and above his common working clothes at the end of term, Jane was to be trained into housewifery, cared for as a member of the family in sickness and in health, sent to school until she was literate, and be given a heifer with all the profits and advantages of ownership. At the end of her term she was to be provided with two suits of clothing for common and Sunday wear. The significance of Henry's case lay in the fact that his parents retrieved him after two years and filed suit against the master for the "heartless and brutal treatment" he rendered his apprentice. He had been whipped, bedded in rags, and insufficiently nourished.66

It must be noted that similar "heavy and severe chastisement" was frequently the lot of pauper and charity children but their plight was met with general disinterest. Take the case of the runaway Percy Nicholls, apprenticed by the Toronto POH in the 1890s. Beaten, ill clothed, and not surprisingly, described as "discontented," this lad found himself "re-sentenced by a Magistrate" to return to the same household with three extra months added to his indenture to compensate for the inconvenience his absence had caused his master. The committee of the Home felt some unease about this incident, but as the couple to which he returned were good friends of a formidable and influential committee member, they chose instead to keep a guilty silence.67

Two years previously, Mary Boston was returned to the London Home by Mrs. Labat after serving her mistress for almost two years. "In rags from head to toe," the child pathetically and fearfully clung to her mistress' letter attesting to her "good character." Mrs Labat offered to make Mary some clothes if she would go back sometimes and help her "gratis."68

Returning to the Home as a result of dissatisfaction was not a cheering experience for a child. Even if not at fault, the inference was made that somehow there had been personal failure. In Victoria such "failures" were segregated from other children and relegated to sewing tasks and domestic work until placed again. When Rudolph Alberstadt, apprenticed for four years, attempted to hang himself due to a depression over another apprentice doing so, the committee of the Toronto POH decided that at twelve years of age he was too old to be readmitted to the Home, and attached him to a party going to the North-West territories. They stated that this was a satisfactory solution to his distress and shame, "as the long journey would divert his mind from gloomy thoughts and the change of climate would build him up." There is no further information as to whether this traumatized lad proved to be the independent and strong young pioneer that the hardships 1897 frontier society demanded.69

It is obvious that most Homes could have advertized themselves as "Cheap Child Labour Bureaus." The Toronto Home, which bound children over at twelve unless "a particularly good situation should offer for a child at an earlier age," refused to apprentice children to a boarding house, or a

171

tavern keeper, and no girl to an unmarried man. The only employer reference usually necessary was that of a clergyman. Originally, indentures lasted until the boys were twenty-one and the girls eighteen but in 1856, this was altered to seventeen years for both. Twenty shillings per annum were paid in the first year for the boy's services, with an additional five shillings per annum thereafter and a good suit of clothing at the expiration of the contract. Girls received fifteen shillings and an additional five shillings per annum thereafter and also a good suit of clothing. A "good" suit of clothing did not necessarily mean a new suit.70

This Home obtained better conditions for its children than its sister institution, the Girls' Home. The terms of indenture here included food, clothing, lodging, medicine, medical attendance, instruction in a Protestant faith and attendance at a Sunday school, "moral and spiritual culture," and instruction in reading, writing, plain needlework and household duties. After an advance fee of $5, the child received $5 per annum until fourteen years when it went to $10 at fifteen, $15 at sixteen, and $20 at seventeen years. The employer could return the child if dissatisfied and the Home could retain her, but the girl herself had no say in either matter. The most frequently abused clauses were those calling for medical care and schooling. The "dissatisfaction" clause was a curious one. Sometimes such "dissatisfaction" took years to be recognized, and then occurred only when the child reached an age that required an increase in payment.71

The Kingston Home did more than most to ensure favourable conditions for its apprentices. It attempted to place girls close to town and boys to nearby and known farmers. After 1870, boys were kept in the institution until they received "the elements of ordinary education" because it was noted that this item was so frequently overlooked by employers. Despite the goodwill in the matter of supervising apprenticeships, the lack of money meant a concomitant lack of pre-placement inspection and post-placement supervision. Mary Jane Ferguson in 1863 had been sent by canal boat to take up her indenture at Smiths Falls, but left the boat with a "wealthy man living near Newburgh." The individual

172

in question may have been a "respectable" man (as he was subsequently described) who had identified a promising and useful domestic servant or a strong and healthy girl, but the fact remains that young Mary was sent to her place alone and subject to all the hazards such a trip entailed. In 1870 Maria Kenny was returned from Pittsburgh to the Kingston Home, although it insisted in its reports that it was reluctant to bind girls out of the town or the county.72

Defaulting on payments was as regular as it was depressing. The reason given by employers and mistresses for non-payment ranged from the facile to the niggardly. All represented the common view that charity children were not to be accorded the same dignity and respect as children with guardians, relatives, or parents who might protest such default. Several employers made requests that were almost identical to that of Mrs. Whittington of Winnipeg, who asked to be "excused" from yearly payments for Carrie until she was "old enough to be useful." Similarly, another woman asked to be excused "on account of the trouble George" had given her.73

Although the Homes' surveillance over the conditions and treatment afforded their children was less than vigilant, this was not usually the case with regard to payments. Although anxious lest the children be defrauded of wages rightfully theirs, the payments handed over by the Homes were so small that they could not be seen as representing a stake for independence. Moreover, children, failing to fulfil the conditions of apprenticeship, lost those wages that had been collected by the Homes on their behalf. The Hamilton Orphan Asylum regularly transferred forfeited wages to the institution's reserve fund.74

It is apparent that some farmers and mistresses preferred charity children because they were easy to defraud and exploit, just as others preferred British immigrant children who were even more vulnerable than the domestic product. Most Homes engaged in acrimonious bickering with employers and insisted on payments under penalty of legal action should they refuse, but it was a rare case, such as that of Alex McClean's of Kingston in 1866, that

173

they took the child out of the situation because an employer was not prepared to do "the apprenticeship justice." Yet the mercenary and avaricious penury involved was sufficient evidence that the situation must have been less than satisfactory. The Kingston Home did not see anything amiss in agreeing to extend David Henderson's apprenticeship to a Pictou farmer from eighteen to twenty years of age. Nobody thought to ask David what he thought of the extension.75

Fortunately, committees did not comply with all requests. A mistress who having paid only partial wages to the Home over a period of indenture, requested the committee to send her the total sum so that she could reimburse the girl at the end of her indenture, would usually be rebuffed. The delays incurred in making final indenture agreements were so common as to be almost endemic. Although all Homes expressed gratification that for children between twelve and fourteen years "the demand always exceeded the supply," this fact was not viewed with either suspicion or forboding.

The failure to investigate applications as well as the lack of post-placement oversight and supervision on the part of the majority of Homes was, in a word, unconscionable. It is quite evident that while Canadian interest groups were noisily and virulently protesting the lack of superintendence on the part of the distributing Homes that placed British immigrant children in the first decades of the twentieth century, they could well have taken a more candid look at their own institutions and agencies. This is not a justification of the calloused British negligence or an attempt to minimize the special circumstances relating to the severity of trans-Atlantic separations, but merely to draw attention to an aspect of Canadian social life all too readily overlooked. The abuses meted out to the British Home child were sometimes no more gross than those meted out to its British North American counterpart. The Canadian dependent child apprenticed to townhouse or farmhouse was no better off materially speaking, although familiarity with the culture and proximity to family and old haunts were qualitatively different.

174

When "one, Alfred Spanton" of the Toronto Home died or when "poor Charlie Davis" was reported by his employer to have been killed by a piece of timber, there seemed little interest in the circumstances surrounding these events. The Ottawa committee effusively observed in the case of Charlie that "he had conducted himself well and given good satisfaction. . . ." There may have been nothing sinister in either cases but neither was there any particular concern expressed. It is, however, comforting to note that when one applicant to the London Home forthrightly asked that she might have a girl to "thrash" occasionally, the committee, scandalized by such a request, refused.76

Although the orphanages were constantly alerted to the problem of exploitation and constantly discussed its possibilities, yet just as constantly they overlooked its presence. The twenty-third annual report of the Toronto Boys' Home noted that there were

> . . . no less than fifty-five boys in
> different parts of the country serving
> their terms of apprenticeship with
> farmers, and the managers endeavour
> by regular and careful inquiry to
> assure themselves that these absent
> children are well brought up and
> kindly treated.

In this institution boys were not indentured until they were ten years of age and their contract did not expire until they were eighteen. "Regular and careful inquiry" normally consisted of a letter to a clergyman or to the family itself.77

In 1872, one visit only was made that year by a friend of the Halifax POH to thirty-five apprentices spread over Colchester and Pictou counties although the western districts were left unvisited. Not surprisingly, little was gained from the expedition which was anticipated by the families concerned, although the committee expressed satisfaction that only two children were not in good homes. In 1855, the St. John's Home insisted that it had a duty to protect "these helpless little ones being exploited by unscrupulous persons" and recommended careful and systematic follow-up procedures and reports to be

175

endorsed by local clergymen. The Hamilton Orphan Asylum attempted from time to time to write letters to its apprentices or their employers to assert "our continued interest in and care for them." There is no evidence these good intentions were particularly followed.78

Very few records were kept of children apart from an initial entry as to when they were admitted into the Home and when they left the Home and under what circumstances. The records of their places of indentures and apprenticeships usually contained only information regarding payments. Even these were far from carefully kept, not because the Home intended to defraud the children, but because record keeping was not deemed of much importance. Transferred from one household to another by masters and mistresses if dissatisfied or if they were reaching an age to demand wages, many children were "lost trace of" once they left the Home. The children who were "indentured" very young sometimes found themselves returned to the Home when they reached adolescence. Beecher Dow was one of these lads returned by Mr. Whitehead of Neepawa "not for any fault but because he was too big to work without wages which Mr. Whitehead did not feel able to pay." This boy was fortunate, for the committee found him a job with the Hudson's Bay Company at $15 a month. Such fortuitous circumstances, however, revived his father's interests, so that Beecher left his lodgings to share his monthly pay packet with a parent who wanted him back.79

Rarely did members of the various committees of Canadian institutions articulate their commitment to the institution and its regimen or to the placing out system in the framework of the broader intellectual theories as occurred in the case of the New York Children's Aid Society under the direction of Charles Loring Brace. The benefits of the placing-out system and the resettling of "children west" on farms, were placed by Brace in arguments about natural selection and gemmule transmission as well as in appeals of "economic charity."

> The change of circumstances, the improved
> food, the daily moral and mental influences,
> the effect of regular labor and discipline,
> and, above all, the power of Religion,

176

awaken these hidden tendencies to good
[gemmules], both those coming from many
generations of comparative virtue and
those inherent in the soul. . . .

Theories of latent tendencies coming to the
forefront when aroused and developed by healthy
family life and the rural atmosphere, were popular
last century. It was believed that even the debased
had hidden gemmules transmitted from their virtuous
ancestors.80

The ladies may have found the case for gemmule
transmission difficult to comprehend, but the
familiar appeal to economic charity that Brace made
elsewhere in his book would have been a matter of
common sense to them. They were far less likely to
believe that the children of ruffians and vagrants
had any gemmule potential except that of
perpetuating a pauper class unless carefully
controlled. Subsequently, they asserted that the
training into usefulness and the apprenticeship
programs their Homes promoted would socialize the
children to "be independent of any further charge
upon charity." Therefore, the appeal to placing-out
was based on both short term and long term
economy.81

In the short term, placing-out was a cheaper
means of socialization than retention in
institutions, and it was believed that surrogate
family life, the rural and domestic virtues and
employer surveillance, could be done as effectively
and a lot more cheaply than within the institution.
Moreover, those "muscular orphans," that is, those
who were disagreeable, independent, and troublesome
- difficult to socialize - could be better
controlled by the firm paternal hand of a good
farmer.82

In the long term, institutionalization followed
by apprenticeship would contribute to the
depauperization of society. That the lessons
learned were sometimes not those of the rural and
domestic virtues - good management, order, industry,
sobriety, wholesomeness, justice and generosity -
did not convince the committees that placing out was
not a desirable system. Those children well placed
and lovingly nurtured as adopted or indentured

177

family members justified the other cases of shameless exploitation which the committees hoped were far and few between. Apart from this justification, the appeal to economy was louder and more compelling than any doubts as to the prudence of the placing out system. Committees could neither afford to keep older children nor supervise them in their situations.

The children's institutions founded in nineteenth-century British North America and in the Dominion of Canada reflected the growing consolidation of new middle class attitudes towards child life and the continuation of old views of lower class morality and dependency. The orphan asylums separated children from the contaminating influences of urban pauperism, alcoholism, crime, and disease, which were represented in many cases by undesirable families and friends. At the same time that educational theorists and medical practitioners were expounding on the formative role of mothers and the need for careful guidance in the proper nurture and education of children, advocates of the new scientific charity were refurbishing the tenets of political economy to argue that indiscriminate relief itself contributed to the incidence of social ills plaguing the cities.

The men and women who founded the Canadian asylums and the ladies who directed their domestic economy were not innovating philanthropists who created new institutional forms or wrote theoretical expositions on charity and society. Instead, they were pragmatic and pedestrian, sometimes pious and religiously motivated, but most often loyal to the institutions they founded and convinced of the value of the work. It is easy, of course, to be cynical of their interest in children since most children "rescued" were destined for domestic and farm service which certainly benefitted the social classes represented by the child savers. Still to write off their efforts in this manner would be to distort their social reality.

It was assumed by the ladies and gentlemen of the Homes that such employment was natural for the classes from which their children came. Moreover, domestic service for girls promised steady work, proper supervision, and respectable marriages; while

178

agricultural labor for boys held the hope of land ownership for those who completed their indentures. As with the British emigration societies that began to send juveniles to Canada in the late 1860s, the Canadian child savers were hopeful that some children would be adopted by the families that received them. Just as Dr. Barnardo and others would claim that emigration was better than anything open to the children in Great Britain, the Canadians maintained that institutionalization and apprenticeship were preferable to the deprivations of degenerate family life or the streets.

Although the Protestant Orphans' Home sought to operate as "total institutions" in their effort to separate their children from undesirable influences (mainly family and friends), their commitment to resocialize the inmates into the ranks of the respectable working classes made the conduct of children's institutions radically different from the mental hospitals and prisons studied by Goffman and others. As much as the ladies and gentlemen wanted to uplift their charges, their enthusiasm and efforts were constrained by the need to place their child in either "adoptive" homes or service. Private philanthropy never enjoyed the security of modern public institutions that whatever their deficiencies could depend on regular governmental funds. In brief, neither funding nor staffing created the conditions under which a professional and salaried personnel had substantial vested interest in keeping their inmates incarcerated for long periods of time.

The Homes also represented the hopes of middle class ladies and gentlemen that personal service and Christian intervention could demonstrably alter the downward course of those they rescued. Unfortunately for the pioneer Canadian child savers, the psychological doctrines underpinning the belief in the power of institutional training were already being undermined in Great Britain and the United States at the very moment they were establishing the first orphan asylums. By the 1890s, the first Children's Protection Acts, by arguing for temporary shelters and foster care, rejected institutionalization and apprenticeship. The establishment of the Children's Aid Society model in Ontario sounded the death knell of the POHs as general purpose

179

children's institutions, and the rise of provincial departments of dependent and neglected children marked the first stirrings of professionalism in Canadian child welfare.83

Whatever their fate, the POHs, by focusing attention on the lot of orphans and other disadvantaged children, and by insisting on practices that seemed eminently sensible to their managers, helped to crystallize public perceptions of dependence and awareness of the means to relieve its consequences. Notions such as adoption and apprenticeship were partially unravelled and mapped by the courts and legislatures as a result of the Homes' claims regarding wardship and placement. As with the later emigration societies, their practices forced Canadians to consider the status and future of categories of children and youths who previously had been lumped together with the failures of British North American societies.

transforming the asylum

15

16

18

17

183

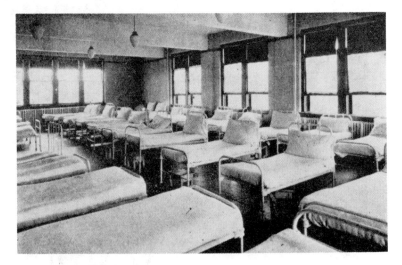

19

20

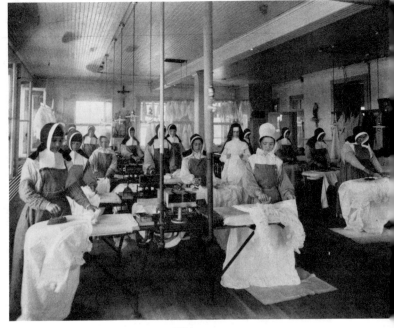

Boarding-Out and Child Emigration: The British Background

6

> . . . we would conclude by calling
> the emigration of pauper and criminal
> children merely an inexpensive
> system of boarding-out in Canada;
> it is a system of boarding out
> without payment.
>
> Birmingham Emigration Home, 1883

For sixty years, British individuals and child rescue societies transported some 80,000 children to British North America. The British Juvenile Emigration Movement is usually dated from the arrival of Maria Rye's first parties of girls in 1869. The movement, losing impetus in the late 1920s, collapsed during the Great Depression. In many ways it provided a catalyst for those child care interest groups in Canada who were opposed to congregate care of dependent children and promoted de-institutionalization and foster care under the auspices of children's aid societies, social welfare professionals, and public welfare departments. The controversy, which child immigration provoked within Canada as well as in Britain, focused on the arguments over the boarding and binding-out of children, and crystallized much of the changing sentiment and practice related to such child welfare concerns as labor, dependency, schooling, state responsibility, apprenticeship and foster care.1

Before large parties of children were brought into Canada under juvenile emigration schemes, some individual boys had been received by the Toronto Boys' Home to be placed out in Ontario for the Earl of Shaftesbury in 1868 and for a "philanthropic gentleman" from London, Mr. Quentin Hogg, a year later. The Home, however, criticized the practice of sending unaccompanied lads over to Canada not only because they were left largely unsupervised, but also because they roamed the streets, with

185

several finding themselves confined to the city gaol as unemployed and vagrant. Years previously, however, the British Children's Friend Society, having approached Toronto's mayor, R. B. Sullivan, in 1835, had reached an amicable agreement to place boys as apprentices in Ontario. A select committee of City Council, impressed by "the exalted patronage" of such eminent gentlemen as the Lieutenant-Governor, Archdeacon Strachan, and the Attorney General, agreed that the request for "the protecting kindness of the Civic Authorities of the chief city of the province of Upper Canada" was mutually advantageous to "so useful and benevolent a Society," to those individuals who would employ the boys, and finally, to the boys themselves in relieving them from distress. The committee's justification for the agreement combined ingredients of fair chance and of dumping ground theses, which for the next century, would provide grounds for supporting or opposing juvenile immigration. The arrangement continued, so it would seem, since "reformatory" boys from Britain were still being apprenticed in 1858 under the wardship of the city's house of industry.2

In some ways, these scattered cases and isolated Canadian objections <u>prefigured</u> the controversy which surrounded the later importation of larger parties of children under the more ambitious schemes conducted by such British child savers as Thomas Barnardo and William Quarrier, or under such agencies as the Liverpool Sheltering Home, the Catholic Emigration Association, and the Church of England Society for Waifs and Strays. Three persistent themes in the subsequent debate had already emerged in the objections presented by the committee of Toronto Boys' Home: the inadequate inspection of the home into which children would be placed or apprenticed as well as inadequate supervision of children once placed; the potential, if not actual, criminality and dependency of the young immigrants; and finally, their contribution to the problems of "urban drift." The purpose of this chapter is to discuss the first objection - regarding supervision at the pre and post placement levels - by relating it to the changing ideas on the proper nurture of dependent children in the British context. The following chapter will further the discussion by considering such Canadian objections

186

as criminality, and dependency, and the accusation that juvenile immigrants contributed to "urban drift."

The evidence of the preceding chapter demonstrates that the criticism from the Toronto Boys' Home referred to above is curious given the similarities of domestic practice. Child and juvenile immigration were, however, to become the centre of an extended and sporadically bitter debate which, while deflecting criticism of domestic agencies in the short term, would eventually draw attention to the home-grown practices of binding-out as well as the related problems of placement and supervision. It is, therefore, necessary to place the Canadian controversy in the broader framework of Britain's "boarding-out" debate to fully understand its intellectual roots and social origins. Although this debate flourished in the last three decades of the nineteenth century, many of its tenets had surfaced in previous ones.

THE BOARDING-OUT DEBATE

At the very time when British child savers were engaged in heated and lively controversy over the success of and the assumptions behind institutional-ized child care, their colonial counterparts were busily founding the first generation of British North American children's homes. The enthusiasm for such institutions was identical to that which had fired British philanthropists in previous decades. Discussion of the boarding-out of dependent children were usually couched in more solicitous language than arguments which supported the binding and placing of children into service, a practice which was more in keeping with apprenticeship customs of former centuries. Indeed, when institutions in Canada or in Britain exercised powers to bind children, their mandate was normally included under the apprenticeship and indenture acts of the provinces or the parishes of the respective countries.

The practice of binding or placing-out clearly involved the socialization of children and their initiation into useful employment because such children were dependent employees within households

and businesses. Apprenticeship entailed mutual
obligations on master and apprentice. Masters were
expected to treat their apprentices humanely as they
would any servant, to supervise their behaviour, to
provide sufficient food, clothing, and shelter, and
to provide for their proper education and
occupational training. Many of these requirements
were met in the ordinary activities of life in
households and business. Often indentures of
apprenticeship included the payment of fees,
provision of tools, or a grant of clothing at the
completion of the service. Since binding-out was
analogous to service, inspection of dependent
children was not normally part of the indenture. It
was assumed that the ordinary legal provisions
combined with customary practice offered sufficient
safeguards. However, the <u>payment</u> of families in
boarding-out schemes represented an economic
reversal that symbolized an important shift in
sentiment and ideology, because the foster family
was obliged to treat the child as a member of an
affectionate family and not as a servant within the
household. In addition, a system of inspection was
required to justify such expenses. The sentiment
and ideology of boarding-out demanded that the child
be educated and socialized <u>not through work but
through participation in a family setting</u>, which was
characterized by the attitudes and sentiment of
nineteenth century middle class family life.
Although the differences between "binding-out" and
"boarding-out" were often confused and abuses
occurred in both situations, the assumptions behind
each practice were quite dissimilar.3

This emphasis on family nurture meant that the
status of children was now radically transformed.
First, children were understood to need special
guidance with regard to their moral and psychological development, which meant that foster parents
were responsible for providing careful instruction
and direction, that children were to be protected
<u>within the family</u> from the more unsavory aspects of
adult life, and that foster parents were to be
models of independent worthy lower class life.
Second, the presumption that children were to be
educated and not worked for profit suggests that the
primary concern of the foster parents was to rear
the children <u>as children and not as unformed adult
workers</u>. In other words, the criteria governing

boarding-out practices were not concerned with initiation into useful employment, although this aspect was understood as a probable consequence of the role models provided by foster parents and the communities in which the children lived. This delay of responsibility in maintaining one's self represented a significant transformation of attitudes towards children. Unlike many contemporary institutional practices, such as those found in the Canadian (and presumably British) orphan asylum that consciously aimed at training dependent children for useful employment, boarding-out operated on the imperatives of educational over occupational aims. This was particularly true in the case of younger children because their placement represented the "ideal" of boarding-out as their relative dependence lessened the likelihood of confusing the criteria of binding and boarding-out. Interestingly, most emigration societies stressed the successful boarding of younger children also but were unable to find as many places for these in the colonies as for older and more useful children.

Although there was a decided preference that boarding-out should occur within the geographical jurisdiction of a particular union (sometimes regulated), there was some provision made for children to be placed outside the area of jurisdiction, that is, "beyond union," which meant that children were placed outside urban districts and particularly the metropolis of London with cottagers and crofters in the countryside. The philosophy behind the system was predicated on the belief that rural life was more wholesome than city life, that the training into horticulture, agriculture and domesticity was superior to urban schooling and to everyday concerns, and that the children would be less likely to return to the cities and exacerbate population and employment pressures. British boarded-out children were seen as competitors for jobs and contributors to urban drift just as their counterparts who were emigrated to Canada would be. Mr. J. Pendlebury, governor of the London branch of the National Children's Homes, founded in 1869 by Thomas Bowman Stephenson, argued for the advantages of rural over urban placements in Britain and extended this to include the Canadian situation. He considered removal "from the streets to the field" to be essential for moral and physical reformation because "the laboratory of nature [was] the best workshop into which to take out the soul of a pauper, and cut off the entail of habitual and inherited idleness." The reports of poor law unions and numerous rescue societies expressed similar sentiments, but all conceded that country homes were limited both in quantity and quality.4

The proponents of the new system of boarding-out (as distinct from the old methods of binding) based their arguments on four major points. First, they argued that boarding-out was necessary for the depauperation of society, that is, the congregate care itself produced those characteristics that perpetuated permanent economic dependency and social disability. Second, they insisted that the moral, physical and psychological risks of congregate care to the child were too great to ignore. These included the prevalence of "serial contamination" and the charge that institutional arrangements, while removing children from unsatisfactory environments, did not satisfactorily remove children from the pernicious influences that often resulted from intercourse between large numbers of children themselves who could not always be supervised. Third, the argument became increasingly more persistent and persuasive that the removal of appropriate children from the probability of pauper taint or from physical and moral contaminations was best realized in "natural" family settings, in other words, that foster family care was more efficacious in both its process and its product than the best institutional setting which remained artificial in environment and regimen. Finally, such psychological appeals were accompanied by the most persuasive argument of all - that of the economy of boarding-out methods when compared with the erection, maintenance and outlay involved in institutional care. Not only would boarding-out prove to be more economical immediately, but when combined with the ultimate "depauperization" that was assumed to result, then boarding-out was clearly a cheaper way for the public to meet its obligations regarding the guardianship of its wards. These arguments, incidentally, would be as essential to the British North American interest in the relative advantages of both systems of child care as it was originally to the British.

It was, however, neither perfectly obvious nor indisputable to all caretakers of Britain's dependent children, any more than it would be to their Canadian counterparts, that the boarding-out method <u>did</u> offer "the best means of educating and providing for destitute children." As in the nature of any debate, there were passionate supporters and bitter opponents on both sides of the question regarding the efficacy of boarding-out methods or congregate systems. In the view of many guardians of the poor, neither did the "stultifying atmosphere" of asylums, workhouses, and district schools obviously produce the "listless and subservient manner" or the psychological and economic dependence in children their critics described. The guardians were proud of the economy and discipline maintained in the public institutions. They were proud of the prosperity and the humanitarianism these impressive edifices symbolized, just as they were proud of Britain's relative genius at staving off riot and revolution by the pacification of the masses through provision of indoor and outdoor relief under the poor laws. Any criticism of the orderly regimens provided by congregate care seemed to be a direct attack on British governance and civilization itself.5

One point, however, that worried even the most complacent guardian of the poor was the mere suggestion that congregate systems for children perpetuated a pauper mentality in a cycle of dependence that produced from a young age those "tribes" of generations and whole streets of "professional" paupers. Consequently, any reasonable claim which argued that placing of children into regular and respectable laboring family life led to the breaking of the chain of dependency and contributed to the depauperization of society was one not lightly dismissed. It commanded a strong case for boarding-out as it did for child emigration.6

What was involved in this so-called cycle of dependence was perfectly understood by the critics of the poor law system and advocates of boarding-out and child immigration alike, and was described by George Bartley in an 1874 pamphlet, <u>The Seven Ages of a Village Pauper</u>, which he dedicated to the "one million of Her Majesty's subjects whose names are now unhappily and almost hopelessly inscribed as paupers on the parish rolls of England." Bartley's position was compatible with that posited in "The History of A Charity Child" printed six years later in the Charity Organization Reporter. The two essays coincided in the view that the charity child followed a demoralizing course. Having been born in a lying-in-hospital at the cost of a maternity society, the course of dependency continued in the obtaining of treatment and accommodation in any one of the various infectious diseases hospitals when required, the receiving of medication from public dispensaries, the attending of clothing charity schools, being trained in and apprenticed from the district poor law schools, receiving alms, fuel, goods and bread from one or several of the innumerable benevolent associations and private charities, and finally in obtaining outdoor relief from the rates to end his days in a poor house followed by a pauper's burial.

> Before leaving the world, he might,
> perhaps return thanks to the public.
> He has been born for nothing - nursed
> for nothing - he has been clothed
> for nothing - he has been educated
> for nothing - he has been put out
> into the world for nothing - he has
> had medicine and medical attendance
> for nothing; and he has had his
> children also born, nursed, clothed,
> fed, educated, established and
> physicked for nothing.7

In addition to the persuasiveness of arguments about the depauperization of society, few British humanitarians were rash enough to question the common wisdom of the day regarding the separation of children from the undesirable elements of their social and family life, or to oppose the thesis that the segregating of children in specialized facilities was necessary. However, the supporters of congregate care believed firmly that the separate district poor law schools urged in the recommendations of the Fourth Report of the Poor Law Board in 1838 were adequate in meeting both the criterion of segregation and the efforts to "depauperize the rising generation." In 1870, Mr. Woodhouse, Her Majesty's Inspector of Schools, issued a report to the Local Government Board which represented the opinion of many other supporters of the poor law schools who advocated the removal of children from mixed workhouses

> . . . in which the mere presence of adult
> inmates, apart from the question of con-
> tamination, familiarizes their minds with
> the idea of a place to which they can
> return in after life, whenever they find
> a difficulty in getting their own living,
> and thus renders it more difficult than
> it would otherwise be to implant in them
> habits of industry and self reliance.

Training in poor law schools built separately from mixed poor houses created "a dislike to dependence on the rates" which repugnance contributed to the depauperization of the children concerned.8

At no time did caretakers of children ever doubt that parental models remained the strongest of all adult influences. Their determination to separate children from such models, and the strenuous effort they put into the resocialization of children so that they might reject the "negative" values of their families and social class are sufficient evidence to support this claim. It was argued that a fatal model of pauperism was presented if it combined familial ties with parental affection. The regimen in the workhouse school itself was also accused of encouraging a form of psychological as well as economic dependence. According to this view, children were socialized into a ready acceptance of charity and an unwillingness to work. In addition to this, the very "taint" of being admitted into and trained in a workhouse or district school was assumed to result in having a low opinion of one's self which made it difficult to break the cycle of dependence, a view which was not lessened by the suspicion poor law children confronted when they sought employment. Inspector Tufnell of the Metropolitan Poor Law Board noted in a report, which discussed the effects of pauper schooling on girls, that even young children were aware of "prejudice" and often did everything to conceal their having been brought up upon the poor rates. This sense of shame was transplanted to Canada when children were emigrated, for there is evidence that many young immigrants, once they left their indentures and struck out on their own, attempted to hide their backgrounds even to their own children and spouses. British prejudice toward those who received poor relief was no less disreputable than its Canadian equivalent toward juvenile immigrants who found it equally difficult to escape from the stigma of pauper or charity child.9

John Skelton, who wrote about the boarding-out of Scottish children, associated "the hang dog look of pauperism" with workhouse children who were regarded by the rest of society as "pariahs"; while Mrs. Nassau Senior, Education Commissioner, said their demeanour bore "the pauper stamp" which effectively cut them off from ordinary life. Mr. Cumin, Assistant Education Commissioner, agreed that workhouse children seemed to be "broken down by misfortune before they entered into life," and F. C. Clayton, an advocate of cottage systems, noted that poor law children were trained like "machines" and rendered quite useless to earn an independent living. Even into the twentieth century such criticisms continued to be publicized, as the case of R. M. Noordin, a young guardian of the poor for the Romford Union, illustrates. In 1925 Noordin was so appalled with the effects of institutionalization upon children that he described the degeneration that occurred within institutions from an inculcation of politeness and civility into "obsequiousness." He continued that, "It is difficult, I know, to avoid the children to be servile when one only wants them to be taught orderly good behaviour"; however, such children were uniformly a little "too subdued and a little unnatural."10

T. J. MacNamara, parliamentary secretary to the Local Government Board, had observed in his 1908 report, "Children Under the Poor Law," that both the character and intelligence formation of those in large congregate systems was far lower than that of boarded children. Moreover, those institutions combined surroundings which excluded normal domestic arrangements with a dependence upon the large scale mechanical devices used for cooking and cleaning. This combination left the children unprepared for life outside the strict confines of an institution.

MacNamara was merely reiterating a similar point of view expressed in a "Report of a Drawing Room Conference on the Boarding-Out of Pauper Children" published in 1876 which commented that even the middle class did not have the opportunities of educating their children in such "palatial institutions" as the great district schools of the Metropolis. The moral result of such "beautiful domains" was that the children were ill-prepared for industrial pursuits, a preparation that could occur within the cottages of laboring foster families representing socio-economic circumstances deemed to match the expectations of poor law children. Reverend William Pitt Trevelyan, who influenced the implementation of the boarding-out system in Calverton, agreed with this premise and enthused that boarding-out placed friendless children advantageously in homes "equal to that born under the ordinary conditions, and in many cases in a safer and better position."11

The Poor Law Unions' district schools operated on a presumption that their residential program of training and education by effectively removing children from those adult moral characteristics that pervaded the workhouses, including the examples presented to infants and little children of nursery care by unlettered and gin soaked "pauper grannies," was sufficient to prevent the development of any spirit of dependence. Although such removal was not thorough enough for boarding-out enthusiasts, there was complete agreement between district school supporters and their adversaries, who were to form the Association for the Advancement of Boarding Out in 1885, that "the chances of a pauper child earning an independent livelihood [were] proportional to the distance of its removal, when launched into the world, from its low relatives and haunts of vice among which it has probably passed several years of its life." These words of the poor law inspector Edward Carleton Tufnell in his first report to the Local Government Board in 1871 were not disputed because it was only the efficacy of the method to be used and not the principle of removal and separation that was in question.12

Yet by the 1870s, the dilemmas associated with the separation of children from their parents were apparent, as were the assumptions which were to eventually ground arguments for parental rights in the twentieth century. The following observation made before a conference on Poor Law Administration held at Newcastle-upon-Tyne in August 1874 suggests an awareness of the pathos, if not the morality, of separating children from parents in situations where familial attachments were apparent to all who cared to observe them.

> Every guardian knows that this is needful,
> but it is painful to learn the small
> duplicities, jealousies and vanities,
> which low ignorant mothers impart; to
> see how they will make small thefts for
> their children, or teach them to get things
> for themselves, how they will try to
> provide little ornaments, or speciality in
> dress, or set the child against its
> teachers, for some fancied slight or
> jealousy.13

Nonetheless, it seemed that removal was usually preferred. That it was a delicate matter even in the nineteenth century is apparent in the numerous examples that ultimately disprove rationalizations about parental indifference and callousness in the workhouses. These examples included the efforts of parents to take their children from these unimaginably dreary environments or avoid their being admitted into them, and parental protestations about the immigration of their children. Parental rights were, however, far from being generally defended with the belief prevailing that pauper children should be taken away "from the travesty of family life to which they [were] condemned." A point of illustration could be seen at the Third International Congress for the Welfare and Protection of Children held in London in July 1902. When the Reverend Marshall G. Vine, warden of Red Hill Reformatory (which sent boys to Canada), observed that as a general rule "boys ought never be returned to their parents" who planned to "sweat them," the audience boisterously responded with a hearty "Hear, Hear!" That parental rights were gaining some advocacy during the second half of the nineteenth century is apparent because the classification of appropriate children for boarding-out stipulated that only the orphan or deserted should be boarded "beyond unions." A manual for poor law guardians in 1890 reminded them of this rule, cautioning them that the "severing" of family ties were to be avoided even when parents were of bad character.14

Another aspect, which comes within the ambit of concern about the contamination of children either by adult example or through an inadequate classification of particular classes of children, deserves mention. Roman Catholic guardians of the poor, laity and clergy alike, expressly considered the possibility of another form of moral contamination from which their children must be rescued - that of proselytizing Protestant tenants or of wilful obstruction in providing Catholic instruction in either poor law district, truant, or industrial schools. Correspondence between Bishop Vaughan and the Colonial Office in the late 1880s indicates that this concern was not exaggerated. In Sheffield, the Reverend L. Burke of the Hollow Meadows Industrial School for Truants had protested earlier that the conduct of the industrial schools in Britain were contrary to the spirit and the law of the 1870 Education Act by representing "not only spiritual privation but violation of the rights of conscience." Burke insisted that the Sheffield board of guardians consisted of "the stern non-conformist type" who were pleased "to call their religious sytem to the school 'unsectarian.'" This concern "for the protection and rescue of poor children who [were] in danger of losing their faith" led to the establishment of duplicate Catholic facilities such as industrial schools, and organizations such as the Salford Catholic Protection and Rescue Society. Catholic children were described by this society as "the prey of proselytizing institutions, which snatched our waifs and strays whenever they were found abandoned and not under proper guardianship." The workhouse schools and industrial schools "rigidly excluded, and indeed, often times held up to ridicule" anything that resembled Catholic belief.15

In Our Waifs and Strays, Father Richard F. Clark, S. J., noted that Dr. Barnardo's homes included twenty per cent, not only of Catholic children without religious instruction, but Catholic children learning to regard Catholic devotions as a form of "mummary." Such suspicions cannot be

197

construed entirely as paranoia. There is overwhelming evidence of British prejudice against both Roman Catholicism and the poor of the larger manufacturing centres who were frequently Irish Catholic. One incident, recorded in the minutes of the Liverpool Sheltering Home, illustrates the point. This Home, which had receiving and distributing centres for its immigrants in Knowlton, Quebec, and Belleville, Ontario, in 1874, decided against receiving children whose parents did not agree to emigration because it could ill afford to run two separate programs of training within the Home. It seems though that such respect of parental rights was not always afforded to Irish Catholic parents for in 1876, Mr. Maloney, a "strong ill looking Irishman," with two equally belligerent and sturdy companions, came to the Myrtle Street residence and forcibly withdrew his three children because he had not agreed to their being sent to Canada. Mrs. Lilian Birt, the founder of the Home, saw such unreasonableness and intransigence on the part of this outraged father as the result of his priests, who consigned him to purgatory or even to Hell if he did not take his children out of a Protestant institution.16

The Catholic Emigration Society, which received children for emigration from various sources, including Father Berry's Homes for Friendless Children, The Catholic Children's Protection Society, and from Father Nugent's child rescue efforts, all found the Liverpool Sheltering Home guilty of highhandedness in its treatment of Catholics. Children were sent to Canada by Catholic rescue societies from Liverpool, Westminster, Birmingham and from the Orpington Poor Law Schools, Southwark. Under the auspices of the Catholic Emigration Society they were distributed from Orpington Lodge and St. George's Home, Ottawa, and St. Antoine's Home, Montreal, with the cooperation of the Grey Nuns and the Bishop in Ottawa, and the Sisters of Providence, Kingston, with Father Godts of Montreal distributing many of these English speaking children in Quebec.17

Not unexpectedly, such placements were far from satisfactory. Father Nugent, who founded the Liverpool Catholic Ragged School in 1853, may have been correct in his observation that "newsboys,

shoeblacks, fuzee-sellers and ballad singers" had
energies and talents over and above average children
because of the "push, the energy and invention which
are called into action by the street children in
their vicious avocations and trades." Nevertheless,
such attributes could not have easily overcome the
fears and bewilderment that Anglo-Irish urban
children confronted in isolated French-Canadian
rural communities.18

   The original principles behind boarding-out,
which would become more systemized in the supervised
methods of foster care, were not only quite
compatible with the concept of childhood in their
faithful reflection of the criteria of protection,
segregation, dependence and in the extension of
these to include delayal of responsibility, but were
actually a consequence of the persuasiveness of the
concept itself. As the attitudinal presumption that
such criteria were essential to child rescue gained
ground, new ways to realize the maximum benefits of
childhood were embraced. The middle class family,
autonomously regulated by its own members, or
labouring families, externally regulated by
representations of the middle class ideal, became
the social unit that was argued to be the most
effective and seemingly humane mechanism through
which to socialize dependent children into economic
independence. Although there is every indication
that the emigration agencies were fully aware that
Canadians were motivated by other than solicitude in
receiving British children into their homes, their
annual reports continued to publicize the family
ideal because such an ideal could not fail but
appeal to the public, thus gaining financial
support. Mr. Middlemore of the Birmingham Childen's
Emigration Homes noted in words which were equally
applicable to boarding-out in Britain that

        . . . the children are taken to Canada
   to be settled in Christian families
   there, the younger are adopted, and the
   elder are settled on farms where they
   eat at the same table and work in the
   same field as the farmer does himself.
   They have the great advantages of
   family life. . . .19

Moreover, accompanying arguments for the depauperization of society through the careful training of its youngest members was one which patently related socio-economic needs to changing patterns of sensibility, thus shaping what may have remained an idiosyncratic interest in childhood into an ideology with definite form. Ideas about training children for a certain kind of citizenship, a particular notion of adulthood, and a definite direction of productivity, labour and social organization, began to emerge more clearly in attitudes towards childhood.

Based on several centuries of precept dating at least from the humanist child rearing manuals and literature which contributed to ideas regarding the making of good citizens, and which came to embrace Rousseauian and Lockean social contract theory, the conclusion by the nineteenth century seemed perfectly obvious - that "the child is father to the man." Boarding-out principles were based no less on this self-evident truth than Victorian family sentiment itself. Mrs. Clara Lucas Balfour, enthusiastic crusader against intemperance and organizer of children's temperance work, was quoted at the 1857 Bands of Hope Conference as positing the following relationship:

> If the child is father to the man,
> childhood is the incipient parentage
> of a nation; as the seedtime is in
> relation to the harvest, so is the
> childhood of the present in relation
> to the manhood of the future.[20]

Drawing upon the plant metaphor of childhood, with all its tendency towards romanticism and cliche that had been in vogue for decades, she argued its tenents that children, being young, dependent and innocent, required "pruning." "They are expanding and active and want training; Like tender plants in the garden they require a sheltering wall and the strengthening prop." Such glowing optimism about the potential of childhood training included not only "the sheltering wall and strengthening prop" of a temperance movement which sought to remove temptation and vice from children's surroundings but also more effective intervention, that is, the removal of children from temptation, vice,

200

dependency, and pauperism, by a complete separation from unsatisfactory surroundings. Boarding-out of dependent children met this need ideally and juvenile emigration proved even more seductive due to the thoroughness of the removal. However, the ideal of such removal could not succeed unless carefully invigilated through scrupulous methods of home inspection and supervision after placement.21

Instituted in 1830, the Children's Friend Society advocated a boarding-out system for the training of pauper children by placing them in country areas, and if obstacles prevented this domestic scheme, then, a well regulated system of colonization for those with "no steady attachments" should be implemented. Indeed the Society had initiated such a scheme between it and the Toronto City Council in 1835. It was strongly recommended that placement whether at home or abroad should be closely supervised. The society rejected the arguments that the training which occurred in existing asylums and workhouses adequately prepared children for future usefulness, and saw these attempts as impracticable, futile and sporadic. It conceded in its first year that "the grand desideratum in the instruction of the children of the working class" was to "temper the development of the mind by the labour of the body," but that this was best effected in natural home settings whether in villages or colonies of cottages. Only through such training into early habits of industry would orphan and street children be prevented from "returning upon society in the unhappy character of Parish paupers."

> From such a system, with a rigid
> attention to their religious and
> moral duties, aided by classifica-
> tion, and a close superintendence
> much might be expected; and a well
> grounded hope encouraged that by
> resorting to early efforts of preven-
> tion, numbers who would otherwise
> invariably fall into a guilty course
> of life, might be trained up, at a
> trifling expense, to become useful
> members of the community.22

The rhapsodizing of the advantages of family life which accompanied the debate was a curious reversal of previous attitudes toward the labouring classes although the cottager had enjoyed several centuries of romanticization. Undoubtedly, the laboring class had been regarded as rude in the extreme, lacking in civilization, and debased beyond imagination, so much so that the founders of children's institutions, whether British or Canadian, believed that their "Homes," with all their defects, were unquestionably superior to that of an average laborer's. The supervision was more thorough, the protection more assured, the segregation was better, and the training more disciplined, in these quasi-family institutional settings, while the resocialization of the inmates was more probable. Yet by mid-nineteenth century, these same attitudes were being represented by an equal enthusiasm for foster care in natural family settings transcending class line. Admittedly, not all biological families - only those with undeniable claims to respectability - were perceived as the ideal setting for dependent childen, and there was some hesitation in returning children ever to these families. For the orphaned or deserted child, however, even the best institution was increasingly viewed as outmoded and unnatural.

SUPPORTERS AND CRITICS

Robert Anderson, a Glasgow advocate of foster care, was not alone in his opinion that the "barracks" systems of child care suppressed "a buoyancy of spirit, a confidence of manner and a happiness of countenance" in its "precise, well disciplined" inmates, and that "the family circle [was] the most natural one for the bringing up and training of children." It appears that either such a transformation had occurred in the actual sensibilities of the labouring classes that the child savers now felt it safe to entrust the young, the orphaned and deserted, into their homes (with meticulous strictures regarding supervision) or the child savers' perceptions of labouring class virtues had radically altered. Perhaps the synthetic filtering down of several streams of popular intellectual thought had contributed to this new perception and changed consciousness - a combination

202

of Rousseauian naturalism, Pestalozzian mother-centredness, and Lockean psychology. Even the persuasiveness of the relative economy of foster care when compared with huge institutions could not have been solely responsible for the reassessment to have occurred in such a short span of time.23

Mary Carpenter, a defender of industrial schools and not particularly an advocate of boarding-out, concurred with Anderson that it was "in the nature of children to be in a home, to feel around them (as the Creator appointed) a family attachment and sympathy" because of their "craving for attention." The scriptural precept that "God Setteth the Solitary in Families" was used to support claims that boarding-out best assured children the "moral, intellectual and physical training" needed to fit them for that "sphere of life which they are likely to occupy."24

Of all the points in favour of boarding out - the severance from pauperism, the removal from the demoralization of institutional life, the prevention of contagion and disease such as opthalmia or scrofula, success at school, and eventual self-support - none was as strongly persuasive as that of the "restoration of family life." T. J. MacNamara, whose approval of child emigration and more particularly of the advantages of cottage systems was well known, nevertheless made the following concession to boarding-out in addition to its obvious inexpensiveness:

> The child is under the continuous
> influence of a fatherly and motherly
> supervisor that approaches good
> parental care as nearly as the circum-
> stances admit, and is brought face to
> face daily with the little cares,
> anxieties, and duties of the artizan
> household such as those which it will
> inevitably be confronted in after life.25

He argued that the insulation of a semi-conventual life within an institution with its concomitant sanitary and economic disadvantages as well as the incessant problem of the "ins and outs" meant that even its quasi-family nature remained totally artificial and that it was always "wholly unlike a home." As Charles Loch of the Charity Organization Society observed, no child ought to be treated "as a denaturalized family-less thing" - merely "a creature" - and that an "institutionalized child without family feeling [was] a monstrosity."26

Among even the most uncritical of the boarding-out advocates, none denied that the key to the success of the method lay in two premises: the careful selection of suitable homes and foster parents and systematic inspection after placement. Both points have been stressed consistently whether in relation to past or present foster care. Not surprisingly, the tenets were easier to urge than to realize. The energetic and sympathetic female inspector of the boarding-out method for the Local Government Board, Miss. M. H. Mason, found that the tenets were routinely neglected. Unlike inspectors such as Doyle or Tufnell, Miss Mason was predisposed toward the method, or at least open to its purported advantages. Neither did she pretend that the matter of motive was easily resolved, given that the majority of foster parents came from that class that needed the extra income merely to maintain their own households. As the children were not permitted to be employed outside the home before the age of indenture, she felt that an honest assertion of income as a motive was sometimes preferable to the treatment children received in the servantless homes of small tradesmen, farmers, or the lower middle class, where their status was often no different than that of a servant's and their treatment worse than if this had been the case.27

Mason's doubts as to the success of the method are apparent in her private reports to the Local Government Board in which she pointed to the anomalies that were discernible. She argued that boarding-out was not a panacea and remedy for pauperism because it was based on two unwarranted assumptions: (a) "that children by merely being boarded out are, as a matter of course 'rescued' from the workhouse and from pauper influences, and introduced to the affection of home and family life; and (b) that there is an unlimited supply of good homes for children."28

Seven years later, she added a telling comment that illustrates the extent of the problem.

> . . . the labouring classes do not trust
> boarding out as a system, and they know
> better than Ladies and Gentlemen how the
> Guardian's allowance is spent by their
> neighbours, and they do not always see
> it expended upon the children. They
> regard boarding out on the whole, as a
> means of maintenance, or addition to the
> income of the foster parents. The
> children are a species of lodgers.

Miss Mason adroitly continued that when she asked
foster mothers if they would want their children
boarded-out if orphaned, she had "never yet heard
anyone answer in the affirmative." Hanna E.
Harrison, who worked with Mason, also doubted the
assumptions behind boarding-out for she was
convinced from her varied experiences during
inspections that most placements "were merely money
making transactions on the part of the foster
parents."29

   Andrew Doyle charged that children were being
"placed out with paupers" for one shilling or one
shilling and sixpence a week and that little regular
inspection was done. Then, as now, the difficulties
that confronted foster care supervision seemed
insurmountable. Without even the present aura of
the social worker "as friend," it is not hard to
imagine the suspicion and hostility such inspectors
were subject to a century ago. In addition, many of
the inspectors, no doubt, postured as moral watchdog
and the bearer of civilization accompanied by
arbitrary decisions and patronizing attitudes. For
instance, Tufnell's view that the country cottages
ranged from "deplorable" and "detestable" to a
"disgrace" was probably not untypical, although it
must be noted that Miss Mason's reports are full of
astute observations about artisan customs and
laboring life which are not altogether
unsympathetic.30

   Sleeping conditions, the number of children per
household, the amount of light work given, diet,
schooling, health, sanitation, and personal
cleanliness, all came under her purview. Mason
showed herself to be unusually perceptive and
flexible on some matters such as bathing which she
observed was generally disregarded after the

children were quite young and was confined to those portions of the body that were visible. She did not venture to postulate what lay "beneath the water mark." An amusing conversation regarding the matter helped her decide that if local custom or lack of facilities required no more than weekly or even fortnightly washing then she would not insist on it being otherwise for the foster children. After Miss Mason regarded a girl's obviously dirty feet she asked when they were to be washed. The reply was as follows:

"Mother says the time's not yet come."
"When will the time come?" I asked.
"In the summer," she said. It was
then the middle of March!31

Although it cannot be inferred that all advocates of boarding-out automatically and unequivocally extended the principle to juvenile emigration, it can be assumed that almost without exception, those who strongly opposed boarding-out also opposed juvenile emigration. Thus there existed an ambiguity in that a fierce supporter of the institutionalization of children, which is now seen as a conservative or even an authoritarian view of child care, nevertheless could be on the more humane and "progressive" side of the question of juvenile emigration even if only by default. Andrew Doyle, whose criticisms of the Canadian movement were much publicized in 1874, proved to be such a person. This poor law inspector's opposition to and exposes of the abuses of the Canadian reception and treatment of the young immigrants were predictable, consistent, and in complete accord with his previous defence of the district school training and suspicion of boarding-out.

On the other side of the dispute, however, was Mrs. Nassau Senior whose provocative report of 1874 criticizing the district school system had caused some dissention among poor law inspectors and guardians. Committed totally to boarding-out for older and non-orphaned children as well as younger ones, she condemned without equivocation the training of girls in workhouse schools and asserted that "no artificial training, however careful, can teach a girl what she learns in family life without any apparent effort at all." She subsequently

206

founded the Metropolitan Association for Befriending Young Servants (MABYS) for the extension of boarding-out principles by placing girls in domestic service in Britain and Canada. MAYBS girls were included in parties under the auspices of the various emigration agencies or in the keeping of philanthropists such as Charlotte Alexander or Annie Macpherson. Mrs. Senior chose to ignore the confusion between binding and boarding-out that she was causing, or the estrangement between her views and those of the Local Government Board generally.32

While enthusiasts like Mrs. Senior were founding private imperial domestic employment bureaus with Canadian middle class matrons eager to receive one of her recommended, trained, and respectable servants, public authorities such as Poor Law Unions were not so willing to give their children over to Canadian households or farms. In the long run, probably no more than ten per cent or so of the juvenile emigrants over a sixty year period came from the Unions, with the remainder coming from private sources. It was the philanthropic child saver who most quickly assimilated the fundamental premises of the boarding-out method by extending it to include juvenile emigration. The Birmingham Emigration Homes, which established a reception centre for its children, the Guthrie Home, in London, Ontario, made the connection explicit by observing that "we would conclude by calling the emigration of pauper and criminal children merely an inexpensive system of boarding-out in Canada; it is a system of boarding out without payment." The cost of an outfit for travel and subsidized ocean fare along with the maintenance of the distributing centre was much cheaper than boarding-out these same children in Britain, even if there were sufficient homes in which to place them, and by far cheaper than keeping them in institutions. Whereas the boarding-out plan practised by the poor law unions involved payments to foster families, the private societies, unable to finance either boarding-out or the inspection necessary, sought to place children in free or workhomes under schemes similar to those of the New York Children's Aid Society which exported many urban children "west" as rural help. If Americans had their western states, Britons had their settlement colonies.33

207

EXTENDING THE BOARDING-OUT PRINCIPLE

Views about child emigration consisted of a complex mixing of various strands of social thought about dependency and depauperization, the restoration of family life for those without it or those whose family life was deemed unsatisfactory, imperial interests in populating the colonies with British stock, Malthusian anxieties, and the training of children into occupational usefulness that would render them self-supporting and good citizens.

The child rescue movement in Great Britain and elsewhere produced effects similar to those of other modern reforms in that the more vigorous and successful its effort, the more it seemed to produce objects fit for reformation. In the case of child rescue, the early legislation intended to eliminate some of the worst features of exploited child labor and to provide for the most destitute and bothersome of children was gradually supplemented by legislation providing schools and then compelling some minimum attendance.34

As various acts defined a normal childhood and brought within the dimensions of the concept more and more children and youth of the working classes, those children who stood outside the <u>norm</u> became increasingly the object of philanthropic and state intervention. As the idea of a stable respectable family became accepted as the norm for the socialization and education of children, the child savers were drawn to schemes that sought to provide for even the most destitute and abandoned children the comforts and strengths of a family life.

With the growing rejection of a psychology that advocated the effectiveness of institutional discipline and training, the new philanthropic movement of the nineteenth century had turned to family sentiment and the careful personal nurture of child life. Sweeping children off the streets and into institutions may have saved their lives or at least improved their physical conditions but in the long run, the philanthropists faced questions as to whether institutional arrangements were satisfactory and what would happen with their charges once they were too old to remain with the societies. The answers to both questions were, of course, interwoven. In many cases, the most successful of the child savers, e.g., Barnardo and Quarrier, found that although it was impossible to deinstitutionalize, it was possible to humanize their institutions. For public bodies, such as the Guardians of the Poor Law Unions, there were the regulations that permitted boarding-out of children. Unlike the Guardians, the philanthropic societies did not have the advantage of the rates and were compelled to use new means of providing for their retrained and resocialized inmates.

A continuing problem that compounded the child rescue movement was the future of most children in industrial Great Britain. Barnardo, along with other child savers, bemoaned the fate of promising boys and girls who were turned into the unemployed or into casual labor upon leaving their institutions or home placements. Prior to the establishment of the various parts of the welfare state, both private and public authorities sought for new positions for children and youths so dearly reclaimed. Thus, the demands of child rescue sentiment and the weaknesses of institutional intervention without the support of the welfare state forced the philanthropists to seek elsewhere for solutions to their problems.

The possibility of placing children in societies that could use their strength and skills while at the same time separating them from their unsavory backgrounds, made the idea of emigration to the colonies appealing. Concerns about inadequate or immoral family and friends, lack of satisfactory employment, and convictions about the virtues of rural family life in a new society, came to outweigh the dangers due to separation and lack of supervision that the philanthropists recognized as part of juvenile emigration.

In the 1830s, several false starts to later boarding-out and juvenile emigration schemes occurred. These pioneering efforts, however, de-emphasized psychological training through family life experiences in favour of occupational training through apprenticeship by arguing, not for delaying of responsibilities, but for economic opportunities in an environment not subjected to the same competitive edge as Britain. The Irish Protestant

209

Orphan Society and the Benevolent Society for the Establishment of Poor Colonies in 1828 were joined by the British Children's Friend Society Report of 1830 in referring to systems of fostering in France, Germany and Switzerland, or to the "agricultural workhouses" and colonization of orphan children in Holland. These societies, believed emphatically, along with the Society for the Permanent Support of Orphan and Destitute Children By Means of Apprenticeship in the Colonies, that "any lot would be better than that which [pauper children] appear to inherit" and that "any change of circumstance would ameliorate their condition." This view, which might be called the "fair chance thesis," was as pervasive to boarding-out arguments as to those which encouraged juvenile emigration. Indeed, the whole ideology of childhood as child rescue reflects a fundamental commitment to the idea of a "fair chance" being the right of society's young members.35

Each of the early societies operated on "the principle of indenture," which in the case of British children became transformed into the principle of fostering, but for those sent to the colonies, it would remain economically based. While the Permanent Support Society received children and funds from individuals, child rescue societies, parishes, foundling hospitals and orphan asylums (a precedent that continued in later emigration schemes), the Orphan's Friend Society chose promising and healthy children (as did the later Barnardo, Quarrier, and Thomas Bowman Stephenson schemes) from its own Asylums - the Brenton Juvenile Asylum in Hackney Wick or the Royal Victorian Asylum, Chiswick.

By the 1880s, fostering flourished in many Scottish parishes and in Edinburgh under its poor law. With Louisa Twining and Florence Hill leading the campaign, boarding-out was adopted in parts of England such as Warminster, Wiltshire and Ringwood during the following decade.36

Two years after the 1868 poor law order was passed authorizing the method, twenty-one poor law unions were reported using it. Child immigration did not continue quite at the same steady pace after 1837 due to a scandal precipitated by the reputed harsh treatment received in Cape Town by the young emigrants of the Orphans' Friend Society. The Society, founded for the "suppression of juvenile vagrancy" indentured children to colonists in New Brunswick as well as the African colony, appointed a committee of guardians to supervise their indentures. The children were said to be used as field hands, replacing the labour previously exacted from free coloreds or emancipated slaves. The reputation that they came from the pauper or criminal classes led to a calloused indifference, as would be the case when juvenile immigration schemes surfaced again in the 1870s. Although such initial experiments proved largely ineffectual, some children were indentured in New Brunswick which continued to receive a trickle of destitute and orphan children so that in 1874, the Reverend George Rodgers, formerly of Bristol, was able to report "quite a little colony of boys" at Shelburne in addition to those residing in the United States.37

Interest in this form of extending the boarding-out method was revived with the 1870 regulations of the Local Government Board that included the possibility of emigrating orphan and deserted children if their consent had been obtained before a justice of the peace. Between the initial efforts of the 1830s and the later schemes of the 1870s, the Seventh Earl of Shaftesbury continued his involvement in the emigration of children from his ragged schools, often using the evidence of destitution, unemployment and vagrancy, so grimly presented before parliament in the 1840 Royal Commission of Inquiry into Children's Employment, to support his claims. In 1848, he received a parliamentary grant of fifteen hundred pounds to send children to the colonies that year. He tartly answered colonial protests that pauper and criminal populations were being "dumped" on them by claiming that he did not "pour out the filth of our streets" but that the children who came from his Homes and ragged schools were carefully trained, thus "passing through a learning and filtering process before we put them forth in a rich and fertilizing stream on the colonies of our country." This claim regarding initial training and careful selection remained constant in all cases of emigration societies. For example, the Barnardo Report of 1885 insisted that all its emigrants were young and "in the most

plastic period of their lives, . . .therefore
conform easily and naturally to radically changed
conditions of existence." They were, moreover,

> . . . picked emigrants, the very flower
> of our flock, physically, morally and
> intellectually. They were also carefully
> trained emigrants, trained to the use of
> their fingers as well as their brains.38

On all counts, the early experiments with
juvenile emigration between 1830 and 1840
demonstrated the weak links which were to remain
consistent throughout future domestic boarding-out
or its extension to the colonies of Australia and
British North America. The weak links consisted of
inadequate pre-placement especially with regard to
the motives of the foster families and of inadequate
inspection after placement. These weak links were
as obvious in the boarding-out practices which were
simultaneously occurring in Britain itself as they
were endemic to the placing-out of children from
Canadian institutions. They remain today the weak
links to the fostering method.

Nevertheless, a crucial, although subtle point
to grasp, is contained in the rhetoric expressed by
the earlier juvenile emigration experiments when
compared with the later schemes. The rhetoric of
the late nineteenth century differed markedly from
earlier efforts represented by the Orphans' Friend
Society or the Permanent Support Society. The new
rhetoric was also unlike the purely pragmatic
policies of the Canadian children's institutions
that spoke so confidently and unconsciously of their
children being socialized into labor at the age of
indenture and prepared for it during their confinement in the Home. The later schemes adopted the
ideals of boarding out sentiment and curiously
combined them with the economics of binding out
practices. The "fair chance thesis" thus became a
hybrid of both views - not only were children to be
rescued by providing them with economic opportunities or by separating them from a tainting environment - but they were to be more satisfactorily
rescued through the assimilation and emulation of
family virtues.

Once again, the reality and the rhetoric of child emigration were not so easily reconciled. Child saving agencies, institutions, avaricious and unscrupulous philanthropic individuals, and various Poor Law workhouses, industrial schools and "great" district schools, attempted to solve insurmountable problems of poverty not by eradicating its cause but by exporting the symptoms in its dependent childen. The managers of institutions frankly saw emigration as the means to relieving the population pressures within their Homes. The categories of "Home Children" that made up the juvenile emigration parties sent from the British institutions included (1) the destitute or neglected child placed by child savers in institutions - those street arabs who were orphaned, homeless, or independent of parental or other adult control and who pursued a variety of occupations, or who were the offspring of negligent parents; (2) orphans - those deprived of parental and familial care at various stages of their pre-Canadian experience; (3) part-orphans - those whose socio-economic expectations had been radically diminished through the death of either parent, and (4) non-orphans - those who were separated from family, guardians, or relatives for a variety of reasons.

Confirming the impressions gained through a perusal of traditional historical materials, Joy Parr's computer-analyzed data base has verified that a generous proportion of British apprentices from the Barnardo Homes at least were not orphans bereft of natural family life but were part orphans, abandoned children, and children from otherwise viable family groups constrained by misfortune or poverty to surrender one or more of their members.[39]

Thus, the juvenile emigration movement provided, in an extreme manner, a custodial function for some sectors of the laboring poor and indigent of Britain and cannot be absolutely and always dismissed as just another form of "philanthropic abduction" practised by child savers; for if many children were "snatched" from their working class familial roots by middle class child savers, some were also deprived of family life by the decisions of relatives or parents. The extension of this view is discussed by Parr who concludes that parents handled their family relationships in ways that minimized for themselves the worse effects of economic dislocation by using their children as home workers, placing them in dead-end but relatively well paid jobs at the earliest possible age, and giving up weak or "useless" children to rescue and emigration societies.40

Some parents reasserted their parental claims at the age when a child was able to earn a living, most often between twelve and fourteen years. Blood relatives who were perceived as determined to drag their offspring "down to their level" were viewed askance by British child savers as "a curse to their children." Miss Florence Penrose Phelp, a poor law guardian, said before the Northern District conference in July, 1903, that

. . . during the years when they are
dependent their relatives lie low but
when they are old enough to begin to
earn, family affection asserts itself,
with amazing vigour, and parents and
relatives appear to claim then with a
virtuous though belated assumption of
responsibility.41

The Charity Organization Review, April 1887, pithily observed that it had been repeatedly startled by the revival, which was as "pernicious as it was phenomenal," of "the long dormant affection - paternal, maternal ataval, and avuncular. . . ." The placing of useless children or children who had become an economic and psychological burden, for whatever reason, either permanently or temporarily, has been demonstrated as common a practice in British North America as it was in Britain. As in Britain, Canadian institutions found themselves pragmatically used by those members of the poor who were often not willing to have their children bound out when they reached an age of being able to contribute to the family maintenance.42

All those who conducted child emigration schemes, from Barnardo to the more modest successes of Maria Rye, Charlotte Alexander, Annie Macpherson, and Ellen Bilbrough, believed in the "fair chance thesis," and one cannot dispute their sincerity while doubting the wisdom of the decision to emigrate children and youth for placement on farms or in households. The literature of the early twentieth century ranging from The Imperial Colonist (1902-11) to James E. Sedgewick, Lads for Empire (1914) applauded such schemes. The Charity Organization Review in 1910 reviewed G. Bogue Smart's "Report on Juvenile Immigration" with glowing praise. Smart, inspector of immigrant children for the Dominion Government, was a long time advocate of the movement. The thesis received further support from the vast literature from 1900 to 1930 regarding the problems of "boy work." The persistent difficulty of providing regular adult employment for older youths as they outgrew jobs taken up as school age leavers was given an empirical base by British Government reports such as the "First Report of Boy Labour in the Post Office" (1911) and the "Report of the Departmental Committee in the Homes and Conditions of Employment of Van Boys and Warehouse Boys" (1913).43

It was even more difficult for ex-charity children to be given employment. The Birkdale Farm School complained that it emigrated its graduands through the Liverpool Emigration Society because of this problem. Imperialist interest in maintaining British populations and sympathies throughout the Empire joined with publicity concerning the surplus of worthy young people to enhance the desirability of juvenile emigration. It was believed by many colonists as well as Britons that "for good or ill England [was] a bigger place than this little island."44

The separation of family members was ultimately justified by a view of imperial philanthropy that saw the "utilization of street arabs," and "infant emigration," as giving the children a new start in life - a fair chance. The exchange was supposedly "twice blessed" - it blessed the nation that gave and the nation that received. Mr. Arthur Chilton Thomas, a Liverpool barrister, who, with Canon St. John of Southwark Diocese, founded the Catholic Canadian Emigration Society in 1902, was firm in this conviction and inclined to somewhat fatuous prose about it.

> We are merely transferring them from part
> of the Empire to another - from our own
> England where they have no prospects, to

our own Canada, where their prospects are as bright as the flame that glows on the maple leaf in the fall.

For those who still remained reluctant to send parties of young children across the Atlantic, there was the terse persuasiveness of advocates of assisted emigration such as Joseph Forster, Stay and Starve; or, Go and Thrive (1884), who asked whether suffering chilblains in Canada's climate was preferable to facing starvation at home!45

Although the separation itself was executed with righteous zeal, nevertheless, it was readily conceded that it was not always a smooth operation. Not surprisingly, it was found, for example, that children often clung tenaciously to their past attachments even if the object of their devotion and loyalty appeared to be quite unworthy. A poor law guardian, Mr. Murray of Tynemouth, observed that in his experience, he had found that "children could not forget their parents however bad they were." In 1874, the Middlemore Homes of Birmingham duly noted that, "It is no small thing to make a girl, even if she is but five years old, forget the mother who bore her and the work that can do this is certainly a thorough one." As a majority of juvenile emigrants were not orphaned or abandoned but surrendered, this point helps explain the loyalty to their families that many children exhibited and that baffled the officials of the Homes.46

Although emigration, it seems, was as "thorough" a work as was deemed possible, even it could not be thorough enough as can be seen in the case of Millie Fairbanks, who had been advertised for adoption in the Weekly Globe, Ontario, in August, 1889. She proved "troublesome" and badly wanted to return to her father in England who could only support himself and his two sons, and whose wife was an alcoholic in a workhouse; or of Ann Scanlon, who, desperate to return to her father who had rid himself of her, proved such "a bad case" because of her discontentment that she was returned to England after having been placed six times.47

If modern psychological research on deprivation is correct, it is a grim irony that those very children who had been abandoned by or taken from a semblance of orderly family life would probably have made what is usually seen as the "best" immigrants, that is, the most assimilable, because they would be able and anxious to form new bond attachments and identify with their new homes and employers if that new home provided an amiable environment and responsive relationships. The cases of rejection in Canada were, therefore, all the more tragic. The 1894-95 annual report of the National Children's Home perceptively but mistakenly observed that the children would be generously welcomed into the colonies because they were "well trained and tested, who after a time will become thoroughly Canadianized, and will cease as grown up emigrants cannot, to be an alien element in the population. Grafted on the new stock, they will be part of the national life."48

A compounded sense of abandonment and loss must have occurred in the case of children separated from their own families but who were amenable to new attachments. To be ultimately rejected by a cold and unsupportive environment, or worse, a contemptuous and exploitive one, must have been particularly traumatic. Moreover, even for those children who were fortuitiously placed in happier circumstances, the general prejudice that prevailed against the "home children," an epithet that had perjorative connotations, was scarcely conducive to feelings of security. This seems equally as probable for the boarded-out child in Britain who also bore the burden of ostracism, prejudice, and the "pauper stamp," to remind him of his antecedents.

Mary Ann Flowerday, taken from "low dancing saloons" in London by Charlotte Alexander was described as a "very poor thing - small and white, a very good, gentle girl, grateful, affectionate and trustworthy." She was overworked for six dollars a month as undernurse in Toronto and there was nothing to indicate that either her trust or affection were returned in kind. The remarks from numerous employers reveal an alarming incapacity to empathize with the problems of immigrant children. One Toronto mistress in 1875 explained why she had kept her young help in her room for several days by remarking that "Polly" had " some little perculations" that required correction. She further observed that

> People as a rule exhibit such a foolish, and not only foolish, but positively injurious sympathy with these children, when they are corrected for doing anything wrong, giving it as an argument that they are waifs and orphans; poor children, is that the reason why they should be allowed to grow up without restraint of any kind? I should very much have liked the receipt for bringing up my own children without punishment and reward, and very much have liked a child that did not require it - let alone Polly.49

Throughout the period some madcap schemes, including Captain Palliser's plan to systematically train some 50,000 poor law boys in a simulated Canadian rural existence on a "few acres set aside in East London," were suggested. Impracticable to the point of eccentricity, Palliser's plan was understandably ignored. Another scheme for the "Education of Pauper Children and for the Reduction of the Rates" drew more attention in 1903. Mrs. Ellinor Close, a gentlewoman of means, proposed that 7,000 two-to-three year olds be trained in Canada at Dominion expense, and after having enjoyed the bracing robust life of the Province of New Brunswick, be returned to England when employable. While the Paddington and Fulham Guardians treated the idea with despatch and the Home Office saw it as thoroughly absurd, The Times heartily praised the scheme because the children were to be the ailing and feeble-minded; therefore, England would not be "bled" of her best stock. Mrs. Close's Children's Farm Association did implement the plan for several years by receiving private cases such as little Arthur Osborn, "the boy the Duke of Bedford [was] paying for" and Sophie Green, "who used to support her disreputable mother by lighting fires for the Jews in the East End at a farthing each."50

Many emigration homes operated on more practical premises by training their children on their own farms, although it is doubtful that such training was anything but minimal. J. W. C. Fegan, a zealous and overpowering evangelical, had eighty-four acres - South View Farm - set aside at Goudhurst, forty-three miles out of London. He claimed that the farm was "a little bit of Canada in England" because he used lectures and lantern slides demonstrating Canadian methods of ploughing, harrowing and milking, and his boys used implements donated by Massey-Harris Company of Toronto. His "hiving off" parties of boys were distributed out of a home donated to him by a Toronto gentleman, Mr. William Gooderham.51

In conclusion, boarding-out was not popularized in British North America until the creation in 1891 of the first Children's Aid Society (CAS) in Toronto. The CAS model operated, theoretically at least, on boarding-out principles, which, however, were undermined because of the CAS practice (like the emigration societies) of sending children to "free" or "work" homes rather than paid homes. The full impact of the British debate was felt in its extension of the method to include the emigration of children, which represented the ultimate removal of children from the moral contaminations and economic strictures of the old world into what was described as a new world of economic opportunity and "the home of happy childhood."52

In part, juvenile emigration was a logical, if alarming, extension of the growing interest in the de-institutionalization of dependent children through foster care. To be irrevocably and indubitably "rescued," morally endangered or economically disadvantaged children must be completely separated from penurious circumstances and pernicious past associations. The first report of the Birmingham Children's Gutter Homes in 1873 insisted that children were not taken to Canada "because they [were] poor"

> . . . but to save them from their bad companions, to whom, were they to remain . . . they would always be tempted to return. Emigration is the only mode of permanently separating these children from their old associations.53

The separation represented by thousands of miles and a vast ocean between Britain and her colonies was, to say the least, as striking, imaginative, and "thorough" a removal as could be conceived and practicably realized. Even then, the Liverpool Catholic Reformatory Association, disturbed by boys returning from Canada, bemoaned the fact that Canada was still not far enough and that "places more inaccessible" would be greater advantage to emigrant children by absolutely preventing their return.54

7

British Children for Rural and Domestic Service: The Canadian Response

> . . . they are not wanted here, don't
> like to boldly tell you they are not
> wanted here but such is the facts;
> they have lots of poor children here
> of their own. Town charges they
> would gladly farm out to anyone
> that would take them to bring up . . .
>
> John Walters to Colonial Office, 1875

Farewelled midst an excess of philanthropoic cant that promised them a "fair chance" in the new world, the young British immigrants frequently found themselves confronting a hostile climate of opinion whether expressed privately by an Ontarian citizen or publicly in the court rooms of Manitoba in 1893 and Ontario in 1896. Although some were adopted by the families that received them, the great majority were placed as laborers and domestic servants in farm homes. After an initially favourable reception, the movement was increasingly viewed as a threat to the social and moral purity of the nation. Even those Canadians who benefitted from their labor professed to see dangerous traits in their farm hands and domestics.

Criticism of the movement, its agents, and the immigrants themselves, united a disparate collection of trade unions, women's organizations, sheriffs and country doctors, and exponents of Canadian child-saving in condemnation of the importation of British children and juveniles as unwise policy and a dire threat to Canadian life. Playing on themes of social and moral degeneracy, unfair labor competition, urban drift, and economic drag, the groups worked to restrict, if not eliminate, the immigration.

223

From the beginning, all organized efforts at juvenile emigration combined an interest in the amelioration of pressing British social problems of destitution, vagrancy, and criminality, with an argument for benefits accruing to the children and the receiving colonies; however, these "fair chance" arguments were less persuasive than those that identified the movement as merely another part of Imperial "dumping ground" policies.1

As the children had begun their lives in the Old World as part of the destitute, abandoned, or orphaned classes, it is not difficult to assume that they had all suffered to some extent from humiliation and indifference before sailing and trans-Atlantic trauma and culture shock during their introduction and initiation into Canadian society. Although the data still remain scanty, it seems reasonable to extrapolate that on an individual basis, approximately one-third were well received and humanely treated, some even with love and acceptance into their respective adoptive homes; another third found their new lives tolerable enough despite difficulties; while the remainder were exploited, defrauded, ostracized or mistreated.

As a group, however, the children were subjected to a Canadian response that requires closer scrutiny than so far received for it was apparently oppressive enough to drive them into historical "hiding" - ashamed of their backgrounds as charity children or as abandoned family members - until the 1970s. Only interest in finding one's roots and the good press given minorities and the disadvantaged in the 1960s have allowed these forgotten immigrants to surface in Canadian history and the popular imagination. Nowhere in the annals of British emigration history is there a more calloused expulsion of children, and nowhere in Canadian history is there a more shameful response to and treatment of the young and vulnerable. Neither country can be seen as blameless in the exchange.2

"THE HOME OF HAPPY CHILDHOOD"

It is not the intention of this chapter to either substantiate or reject the Dumping Ground or

Fair Chance theses, which are not always incompatible, but to approach the problem of juvenile emigration by examining the Canadian response to it. To take the view that Britain merely "shovelled out" its juvenile paupers to relieve its alarming industrial problems and that the emigrant children were indiscriminately snatched from their working class roots by evangelical philanthropists, or that once in Canada these same children inspired working class interests to righteous indignation against their exploitation and that progressive Canadian social elements expressed their more sensitive attitudes toward childhood in a humanitarian crusade against the movement is to simplify a complex historical subject. One aspect that needs analysis is the fact that individual cases of exploitation were often used to justify a virulent attack not on the brutalizers but on the victims. Ironically, too, raising the age limits for emigration to coincide with Canadian school leaving requirements meant that by the 1920s, the young people increasingly were being brought over as cheap labor.

The movement had been uncommented on for the first half dozen years until British concerns about Poor Law children emigrated to Canada resulted in the visit of Andrew Doyle, Her Majesty's Poor Law Inspector for the Local Government Board, in 1874. His report on Poor Law emigrant children, which expressed grave concern regarding the more strenuous living conditions in Canada and the "loneliness, homesickness, recollections and attachments" of children isolated from kinfolk and homeland, precipitated both a spirited defence of the movement by its advocates, and individious comparisons of social conditions in the Dominion and Great Britain by Canadians. The controversy over Doyle's Report was only the first in a series of skirmishes in the next half century between advocates and critics of child emigration.3

In rejecting Doyle's recommendations for improved reception, training, and supervision, Canadians and their government officials argued that the physical and moral situation of the children in Canada had to be better than their lot in Britain. It is also likely that they knew that Canadian institutions regularly placed out Canadian children in similar circumstances.

In 1875, the Local Government Board (LGB) decided to end the emigration of pauper children under the auspices of the philanthropic societies while the Canadian government undertook to examine the conditions of every child immigrant in the country. When the report on 2,301 pauper and arab children finally reached the LGB in July 1878, it still failed to satisfy British authorities. Consequently, the LGB refused an offer of the Department of Agriculture to inspect each child once during its first year of Canadian residence. Only after a great deal of lobbying was the LGB finally persuaded in 1883 to accept the assurance of the Canadian government that annual inspections would be carried out by government immigration agents. In spite of persistent complaints by the LGB, Canadian reports were generally prompt enough to forestall any further prolonged suspension of the pauper child emigration.4

After the Doyle controversy, the movement remained relatively unnoticed in Canada until more ambitious schemes again publicized it. Dr. Thomas Barnardo, whose first party entered Canada in 1883 and who, in addition to several distributing homes, established a training farm at Russell, Manitoba, soon became the most successful and notorious of the juvenile emigration promoters. The notoriety of his schemes were equalled only by those of the Salvation Army and to a lesser extent those of the Anglican equivalent, the Church Army.5

Beginning in the 1880s, the enlarged juvenile immigration movement was challenged by Canadians who opposed the importation of children and youths not on grounds of real or potential hardship and exploitation, but because it represented an undesirable addition to the nation's population. Among the Ontario critics in the 1880s and 1890s were country doctors who were members of the Dominion Parliament and county sheriffs and gaolers. Emphasizing the notion of "hereditary taint," these spokesmen of rural and town life identified juvenile immigrants as transmitters of the worst characteristics of Old World life, i.e., urban degeneracy, immorality, criminality, and syphilitic tendencies. In federal and provincial parliaments and in representations to committees and commissions, they helped popularize beliefs regarding the undesirable nature of the child immigrants.6

Trade unions such as the Dominion Trades and Labour Congress (TLC) organized in 1883 consistently opposed the movement on the grounds that any immigration that contributed to urban drift was unacceptable. TLC leaders such as Daniel J. O'Donaghue specifically objected to juvenile immigration because such children, many of whom "sported a fair growth of whiskers," not only competed with agricultural labor and Canadian dependent children for rural employment but also showed a decided preference for city life once their apprenticeships were served.7

Charges of urban drift and replacing of mature adult farm hands by child immigrants were consistent with the TLC's obsession with unemployment in Canada; however, when the TLC suggested that the wards of Canadian asylums could have filled those places, the recommendation is odd. First, if TLC's opposition were based in part on "empathy" or concern for "the rural apprentices' working conditions," it seems strange that Canadian children should suffer the same deplorable working conditions as the apprentices. Secondly, the supervision of children placed by Canadian institutions was no better, if not worse, than that provided by the Emigration Societies. Finally, Canadian children could not have been more acceptable competitors for jobs usually filled by adult farm labor if the objection had been on grounds of child labor undercutting adult wages.8

Moreover, statements by O'Donaghue and his TLC associates on every aspect of the movement were consistently exaggerated. Their comments on the publicity surrounding the death of the fifteen year old "Home Boy" George Green in 1895 is a good example of the tone of organized labour's "empathy" for the plight of juvenile immigrants. Placed on a farm near Owen Sound, Ontario, by Barnardo's, Green had died under suspicious circumstances. His employer, Miss E. R. Findley, was later charged with manslaughter in connection with his death. The subsequent trial included a post-mortem report that Green's "body was very much emaciated and covered with wounds and bruises" and the testimony of witnesses regarding beatings, lack of proper clothing, and care. In a prolonged exchange with the Department of the Interior, O'Donaghue first denounced Barnardo's activities, but then, with the failure of the jury to convict Miss Findley for manslaughter, mixed solicitude for the welfare of rural apprentices with a description of the boy that pictured him as "humpbacked and crosseyed; his mouth was crooked and he was short-sighted and weak of intellect." Poor George Green may have been all these things but they hardly made him a prime candidate for maltreatment and death.9

Grand jury presentments at the Brandon, Manitoba, and Hamilton, Ontario, assizes, in November 1893 and September 1896 respectively, also reflected much of the profound hostility experienced by juvenile immigrants.

At Brandon, the grand jury, after commenting "upon the apparent increase of crime," observed that

> We may be permitted to add that in our
> opinion some action should be taken by
> the authorities having in charge the
> immigration of foreign population to
> this country towards preventing the
> further importation of boys from the
> slums of the large cities of the Old
> World. We need not state that they are
> referred more particularly to the class
> of youths which have been brought to the
> 'Barnardo Home' from the Old Country.

The subsequent publicity given the allegation resulted in a full-scale Dominion investigation not only of the Russell Farm operation by the Barnardo's and of the incidence of criminality in Manitoba and the Northwest Territories, but also of the distributing homes and operations of all the Emigration Societies.10

The National Council of Women organized in 1893 found the issue on the proposed agenda for its May 1896 national conference when the London Local Council resolved:

> That in view of the establishment of
> Children's Aid Societies in Canada the
> Women of the NCW be asked to investigate
> the effects on the social conditions of
> Canada by the importation of pauper
> children. There are now several old
> country agencies shipping children to
> Canada and it is believed that in many
> cases they are productive of much evil in
> the communities where they are placed.

In preparation for the meeting, Lady Aberdeen, NCW
president, requested information from the Department
of the Interior that might refute the charges
against the children and the emigration societies.
A substantial part of the information supplied by
Deputy Minister A. M. Burgess to Lady Aberdeen came
from the reports of Dominion inspections conducted
during the Russell Farm investigation.11

At the 1896 meeting, the London Local Council
proposed that if other Local Councils elicited
similar facts "that the National Council of Women in
Canada in Council in Halifax in June next will call
for a resolution calling for the suppression of this
system of immigration." The views of the London
Local Council, while representative of the
antijuvenile immigration sentiment of Western
Ontario, hardly agreed with those of the NCW
president. Lady Aberdeen objected to the suggestion
that the government should insist that only
"mentally, morally and physically desirable
children" be admitted, since she and the Governor
General had visited the docks at Quebec and found
the children to be so. The controversy at the 1896
NCW meeting was, of course, not the end of the
debate over the desirability of juvenile immigration, and along with resolutions on feeblemindedness
and venereal diseases, the topic sporadically found
its way on agendas during the next two decades.12

With the expansion of juvenile emigration in
the 1880s, Canadian perceptions of the emigration
societies and their wards were established. Three
dominant arguments ran through the controversies of
the next half century. The most persistent charge,
vulgar or sophisticated, was that the children were
the products of a physically, morally, and social
degenerate population (i.e., "the biologically

inferior strata of British life"), and thus posed a threat to the well-being of Canadian society. The second was that regardless of their moral and social deficiencies, the children were inappropriate settlers because they would not remain on the land and were potential competitors for scarce desirable urban jobs. The third charge was that emigration worked a two-fold hardship on the children by separating them from families, friends, and homeland, and by failing through imperfect supervision to insure their proper care, education, and happiness in the colonies.13

In Ontario, the passage of the Children's Protection Act in 1893 provided a focus for actions regarding juvenile immigration through the work of J. J. Kelso, the Ontario Superintendent, who organized the First Conference on Child Saving in 1895, which brought together the friends and foes of the movement. By combining a provincial Department of Neglected and Dependent Children with a system of semi-voluntary children's aid societies, the Ontario Act created a paper system for the supervision of Canadian children and laid the basis for the 1897 Immigrant Children Act. Superintendent Kelso, who also functioned as the Inspector of Juvenile Immigration Agencies, saw the 1897 Act as espousing "three great principles: First, that only respectable children of sound physical condition be brought to Ontario; second, that each agency should have a thorough system of supervision during the minority of their wards; and third, that the work should be conducted under government inspection." The Ontario legislation was quickly copied by Quebec, Manitoba and Nova Scotia, which, however, also lacked the necessary child protection agencies to provide even minimal supervision of their Canadian neglected and dependent children.14

The 1897 Act insisted that the supervision of children include a medical and general examination in Britain and again at the point of debarkation in Canada, as well as the extension of the government inspections in practice since 1875 from an annual to a quarterly basis with adequate record-keeping. Most of the agitation during this time concentrated on selection processes rather than aftercare superintendence. Selection continued to be a point of controversy for the next thirty years. Most emphasis was placed on medical inspection of the children than any other kind. In addition to the inspection implemented by the emigration societies themselves for their own private wards, the Canadian government gradually began to strengthen its service. By the turn of the century, a Dominion inspector, G. Bogue Smart, who was to champion the children's cause and defend the movement for several decades, was appointed. By 1903, the distributing and receiving homes of the philanthropic emigrating societies were also included under his inspectorate. It was not until 1920, however, that all immigrant children, both pauper and private, were inspected by an expanded juvenile immigration branch of the Dominion government. At no time during the movement can it be argued that inspection at either the pre- or post-placement levels was ever thorough enough or even adequate. Subsequently abuses crept in or were permitted to flagrantly exist.15

As noted in the previous chapter, child savers had understood quite early that the inspection of foster families at two crucial stages - that of pre-placement and post-placement - was essential to the ultimate success of any boarding-out program, and it was always at these points that failure occurred both in boarding-out and in juvenile emigration. This was especially the case when foster families preferred older to younger children. In fact, the boarding-out of young children was always recognized as preferable by those who argued for either boarding-out or emigration because of the risks of exploitation involved in placing older children. If the principles of boarding-out of immigrant children were abused in British North America, the blame must be shared equally between British callousness and Canadian crassness. That Canadian householders blatantly sought older children, and that British emigration agencies eagerly provided them, maximized the potential for abuse of the system. When Canadian legislation prohibited very young children, the likelihood of adoption and real fostering lessened in proportion to the numbers of older children entering Canada. These were then identified as workers - urban children for domestic or rural service - and ironically, their exploitation was assured by the very means whose purpose was to provide protection for juvenile immigrants.16

231

As long as the actualization of the boarding-out ideal depended solely on the goodwill of minimally supervised individuals and not on state legislation, the confusion between binding-out economics and boarding-out ideals was compounded in both the Canadian and British domestic placements and the juvenile immigration movement. Neither should it be forgotten that even when boarding-out was adapted as a state responsibility and family intervention labelled "foster care," the weak links of inspection and, to some degree, motive have remained as demonstrated by both Ontario and Alberta in their continuing struggle with the dilemmas of fostering dependent children.17

There is scant evidence that employers sought to adopt, foster, or indenture siblings even in those cases where there had been a conscious effort to keep them together. For those children, the wrenching separation from a sibling meant that they would rarely, if ever, see the other again for contact was almost invariably lost. Thus, the original separation from parents and homeland or from the Home in England was callously and indifferently reinforced.

The four year old twins, Winnie and Jimmie Ferguson, were fortunate children who won the hearts of their adoptive parents with their endearing little ways, but it is pertinent to observe that in this case they had come from what was seen as unassailably respectable parentage. On the other hand, Harry Dowson and his twin were separated, as were the Butts children who were brought to Canada by Charlotte Alexander in the 1880s. The four Butts children were advertised by relatives after the break-up of the family due to the death of their mother and the father ruining his prospects by gambling debts. They were separated variously in England and Canada. Edith, who was described as "rough and free with the boys" and "forward," was returned to England after failing in several situations. Sister May was adopted, renamed Lily, and remained in Canada. Lily, however, was to become the centre of an avaricious tug-o-war when she inherited a little money from her coal-merchant grandfather who had, it might be added, orginally arranged emigration. Her neer-do-well father decided at that point that he wished her to return to the paternal roof after all. One must ponder on the emotional havoc such events caused.18

Moreover, in addition to isolation and psychological alienation, the immigrant child had to contend with an ugly and frequently articulated prejudice. Thus, in 1875 the Andrew Doyle report on child immigration quoted the complaints of "S.M.," a brooding and resentful girl.

> As long as they bring our poor children
> to be pounded half to death and slave to
> the utmost . . . I was not going to be
> told that I was glad to come to Canada
> for I was half-starved, and was picked
> off the streets in London and my parents
> were drunkards. Dear Sir, nobody knows
> what a girl has to put up with that comes
> from the Old Country, for they know we
> have no parents to take our part and they
> do as they like.19

Charlotte Alexander, a philanthropic gentle woman, who brought girls to Canada last century, admitted that even adoption was frequently a "cloak for service without wages." Some forty years later, Mrs. Eleanor Stuart of Simmonds, Ontario, a critic of the movement, protested that the older age limits that had been introduced in keeping with school leaving laws were still not old enough.

> Even in the most satisfactory cases they
> were lonely, hardworked under different
> and very severe climatic conditions and
> sometimes in barren and unlovely surround-
> ings with scant pay and consideration . . . .
> They have at the best a vague conception
> of being exploited and indignation
> without force, misery without vent, the
> butt of mockery and abusing from employers
> often without pity or conscience.

"Misery without vent," and "indignation without force" - these are two graphic descriptions of frustration, oppression, and impotency that were felt by many of the immigrant children.20

Phyllis Harrison's moving biographical essays record some of their memories as adults and it is noteworthy that some of her interviewees still felt the pain keenly enough to withhold their identities or to refrain from sharing their pasts in any but a superficial manner with their own children. One child, brought over at nine years between 1911-12, observed that Canada has been promised as "one big apple tree" where all one's worries would cease for life, but wryly concluded that "it wasn't my fault that I picked a wrong apple. . . . I damn near died of loneliness. I was sure I would die, but little boys don't die easily." Another bitterly said, "The whole family ridiculed my accent and jeered at my clothes" and another observed that what hurt most was "the fact that the people would not believe me or trust me." William Wood who came to Canada at eight years of age, having been born in a Union Workhouse in 1897, was exploited, beaten and, as his wife sadly remarked, had been "owned by a beast."21

Many were like Joseph Welsh who after three years in Canada was described in 1927 as "disrespectful" and "hotheaded" because he refused a situation chosen for him at the age of sixteen. His combative nature apparently got him into difficulties with a new employer who handled him roughly. Joseph was obviously a plucky and resilient lad but not all children were so. Enuretic children normally had less of his ability to express his rage.22

Another boy could not escape after four years of service although he had turned eighteen. His employer said he was reluctant to have him "freed" because he had the mind of "a mere child," although he admitted that the boy himself was "hankering for a move." One cannot tell anything about the lad's mental abilities in this self serving remark, but one can certainly speculate about his psychological state. Some children's medical bills and deportation costs were squabbled over by the Immigration Department, the Emigration Society, or the Board of Guardians in England with each disclaiming final responsibility as with the cases of the tubercular Margaret Gaskin and another deportee, Dora Rooker. Nobody wanted these girls.23

In the 1878 minutes of the Liverpool Sheltering Home, there is a record of a letter received from Sarah McNaughton, placed in Nova Scotia, answering the Home's suggestion that she send a portion of her wages for her mother's relief. The letter to her mother declined the suggestion by pointing out that being "adopted," Sarah did not receive wages. Indeed, the young girl's insistence that she would not receive them even were they offered to her because "I would far sooner be as I am" had a strangely hollow ring to it. Adoption, an extraordinarily loosely defined process in much of Canada until 1930, and described by Whitton as "a somewhat glorified indenture process carrying no claim of inheritance," was often an insidious means of defrauding children sent to rural areas of their wages while masquerading under humanitarian sentiments of family life and rural romanticism.24

As noted with dependent Canadian children, girls were helpless not only against seduction but also the narrow confines of social expectations set for them as household helps. As observed previously, domestic service was no less rigorous an occupation than agricultural service but opportunities for mobility, self-expression, and variety were far fewer on the presumption that all dependent girls, whether Canadian or immigrant, were temperamentally suited for and socially born into domestic tasks. When Mrs. Despard of the Catholic Workhouse Association visited Canada in 1902, she deplored the attitude that these children were fit only to be a "helot" class and questioned the principle that girls should only be domestics. She articulated the frustration of those girls not adept at such work or disinclined toward it. "There are mechanical hands," she said, "there are inventive brains, there are talents for organization amongst our girls as well as amongst our boys."25

The female child's circumstances were especially vulnerable, and a number of girls were indecently treated or impregnated in the very homes they were placed. Feelings of helplessness, fear, humiliation, and anxiety could only have been further distorted by such risks. In 1902, Annie Garwood was returned to her receiving home by the highly regarded Maritime family in whose household she had been placed. The family had left on an extended trip leaving her alone with the hired hand who had exploited her unprotected situation. The remark made of her - and not the predatory hired hand - was that "the girl is not bad - only weak and foolish and rather irresponsible."26

Two years later, fourteen year old Alice Britnell was sent alone and unprotected from New Brunswick to her sister in Winnipeg because she was found to be pregnant by a boy from the household where she was placed. Gladys Hunt was harrassed by her master but felt it impossible to share her ordeal with anyone and instead locked herself in her room constantly, abject and afraid. The Saint John Star, 13 November 1907, reported the case of a man who had "carnal knowledge" of twelve year old Ada Francis and who skipped bail and was not rearrested.27

In one case, at least, an immigrant girl was not even protected from the profound psychopathic disturbance of a governor of the Middlemore Receiving Home in Halifax which distributed approximately 4,000 children in New Brunswick and Nova Scotia between 1872 and 1915. Mr. J. Sterling King, the governor concerned, defended his own lax supervision and questionable conduct by claiming that the dismal failures the Home appeared to place were due to Mr. J. T. Middlemore's dumping of undesirable children onto the Maritime provinces. His descriptions of the unfortunate children were gross, inhumane, and reprehensible, but he apparently knew that they would touch a sympathetic chord in Canada.28

As with any significant historical phenomenon, the juvenile immigration movement cannot be totally judged according to negative criteria. Although the "home of happy childhood" version of their trans-migratory experiences at the time was unduly optimistic and undoubtedly exaggerated, nevertheless, the positive aspects of this experience cannot be ignored. The positive aspects do not ultimately deny the collective ordeal of the children's experience but rather complement it as a prism which highlights a complex, contradictory, ambiguous and variagated spectrum. Joy Parr's Labouring Children successfully discusses this complexity and points to the beneficial consequences of the movement for many of the children concerned.29

The heart of the Labouring Children is a scrupulous quantitative analysis of a sample of 997 boys and girls out of the nearly 20,000 emigrated by Dr. Barnardo's Society between 1882 and 1902. The sample was generated by selecting every twentieth juvenile name on Barnardo's sailing party lists. Since the lists were not alphabetical and since the parties included both Barnardo's wards and Poor Law children assigned to it for emigration, the sample seems to provide a fair cross-section of children emigrated. Dossiers for each "apprentice," which include all relevant data, formed the basis of a computer assisted analysis.30

Parr establishes several interesting points that enhance the reputation for the prudence and pragmatic genius of the most successful emigration societies. First, the practice of indenture, which Parr had initially likened to pre-1800 indentured labour, proved to have served "more to define the rights of British immigrant children than to extinguish their rights." Second, the practice of offering a monthly support payment for children under ten years opened up reasonable homes for the wards of Barnardo's and the Catholic agencies. In other words, where the boarding-out principle was correctly carried out there was greater insurance regarding the care of children. Although Parr does not mention it, this "competition" for homes compelled some CASs to more rigorously implement and supervise the homes in which their own wards were placed. Third, the movement of children, especially boys, was often related to the need of matching the increasing economic value of their labour to land productivity. Consequently, the apprentices moved from the least to the most productive agricultural lands as they progressed from being boarded-out to earning their keep and schooling by helping with farm chores to earning wages as farm hands. The various forms of indentures devised by the emigration societies were innovative means of insuring under existing social conditions the welfare and interests of their wards. Fourth, the study supports the contention of the emigration societies that the younger children made a better adjustment to Canadian life. The results cited by Parr suggest that on the grounds of consistent schooling and lower incidence of illegitimacy, the young immigrants were fairly typical of rural

Canadian children. Such a reconstruction of the rhythm and routine of rural life cycles actually substantiate many of the most optimistic claims made by "the fair chance" proponents both at home and abroad.31

It is obvious that immigrant children bore an onerous psychological burden by being deprived of the ordinary ties of blood and being denied the usual support systems of even the most desultory family life. Those who had truly been "adopted" as part of a family group were rare with the majority merely serving out their indentures. The physical demands regarding labor were possibly no more strenuous than those required of biological members of a family of the same age but, as Parr also observes, the immigrant child's absolute dependence upon the new family was of quite a different kind since it was entirely bereft of the usual bonding processes. Although many of these children worked no harder than family members, they lacked any compensating potential share in the family's success. Superficially, the only connection seemed to be economic, i.e., cheap and relatively defense- less labor exploited by a self-righteous and dominant landowning class. There were, of course, more than economic advantages for the householders. Domestic servants were always scarce, and their presence not only relieved the female family members of undesirable tasks but also confirmed the family's social standing.32

Much opposition to the juvenile immigrants was based on the realization that with completion of their indentures, most would leave domestic or agricultural service and compete for scarce urban jobs. As late as 1924, the Canadian Council on Child Welfare, in its analysis of a report submitted by the British Delegation examining child immigra- tion quoted a judge of the British Columbia juvenile court, Helen Gregory MacGill, as insisting that the social service workers of Vancouver "would like some certainty that these children will stay on the farms or in agricultural life" even after their superintendence was terminated at eighteen years, otherwise they would "drift to the cities." The Council was in good company with labor sentiments such as those of J. C. Walters, President of the Trades and Labour Council of Canada, who rejected

238

all forms of <u>assisted</u> immigration because "through some natural process we find it gravitating to the cities and the cities bear the brunt and burden of it anyway" when assisted labor, correctly should go to and remain on "the land." He hastily assured the British Commissioners compiling the Fifth Interim Report of the Dominion Royal Commission of 1917, that he was not against "voluntary" immigration, because most labor spokesmen, including himself, were part of that phenomenon anyway.33

"LITTLE BETTER THAN BRUTES"

What is most interesting about the movement is less in its detail and more in the various responses that it evoked. On the one hand, there was the cloying, sentimental child-rescue rhetoric justifying it as represented by the effusive and florid verse of a 1884 poem, "Canada's Plea for the Waifs and Strays."

You have homes and schools of training;
take these children from the street;
Show them what God meant they should be;
clear a pathway for their feet,
Make them feel that work is noble; teach
them what their lives may be;
Then we'll give them hearty welcome in
our homes across the sea.

On the other hand, there was the vulgar use of pseudo-scientific hereditarian theories to describe the children of paupers as degenerate stock who ought to be separated from pure blooded Canadians and as "children from the streets who are not wanted here."34

The bitterness of the response that rejected the young Britons can only be understood in light of the new and powerfully seductive eugenic theories which gained considerable ground in the last decades of the nineteenth century and the first half of the twentieth. Indeed, they are still not put to rest, and probably will never be, as long as arguments about "nature versus nurture" remain intrinsic to ideas about childhood and of environmentalism. The opponents of juvenile immigration gave voice to concerns of moral degeneracy, genetic criminality, female immorality, physical defectiveness, social incompetence, and chronic feeblemindedness.

By the 1920s, there was an effective and organized campaign based on pseudo-scientific principles derived from the work of international authorities in eugenics and the statements of "experts" in public and mental health, criminal statistics, juvenile delinquency and charity institutions. Studies of racial degeneration and the horrors of "city drift" were produced, and immigrant children accused of contributing to both. The extravagant claims about the eugenic deterioration represented by the "Juke," "Kallikak," and "Ishmaelite" families popularized in North America along with Dr. Goddard's figures on heredity, and Dr. Tredgold's similar conclusions in Britain were liberally quoted to restrict their entry.35

If the first shifts in family and childhood sentiment that occurred in the eighteenth century were logical extensions of the prudential literature for parents and guardians dating from the Renaissance, this understanding was further enhanced by nineteenth century pedagogical literature that emphasized the benefits derived from careful nurture and guidance of children in home and school. The advice literature, which was based on a fundamental belief in environmental forces when related to the right social classes, was now united with a belief in the power of psychological and institutional practices to effect significant character formation.36

The earliest efforts of the middle classes to insure a childhood for their children stressed the need to separate and protect them from the vulgarities and contamination of public life, which was largely achieved through the life of the reformed school and increased family privacy. Despite these changes, many were convinced that society still required substantial ordering. As legislation and social convention sought to impose notions of good order and discipline on society, reformers confronted dependent and pauper classes who failed to conform to the new social norms - particularly with regard to childhood and family life.37

The subsequent failure of philanthropic and
state intervention by the late 1800s reinforced old
ideas of bad blood and inferiority, and prepared the
way for the acceptance of scientific theories that
emphasized the predominance of heredity over
environment. If advice literature was intended to
assist parents in better ordering their family life
and rearing their children, ideas of nationalism
gradually intertwined concern with the proper
development of children with the state's interest in
the making of citizens. Under the notion of the
parenthood of the state, national governments moved
to implement ideas of citizenship that included the
promotion of the well-being of its members and their
efficient participation in all aspects of national
life.38

With certain writers and intellectuals, these
ideas of good and efficient citizenship were linked
with beliefs in the need to encourage the best
"stock" and discourage the worse. Genetic theories
connected with plant and animal life and the
apparent successes of selective breeding were used
to support campaigns to promote the proper
development of national populations. Expressions
such as "race suicide" were used to mobilize public
sentiment in favour of private and state intervention into the most intimate aspects of human life.39

In a general way, the efforts of eugenicists
and other advocates of hereditarianism were
compatible with the basic criteria of childhood
since protection and segregation could be extended
theoretically, at least, to issues of heredity as
well as psychology. Nevertheless, the insidious
nature of the theories meant that they could be
easily vulgarized and exploited by exponents of
racism, xenophobia and anti-democratic views. It is
not remarkable, therefore, that a disgusted William
Quarrier, who emigrated children from the Orphans'
Homes of Scotland, could comment in 1897 on the
surprising "amount of cant one hears about the
danger of corrupting Canadian morals, or indeed
causing a mental or physical deterioration of the
race by the importation of these children."40

If in 1885 Dr. Barnardo had reported that the
Canadian press was willing to perpetuate the view
that the juvenile immigration movement was "a whole-

241

sale dumping of moral refuse on its shores," then by 1907 his society was noting that Canadians cited the laws of heredity "to demonstrate the degenerate characters of our young people, and the alarming results that might be expected to follow from the contamination of their presence among Canadian youth." James S. Woodsworth, a progressive social reformer, could observe in a popular 1909 critique of Canadian society that such children "inherited tendencies to evil" which must lead to the "degeneration of our Canadian people." If Canada was to receive juvenile immigrants, Woodsworth expressed a decided preference for the pink-cheeked, fair haired, blue-eyed young Saxons and the sons of refinement and education over the grubby little street urchins of uncertain parentage who threatened to pollute Canadian stock.41

The Montreal Gazette, 25 July 1895, published remarks from Ontario farmers which included epithets such as "the scum of Europe," "little better than brutes," a "curse to the country," "good for nothing pauper and criminal classes," and "a contaminating influence on native born Canadians." As one dour observer commented - "they cannot help it; it is in their blood and it will tell. . . ." The Toronto Evening Star demanded that England look after its own "syphilitic paupers" and not continue the practice which lent itself to "physical corruption of a pure blooded people." Three years later the Ottawa Citizen, September 1899, said that they were the "physiological off-scourings of the Old World dumped on [Canada's] shores" and archly added that the least the philanthropists could do was to give them a bath before they left "'ome."42

In 1897, James C. Moyal, Chief Inspector of Penitentiaries, objected to the transplantation of "exotics unsuited to the soil and moral atmosphere of the Dominion."

> Cockney sneak thieves and pickpockets
> are numerous. These pests are gathered
> from the slums of St. Giles and the East
> End of London . . . with a few exceptions
> these street arabs . . . speedily
> returned to their old habits on arriving
> in Canada, and in consequence became
> a burden and an expense to the taxpayers

of the Dominion in reformatories, gaols,
and penitentiaries where they are found
to be the most troublesome and worse
convicts in Canada, their evil influence
for the corruption of others being
potent and pernicious.

As late as 1929, the Acting Deputy Minister for
Immigration was still speaking about "picking out
the culls" and asserting that "van boys from
Glasgow, butcher boys from Dundee and newsboys from
Bristol" were unsatisfactory material for Canadian
social life.43

    The Canadian labor press was in perfect
agreement with the 1887 comment in the Charity
Organization Review which criticized boarding-out of
workhouse children in Britain by saying that the
placing of such children in private homes after a
residence in some institutions was "to take your
bleached linen, hard enough to keep spotless and
throw it in dirty water." The Hamilton Palladium of
Labour in 1894 charged that Maria Rye was "dumping
the refuse of British jails, slums and workhouses."
With such bad press, it was no wonder that in the
same year Miss Rye summarily returned young Annie
Fidgett to the Chelsea Workhouse because she was
"given to thieving, lying, and in everyway was
unsatisfactory," according to her mistress, Mrs.
Shaw of Mansfield, Ontario. The Toronto Trades and
Labour Congress weekly, The Toiler, releasing a
litany of horror stories of the poverty and disease
of the young Britons, stated in 1903 that these
waifs were still being imported "regardless of the
injury done to the country by the lowest scum of the
earth." In 1904, it deplored the undermining of the
"present standard of health, physique, and
mentality" by the importation of waifs.44

    Finally, it should not be overlooked that the
farmers who benefitted from or even exploited the
young immigrants frequently expressed an intolerance
and prejudice that was singular. The language used
to describe them was as immoderate as the language
condemning masturbation and enuresis. The Ontario
Agriculture Department Bulletin of 1895 published
remarks from farmers that were widely quoted in the
press. Moreover, several parties of children
learned their first lessons in rejection and

prejudice when they were treated with contempt and harshness at their points of debarkation.45

On the evidence, one must agree with William Quarrier that "we do not claim to have brought angels into the country, nor do we place them among angels," despite the reply of the Premier of Ontario, Arthur S. Hardy, that he intended "to guard against the moral or physical deterioration of our people."46

With such abundant misrepresentation, it is not surprising that little girls who were "addicted to self abuse," or young lads, who were enuretic or encopretic, were deported because of their "filthy habits," or that children who proved "unequal to their position" were returned to their original orphans' homes. These are not isolated examples since the immigration records are replete with others. The willingness of the Immigration Department authorities, who were normally sympathetic to the apprentices and champions of their cause when they were unjustly treated, to deport masturbating and enuretic/encopretic children, suggests that they too deemed such behavior as irrefutable evidence of genetic and cultural taint.47

It is against this Canadian context that the many cases of deportation due to masturbation or enuresis or encopresis must be placed. Moreover the shame, rejection, and burden of failure that children and youths took back to their British institutions or families cannot be minimized. How these children explained their failures when they returned and how they were subsequently treated by the authorities of their respective Homes can only be speculated on.48

In all honesty, the propaganda methods of the societies themselves contributed to misunderstanding regarding the characters of the young Britains concerned. Nineteenth century societies were excessive in their child saving claims. The greater the wickedness, the more spectacular the rescue, and the more spectacular the rescue, the greater the likelihood of attracting funds. Case histories were calculated usually not to edify or inform but to alarm. Voluntary societies depended on the credulity of their subscribers, and incoming donations were usually in proportion to the misery their advertisements, appeals, brochures, magazines, annual reports, and tracts depicted.

Barnardo, who was a prolific and colorful writer of child saving literature such as Rescued for Life: The True Story of a Young Thief, depicted children in their worst aspect, sold his fiction as penny magazines and chapbooks, and then wondered that many Canadians actually believed his claims. The pamphlets and publications of J. W. C. Fegan, Hiving Off and Loving and Serving, and of the National Children's Homes or the Liverpool Sheltering Home, to name only a few, are fine examples of the genre of child saving sentiment which was mawkish and banal to the extreme. And just to prove that Catholic child depravity was equally alarming as its Protestant variety (a fact about which few English Canadians needed to be convinced), the Birmingham Diocesan Rescue Society for Friendless and Destitute Catholic Children published The Fold, which depicted the disreputable activities in which candidates for emigration had formerly engaged. Delving and Diving: or Voices from the Slums of Manchester and Salford regularly contained a penny's worth of lurid stories about street children rescued by the Children's missions or who attended Deansgate Boys' Home.49

In "Arabs of the City," an address which typified many similar ones delivered before child savers, W. Morgan, Birmingham town clerk, described street children as "dabbling in gutters, leaping over posts, laughing through their filth and rags, with the indomitable freedom of the child, but left to grow up ignorant of everything except the most revolting aspect of human nature." Unless rescued and removed from the gutters, these puckish urban scalliwags would grow up into degenerates and felons.50

While such stories, along with Annie Macpherson's unrestrained tales of little street arabs and matchbox makers, were voraciously consumed by a credulous and censorious public, they did little to alleviate Canadian anxiety, and at the same time underestimated the degree of Canadian prejudice. When such depictions were juxtaposed with views such as those expressed by Mary Carpenter in "What Shall We Do With Our Pauper Children?" that street children were destined to become "a drag and incubus on society," and that they would "carry elsewhere a degraded race" if allowed to emigrate, were scarcely bound to fill Canadians with eager anticipation for those who did.51

Mrs. Nassau Senior's description of workhouse girls as "disreputable, slovenly, feebleminded and criminal," although made to promote boarding-out over congregate care, nevertheless provoked concern because she advocated emigration of such girls for domestic service. The Emigrant, a magazine avidly read by Canadians, while praising Barnardo's Russell Farm in Manitoba, included the offhand remark that it was for "the rougher sort of boy," while the Superintendent of the Waifs and Strays Society heartily endorsed the belief that although his children were the offspring of "habitual criminals and confirmed paupers," they became honest citizens in a new environment. Certainly none of this can be viewed as salutary advertising.52

Some Canadian societies desired to advertise in a more efficacious manner. For instance, the British Columbia Development Association wished, in 1910, to alter the nomenclature of "reformatory" attached to its emigrant lads as these were merely "destitute, vagrant and sleepouts." The point here is that it publicized what Canadians suspected anyway - that they were receiving reformatory cases. Canadians were not about to examine the differences between British industrial training schools and reformatories, or laws concerning children which led a quite different class of child frequently to be institutionalized in Britain than in Canada.53

They were not about to be convinced that many were not bad lads especially as the Redhill Farm School of the Philanthropic Society in Surrey stated every year in its published report that it aimed at protecting "children who had themselves been engaged in criminal practices." Redhill sent trained older boys to Canada along with a small number of reformatory boys who had been discharged from industrial training ships such as the Formidable, the Clio, and the Cornwall - boys who had mostly been convicted under the clauses of the 1866

246

Industrial Schools Act. Such children were quickly labeled "moral defectives" which was synonymous "with the term institutional psychopathic inferiority," that is, "destined to become a charge on the community." And if Canadians grimly shook their heads as they read the early tracts of Annie Macpherson informing them that the young emigrants lived "as much by thieving as shoeblacking, and considered themselves too bad to be reclaimed," we ought not to be surprised at the reception accorded the children in British North America.54

Neither did government agreements in the 1920s with the Oversea Settlement Office about more careful selection procedures, the compilation of case histories, the inclusion of psychiatric examination, and more rigorous placing and inspection standards, pacify pressure groups. The Church of England Council for Social Service, the Canadian Association of Child Protection Officers, the Committee for Mental Hygiene, the Montreal Women's Canadian Club, the Montreal Society for the Protection of Women and Children, the National Child Welfare Association, the National Council of Women, and other societies wanted nothing less than a complete cessation of the movement. Tom Moore, President of the Toronto Labour Council, the confrere of Whitton and the labour representative of the Canadian Council on Child Welfare (CCCW), who replaced his nineteenth century predecessor O'Donaghue in the extravagence of his claims, was aided and abetted by "professional" interests as represented by Charlotte Whitton and the CCCW.55

Whitton, Canada's foremost figure in scientific child welfare in the 1920s, organized a survey of immigrant children which sought to unearth as many examples of "taint" as possible through records of charitable agencies, asylums, reformatories, penal institutions, the Toronto General Hospital, psychiatric departments, and female rescue homes. Although the CCCW survey of 1928, Several Years After, bore all the outward signs of a humanitarian document condemning the exploitation of unprotected British child life, its data base was generated from a profound belief that such children also represented undesirable immigrants.56

Whitton's views that the major task of immigration policy was to keep Canada "strong, virile, healthy and moral, and we insist that the blood that enters its veins must be equally pure and free from taint" were in keeping with the sentiments found in the journal Social Welfare of October, 1918, with whose publication she was actively involved as assistant editor while working for the Social Service Council of Canada (SSCC). The journal warned against intermarriage of imported British domestics when Canada was in a vulnerable state with its depleted male population after World War I. It continued that "this must be constantly born in mind lest the reborn Canadian of the future be a weakling race, and a menace in its [eugenic] constitution."57

Whitton freely used the expression "the backwash of juvenile immigration" in her own correspondence, quoting from a 1925 SSCC report, which deplored "the eugenic effects of bringing in thousands of boys and girls, a considerable proportion of whom have sprung from stock, which, whatever else may be said of it, was not able to hold its own in the stern competition of the motherland." The "backwash" represented those unsuccessful and statistically few young Britons who, during their minority or well into their majority, added to Canada's figures of mental defect, illegitimacy, gonorrhea, prostitution, crime, or charity. Whitton vigorously defended psychiatric examinations as a qualification for juvenile emigrants when such examinations were still primitive and frequently punitive, if for no other reason than to prevent children who might be, or might become, "sex morons" from entering Canada.58

In order to accumulate as many cases of "degeneracy" as possible, Whitton queried the veteran Superintendent of Neglected and Dependent Children about Ontario's figures on "unmarried parents" especially with regard to immigrant girls. Although he had impetuously and indiscriminately used data collected from the records of the Toronto General Hospital dating back to 1907 at the 1924 Juvenile Immigration Conference, Kelso proved unwilling to give her the figures she sought on illegitimacy and "social disease." Kelso compassionately defended the girls whom he

248

unequivocally identified as "victims" of their vulnerable and precarious position.

> It is natural and indeed inevitable that many of our unmarried parent cases should come from the immigrant classes and also from wards of Societies and juvenile institutions. All experience shows that when a man wishes to betray a girl he usually selects one who has no father, or brother to defend her. Accordingly, the "openly and brazenly immoral" are a small percentage.59

Later, Professor G. D. MacPhee scurrilously exploited similar figures from the Hospital at the Conference of Child Welfare held in Ottawa, 1925. Although his statements were enthusiastically received by Whitton who recognized their implications for the campaign against juvenile immigration, the data were so inaccurate as to force the professor of psychology, who was then at the University of Toronto, to withdraw his claims and offer a public apology to the Barnardo's who had objected strenuously to the fact that the "immorality" of their girls had been particularly pinpointed.60

Sensational and inflated figures from asylums, gaols, rescue homes, child welfare department, venereal disease clinics, reformatories and industrial schools were collected deliberately by the CCCW. Then, as now, the "statistic" was compelling evidence for whatever was needed to be proved. Sometimes the data was unreliable as in the case of the Juvenile Immigration Survey conducted by Mrs. Hazel Breckenridge McGregor, who, having valiantly struggled to accumulate sufficient damning information from the understandably reluctant and suspicious agents from the various societies, submitted her conclusions to Whitton with the following comment.

> I am struggling with my report and I am afraid it is just going to be a jumble of unrelated statements and impressions and shall have to give it to you to dish up in you usual masterly style.

The final report was consequently the result of their combined efforts.61

When Gladys Pott of the Oversea Settlement Committee, which had conducted the British survey of juvenile emigration, questioned the validity of both the CCCW statistics and the psychiatric testing of immigrants by means of detailed case histories, Whitton responded by referring to the case of a boy in trouble with a little girl. Such tests, she asserted, would have revealed the boy for what he was - "a sex moron."62

Moreover, it was not paranoia which induced James Webb in 1924 to write to George Bogue Smart, the Inspector of British Children, to inform him that he was "an Old Home Boy from 1882" who now owned his own business, having been apprenticed to a decorating firm after his agricultural indenture. This contributor to "city drift" had organized an Old Boys Society with one hundred members. They intended to confront head-on the adverse publicity given to their backgrounds and the subsequent slander upon their characters. At the 1924 annual meeting of the neophyte society, he said that the "old boys" recognized that

> . . . there seemed to be a dead set on Home Boys by the public press. We were blamed for all the ills of the country and anything done in a community for which the perpetrator was not identified was landed at the door of the Home Boy.

Such solidarity was understandable after several decades of bad press.63

STEMMING THE TIDE

The anti-juvenile immigration protest took on the form of a crusade in the 1920s; a crusade that united heterogeneous groups in an unanimity of purpose if not of interests. Nevertheless, after thirty years of sporadic antagonisms and irregular and factious hostilities, the movement had proven durable. The movement became especially problematic when a resurgence of emigration occurred with the Barnardo's and the Salvation Army resuming it on a grand scale after World War I. The war had left a legacy of British orphans and unemployable youth competing for scarce post-war unskilled jobs. An irresistible incentive was presented to emigration societies, whose activities had laid fallow during the hostilities in Europe, when the Canadian government offered subsidies to the tune of a $1,000 grant to any agency that transported over one hundred children per annum, with an additional $500 for each subsequent one hundred. As those agencies which transported less than one hundred children were ineligible for any grant, even the more modest philanthropists became more aggressive in recruiting children. This resurgence provoked those Canadian groups which had been, for whatever reasons, traditionally opposed to the movement. The tide had to be stemmed.64

It is tempting to conclude that the renewed opposition to the movement was a reflection of the changing concepts of childhood. Since the six decades under examination were crucial ones in the emergence of child welfare from earlier Canadian child-saving sentiment, the attitudes toward the child immigrants might be interpreted as an expression of solicitude for their well-being or an abhorrence for the harsh living conditions to which many were subject. Although this is more plausibly the case between 1920 and 1930 when child labor and protection laws were being implemented and child welfare departments intervening in the lives of more children, it does not adequately explain the hostility which was apparent by the 1890s. Neither does it adequately explain an opposition that more often than not included personal attacks on the type of child being emigrated, and whose rhetoric lacked sentiment of childhood that was part of progressive attitudes.

Even as part of the dumping ground thesis, the phenomenon is singular, for in a time when optimism abounded regarding the efficacy of child-rescue and when child nature was seen as increasingly redeemable, these young emigrants, who as Denis Crane expressed "began life under the minus category," were excluded from the usual advantages of child rescue sentiment. The intellectual climate with its emphasis on new psycho-physiological theories of

251

heredity merely provided a rational basis for the deep-seated resentment.65

Canadian child-rescue sentiment manifested itself in new perceptual criteria that increasingly defined the status and role of children and youth by segregating and protecting them from the rigors of adult life. Beginning in the 1850s, dependent, neglected, and delinquent children and adolescents were removed slowly and unevenly from houses of industry, poorhouses, and common gaols and lock-ups, and placed in orphanages, children's villages, reformatories and industrial schools. By the end of the century, sentiment for family life over institutional reformation was reflected in the stress on placement in foster homes under the supervision of newly forming provincial departments of dependent and neglected children and their local agents, the quasi-public children's aid societies. Since, except for Ontario, little machinery existed prior to 1914 for the enforcement of child protection legislation, the early criticisms of the failures of the emigration societies were not based on superior performances by Canadian institutions and agenices. Indeed, the drive for systematic and professional child welfare in Canada awaited the genius of Charlotte Whitton and the CCCW in the 1920s.66

It was the CCCW, under Whitton's guidance, which sounded the alarm against the immigration movement in that decade by producing a series of reports, responses to official immigration reports, and questionnaires. The Council represented its cause at child care, immigration, and women's conferences, and effectively coordinated disparate groups and diverse interests into a common cause with a humanitarian appeal. Whitton's consummate skill at coalescing various professional child care groups under the aegis of the CCCW resulted in a highly politicized lobby that proved a major tour de force in expanding the Council's influence nationally and advancing her own career.67

Far from representing a consensus of child welfare opinion or an altruistic and progressive statement on the state's responsibility for dependent children, the signatories of the various petitions, resolutions, and questionnaires circulated by the CCCW were as much bound by particularism as by humanitarian disinterestedness. The lobby consisted of various groups - tenuous associations drawn together by a common interest - and individuals fitting into one or more of the groups but who allowed a formal representative, in this case the CCCW, to speak for them and coordinate their interests. These groupings were preponderantly opposed to juvenile immigration for various reasons, although they were not all active from the beginning of the movement. Nativists, nationalists, and labour groups had demonstrated a sustained and predictable opposition from the 1870s, whereas in the 1920s, several groups such as politicized women's groups, superintendents of dependent children, child protection officers, social workers, and organizations such as the CCCW and the Social Service Council of Canada, were added.

Included, of course, were those humanitarians who sincerely and unequivocally sought to improve the conditions of child life whether these applied to immigrant or native children. Each group had its particular raison d'etre for participating in the lobby. To conclude that the lobby represented a major shift in child rescue opinion would be to oversimplify gravely the matter, although it did present a common front on one particular issue whose significance had implications for similar domestic practices.

For the sake of illustration, four major groups of these loose associations can be identified. Although their interests were somewhat transparent, this is not to suggest that they were capricious. The first group consisted of those with centralist philosophies regarding the organizing of child welfare either at the provincial or the Dominion level. The second group represented those who belonged to provincial or national woman's organizations and whose opinions and support were called upon by professional child care groups to add strength to a lobby whose prime aim was not to improve either selection or supervisory procedures but to abolish juvenile immigration altogether. The third major group included members and sympathizers of the CCCW itself which was engaged in its own dramatic bid for national recognition and influence. The fourth group represented all those anti-philanthropic "professionalizers" who were steadily staking out their social work domains during the first four decades of the twentieth century. Although the last two groups will be touched upon in this section, a full discussion will appear in later chapters.

It will come as no surprise to those familiar with the problems of Canadian confederation that even in the area of child welfare, tensions existed between Dominion and provincial jurisdiction. Much justified criticism was levelled at the inadequate inspection procedures and under-staffed juvenile immigration branch which carried out these procedures for the Canadian government. Accompanying this criticism was an equally considered view, less obviously justified, that the selection processes, especially in matters of psychiatric and medical examination, were grossly inadequate. The reasons behind such criticisms can be more easily understood, however, if approached from a perspective that does not take them merely on face value - that of the jockeying between provincial and Dominion child welfare officials and authorities over rights regarding the supervision of the receiving homes established, and the children placed from these homes in the various provinces. After the Ontario Act to Regulate Immigrant Children was passed in 1897, William Quarrier observed that the insistence on provincial laws about immigration suggested that the Dominion government was "not doing its job" and that "Canada will never stand as a Dominion . . . by adding sectional laws to this and that part of the country."68

Superintendents of dependent children, such as F. J. Reynolds, Commissioner of Saskatchewan's Bureau of Child Protection, Mr. A. Percy Paget, Director of Child Welfare, Winnipeg, Ernest H. Blois, Director of Child Welfare, Nova Scotia, Mr. K. C. McLeod of Edmonton, and representatives of provincial departments such as Huilota Dykeman, from the New Brunswick Department of Health, felt that the provinces concerned ought to superintend the rural placements and after care of the immigrants. They argued that the procedures and regulations should come under those concerning their own delinquents and state wards, and that the transfer of the "foster" (i.e., "indenture") agreements of

such children should be given into a judge's order
in those western provinces where this was the
custom. Such a position was submitted by the
executive committee of the CCCW to the Dominion
authorities in 1924 in the form of an <u>Analysis of
the Report of the British Delegation [the Bondfield
Report] on Child Immigration</u>. Arguing that as the
Ontario Province had thirty CAS visitors and a
corresponding number of agents dealing with mothers'
allowances, it insisted that

> By utilizing these services, and by
> systematic cooperation between the
> federal department and the provinces,
> the officials and standards deemed
> adequate for the protection of our own
> dependent children can be utilized to
> perform or supplement the inspection
> services necessary.69

Apart from the mistaken presumption that
Ontario had sufficient staff to adequately deal with
the problems relating to its own CAS wards, let
alone several hundred more young Britons, the CCCW
consistently supported the proposition that the
immigrants ought to come under the CAS system where
it operated or a central provincial unit where it
did not. The provincial governments in either case
should register and licence the societies, their
homes, and their children and remove and replace
children in unsatisfactory circumstances. The <u>in
loco parentis</u> claims of private philanthropy were
totally rejected in a belief that the importation of
children into Canada's national life was "a
responsibility which civilization and humanity
demand is the first duty of the State." The
Dominion position, and particularly that of
Inspector Bogue Smart, rejected the premise by
tersely pointing out that the children were the
wards of the societies and had done nothing in
Canada to warrant their becoming "state wards." The
claims of the societies as guardians of the children
could not be violated by a presumption of provincial
jurisdiction.70

The claims for provincial jurisdiction had been
raised first during the mid-1890s by Ontario's first
Superintendent of Neglected and Dependent Children,
J. J. Kelso. At child saving conferences and in his

annual reports, Kelso argued that CASs should supervise the young immigrants and that in addition to federal regulation, provincial legislation was needed to control and supervise the children. What is curious about this statement is that while criticizing the lack of safeguards for British children, Kelso, who was always in touch with the Toronto CAS he had helped organize five years before, could not have been ignorant of that organization sending its own "rescued children" in the form of sturdy boys to Manitoba under the care of the same people who were pleased to exploit imported labor. The report of the CAS for 1896, which recorded the work of the previous year, observed that Hon. Thomas Greenway, the Premier of Manitoba and the Secretary of the Northwest Territories, was happy to receive Toronto's male waifs and strays, although their unaccompanied travel arrangements caused the CAS some anxiety. They were met at Winnipeg and cared for by Hugh McKellar, chief clerk of the Agriculture Department. These boys were being sent across only two years after the Brandon Assizes had denounced Home boys in Manitoba.71

While Kelso and others argued that the children should be deemed state wards, the philanthropic societies continued to defend their right to privacy. They consistently argued that increased supervision would put otherwise free citizens in the same category as the delinquent, abandoned, or dependent children of Canada. Many years after Kelso's recomendation, The Hamilton Spectator, 3 May 1924, in a succinct summary of the issue, stated:

> Does one think they will become better Canadians by retaining the tag of 'State Ward' until manhood than they would if placed in the care of responsible employers and left to their own resources? Why ought they be constantly reminded of the handicap of an orphanage instead of a system being provided to forget their misfortune?

This summary of the matter was in keeping with Quarrier's observations twenty-seven years previously that "those who are not criminals ought not to be dealt with in any other way than as full born subjects of Canada and Britain. . . . We will

256

not have our children bearing the additional stigma of being Government children." The rescue societies' heartfelt sympathy with this statement was based on the premise that such emigration was intended to decrease dependency whether in Britain or in Canada. To be automatically included on the poor law rolls, or for that matter on the CAS registers as a "state ward," were equally social stigmas.72

Recommendations that all children should be subjected to provincial superintendence were also based on the curious argument, not dissimilar to the familiar one of "unfair competition" used by labor leaders, that immigrant children "took the places" of Canadian dependent children. Although in 1924, Mr. Nickle, the Ontario Attorney-General flatly rejected Miss Kate Dixon's representation for the CCCW when she argued for this position, the view was nevertheless taken up again by the Council in a memorandum called "Summary of Present Day Problems With the Council's Consideration." The memorandum objected to the free agricultural training programs being proposed for British youths under the conditions of the Empire Settlement Act. The Council argued that programs were patently unjust when 5,000 Canadian children remained "cooped up" in domestic institutions and condemned to an urban existence.73

During the years 1924 to 1928 when the CCCW was so active in its campaign against British agencies and their lack of supervision, and Hazel Breckenridge McGregor was denouncing these "antiquated old creatures [for] spreading children over the country like cattle," it is interesting to note that at no time did she, Whitton, the CCCW, or any Canadian child welfare groups similarly condemn the incompetent but well-connected British Immigration and Colonization Association (BICA) which operated out of Montreal. This Canadian association, while dealing with older boys, was so incompetent as to go into receivership under the Immigration Department because of bankruptcy, and its supervision and placement procedures were so negligent as to verge almost on being unconscionable. Its records are full of stories of boys who were carelessly placed out and promptly forgotten, and whose serious grievances were ignored.74

Sometimes it was clear that arguments about child immigrant labor were less crucial than the fact that the supervision and placement of such apprentices was carried on by British agencies and under the superintendence of Dominion authorities, because this meant that many potential "wards" were excluded from provincial statistics which gained CASs and child welfare departments additional funds. Although conferences on child welfare continued to protest the child labor abuses intrinsic to the movement in an indisputably genuine manner, the insistence on supervision by Canadian agencies represented a complex issue.75

Child welfare interests across the country refused to relax their claims for wardship, and the British societies refused to relinquish theirs. As the deputy Minister of Immigration observed in 1926, if the provinces had been given such authorization, they would "likely [have made] life unbearable to the Societies." The consistent defence for the Societies' refusal to cooperate with provincial government authorities and social welfare agencies in giving access to their records was best articulated by John Hobday, Manager of the Barnardo Training Homes in Canada.

They are the records of the children
rather than the records of the Home and
they are certainly not intended for the
public. The view taken by Dr. Barnardo's
homes has always been that these, usually
humble members of society are entitled to
demand the history of their childhood
should be as much shielded from public
curiosity as the history of more fortunate
children who have been brought up in the
privacy of their own homes.

Lack of cooperation, however, was interpreted as confession of incompetence and defensiveness as having something to hide.76

The children's aid societies had expressed objections to British children not coming under their jurisdiction as early as 1902-04. An Ottawa complaint was recorded in the reports of these years in a fretful observation that the Barnardo agency placed young children "under less onerous

258

conditions" than CASs could afford, that is, in keeping with the boarding-out principle - for a payment. The payment meant that such children took the places of Canadian wards. In contradiction to the stereotypes of criminality, feeblemindedness and degeneracy, it was observed that the difficulties in placing Canadian wards were compounded by the fact that immigrant children were "better trained and educated." The Toronto CAS in 1912 also objected to the payment of $5 a month by observing that little boys (probably Barnardo's) were preferred to its own because of this payment. The CASs, while believing in principle in boarding-out, felt the method's efficacy was thwarted by British children being so readily absorbed into Canadian homes and given the advantages of rural life, with or without payment. It cannot be overlooked, however, that such absorption and even preference for Britons was based as much on the isolation of the children from relatives or oversight as on any other factor.77

Similar sentiments were reiterated in the Immigration and Travellers Aid Survey of 1928-29 which reported the recommendations of Judge MacLachlan and Mr. Reynolds of Saskatchewan before a recent Child Welfare Conference. These recommendations included provincial supervision of British children, and urged that the "21,000 dependent children" in Canadian institutions or under CASs should be placed out first into situations that would be otherwise taken by immigrants. These views had been first formulated by the Trades and Labour Congress in 1886 when it wrote to the Reformatory Refuge Union in Britain that immigrant children were being placed with "merciless taskmasters and slave drivers," while rather incongruously adding that Canada had its own orphans to place.78

It is not certain as to what extent provincial departments or CASs were cognizant of those Canadian institutions that received British immigrant children for a fee and distributed them after a short period of acclimatization. This is known to have occurred in cases of the Toronto Boys' Home, the Halifax Industrial School, and several Catholic homes such as St. Joseph's Home, Ladysmith, British Columbia, St. George's Home, Ottawa, and St. Patrick's Orphanage, Halifax. Saskatchewan received emigrant children from the English Rescue Society in

1908 when the Society agreed to provide the buildings for the St. Patrick's Orphanage, Prince Albert, where Father Brueck promised to train sixty destitute English children in agriculture and trades.79

A good measure of the success of the 1920s lobby must be laid at the door of the women's groups who supported Whitton and the CCCW. By giving addresses at various conferences and meetings, Whitton had managed to convince many that it was in their self interest to end juvenile immigration. Her awareness that a lobby could not be successful unless it included "the consciousness of the woman electorate" is evident in a comment made before the 1925 Canadian Conference of Child Welfare in which she described women as that "vast body of citizens, now possessing an electorally as well as socially active voice in public affairs." Moreover she was convinced that "the public men of Canada had their ears to the ground and realized the appeal of social measures to the woman citizen." Her efforts were rewarded by the support she received from female child protection officers such as Judges Ethel MacLachlan of Regina, Emily Murphy of Edmonton and Helen MacGill of Vancouver, Adelaide Plumptre, Convenor of the Immigration Committee of the YWCA, Professor Carrie Derick, Convenor of the Committee for Mental Defectives and President of the Local Council of Women, Montreal, and Dr. Helen MacMurchy of the Dominion Department of Health.80

An active member and often executive officer of several women's groups including the Canadian Women's Club and the Imperial Order Daughters of the Empire (IODE), as well as Secretary of the NCW and President of the Women's Institutes of Ontario in 1925, and frequently a spokesperson at their meetings or convenor on their sub-committees, Whitton was able to exert considerable influence because of her talent for directing their concerns and anxieties about two matters - the supply of domestic servants and surveillance of the feeble-minded. In the juvenile immigration debate, these two concerns converged midst the plethora of other diverse interests. The argument that insisted on the monitoring of immigration schemes so that the "right class" of domestic help might be brought over was a strong one. The rejection of juvenile immigration, therefore, was made not on grounds of exploitation (for women who employed domestic servants of any type were hardly noted for their altruism) or even on grounds of progressive child welfare, but rather that the young female Britons were not carefully screened by their sponsors and came from "biologically inferior strata of British life." They were reluctant to have in their households such girls, whom they believed, were prone to immorality, feeblemindedness, hereditary diseases, criminality, irresponsibility, slovenliness and improvidence.

It is less obvious in their lobby against juvenile immigration than in their support of child welfare generally that the women's groups involved were expressing purely solicitous interests. Their sincerity as delegates from the National Council of Women, the various Local Councils, women's clubs, service clubs and women's institutes, the YWCA, the Girls Friendly Society, and the IODE, in the child welfare conferences or as affiliate members of the CCCW is not in question. They had frequently demonstrated genuine concern over matters of infant mortality, playgrounds, legislation concerning women and children, the "circulation of deleterious literature" and "unpurged picture shows" among others. Neither is their involvement in resolutions coming out of national provincial child welfare conferences in question.81

Nonetheless, women's groups also appeared to be concerned in quite another matter - one close to their middle class aspirations - that of employing domestic servants. The observation made almost a century previously by a similar group of middle class women in Montreal, the Ladies Benevolent Society, that domestic servants were a "class important to the community" remained a constant preoccupation of women's groups in Canada. The "community" in the 1920s, as a hundred years earlier, can be understood as middle class female employers of such service. It would be of interest to know how many of the women involved in general child welfare activities received young British girls into their homes as household help despite the 1924 judgement of the CCCW that "it tended perilously close to a peonage system."82

No matter how desperate to procure domestic help in a country where there has always been a shortage of such service, such women were just as anxious to procure "the right class" of servant. As domestic servants traditionally had come from the laboring classes, "the right class" could not have meant them. The fine lines between "worthy" and "unworthy" were being drawn once again, with the reputation that preceded the young Britons suggesting that they were the ignominious products of British slum life. As early as 1907, the NCW complained that social mobility in the new world had led to a depletion in the supply of domestics alongside a rise in the demand. Consequently a resolution was passed that something ought to be done to attract more to Canada due to a situation that "threaten[ed] to entirely annihilate our homes." This concern was articulated constantly by Mrs. Charles Thorburn, the president of the CCCW in 1925 and long time patron of the Ottawa POH, when she became honorary government commissioner in 1923 to examine the possibilities of immigrating "a superior type."83

The emphasis on the right kind of immigrant girl or young woman was repeated often by Miss Burnham, superintendent of the Women's Branch of the Immigration Department, and by the managers of the several girls' immigrant hostels and various reception committees across the country. At the beginning of her career with the Social Service Council of Canada, Whitton was an active member of the Canadian Council of Immigration of Women for Household Service and therefore attuned to the anxieties and concerns of middle class women, although she remained aloof from employing such help herself if we can judge from her later criticisms of the practice.84

Historically, women's groups had expressed concern about "girl immigration" especially with regard to the type of girl who would become part of their households. They stressed a careful selection process, medical and psychiatric examinations, and as thorough a training program as possible before emigration. While their preference was probably for an older girl - well trained, responsible, and above all, committed to the status of servant - the common grievance was that the relative freedom in Canada,

262

the opportunities for factory work, marriage, and social mobility, as well as the inducements of higher salaries in other households with less surveillance, militated against older girls remaining or constituting a permanent menial class.

As in the case of agricultural labor when such issues were taken into account, younger workers were in the long run more satisfactory. Brought over under indentures and with societies operating in loco parentis (therefore assuring such indenture arrangements would be kept), the young girl involved would be captive so to speak, able to fulfil household duties on a full-time basis rather than casually or as a daytime servant, nurse, or companion, and more likely to remain until the age of eighteen when their indentures commonly ran out. As requests for girls over fourteen, who were no longer required to attend school, were prevalent in CAS files, girls between fourteen and eighteen were probably in demand, being strong and dependable and available during the day.85

Women's interest in maintaining order and gentility in their own households was as important a factor to their group participation in the juvenile immigration crusade as was any appeal on national-istic grounds regarding the preservation of Canadian stock or on the appeals of Labor that immigrants by drifting into the cities usurped Canadian jobs. The preoccupation with domestic help was reflected as much in a publication like the Imperial Colonist, which studied the colonial needs and concerns over immigration for the years 1900-1920, as it was in the minutes of many of these women's organizations during the same period.

Alongside the problems of obtaining domestic help, a second matter that loomed large was the obsessive preoccupation with feebleminded females as a particularly threatening eugenic problem. Women's groups were as equally committed to the state controlling this aspect of social life as they were to the state implementing immigration schemes which would being over sufficient numbers of the "right class" of girl and woman.86

The two remaining identifiable interest groups may be loosely described as the "professionalizers."

Their opposition to the movement is grounded on several factors, none of which is mutually exclusive. As this group requires more extensive discussion than can be permitted at this stage, the following comments must suffice.

Due to the shift from scientific principles in child welfare, a new class of social worker, which participated vigorously in the anti-juvenile immigration campaign of the twenties, had arisen. This emerging class of social workers and the CCCW were committed to qualifications, training and expertise, that is, to the professionalization of charitable efforts that had previously been controlled by volunteers and funded by philanthropists. The Council exemplified the shift towards professionalization and the coordination of child welfare problems by expanding its function, promoting scientific philosophies, and opposing vestiges of the "old charity." Mrs. Thorburn noted that "the history of the five years of the CCCW might be called the autobiography of an infant prodigy." And indeed it might, for in that short span of time the Council had embraced nineteen national, fourteen provincial, and sixteen municipal organizations, and 191 individuals as affiliated members.87

The new professionalizers were opposed, on principle to philanthropic endeavours and were determined that such endeavours should not be imported into Canada which already retained an excess of its own who stubbornly resisted coordination, systematic and preventative investigation, and business methods of charity organization. The Salvation Army's "relief without cure," and the enormous success of the Barnardo's in organizing and coordinating a philanthropic enterprise into a remarkably efficient charity-machine at a time when such methods were viewed with dismay, epitomized the worse aspects of charity giving. The prospect of the Barnardo menace of never ending sailing parties appalled its Canadian critics. Barnardo in many ways bore the burden of being too successful at philanthropic child rescue and the opposition at home and abroad was the price extracted for such success.88

As important as humanitarian motives were in developing this opposition, equal weight must be given to the growing "professionalization" of charity with its manifest urge to include all aspects of child life under its aegis. Hazel Breckenridge McGregor expressed this growing urge toward professionalization in 1927 when she wrote to F. C. Blair, Deputy Minister of Immigration, that "the social workers in Canada now constitute quite a large proportion of the population and they are people who carry considerable weight in matters of this sort." Blair had been quite aware of their "weight." Having been subjected to constant petitions and deputations from social agencies, he grumbled to the Minister in 1924 that "most of the agitation I think comes from a bunch of busybodies who are seeking to establish influential organizations."89

It is conventional wisdom that Canadian child welfare groups had reached a level of efficiency which surpassed their British counterparts in philosophy and practice regarding pauper, orphan and dependent children under professional care. These groups included the Canadian Association of Child Protection Officers, the CCCW, a score or so of CASs, the Social Service Council of Canada and various provincial departments of neglected and dependent children. Although this view, gleaned from self congratulatory claims of the CASs, child savers, and child saving conferences, has been handed down by recent studies of Canadian child life, it remains unfounded as a contention and largely unsubstantiated as a generalization.90

Indeed, it is doubtful that even Ontario had reached the presumed level of efficiency as far as supervision and boarding-out of state wards or the care of private wards in the various orphanages was concerned. To judge Canadian standards as uniformly superior or more progressive than their British counterparts is doubtful if one takes into account the evidence accumulated in previous chapters of this study and which will be further elaborated in the following chapters. This is not to assert, however, that they were any worse. It was to take many years after the decade between 1910 and 1920 before such a claim could reasonably be made, and even then a comparison with British child welfare would be rendered superfluous when one considers its massive intervention on behalf of its children under the welfare state. As the boarding-out method was never properly practised until almost mid-century in Canada with the child welfare departments and the CASs seeking "work" or "free" homes while British poor law guardians were using "paid" homes, the claim is doubly tentative. Alberta continued to make rural placements without much attention to supervision into the 1950s.91

Most of those who were involved simultaneously with the professionalization of child welfare and the anti-juvenile immigration lobby had little empirical evidence that Canadian standards of child care were more progressive and superior than those of Britain. While they had made such claims with regard to juvenile immigration, they were very soon after its cessation forced to confront major flaws in the domestic situation. Protests about child labor is a point in question, for the lobby flouted its abuses almost to the point of embarrassment considering the actual situation in most of the provinces regarding child employment. Writing in 1927 to Tom Moore of the Trades and Labour Congress, Whitton observed that - despite the League of Nations devoting this year to the problems of child labor - "until the Canadian Provinces can agree on common principles of adherence to these standards, we are denied any recognition of equal or higher standards even in those provinces where they do exist."92

Both Canon Vernon of the Social Service Council and Judge Helen MacGill were well aware of the dilemma at the very time they were insisting that the philanthropic societies must improve their standards regarding the apprenticeship of their wards by coming up to Canadian standards. Vernon, at the Child Labour Conference held in Winnipeg in the Fall of 1923, observed that fourteen years of age commonly seemed to be the school leaving age "at which our legislators think it is quite all right for other people's children to become wage earners or workers in their parents' farms. Few of them, I imagine, would regard it as desirable time for their own offspring to become self supporting."93

266

The age differential at the time of going out to work between Canadian children and the young Britons could scarcely have been much different. Several decades of protest did induce the British Societies to gradually raise the emigration ages, although it was not until 1924 that fourteen years became the official age. Later, in 1933, the CCCW was still working for the ratification of the Geneva and White House conventions. Not only was provincial standardization impossible to assure, but in some provinces such as New Brunswick the age and conditions of employment for children differed from city to city.94

In 1925, the Conference on Child Welfare received a report submitted by MacGill full of figures that can hardly be said to reflect the superiority of Canadian standards. In Ontario and New Brunswick, children under fifteen worked ten hours a day for sixty hours a week. In Manitoba, it was not unusual for them to put in a fourteen hour day, and in British Columbia sixty-six and a half hours a week in shops was commonplace. Almost all provinces were guilty of relaxing compulsory school laws in favor of children performing necessary household tasks or farm duties. Consequently, the following comment must be carefully weighed against any claimed superior standards (although for those whose prime interest surrounded the problem of child labor, it is reasonable that they found exploitation and abuses reprehensible for both class of child, the unaccompanied immigrant and the native born).

> Though Canada is a young country, yet
> child labour with all its sinister accom-
> paniments is already raising an ugly head
> in the Dominion. . . . We have enacted
> some legislation that looks well on books,
> and other laws that do not look so well.
> But even that which makes the best appear-
> ance in theory is frequently defeated in
> practice through the administration clauses
> or final sections making them inoperative.
> The logical conclusion therefore is that
> while idealists (using this in its highest
> and best sense) have obtained some ameliorat-
> ing legislation they have not succeeded in
> securing general public support, or persuaded
> their fellow citizens of the evils of child

labour or that the question is worthy of
serious notice.

Child welfare legislation <u>in theory</u> was admirable
but, as in the cases of the CAS and the various
child welfare departments, the practice was less
so.95

Without a doubt, the new social worker was
committed to replacing all forms of philanthropic
child rescue by modern child welfare principles. It
is in this context that their participation in a
lobby that crudely caricatured children as degenerates, and their movement as a scourge to be
eradicated can be largely, but not completely,
understood. Their reputation as "the indefatigable
social workers" preceded their efforts in the
juvenile immigration campaign as far afield as the
Colonial Office in Britain. In 1926, the Oversea
Settlement Office was discouraged with the extent of
discrediting the Barnardo girls that both "the
Toronto Hospital and Social Workers" had engaged in
by trying to prove that 125 out of the 500 unmarried
mothers who passed through their hands in a given
period were Barnardo girls. Even when a public
apology had been forced from them which reduced the
numbers to seventy-nine, Whitton and the CCCW
continued to malign the girls. W. Garnett, who
attended to matters of boy and girl settlement
schemes, observed ruefully that "Miss Whitton
persists in the error of her ways" and that he was
afraid that she had "started off with certain
preconceived ideas on this matter and the facts are
of little importance."96

This chapter has described the background to,
and the nature of, these preconceived ideas, a
background that shaped perceptions which stand
starkly at variance with the overall softening
attitudes toward child life generally and a belief
in its potential to flourish under suitable
environmental conditions. That social workers could
claim a concern for the protection of children yet
participate in an ugly campaign that denigrated
them, is cause to note again the dissonance to which
individuals and groups are prone.

Only in the context of Canadian anxiety about
parties of children bringing to its shores criminal

268

taint, promiscuity, scrofula, illegitimacy, physical defect, feeblemindedness and a general moral contagion can we come to understand the significance of the last crude expressions of such anxiety. The words of a parody of "Britons Never Shall Be Slaves," whose chorus was boisterously repeated at the 1928 annual review of the Canadian Association of Social Workers (CASW) in Toronto, demonstrate the pervasiveness and persuasiveness of a sixty year controversy.

> O there was a London urchin of feebleminded strain,
> His parents both were in the clink and he was raising cain,
> Till Poor Law Guardians got him but he drove them near insane,
> Till an Emigration Home got a subsidy for shipping him across the main.

Singing -

> Rule Britannia, Britannia rule the waves,
> For Britons never, never, never shall be -
> Made to care for their dependent poor
> If Canada will do it free.

Surely these words reflect more than solicitude toward the child life the CASW said they were protecting? They can be seen as a finale to the "sweeping, sensational, and wholly inaccurate statements and imputations" Lady Aberdeen had deplored in 1896.97

23

24

25

26

Boarding-Out in Canada: The De-Institutionalizing of Dependent Children

8

> Child Welfare! That is the beginning of
> the nation. Let us save those we have
> and see that we have a lot more . . .
> The potentialities of every child is
> something we cannot measure and we do
> not know what we lose. The foundation
> of all of it is the home. Let us have
> homes!
>
> Dr. Amyot, Deputy Minister of Health, 1923

Arguments regarding the de-institutionalization of children, the depauperization of populations, and the scientific organization of charity and child care, were not evolutionary either in articulation or implementation but ran parallel in different periods or countries. In Canada with its regional disparities, rhetoric and practice differed markedly across the country. Consequently, a variety of socio-economic and demographic conditions may have manifested similar moral imperatives but at different times. Nevertheless, at the time that Britons were debating the merits of boarding-out against the institutionalizing of dependent children, similar arguments were resounding across the Atlantic, although British North America had engaged in the institutionalizing of its dependent children much later than Britain. Not surprisingly, then, just as colonial institutional models were miniature versions of the British experience, Canadian boarding-out rhetoric quickly assimilated and echoed the sentiments found in Great Britain.

This chapter traces the initial stages of the transformation of child rescue into child welfare, a transformation which was facilitated by the commitment to boarding-out practices exemplified by

the Children's Aid Society (CAS). The interaction
between the CAS and Protestant Orphans' Homes (POH),
which represented fundamentally opposed philosophies
of child care, will be examined to understand the
tensions, contradictions, organizational imperfections, and societal constraints inhibiting the
successful implementation of the fostering paradigm
in English-Canada and to describe the transformation
of the asylum into specialized facilities for new
categories of children requiring "rescue."

A NEW PARADIGM, NEW PROBLEMS

The children's aid societies, which sprang up
in all provinces during the period 1890 to 1914,
were committed to the new paradigm of child care -
the boarding-out or fostering of dependent children
- and profuse in their praise of family homes as
"havens of rescue." Their proliferation, their
public support, their polemic, and not least of all
their legal status in having guardianship rights
under provincial children's protection acts
encroached upon the traditional spheres of child-
rescue that had evolved with the establishment of
the orphan asylum. As sympathy for the fostering
ideal became more pronounced, a dislocation of the
former centres of child-rescue support occurred just
as the legal claims of the CAS and greater provision
of child welfare legislation diminished the
attractions and credibility of the orphan asylums.1

Theoretically, the CAS model was committed to
two major substantive principles: family protection
(that is, to give care to the child in his own home
wherever practicable) and fostering where the
natural environment ceased to be safe for the child
or the community. Its sphere normally included
attendance at trials of juveniles and the provision
of shelter care during remand; investigation of
cruelty and neglect cases; reception of "uncontroll-
able" children surrendered by parents or reported by
truant officers; the approval of adoptions and
supervision of the maternity act (in Ontario); cooperation with other institutions at the provincial,
Dominion and even international levels; and finally,
home finding and fostering. The CAS could take over
children upon application, that is, through a
voluntary admission process for care only, without

transfer of guardianship; for temporary care prior to court hearing on the transfer of parental guardianship; and as "wards" through regular judicial procedure which granted legal custody to the CAS. Children placed in private homes were technically "neglected" under provincial statutes, and superintendents of departments of neglected, dependent or delinquent children, were given the same powers as if they were a CAS.

The foster homes themselves were of four types: (1) adoptive homes; (2) supervised free foster homes which provided maintenance care and received only funds for clothing and school books; (3) wage homes, usually in rural areas, which offered a contract similar to indenture at nominal wages, with some provinces restricting these to children over school age; and (4) paid boarding homes which met the needs of special cases including those with defects, speech impediments, social problems or delicate health. Since boarding parents were hired as "employees," supervision of these homes were the least difficult to maintain. Therefore, the CAS model was clearly one which, if perfectly actualized, must erode the former spheres of traditional child rescue, the orphan asylum.

The POHs of Central Canada, which had enjoyed their maximum social usefulness and largest populations in the nineteenth century, experienced in the first two decades of the twentieth century a considerable decline in numbers of inmates. The result was a series of economic crises which greatly undermined their morale. At the same time in Manitoba, however, all asylums, Catholic and Protestant alike, reached their maximum social usefulness. As Ontario with its increasing urbanization enjoyed an affluence that, though unevenly distributed, absorbed some of the former residue of acute poverty, more children of the poor remained with their families. Disease control, public health programs, vaccinations, improvements in water supply, ventilation and sanitation, resulted in conditions that produced fewer chronic cases of need due to the death of either parent just as the immigrant population was tending to bypass the province and settle in Western Canada.2

Much of nineteenth century poverty and subsequent child dependency had sprung from the needs of the immigrant working classes, a pattern that was repeated in twentieth century Manitoba. Therefore, as Kingston and Toronto POHs began seeking new ways of administrative organization and receiving new clienteles for care (temporary cases), the Winnipeg POH was growing under the burdens of migrant hardship in a turbulent and transient society. Although the later settlement of Saskatchewan and Alberta led to a different adaptation in the form of government controlled child welfare, the institutions such as the Wood's Christian Home of Calgary established in 1915 the Orange Home at Indian Head, Saskatchewan, in 1923, reflected organizational patterns that were remarkably traditional. Since George Wood had worked in the Quarrier Orphan Home at Bridge-Of-Weir, Scotland, his transference of the traditional model to Innisfail, Alberta, was not unexpected. The smallness of these institutions, however, prevented many of the negative consequences of congregate care, although the philosophy on which these homes were founded and operated had roots in a previous time.3

As the emerging CASs began to drain the formerly placeable children away from the asylums, the POHs, concerned lest the demand for their services should disappear altogether, became less discriminating in matters of admission. Probably there were no more defective children in the twentieth century than there had been in the Homes' founding decades of the mid-nineteenth century. Such children simply were not usually included among the clients of the POHs and were instead confined to the public institutions. Therefore, a problem, always present but previously muted, became more pronounced as CASs and POHs alike found themselves confronting the demands of certain "unplaceable" categories - the defective, the deformed, and the delinquent. Thus, as normal children were being de-institutionalized, arguments for new institutional arrangements such as cottage systems, industrial schools, farm colonies, and homes for the feeble-minded, flourished side by side with arguments for increasing and improving fostering methods.

In receiving government grants, the POHs compromised their selection policies as they became obliged to receive public wards especially through arrangements made with the local CAS. Congregate systems could not operate without residential members and as the previous sources of dependent children dried up, they were forced to operate as temporary shelters for the CASs. Therefore, the CAS, by using POH facilities for economic and pragmatic reasons, became a new supplier of inmates. Unfortunately, the CAS was inclined to supply the POHs with shelter or remand cases under wardship of the juvenile courts, or unplaceable children, that is, the defective, handicapped or anti-social. During these transitions, the records of POHs expressed concern about such children and contained recommendations that the publicly supported specialized institutions be used for delinquent and defective children. This is evidence that the changing clientele presented problems with which the asylum was inadequately prepared - profession- ally, financially, or philosophically - to cope.

At the same time as CASs and POHs were express- ing identical concerns about their unplaceable children, the public was becoming more informed regarding the problems of mental defect, social deviance, criminal conduct, venereal disease and feebleminded fertility, as the response to the juvenile immigrants demonstrates. One plausible explanation for this tendency toward more intense social analysis and intervention in social affairs was that alongside the practice of preventative medicine, a transformation of progressive thought occurred which sought to apply the metaphor of diagnosis and cure to the examination of social and, particularly, urban problems. Mistakenly, it was believed that identification and diagnosis of a social problem such as mental defect would lead to its cure, or better still, its ultimate prevention. New and obsessive public discussion about defect and deviance, which took up much of the attention of CASs, POHs, women's groups and child protection officers among other socially concerned citizens, was raised repeatedly in a monotonous, repetitive and unoriginal polemic.

The twentieth century, building on theoretical roots from the previous hundred years or so, saw a

277

growing consciousness regarding problems of the adult feebleminded and the defective child. This mounting general awareness and societal anxiety sometimes resulted in exaggerated and even semi-hysterical responses and new efforts to further classify and categorize people, which amounted to varying degrees of dehumanizing labelling. The POHs had not been unaware of the problem of the defective child but had been able to avoid the issue due to careful admission policies. If undetected during the screening processes, such children were easily dismissed from the institution afterwards or care-lessly placed in mental asylums such as Orillia in Ontario or reformatories such as Victoria, Mimico, or Portage la Prairie. Since the average asylum had neither the staff or expertise to treat certain physical, mental, or behavioral problems, many epileptic, retarded, handicapped, or anti-social children found themselves as the flotsam of dependent child life, abandoned to inhumane institutional care for what were often life sentences.4

Childhood criteria of separation and protection justified the abandonment of the weak and least useful members of society, who became identified as contaminating and disruptive forces in the moral economy of institutional life. Female children were particularly subjected to such a fate, being handicapped by their biologies and reproductive potential. Male children were more easily absorbed in rural life and agricultural labour where their presence elicited less comment.

At conferences of charities and correction, child saving, or mental hygiene, at public meetings, in the press, and in the newly organized psychology and sociology departments at the universities, the discourse about the defective resounded. The discourse itself reflected a morbid and vicarious fascination regarding the sexuality and reproduction of the "unfit." The discussion had far reaching consequences in the form of insidious state directed control of populations as part of the growing emphasis on "scientia sexualis" which had become urgent since the impact of the initial crude forms of psychiatry and application of eugenic theories of the nineteenth century.5

278

The language of sexual deployment was the
language of power whose moral suasion articulated
arguments for the medicalization and the eventual
psychologization of the population under state
aegis. The inventions, the recourses, the methods
and the tactics of the ideology of sexual deployment
has been best described by Michel Foucault, whose
compelling interpretative thesis is as applicable to
Canadian child saving sentiment as it is to the
patterns of charity and relief generally observed in
other Western societies.6

The preoccupation with mental defect and
feebleminded fertility, which spilled over into the
history of childhood, was part of "a science
subordinated in the main to the imperatives of a
morality whose divisions it reiterated under the
guise of the medical norm. Claiming to speak the
truth, it stirred up people's fears; to the least
oscillations of sexuality, it ascribed an imaginary
dynasty of evils destined to be passed on for
generations" and, therefore, dangerous to the whole
society. The discourse on "scientia sexualis"
established a mendacious and morbid anxiety which

> . . . set itself up as the supreme authority
> in matters of hygienic necessity, taking up
> the old fears of venereal affliction and
> combining them with the new themes of asepsis,
> and the great evolutionist myths with the
> recent institutions of public health, it
> claimed to ensure the physical vigor and
> the moral cleanliness of the social body;
> it promised to eliminate defective indivi-
> duals, degenerate and bastardized popula-
> tions. In the name of a biological and
> historical urgency, it justified the racisms
> of the state, which at the time were on the
> horizon. It ground them in 'truth.'7

Given the power of the discourse which sought
to control behaviour through the application of
sexual norms under the guise of science and
ultimately by technological means, it was no wonder
that the juvenile immigrant faced prejudices which,
although only minimally grounded in "scientific
truth," were powerfully driven by anxieties
exacerbated by such "truth." Neither is it
surprising that the CASs and POHs reflected the

power of the discourse in their concern about defective children.

The discovery or invention of the "problem" of mental defect was the outcome of the recently emerged public nature of social organization in the west itself. A society that insisted on compulsory public health standards (such as inoculation), intervened in pre- and post-natal affairs represented by well baby clinics and fresh milk campaigns, organized conscript armies where doctors could detect physical, mental, venereal defect, financed a whole system of compulsory schools with systematic examination, testing, and inspection, was a society, whose members, young and adult alike, found themselves thrust into a non-traditional visibility. The requirements for skills and literacy in an industrialized urban social system led to the detection of inadequacies and deficiencies more readily ignored in a different kind of social organization. Modern society established new norms of social acceptability, and what had been tolerable in the past was slowly assimilated into what was initially a nebulous category of defect to be feared and then contained. The criteria for inclusion as defective became hardened as the scientific viewpoint purported to identify and delineate its boundaries. What began as a vague apprehensiveness grew into a systematic application of the new criteria with a further categorization of people.

Canadians were reminded by Dr. P. H. Bryce in his 1917 address before the Conference on Charities and Correction that everyday the feebleminded "transgresses what is proper in action or manners." Vague and amorphous societal anxieties became monstrous spectres that affected child savers and orphan asylums. Like the dependent child of the nineteenth century, the defective and delinquent child of the twentieth century required specialized facilities and even new institutions. Ironically, the drive to incarcerate the deviant occurred at the time when institutionalization for "normal" children was losing its appeal.8

If the specialization of children occurred in the nineteenth century through their institutionalization, a re-specialization took place in the twentieth as more dependent children entered the mainstream of society through the fostering paradigm. However, the new paradigm placed fresh pressure on both its organizational expression, the CAS, and its antithesis, the POH, by demanding that they either absorb "unplaceable" children or provide appropriate structures for them. As a result, more categories of specialized children were created with appropriate institutional forms to receive them. The protection and segregation of the defective and the handicapped child became urgent at the very time normal dependent children were becoming increasingly assimilated into the society. While the problems of defective children began to provoke discussion and concern, the imperfections of the CAs practices promoted various other problems.

From the beginning of their history, many CASs deflected their energies and efforts, not to mention their funds, by involving themselves in an inordinate variety of "causes" including the support of a "dumb animal department" in the Stratford, Perth County and St. Mary's society. Already overburdened by the hundreds of cases of real neglect or cruelty requiring protection and separation from morally corrupting influences or degraded physical conditions - those cases with which we are so familiar today such as sadism, incest, insanity, alcoholism, abuse or exploitation - the CASs took children into custody for numerous trite reasons. Sometimes acting as a "warning," sometimes acting as a temporary punitive measure, sometimes acting in collusion with frustrated parents unable to control their children, and sometimes acting as a pious watchdog over parental morals or children's manners, CAS volunteers, juvenile courts, and fragile organizational child care structures groaned under excessive case loads.9

Trespassing on railroad tracks, spitting on pavements, shooting pigeons, stealing "brass from the CNR," selling newspapers, riding bicycles on sidewalks, drawing graffiti on alley walls, obstructing public places, bathing in streams, and playing ball on streets were all activities from which children apparently required protection. Sometimes these were, incongruously, taken almost as seriously as destitution, degradation and neglect.

The fact that CASs specifically received government funds for the delinquent cases contributed substantially to such an imbalance. The proviso that a child could be taken into custody if his circumstances were judged as presenting a danger to the community made such indiscriminate custody possible.10

Without justifying the indifference or incompetence of British emigration societies with regard to the supervision and placement of their children, it is nevertheless essential to recognize that if their Canadian counterparts had fewer problems given the domestic nature of their enterprise and the indigenous character of their children, the inadequacies of such agencies were all the more glaring. The negligence of their inspection, the arbitrariness of their pre-placement investigation, the absence of efficient record keeping, the loosely controlled responsibilities of guardianship, the underfinanced and rude shelter facilities, the lack of family and case histories, are all common denominators in child care at both the institutional and the CAS levels in the first three decades of the century. In some cases, such as Alberta and New Brunswick in particular, no less could be said regarding provincial inadequacies into the 1950s. The British child rescue societies may have been more constrained to provide minimally satisfactory services and apply minimal investigative placement and post-placement procedures than their Canadian counterparts if for no other reason than that they responded to the scrutiny and criticism they received from hostile child care workers and government inspectors.

A cursory glance at the CAS model for the appropriate period of the juvenile immigration movement, that is, from 1891 when the first CAS was founded in Toronto to 1930 when the movement had virtually ceased, will illustrate that boarding-out principles were imperfectly understood and minimally practised in Canada. Even as Whitton, the Canadian Council on Child Welfare, and other child welfare groups were decrying British abuses in Canada, they were being forced to contend with similar abuses in the provinces. Since the protests against juvenile immigration can only be understood in light of this overall concern, it necessary to examine what was actually the case regarding CAS work and foster care, and not accept their public statements about the efficacy of their own work.

It would, of course, be unjust to assess the effectiveness of the CAS model by stressing only their first decades as the societies struggled into existence. During this time in some centres such as Ottawa, police officers detained children, and girls from the Hamilton society were placed out as "servants" in large families because the majority of applicants for their services did not understand the differences between a CAS or a POH and a cheap labor bureau. Ironically, the Reverend Wallace, who superintended the Marchmont Distributing and Receiving Home which placed British immigrant apprentices for Lilian Birt of the Liverpool Sheltering Home, was also the president of the Belleville CAS. That his perceptions of the role of the CAS were somewhat confounded by this dual role can be seen in his observation that since there were always "ten times as many homes" for children as there were in Marchmont the placement of CAS wards should present no difficulty.11

At the turn of the century, the Owen Sound CAS was not exceptional in the number of cases it took into wardship for "truancy" solely because of the lack of accommodation in the schools. The policing of school attendance in the first years of most societies was their most onerous task. The CASs were also forced to spend considerable effort in the supervision of the school attendance of their own wards, for the public, accustomed to circumventing the attendance laws in the case of British or POH children, were adept at doing the same with CAS wards.12

The softness of procedure that is evident in the Brockville CAS until the first world war cannot have been unique. Most outgoing letters "hoped" that their wards, placed in country homes, were attending school, and were most obliging indeed in providing over school-age girls as domestic help to applicants who were anxious to avoid having a younger and more useless child. When the secretary wrote to Robert Lathans in 1913 asking "if Leonard is still with you, if not, kindly let me know where he is at present [because] I am anxious to keep in touch with him," this was scarcely an exceptional piece of correspondence.13

However, no matter how tolerant one might be of the first decades of the CAS, that is, from 1893 to 1914, it is more difficult to maintain such impartiality when one examines the results of Canadian Council on Child Welfare surveys conducted in New Brunswick, various centres of Ontario, British Columbia, Nova Scotia, as well as commissions of inquiry in Manitoba and Alberta from 1927 to 1947. Uniformly the CASs in these surveys were identified as weak links in the realization of professional and "scientific" child care.14

The CAS arrangements in Winnipeg and Manitoba as a whole were far from satisfactory and received scathing condemnation by Charlotte Whitton when she was invited in 1928 to make a study of child welfare in the province for a Royal Commission that led to the reorganization of social services. The first major criticisms of CAS conditions had been heard over a decade earlier when the Manitoba Free Press, 20 November 1915, reported deplorable shelter facilities and inadequate dietaries. Incidentally, such disclosures must have given the committee of the Children's Home some small satisfaction because of the criticism to which it had been subjected. The 1912 Children's Protection Act had granted powers of wardship to the Superintendent of Neglected and Dependent Children, Mr. Billiarde. who required the Home to receive CAS cases into temporary custody if it were to continue to receive government aid.15

The CAS model in Manitoba constituted the oldest protection agency of its kind in Western Canada with its inception under the child protection legislation of 1898; however, age and size (the Winnipeg CAS was one of the largest in the country) had assured neither strength nor efficiency. It was not until the 1928 Royal Commission of Inquiry was called to examine allegations made in the Manitoba legislature against the Department of Health and Public Welfare that child protection became scientifically organized in that province. Even then the recommendations of the Commission report were not always implemented, and the economic restraints caused by the depression years slowed the process considerably. Neither the Department of Health and Public Welfare nor the CASs at Brandon, Dauphin, St. Adelard, and the Catholic CAS and CAS of Winnipeg could boast of using any particular system of fostering. Admittedly, few children were kept in their shelters although this was not due to an emphasis on fostering but because most dependent children who could not be placed on farms were institutionalized in the many congregate systems of the province where facilities were utilized as shelters.

Whitton observed that since "foster home finding, boarding home placements, and foster home inspections, are all in a semi-organized state, that makes it impossible for the Division to say what children are or are not wards, and where they are." Although she preferred the CAS to be a local unit of a decentralized child welfare administration as in British Columbia, Ontario, Nova Scotia, New Brunswick, and Prince Edward Island, she worked pragmatically within the confines of the Manitoba situation with its highly codified child protection legislation and emphasis on the centralization of welfare provision. The Manitoba model was imitated to a greater and lesser degree in Alberta and Saskatchewan.16

Whitton's report to the Commission insisted that at both the departmental and the CAS level, the "serious and blameworthy lack of efficiency and organization" of foster care could be partially rectified by the introduction of a record system, a centralized registry for adoptions, more personal investigation of foster and adoptive homes (including a probationary period for the latter) and a generous injection of government funding. At the same time as she was exposed to what often amounted to deplorable child care conditions while serving on the Manitoba Commission, Whitton was busily investigating the Barnardo placements occurring out of Winnipeg and publicly denouncing the inadequacies of the emigration societies at the conferences on juvenile immigration held during 1928-1930 in Ottawa.17

Too often, the relatively smooth functioning of the Toronto CAS, the largest and oldest Canadian

children's aid society, after its reorganization in
the 1920s was used as the exemplar of the CAS model
in Canada with the assumption that a majority of
CASs elsewhere in Ontario operated similarly.
Nothing could be further from the truth, and
considering the numerous exceptions, it must be
concluded that the CASs remained largely
ineffectual, under financed, non-professionally
staffed, indifferently supported by public, and
poorly funded by governments. Lack of salaried
officers or poorly salaried full-time staff led to
constant change-over of personnel and superintendence. The spirit of the CAS model and the good
intentions of its supporters are not in question,
but the mere existence of an agency did not assure
its effectiveness.

The purposes of a CAS may have accorded with
the spirit and letter of relevant child protection
acts or statutes, but the practices generally were
different. For instance, the great majority of CASs
did not provide a shelter for their wards and were
operated by volunteers. Even where paid agents were
used as in Ontario, their offensively low salaries
tell us again just where dependent child life fitted
into government policy and public aspirations. It
is not difficult to comprehend the limitations of
such input and involvement from the active clergy
and the public spirited or philanthropic citizens
that served on CAS committees.

Saskatchewan and Alberta both began an
embryonic system of CASs after the declaration of
their respective Children's Protection Acts in 1909
but within a dozen or so years the CAS in these two
provinces was virtually defunct. In Saskatchewan
between 1909 and 1911, fourteen centres had
societies but by 1917 Judge Ethel MacLachlan of the
juvenile court reported only four survived - in
Regina, Saskatoon, Moose Jaw and Swift Current, none
of which had paid agents. Moreover, existing
institutions were used for "transition" cases, and,
although public welfare departments in these prairie
provinces were responsible for dependent children,
boys were placed with farmers in no different a
manner to that criticized by the proponents of
scientific child care campaigning against the
British societies.18

Despite the legal provisos in the various provincial children's acts that the CAS maintain a shelter, the use of existing facilities for CAS cases was commonplace. The failure to provide shelters was often justified on the grounds of duplication of services; however, it was more to the point that existing institutions were a cheaper means of caring for those children who had been made state wards under the care of a CAS. Furthermore, as city and provincial governments gave at least minimal grants to both the CAS and the children's institutions, they did not see the necessity for building and maintaining another shelter when ones were already available. A Toronto CAS report feared that "mail order" placements were the order of the day merely to get children out of the shelter.19

London, Ottawa, Toronto, Kingston and Hamilton Homes all served as a CAS shelter for the overflow if there was an actual shelter, or for CAS "unplace-ables" as did the POHs in Manitoba and Prince Edward Island. The POHs themselves were somewhat reluctant to indiscriminately open their doors to CAS children and transient cases, but constant penury and government pressure constrained them to relent. Consequently, those very societies that argued for the de-institutionalization of children through fostering practices and under quasi-government CAS provisions were in effect aiding in the maintenance and perpetuation of the same congregate institutions they so energetically deplored.

Just as many governments reflected an indifference to the moral imperatives behind their children's acts by not financing CAS shelters, or by inadequately supporting the CASs, or by not insisting on full-time and salaried agents, neither were they reluctant in overloading the societies with tasks that should have been performed by new government bureaus. For example, in addition to chronic overdrafts as a result of a dependence on voluntary subscriptions as well as insufficient and unqualified staff, many societies were required to handle the administrative apparatus involved in the unmarried parenthood and adoption clauses where operative. Admittedly, to prove their viability, if not indispensability, the societies were far too anxious to take upon themselves such additional loads which they could not under the circumstances possibly execute effectively. If the societies believed that either an increase in manpower or funds would follow, they were often mistaken.

The Ontario CASs, like the new class of social worker generally, wanted to extend their professional influence and expand their social functions. Not unexpectedly, most CASs were opposed to the proposals of 1923 that a Minister of Child or Public welfare be appointed to coordinate the Children's Protection Act, and the legislation which covered Apprentices and Minors, Children of Unmarried Parenthood, Legitimation, Industrial Schools, or the Hospital and Charitable Institutions. Not unnaturally, the least enthusiastic about this suggestion was Kelso because the department would also take over many of his responsibilities. Nevertheless, on 7 May 1924, a Deputy Minister of Social Welfare was appointed.[20]

In British Columbia, neither Victoria nor Vancouver were examples of efficient CAS work. The 1927 survey of B.C. children's services and social agencies conducted by the CCCW and its counterpart in Victoria five years later illustrate the point. Both the CASs of Vancouver and Victoria were run as if they were orphanages. In Vancouver, 180 children were under care with only nine in boarding homes and "an unknown number in free family homes." The facilities could not cope with such numbers, but the survey could offer little sympathy for requests regarding an expansion of the plan when CAS policy customarily stressed fostering as the replacement of congregate systems. The survey team compared this society with the Toronto CAS which at the same time had 1,050 children in care but only forty-five were temporarily in its shelter. Vancouver's supervision of placements was described as "almost negligible," with case records absent and pre-placement investigation and control of placements "a grave matter." As if this indictment were not damning enough, the report noted too that most placements were not visited and many children's whereabouts were unknown.[21]

From its incorporation by fourteen Victoria women the capital city's Society, although smaller, operated similarly. Sarah Hayward, whose family was socially prominant and involved in the POH, was included on the original act of incorporation of the CAS under the British Columbia Children's Act of 1901, and Charles Hayward continued as its president for many years. Although it had no home for the first nine years, children were fostered or placed under wardship of the society in the provincial industrial schools. Although in 1912, two thousand invitations to attend a lecture given by J. J. Kelso were sent out accompanied by an appeal for funds, by 1917 the Home, which changed locations on several occasions, was in grave financial difficulties and suffered under recommendations submitted by a committee of retrenchment. At that time, all children including those attending the day nursery conducted in the CAS buildings were transferred to the Detention Home for Delinquents, which further confused the categories and needs of dependent and delinquent children. As with the Vancouver CAS, the Victoria one was subjected to harsh criticisms regarding management and accused of extravagant and profligate use of funds by receiving other than Victoria's children. It was not until the home on Pandora Street was finally condemned by the fire department in 1930 that policies of fostering were seriously contemplated.22

The Victoria CAS Home, while operating on a shoestring budget, managed under a matron of many years, Miss McCloy, to exude a warmth and homeliness absent from the larger institution; however, were it not designated as a CAS, little in the minutes and reports would have suggested that it was not a small and traditional orphanage. The Home in 1931 had only two toilets and bare washrooms with only one handbasin for three dozen or so inmates. Sleeping quarters were outmoded and overcrowded, and the babies shared the nurse's bedroom. The secretary assumed duties of a probation and apprehending officer until these positions were separated in 1918. A female police officer was appointed as probation officer in this year, an event which caused some consternation in the CAS committee, but Mrs. Clayards remained in the position for the next decade. Not surprisingly the probation officer was frequently called into homes to give wayward children "a scare."

The case histories of the children in the CAS Home were a curious mixture of sordid family life, personal tragedy, and triviality, as in the cases of William Cross, who in February 1911 was remanded before the juvenile court for riding his bicycle on the sidewalk, or boys reported by the probation officer for having bought "cigars." Adoptions remained as loosely governed in this particular CAS as in any of the POHs. In 1915, a couple was merely sent to visit a mother wishing to surrender her six month infant. In this instance, all parties concerned came to an amicable arrangement of "legal" adoption for a fee of $2.50. In the same year, advertisements for babies for adoption were put into the city newspapers. On several occasions "real parents" were known to "kidnap" their children from the home or on their way to school if they had been fostered.

In Nova Scotia too, the CAS hardly practised the scientific principles it advocated. The CAS movement got underway in 1905 after the Halifax Local Council of Women invited J. J. Kelso to advise them and publicize the cause. Ernest H. Blois was on the original committee representing the Industrial School of which he was superintendent. His energetic involvement subsequently gained him the superintendency of the Neglected and Dependent Children's department in 1912. The 1906 Children's Act, which incorporated the CAS, stipulated the provision of temporary shelter for boys under fourteen and girls under sixteen as well as "indenture" into free homes. By 1914, the Society for the Protection of Cruelty to Animals, which had always been involved in child protection in Halifax, was granted the powers of a CAS in towns without one. It was not until 1927 that the CASs met at a conference to consider ways and means of having full-time and paid agents.23

Meanwhile in New Brunswick, the 1919 Children's Act, which did not lead to CASs being set up at all, was implemented even partially only in Moncton and Saint John. Societies, however, were organized despite this impediment. In 1930, Professor Kierstead of the University of New Brunswick was forced to admit that not only did the Fredericton CAS operate as a Home but it also accepted surrendered children whose parents paid $2 to $3 weekly. While there was no juvenile court in operation, "incorrigibles" were sent to the Maritime

Home for Girls in Truro, Nova Scotia, or to the New
Brunswick Industrial School for Boys in Saint John
under the auspices of the CAS, which was somewhat
extraordinary as the society had no actual guardianship rights to do so.24

After the British Columbia survey, New
Brunswick was subjected to a vigorous CCCW survey in
1928-29 that condemned its child care system on the
whole as well as criticizing the government's
cavalier attitude towards its faltering CASs.
Subsequent surveys between 1930 and 1949 continued
to describe the CASs in that province as having ill
defined functions, inadequate funding and staffing,
and rudimentary shelter care. In New Brunswick, not
even its provincial welfare programs overcame the
diffusion and the deficiencies of child care,
investigation, placement or case work as was the
case with the prairie provinces which evolved a
governmental centralization of services. Instead,
New Brunswick clung tenaciously to its ill managed
poor law model.25

In the 1920s, the Charlottetown CAS was not
given wardship payments by government, and the St.
Vincent's and the Orange Order orphanages, which had
agreed to receive CAS wards, were expected to pay
for their subsistence. Since the CAS officer in
Charlottetown had a joint salaried appointment with
the School Board as truant officer, it is not
surprising that the CAS files disproportionately
recorded truancy cases, which suggests that to
maintain his salaried position with the school board
the officer devoted more time to apprehending
children than to CAS work. Both the Charlottetown
and Summerside CASs rarely knew the exact number,
status and whereabouts of wards and supervision of
placements, homefinding, and investigation of foster
parents were not evident.26

Since its inception in 1909, the Charlottetown
CAS had always operated more as a punitive agency
which engaged in few or no efforts at fostering.
Older children under the delinquents' clauses of the
Children's Act implemented in 1910, were placed in
free country homes which secured the labor for which
farmers would otherwise have to pay. In 1918, the
CAS protested that police officers "humiliated" boys
by "arresting" them before their classmates at

school if they were suspected of delinquent acts. In turn, the police department claimed that CAS efforts to implement curfew by-laws and laws prohibiting unaccompanied children in pool rooms and movie theatres increased police work. In that year, the police adamantly refused to apprehend juvenile thieves, claiming that sentimental interference on the part of the CAS meant the Society was loathe to punish children by sending them to the farm school at Sherbourne, Quebec, the Montreal Reform School, or the Maritime Home for Girls.27

Lest one is tempted to dismiss Prince Edward Island as irrelevant to the argument, the nation's capital demonstrates that not all was well in Ontario either. In a 1929 CCCW survey of social agencies in Ottawa, Whitton was relentless in her condemnation of the CAS's practices and facilities in her own city. The detention home and the location of the juvenile court in the police building were described as being "quite contrary to the spirit and purpose of the Juvenile Delinquents Act." The CAS made little attempt to separate neglected from delinquent children.28

At the same time, in Ottawa as in Manitoba and New Brunswick, much of the chaos in the CAS structure was exacerbated by tensions and debates over the handling of children from the various factions of the Anglophone and Francophone communities and the Protestant and Roman Catholic interests of both. Nevertheless, even taking these problems into account, the management of the Ottawa CAS was, as Thelma Williams of the Welfare Bureau observed to Whitton in 1929, "unprofessional." The same comment could have been made of any number of Ontarian Societies at the same time.29

Roman Catholic CASs had come into existence in Ottawa and in Vancouver because of accusations of the proselytization of Catholic children by societies over-represented by Protestant sympathies. In the first decade of the century, Father Madden of the Vancouver Roman Catholic CAS protested to W. L. Scott, the architect of the 1908 Juvenile Delinquents Act, on whom he could depend to give accurate legal advice to Catholic groups. He claimed that the president of the CAS, Mr. South ("an Orangeman," of some influence because he was also Superintendent of Neglected Children under the Children's Protection Act of British Columbia) was arbitrarily placing children in Protestant homes and deliberately withholding their rights to religious instruction. Father Madden protested that in a city like Vancouver where the Catholic population was a minority, the only thing to do with "a man who considers defenceless children legitimate subjects for proseltyzing" was to "fight him," and when he was thoroughly beaten he would become "as accommodating as the Barnardo folks." Scott agreed with the reports of Mr. South's activities and wrote to Kelso of his reservations about this man's suitability for his joint appointment stating that Mr. South was "more bent on proseltyzing or on fighting generally those whom he considers his opponents than on furthering child rescue work." Mr. South and his supporters provoked sectarian feelings in Vancouver that were to obstruct positive improvements taking place in policies and structures of the CAS.30

In Ottawa, Scott faced a similar problem when Archbishop Brunet accused the CAS of similar prejudicial placing and policy. In this case, however, such blatant abuses of principle were less likely than in the Vancouver case because Scott, a prominent Catholic and influential CAS member, was a champion of rights of Catholic children at several levels including industrial training schools, separate schooling, CAS representation and legislation.31

The assumption that, as with other aspects of Canadian life, all good things came out of Ontario and that where other provinces failed, it did not, cannot be substantiated in the CAS case. CAS principles were articulated forthrightly by Ontarian child care workers especially after 1912 with the formation of an Association of CASs with Scott as President, and Kelso as honorary president. Although Toronto was held up as a standing reproach to the tardiness or incompetence of the other provinces, and although Ontarian professionals represented it at child welfare conferences as a model worthy of imitation, the truth of the matter was that Ontarian CASs also left much to be desired. The most fervent advocates of the CAS system of child care (among whom we must include Scott and Whitton) found much to be critical of regarding fostering and inspection procedures of the best managed societies.32

While publicly defending the model's potential if operated with generous public support and government funding, the consistent anxiety about the actual practices tells us that all was not well. CASs remained inefficient child welfare mechanisms up until mid-twentieth century, after which their effectiveness is less easily assessed as greater government centralization of welfare services at both the federal and provincial levels finally assumed many of their functions and subsequently lessened their significance.

After 1923, when Robert E. Mills took over as director of what was described later by Whitton as a "venerable but disintegrating private agency," there were some advances made in the structural and personnel features of the Toronto CAS. Kelso's condemnation in 1915 indicates that the shelter on Simcoe Street was used as if it were an institution, with home finding at a stand-still (indeed if it had ever begun) and delinquent, dependent, and defective children ranging from eight to sixteen years were mixed together and housed in scandalous conditions. Boys taken into custody found themselves locked in a basement room sometimes for a week or more.33

It was on the Board of Mangement of the Toronto CAS in the early twenties that Mills and Whitton first became colleagues and loyal confidants. She was an enthusiastic neophyte in child welfare representing the Social Service Council, while he had been involved in child care aspects of the Department of Health. In what was to become a pattern of cooperation for the ensuring three decades, they prepared a report on a scheme for farm placements for juvenile delinquent boys after Judge Mott had raised the possibilities of such a program which he believed would keep them in the country away "from the allurements and temptations of the city." At the same time, CAS girls were still being put out to service.34

Because of the close liaison which was forged between these two reformers in Canadian child reform work and which did not lessen after they went their separate ways, she to the CCCW and Ottawa, and he to be director of the Toronto agency, the constant reiteration in Whitton's reports and addresses about the astonishing recovery of the Toronto's CAS and its use as a exemplar for CASs across the country, must be viewed cautiously. Whitton was both a formidable foe and a very loyal friend.

If the Toronto CAS transformed into the shining example it was held up to be after Mills' succession to its leadership, such a metamorphosis was truly miraculous given the deficiencies he took over. Although the matter of home finding always was of great concern to Mills, who even represented its cause on the League of Nations Child Placement Committee from 1937 to 1939, he was not overly concerned about "the artificial distinctions between cases of delinquency and dependency" nor the multiplicity of functions allowed the Ontario CASs under the Children's Protection Act. Indeed, he welcomed these functions as a means of extending CAS influence and powers.35

In a pamphlet on child placing in 1925, Mills praised the virtues of the Canadian CAS model over the American one by noting that unlike its southern neighbor, the distinctions between the two categories, delinquent and dependent, were not legally defined. A 1931 survey of the Hamilton CAS, which included Mills as an advisor, pointed to such a lack of distinction. In this instance, the Society took on all juvenile court probation cases, subsequently using funds from private philanthropic sources on what were technically legal and government cases. The police wagon brought all children to the Hamilton shelter where they were virtually "incarcerated" in "unattractive quarters without recreation, education and inadequate sanitation."36

At Mills' retirement in 1947, the CAS had grown in almost twenty-five years from a staff of three under a superintendent to a staff of eighty-eight, with forty-seven of these involved in field work, under a director who managed an annual budget of $700,000 for over 5,000 cases. Mills, however, spent the first decade following his appointment as superintendent in 1923 in overhauling the basic organizational mechanisms of the society and

295

generally attempting to put into practice some small measure of boarding-out preachments. Replacing J. K. Macdonald, who had been the president of the CAS since 1892, Mills found his first problem was how to adequately process and investigate 700 Toronto wards under the care of only two workers while the CAS had only three filed workers for family and case work in a city of 550,000 persons. He developed a family work department under the direction of Miss Nora Lea, initiated an index and record keeping system with case histories, a child placement department, and for the first time boarded-out older children, some of whom had been in the shelter for two to six years. Between 1926-28 he had encouraged a 109% increase in placements.37

Unable to obtain provincial support for other than government wards under the provisions of the Juvenile Delinquents Act and Child Protection Acts, and depending on city support and public funds for home finding, preventative and non-ward work, Mills told the founding meeting of the Welland CAS that not only were shelters a "menace" because of the effort put into financing them but because of the temptation for making children wards unnecessarily. Shelters were also a menace because children were being admitted too readily so that the investment would "pay off" or so that the appeal for funding could be justified by numbers in the shelters. Children becoming wards unnecessarily was the result of funds not being available from the municipality for non-wards, although government monies could be obtained under a court order. Mills bitterly observed that "from the beginning Ontario has organized its child caring work 'on the cheap,'" and that even the passing of the 1893 Children's Act was finally approved only after the government had been convinced that its implementation would not cost much. Moreover, adoption was used only when it was obvious that it would cheapen a CAS's work, and home finding was stressed only after it was proved to be more economical.38

Mills also noted that CAS placing out practices (dignified by the new name of "fostering") still forced boys and girls into the two forms of service customarily apportioned them, despite individual aptitude or preference, thereby "breaking them into conformity." He repeatedly emphasized that

Ontario's chief claim to leadership in dependent child care was based on a policy of "cheapness." Thus, it seems that while the placing out of dependent children from POHs into household or rural life was viewed as archaic, there was no fundamental difference between these practices and the new "scientific" ones the CAS represented, although the latter's emphasis on "keeping families together" and that "natural children ought to have natural homes" suggested a new policy and philosophy.39

Obviously, Mills did not approve of placements that continued to "break" dependent children and state wards into conformity, but in almost ten years under his direction, the Toronto Society was apparently unable to alter the existing arrangements. Indeed, the term "free" homes suggests that the dependent children of previous generations came out of the equivalent foster homes better off - for even minimal payments into trust with POHs under ludicrous indenture agreements placed into the context of Apprentices' Acts rather than under Children's Protection Acts was surely better than no payment at all. The tendency for Societies to operate antithetically to their preachments regarding family break up and the keeping of children within their own homes can be understood in light of the fact that full wards aided the financial situation of a CAS because it received full overhead costs for them as shelter cases. If shelter care was brief and placement quickly facilitated, such money could be used as carry over.

The most common denominator in child welfare work, whether performed by CASs or by provincial departments, was, as Mills quite accurately observed, the policy of cheapness. The few and somewhat abortive attempts at establishing effective group homes or cottage systems all faltered because of financial restrictions. The 1923 Child Welfare Conference in Winnipeg passed a motion which expressed impatience with institutional child care.

> Be it resolved that this conference urge
> its members to use their influence as widely
> as may be against the establishment or
> continuance of congregate institutions, and
> in those cases where it is naturally impos-
> sible to place all charges in foster homes

297

or private boarding homes, members of this conference be urged to use their influence in favour of an institution which will approximate as closely as possible the normal home, preferably by means of the adoption of the cottage system.40

It was the defective and delinquent unplaceables who enjoyed the dubious benefits of the various "cottage systems" that sprang up during the following decades.

Dubious, because by all accounts, the cottages barely resembled cosy little dwellings at all, but rather had all the familiar marks of institutional dreariness and parsimony. The Maritime Home for Girls at Truro is an example of such a system and consisted of several large stone buildings with thirty to forty inmates each, and the Girls' Cottage Industrial School at Sweetsburg, Quebec, retained dormitories for these English speaking girls who were mostly "low mental types with highly developed emotional tendencies." A "cottage" for seventy-five girls, it was argued in a report for 1923, permitted "a normal life," made for "a normal atmosphere" and could not but help "to normalize any girl" - even it seems, sexually active low mental types. If institutional care had proved itself costly, then the costs of ideal cottage systems were far more prohibitive. Foster care, as with boarding-out, had great weight in English-Canada, not only because of its humane principles, but because these were rather too conveniently supported by economic justifications.41

KELSO - HELP OR HINDRANCE?

The first forty years of Ontario's CAS work and child welfare coordination was subjected to a constraint that cannot be overlooked. J. J. Kelso's administrative abilities and socio-political vision while provincial Superintendent of Neglected Children from 1893 until 1934 did little to improve structures, enhance public policy, or strengthen personnel and fiscal arrangements. Believing as he did that government's role in social welfare was "to legislate and supervise but not to operate," Kelso's support of government control over child care, and particularly in relation to the CASs, was always lukewarm. In 1915 it was apparent that he was difficult about increasing the responsibilities and salaries of paid agents, a position which estranged him from his own department and provincial child care workers. Kelso was a child saver more in the old mode of personalism, sentimentality, and spontaneous charity and less in the emerging one of organization, method, and the application of scientific or professional principles.42

Able to organize fresh air funds and playground associations and talk effusively to charitable groups as well as give cautionary advice and psychological support to boys in reformatories, Kelso was less in touch with the shifts towards professionalization. His work with the Pentaguishine Reformatory in 1904 and the manner in which he found situations for delinquent lads was commendable, but these ill-disciplined enthusiasms were not the prerequisites that were essential to his task as head of a government department. The organization of a growing network of CASs and other child care agencies, the superintendence of institutions, record keeping, the management of unmarried parenthood act provisions, and keeping track of funds covering a multitude of services were a far cry from crusading for curfews, improving conditions in industrial schools, licencing newsboys and girl peddlers, or organizing children's visiting committees - activities he had pursued in the late 1880s and early 1890s while an energetic young newspaper reporter.43

His emotional response to unprotected child life was a genuine one that came out of a background which lent itself to the "romance" of child saving. The excesses of his sentimentality can be seen in his 1910 pamphlet that spoke of "true charity" as "love with discernment." Although operating within the emerging framework of charity organization principles and adhering technically to the "progressive" ideas of child care, Kelso was temperamentally and emotionally more of a sentimentalist than a progressive, a situation that caused a great deal of ambivalence and anxiety in his perceptions of his own leadership and worth and of the contribution of others.

Helen R. Y. Reid might have been describing Kelso's characteristics when she delivered an address on "Volunteer Values" before the 1927 Canadian Conference on Social Work. She analyzed the motives of "traditionalists" and "sentimentalists" and compared their usefulness to child care with that of the professionals. While traditionalist was synonymous with "obstructionist," professional was synonymous with "thinker." Kelso, however, cannot be included among the traditionalists who manifested a "let well enough alone" point of view, which induced them to cling to anachronistic practices and attitudes "not because of the treasure that was part of their past but because of their ignorance, their lack of initiative, and their fear of the unknown." Had Kelso been one of these, he would never have become involved in the 1880s and 1890s in organizing child protection services at all, nor involved in 1891 in the founding of the Toronto CAS. No, Kelso belonged to the second category - the sentimentalists - who "with little habit of thought . . . were emotionally quick and ready at the first heart rending appeal to respond with a cry of 'for God's sake why don't we do something.'"44

There is no need to resort to sophisticated and convoluted psychological or personality theories to support claims regarding Kelso's low self-image. The records he left behind testify to them. So much of the laudatory comment regarding his work, the introduction of child care innovations he claimed to have initiated, and the analyses of his historical significance were written by himself in a poignant attempt to win recognition for his work and respect from his colleagues and the public. The former cash boy for Timothy Eaton's in 1876 was, in effect, out of his depth some four decades later. Moreover, Kelso was fully cognizant of the embarrassment he caused some of the social work professionalizers because of his mixture of sentiment, traditionalism, and in some opinions, even obstructionism. With untypical irony, on the eve of his retirement, he wrote to Whitton, who along with W. L. Scott, was one of his firmest critics, that he was not unaware of her attitudes towards him and his work.

You know I thought for a time that you were like the little girl who spent a year at

300

the Social Service class and remarked to a friend, 'Isn't it too bad that Mr. Kelso is not a trained worker for he is such a nice man.'45

It would be easy for us in the late twentieth century to caricature Kelso. Indeed, it was easy to do so in his own time as the satirical and mocking articles in Toronto newspapers, Life, 26 May 1886, and The Globe, 11 December 1890, so cleverly did. But to reduce someone who was a representative of a particular philanthropic mode and a peculiar Victorian mentality as well as a product of his own social circumstances to a "Motley Fool," as the press did, is to trivialize history. The following extract which was included in his autobiographic files indicates the problem. He prefaced these comments with the view that he "was given a vision of social reform far ahead of his time" and that "the object of this publication is to trace present day social advances back to their source."

With an early realization of the many social reforms that were needed and with a keen determination to accomplish the seemingly impossible, Mr. Kelso set aside every other interest, sacrificing leisure, personal comfort, friendships, financial opportunities, everything in fact that might in any way distract attention from the main purpose of his life. Even his nearest and dearest scarcely knew him, so completely was he absorbed in the great work he had undertaken. Quietly and secretly, consulting no one, he achieved one success after another and few indeed were those who knew just where the energy was coming from. Working strenuously for juvenile courts, for playgrounds, for financial aid for widowed mothers, for social settlements, for university training in social service, for better housing, better wages, for shorter hours of labour, for fairer distribution of the world's wealth, for intellectual treatment of the unwed mother, for family life for every dependent child, for a hundred other minor reforms, he strove night and day, without recognition, without appreciation,

301

without adequate recompense, gladly giving
his all for the public good, conscious that
he was fulfilling the sacred obligation that
was imposed upon him.46

Yet this was the same man who had been
described by Scott as "not competent" to present a
paper before a prison congress in Baltimore, and in
1924 by Mr. Wright, the president of the Stratford
CAS, as "having very little executive ability" at
either the organizing or administrative levels.
Round about the same time, the Association of CASs
in Ontario felt that his duties should be largely
subsumed under the proposed minister of public
welfare which suggested some lack of confidence in
his abilities. A year before, the law clerk of
Public Bills in Ontario, Allan M. Dymond, said that
Kelso had "allowed the management of his office to
slip out of his hands." In 1922, Whitton cautioned
Judge Ethel MacLachlan of Regina to dissuade western
delegates to the Canadian Association of Child
Protection Officers from nominating Kelso to the
executive because it "would hurt the prestige of the
group in Ontario." Kelso himself wrote in a
notebook that on "looking back over fifty years of
earnest toil I can now plainly recognize that as a
lad God set me apart for a Great Work - His message
for a new era of child welfare."47

In 1934 after retirement, Kelso concluded
bitterly and regretfully:

Throughout my long civil service career
I met chiefly with coldness and indifference from those in authority. Anything
accomplished was the result of sheer driving
force and without the backing and encouragement that might naturally be expected . . .
First of all there was the natural dislike
of reforms or innovations, the opposition of
other officials to undue activity, the general
rule in official circles that individual option
or prominance should be suppressd, the whisper-
ing of useless busybodies, the unwillingness to
incur unusual expense.48

Of all these comments, the one that was based on
hard and objective reality was the last - "the
unwillingness to incure unusual expense."

It is suspected that Kelso's diffidence about facilitating professionalization and state interventionest policies emerged from an early realization of his own administrative limitations to carry out the details. His loyalties to his co-workers, whose abilities were often minimal at the same time as their positions were tenuous, made it difficult for him to make sound judgements about social and child care work. For example, when Scott inquired in 1922 about the secretary of the Ottawa CAS regarding the efficiency of his returns and reports to Kelso's office, the superintendent replied:

> It would be rather embarrassing for me to say anything about my friend, Mr. Keane, whom I have known now for over thirty years . . . Of course there has been more or less delay right along in getting replies but I attributed this to the many duties resting on Mr. Keane and the fact that with advancing years it has been rather hard just to keep everything up to the highest point of efficiency. You will, I am sure, appreciate my feeling when I say that Ottawa has no worthier citizen, and should make Mr. Keane's last days comfortable.

To which Scott righteously exclaimed:

> It is your view that the work of saving children should be according to personal considerations? I would not have the future of one child sacrificed or even jeopardized for any personal considerations whatever, however worthy of esteem the person in question might be.49

There can be no question that Kelso either willfully "jeopardized" or "sacrificed" children, but as a consistently soft hearted child saver, a loyal and partial colleague, and a very humane man, he lacked the political acumen, the spirit of the crusading professionalizer, or the tough pragmatism that the position required. On several occasions, there was a good deal of talk about his replacement, but this was never affected until his retirement in 1934, and by then the economic depression had set in with its societal dislocations diverting attention

303

to large scale relief programs and intense economic
anxiety.

The CAS model in Ontario under Kelso's
direction unfortunately floundered in its crucial
years from infancy to maturity with the consequence
that its progress remained arrested. A more
resourceful and aggressive reformer and a more
politicized leader in these forty years was
necessary to build the CAS structure into a cohesive
and articulate pressure group and child care agency.
Kelso's failures, although rooted in his own
limitations which did not include conscious obstructionism, ingeniousness, or ill will, can partially
be understood at the level of his self-image, which
was not improved by government indifference and
professional or official contempt for the significance of his task. Kelso's salary, for example,
remained so paltry as to once again reflect governmental parsimony and attitudes toward child care
services.

When he initially took up the superintendency,
Kelso was dismayed at the government salary being
only one thousand dollars which was five hundred
less than he had earned as a journalist. This
salary caused him both great personal shame and
domestic distress; however, the provincial
secretary, J. M. Gibson, offered him cold comfort by
informing him that he ought to be grateful for the
position could have easily gone to a retired clergyman. Apart from the symbolism of the salary itself,
the remark dispels any illusions that child welfare
was deemed an important area of social concern on
the part of the government. If there was any lack
of genuine concern for children or indifference to
the social and national importance of child life, it
cannot be laid at Kelso's feet. At one point in the
early 1920s, he remarked on his own status and
salary in words that are arresting in their pathos.

> The Ontario Government pays me a salary of
> $2850 per annum. Have not had enough
> money to take my wife on a vacation for
> the past three years. Could not even
> afford to hire a motor for a day.50

Given official reaction to the newly created
department in Ontario and the renumeration attached

to its superintendency, it cannot be construed to have been as prestigeous a position as the child savers, who acclaiming it was a major victory and recognition of their work, believed.

However, the appointment of a relatively young and unmarried man proved to be a Pyrrhic victory. Had he been older than twenty-nine and probably married, the five hundred dollars difference in salary would possibly have been a deciding factor in his refusal of the appointment. Had he been a much older man, even a retired clergyman, he would have remained in the position for a much shorter period of time. But history does not concern itself with "might have beens," and the fact remains that his was a lengthy superintendency that groaned to a stand- still as far as innovation, creative coordination, and energetic or intellectually significant leadership was concerned. Perhaps the choice of Kelso for the position was not an error of judgement at all but rather a cynical and astute political move to keep child welfare problems in the background so that it would not unduly call upon the provincial purse. Although many were arguing that children were "the nation's greatest asset," in truth both public and government alike at no time have seen dependent children as anything but unprofitable and unproductive. This is no less true today than it was in the past.

Just as Ontario's initial promise was not fulfilled due to lukewarm leadership, Nova Scotia suffered from a similar impasse with Ernest Blois as superintendent of neglected and delinquent children. Having been appointed to this office in 1912 on the halo effect of his child saving crusades and super-intendency of the Halifax Industrial School, he finally retired from the directorship of child welfare in 1947. Although Blois was more able than his Ontarian counterpart, his thirty-five years in office led to stagnation of ideas, inflexibility of structures, and a lack of innovation. In his earlier years, Blois had been one of the first to articulate a need for a Federal Children's Bureau to coordinate major child care matters. When Mrs. Colin (Minnie) Campbell of Manitoba began to campaign for this bureau several years later, Blois was quick to insist on being given due recognition for his work.51

Criticism of his superintendency was less vocal than of Kelso's but this was most likely due to his comparative lack of visibility. When the CCCW (by then the Canadian Welfare Council) conducted a survey of social needs at Glace Bay in 1940, Jane Wisdom, a consultant, wrote to Whitton of Blois' obstructionism and resentment of professional incursions into his domain. She observed that his staff assistants and workers were far in "advance" of him in responsiveness to new ideas. Wisdom made a comment about CAS work which was as applicable to most other Canadian centres at that time and as applicable for the preceding half century. She noted that there was "a good deal of apathy and no little real antagonism" throughout the community to the CAS. There was also a suspicion that a great deal of money was being spent and "none too wisely" accompanied by an attitude that was pervasive of "let the Government do it [child welfare work] - it's their job." Despite her defence of CAS work, Whitton could only have agreed with the comment.52

There could have been no one in all of Canada more knowledgeable than Whitton as to the <u>actual</u> child welfare conditions which prevailed in most of the provinces. She represented the CCCW on many occasions as an investigator in British Columbia, New Brunswick, as well as in Manitoba, and consulted with the majority of crucial child saving agencies across the country. She was also the Canadian delegate for child welfare at the League of Nations. Commenting on Mlle. Chaptal's laudatory report on Canadian child welfare for the League of Nations, Whitton observed that some CASs were excellent

> but to the present time, allegedly
> fiendish conditions are under judicial
> investigation in one; the CWC of Toronto
> is pressing for open inquiry into another;
> we have privately urged inquiry into a
> third; and have been responsible in five
> years for the entire recasting of four of
> the largest. We try to do our best but
> conditions are deplorable in several. We
> cannot allow a panegyric of what may 'break'
> any minute in some places.53

Whitton pointed out that exploitation was still rife, children were still to be found in poor law institutions in the Maritimes, institutional care standards were uniformly and "unjustifiably low," and farming-out rather than fostering was still prevalent. She also noted that because the free foster homes were often in rural areas or in urban homes where children were placed as "mothers' helpers," there was much abuse of the system and loss of schooling despite the fact that theoretically "this type of placement is viewed askance today, unless careful investigation has shown that the child is really offered a home for his own sake and not as a subterfuge for cheap help."54

As advisor in 1930 to the Ross Commission (Ontario) which led to the organization of a Public Welfare Department, Whitton advised the chairman, P. D. Ross, on the inadequacies present in the provincial CAS system and made recommendations regarding the children's welfare section on the report. She pointed out that the Children's Protection Act, while insisting on shelter provisions, had contained no enforcement clause or any provision by law for the Superintendent of Neglected and Dependent children to enforce shelter standards. Fifty-eight CASs in 1930 had the care of 10,650 children over a three year period while the "recognized standard" in international child care was that sixty-five children was the number that a worker could cope with. As the government only paid the full salary of one executive officer per society while providing no other fringe benefits such as superannuation, the salaries of other full-time workers came out of the society's funds. Volunteer staff, therefore, became indispensable to the CAS model and funds used for salaried officers resulted in accusations about "extravagance" and administrative financial waste.55

Always a supporter of community cooperation in the form of volunteer involvement under professional supervision, Whitton actually played into the government's hands in the Ross Report by resisting the move towards greater municipal control of the CAS because voluntarism would virtually "cease" as a result. Obviously it was to local and provincial governments' advantage that they be relieved of total control over the CAS as long as volunteers were prepared to take such responsibilities. In short, The Ross Commission's findings did not present a particularly optimistic picture of Ontario's CAS system especially in light of the enthusiastic support it gave to a provincial "tag day" to raise funds - a suggestion that hardly received applause from the Ontario Association of CASs which felt the public was subjected to too many "tag day" appeals for a variety of charitable causes.

Nevertheless, Whitton remained unwavering in her support for the ideal of the CAS model throughout the thirty years she was involved in child care reform in English-Canada. The following sentiment can be found in many statements she made throughout these three decades.

> The uniquely Canadian system of a combina-
> tion of private philanthropy and effort
> organized on a sense of community responsi-
> bility, and working through and with legisla-
> tive sanction and government cooperation
> which the CASs afford, form the very kernel
> of the Children's Protection Act of Ontario
> of 1893.56

Whitton never doubted for an instant the efficacy of the Ontarian CAS model or its adaptability and appropriateness for all provinces in the Dominion. However, when reforms in child welfare and CASs seemed imminent and even likely to reflect her own philosophy supporting voluntaristic effort much lauded in the many Council surveys, the government relief programs necessary for the depression crises, and the national coordination of social programs during the Second World War led to a different perspective of social reconstruction after the war. The CAS model originally formulated in the 1890s, and promulgated by Whitton and others until the war, never remotely achieved its ideal in prevention, organization or fostering.

SERIAL CONTAMINATION AND MORAL TAINT

Once the fostering paradigm had received formal public support and legitimation under the 1893 Children's Protection Act of Ontario, the uneasy attitude toward institutional arrangements became

more vocal. The boarding-out debate may have been
less heated in English-Canada than in Britain, but
those who felt its impact first were the POHs, to be
followed much later by the Catholic orphan asylums.
The loci of traditional forms of child care - the
asylums - clung to attitudes and practices which had
served well for nineteenth century dependency, but
the draining away of traditional sources of normal
children and the impact of unplaceable children had
serious implications for institutional policy and
philosophy in the twentieth. Although the mutual
dependence of CAS and the orphan asylum provided a
brief and illusory regeneration for the institution,
the POHs were never to experience again the vigor of
their nineteenth century growth.

Paralleling the de-institutionalization of
dependent children, another configuration is
discerned in the transforming institutional patterns
of the POHs. Catholic asylums retained their
charity-giving characteristics, institutional
integrity and congregate systems for a much longer
period, a matter which, while not within the scope
of this study, does require careful analysis.

English-Canadian orphan homes came under the
same attacks as did the asylums and the district
poor law schools in England, for the Canadian
advocates of fostering rarely proferred original
arguments to support the superiority of boarding-out
methods or original criticisms of institutional
life. The repetition of the arguments since the
early part of the previous century is almost as
monotonous as those arguments regarding the dangers
of mental defect. Indeed, a striking feature of
such criticisms is how constant they have been for
well over one hundred years. At the same time, the
inadequacies of boarding-out methods have proven to
be just as constant. There is certainly nothing
about contemporary concerns that are in any way
different to past ones. It seems that we have all
been there before.

The supporters of fostering in Canada agreed on
the basic premise that home life was the "finest
product of civilization" and that "children should
not be deprived of it except for urgent and
compelling reasons." This fundamental assumption
was given additional weight by other criticisms

which usually reflected an objective and psychological critique of institutional arrangements. The objective arguments were based on grounds of economy - that the institutions were "monuments of brick and stone" which wasted resources, dissipated effort, and led to the duplication of personnel and facilities. Moreover, they offered infelicitous care because of their overcrowded, unsanitary, and unwholesome physical conditions, and the massing together of large numbers of children aggravated the dangers of "serial contamination."57

The psychological arguments of the wholesomeness of regular family life were equally familiar - that institutions could not provide "training into real home life" no matter how much they professed to simulate it. In answer to the popular objection to desegregation and fostering which seemed based on "fears of the dangers of propinquity without the protection of consanguinity," fostering advocates were quick to point out the moral dangers of closely confined aggregates of children mixing and sleeping in the claustrophic quarters and dormitories of the asylums. If protection could not be perfectly guaranteed in a foster home, neither could it be in the asylum.58

The case for depauperization was as pervasive in the Dominion as in the Mother country. In "First Principles of Social Work," presented to the Ontario Legislative Assembly in 1909, Kelso argued that indiscriminate charity not only fostered and pampered the recipients, but also inflicted "upon the community a long and ever increasing succession of degenerates to fill the brothel, the poor-house and the prison." Although not directly aimed at the orphan asylums, the connection, given Kelso's frequent condemnation of institutional child care which was typified by the conviction that the orphan asylum "practically converted each little inmate into a . . . helpless dependent upon public charity," can be inferred.59

Moreover, Kelso felt strongly about the psychological repercussions of institutional care when he described the regimen as urging children to conformity and as being senseless and inflexible.

The children, he argued "were moved about all day like pieces of machinery"

> . . . and their education consisted
> chiefly of scolding, fault finding, and
> lectures on behaviour, humility and
> respect for the good ladies who were
> doing so much for them. No real attempt
> was made to find homes for the children
> until they reached the age of twelve
> when they were apprenticed out as servants.60

The most compelling argument for the de-institutionalizing of dependent children must be subsumed under the general nomenclature of "serial contamination." Even in times when children lived a tenuous existence and quickly succumbed to the ravages of childen's illnesses, when few families could boast of all siblings having survived their first crucial years, when rich and poor alike lived in dread of the next catastrophic contagion of typhus, cholera, or diphtheria, and when scurvy, rickets, tuberculosis, and scrofula among numerous other disabling diseases were prevalent, the problems of serial contamination were rife in children's institutions. It cannot be argued that children's diseases were no more dangerous nor any more frequent than in the general population, for the very fact of congregating young children together and regularly subjecting them to the admission of new children from the general population enhanced the ordinary and generalized risks of children's diseases.

A bad winter of outbreak of infection in 1926, which had quarantined children for several months at a time, inspired the Children's Bureau of Montreal, a home finding agency for Protestant children, to disband its receiving home and substitute it with four foster homes; two apiece with four beds for girls and boys between six and fourteen years; one for children between two and six years and fourth for three sick infants. Not only did this arrangement save $1,231.68 in eight months, but it could care for two or three more children. In short, the history of children's homes is also a history of "bitter chastisement, of grievous sickness, and fearful mortality."61

The previous comment was in fact a lamentation for eighteen children at the Toronto POH who had died from whooping cough, sixteen in one month, and for the ninety-four inmates who suffered from a scourge of measles and dysentery in 1866. The cause was attributed to the drainage system which provoked a public outcry. As a result, the drainage system was repaired and the matron removed for negligence. To what extent the etiology of epidemic was dealt with in this incident is doubtful, however, for only five years later, twenty children contracted typhoid and an infirmary was just built in time to receive young patients suffering from whooping cough.62

With depressing regularity, outbreaks of measles, mumps, diphtheria, bronchitis, scrofula and poliomyelitis were recorded in all Homes, and in Newfoundland, tuberculosis was added to the list. Milder diseases, but no less serious as far as their contaminating potential was concerned, such as ringworm, scabies ("the itch") and ear discharge, were always present.

Although the question of moral contagion with regard to visitors and the circumvention of visiting privileges have been raised previously, another reason for these exclusions was, as the Ottawa POH observed, that "after many experiences with epidemics we learned that too great care could not be taken about infection in the home." When outbreaks of disease occurred, such visits were prohibited altogether, sometimes for months, just as the children were isolated under quarantine regulations for long periods of time. At the Kingston Home in 1863, parents were permitted during an outbreak of scarlet fever to see their children "from the windows," a gesture that contains a certain amount of pathos. The Winnipeg Home between May to December, 1905, was quarantined for measles, chicken pox, and typhoid, only to be followed in 1906 with a vermin plague. A similar sequence occurred in the Church of England Asylum of St. John's, Newfoundland, in 1860, which was quarantined on and off within a half year period due to whooping cough, scarlet fever, and measles.62

The St. John's Methodist Orphanage was quarantined for several of the winter months of 1912 when twenty-one girls of thirty-three contracted diphtheria. The Toronto Boys' Home in 1897 had thirty-one inmates down with scarlet fever in October, followed by an outbreak of mumps in December and severe chicken pox in January. The consulting physician of this institution deplored the "effluvia" ascending to the different apartments in the building as not being "conducive to health, not to say anything of comfort." Dr. Bruce, physician to the Toronto POH, claimed in April 1909 that the 150 children had not been out since December. Eight years later, this isolation was repeated for many of the inmates, not due this time to protracted quarantines, but to the fact that "rubbers" were too expensive to purchase at forty cents a pair, and children could not be expected to withstand the severity of outdoors without them in the winter months.64

Not only did the children experience a sense of hopelessness about their separation from parents or relatives, but such emotional deprivation was exacerbated in those, who at their introduction into the homes found themselves quarantined in isolation wards before being permitted to join the other children. The first shock of isolation was reaffirmed by the cropping of their hair in order to prevent that from which young Willie Slack of Toronto suffered - "a gathering on the head" - as well as an undignified dipping into a disinfectant bath. Moreover, the bonding processes that developed between individual members of a Home during longer periods of residence could be broken "in the twinkling of an eye with death of a companion from a disease to which all had been exposed." And, indeed, the records are full of sad notations such as "our little Stewy . . . the pet of the household" dying of whooping cough during the night in the Saint John POH in 1887 or "Helen Gilbert, four years," in 1860, taking fever and dying at Kingston.65

The fear of epidemic and the insistence upon physical and moral segregation in an effort to protect the children explains the initial reluctance of POHs to receive CAS children although such admissions brought with them provincial and municipal funding. Besides the concerns over the loss of institutional autonomy in relation to admission, demission, inspection and domestic arrangements, and the moral contagion the children from the poorest quarters of the cities were purported to bring with them, the over-riding fear of physical contagion cannot be minimized.

Those orphanages that accepted public grants had always done so with a certain amount of ill ease for their managements, jealous of their autonomy, understood the compromising nature of the gesture. Frequently, they were obliged to submit to government inspection and render themselves accountable to their benefactors. For example, when Kingston responded to the request to receive temporary CAS cases, they were summarily prompted to purchase iron beds to replace their wooden ones which presumably were not free of lice.66

It is not difficult, therefore, to understand the concerns of staff and committees, who, by accepting CAS cases, were required to accept government regulation by raising the standards of their institutions. Improvements in fire protection, kitchen and food standards, the erection of isolation areas, the allowance of so many square feet per child, improvements to ventilation, sewage, and bathroom facilities, all called for ominous and impossible increases in expenditures. Not only were inspection and standardization unavoidable once CAS cases were received, but additional agreements required that these children would be only "temporarily" sheltered prior to being fostered or boarded out, a policy POHs had been unwilling to embrace at any time.

The fear of government intervention grew when CASs insisted that under the various provincial children's protection acts, they alone had legal wardship over full orphans as happened in London in the 1890s and in Winnipeg in 1912, when the CASs insisted on controlling the wardship of the children they admitted to local institutions. The Board of Management of the Winnipeg Children's Home simply could not grasp the idea that the children they received, although admitted through CAS auspices, were not in effect the Home's wards with the Home acting as with its own clients, in loco parentis. The Board refused to consult with Mr. F. J. Billiarde, Superintendent of Neglected Children, about admissions or adoptions. Not until 1919 did the Board agree that deserted children, privately admitted, would be handed over to the CAS. This concession was due in no small part to legal difficulties encountered regarding adoption procedures when parents, after years of what the Home saw as neglect, claimed children that had been adopted.67

Matrons, superintendents, and management not only saw the reception of temporary cases as interfering with the usual domestic arrangements, but viewed the CAS children with some hostility as a disruptive influence coming frequently from environments and circumstances that had not been carefully scrutinized before admission. As observed previously, admission policies were uniformly selective, and, in the case of the POHs, the children admitted were generally from the respectable poor. CAS children were not seen in this light at all, but rather as the spurious offspring of the unworthy, the degenerate, and the criminal, whose home life had been disrupted not through misfortune - disease, death, or poverty - but by moral flaw. The committee of the Ottawa POH in 1896 discussed the necessity of setting aside separate rooms for CAS "transients" because they were "not fit to associate with our children, using as in the case of Agnes S. Kroog, most filthy language." As the Ottawa Home had been less than enthusiastic about their orphans mixing with respectable local children at Sunday School picnics, it was quite in keeping that they would be disturbed at the possibility of these hot house plants mixing with such noxious weeds as government wards.69

The Kingston POH, which had been used as a CAS shelter since the 1890s, made the following illuminating comment.

Besides sheltering children without either parent, we take under our care children whose parents are degenerates. There is always a kindly soul who will help an orphan, but a child with degenerate parents is like an atom before a wind storm tossed hither and thither. . . .69

In 1925 when these words were spoken, "a great many such as these" formed the POH's clientele.

315

Defective children and delinquent shelter cases, as well as CAS temporary wards before placement, before being "tossed hither and thither" sometimes from one home to another, were all part of the degenerate class.

A per diem pittance from the authorities did not convince the managements of some Homes that the income would outweigh the possibility of an insidious moral contagion seeping through the institution. CAS children were seen to be tainted with the "worldliness" of the urban young which would infect the young inmates so assiduously protected from any awareness of social and moral ills such as drunkenness, prostitution, physical abuse, deplorable neglect, and the example of criminal and vicious practices. Their fears were further magnified because temporary cases sometimes included delinquents awaiting trial. Just as they had refused formerly to receive feebleminded, handicapped, or epileptic children whenever it was possible to do so, POHs scrupulously avoided providing refuge to the delinquent or even the troublesome child. Such cases, however, were part and parcel of the CAS clientele.

Many of the CAS youngsters had been taken off the streets by zealous child savers who viewed askance their street-trading, truancy, and unchildlike demeanours and surroundings. All these were now sufficient reasons to make them wards of CASs under the various clauses of the widesweeping children's protection acts. The acceptance, therefore, of CAS children meant an erosion of the controls of boards of management so vigilantly maintained over matters of admission and demission and which they were reluctant to relinquish. As in the case of the juvenile immigrants, a persuasive but specious relationship between moral "taint" and physical degeneracy was frequently articulated in nineteenth and twentieth century eugenic theories, just as it pervades everyday psychology in our own times. This relationship between moral taint and physical contamination helps illumine the basis for many of the reservations expressed about CAS children who were also identified as the children of lower class failures or worse. These reservations were couched in similar, though more restrained,

316

expressions of horror that were used to label the young Britons.

When the Halifax Protestant Industrial School referred to the CAS children as being "dirty and verminous," this was ironical given that three years before, the Home itself was forced to purchase iron beds because their wooden ones were almost without exception crawling with vermin. However, efforts to withstand the pressures of CAS demands in spite of the seductions of financial compensation suggest that the fears of moral contamination, and the implied relationship to physical defect and infection was a spectre always close to the surface.70

Decades of the realities of morbidity and morality had provided the orphanages with a scarring cumulative experience in which the "angel of death" hovered over the children, waiting to strike them down and perhaps subject the Homes to the ritualistic vilification they came to expect during instances of infection. This cumulative experience, which included lonely crying children affected by juvenile diseases, the discomforting odor of epidemic curtailed within the sparse privacy of decrepit and antiquated buildings, and the appalling shortage of nursing staff in times of emergency, must have led to stubborn attempts to ignore the claims of social conscience placed upon them to accept transient children.

With the 1910 Prince Edward Island Neglected Children's Act, the orphanage at St. Vincent de Paul and the POH of Charlottetown both agreed to receive CAS children but only on condition that they have "a clean bill of health." The risks of rapid infection were enormous in circumstances where few wards received medical attention or had been vaccinated against smallpox. Government action could be merciless, as happened in the case of the London Infants Home which was swiftly closed in 1916 after fifty years of operation when a measles epidemic was traced to an incoming case that had not been isloated, a failure for which the staff was deemed culpable.71

In the west, the Winnipeg Home had several frights when parents threatened legal action after the death of a child, a death they saw as the result of carelessness. In 1912, a year of several such threats, Dr. Harvey observed that the physical plant itself could not "withstand close scrutiny" as it did not keep abreast with "scientific standards." Even in 1923, the Home was criticized by a grand jury investigation which observed the inadequacy of its bathroom facilities for 180 children; however, the cost of installing six showers, amounting to $200, proved insurmountable.72

Further west again, the Annual Report of the Vancouver CAS in 1923 observed that few of its children were vaccinated. This observation is suggestive, and helps us understand the conflict between it and the Alexandra Home some twenty years previously, when the non-sectarian orphanage objected to the suggestion that it amalgamate with the CAS for the sake of economy. The Alexandra Board felt that "a wide gulf" existed between them as they did not deal "with the same class." In addition to the moral contagion that Reverend R. J. Wilson of St. Andrews feared if the handpicked Alexandrans should associate with the offspring of "criminals," there must have been equal reluctance on the grounds of fear of actual contagion.73

Not only did the congregating of many children contribute to the risks of serial contamination, but so too did the actual physical conditions of most of the institutions. Inadequate funding prevented the Homes from maintaining proper standards of hygiene, ventilation, sanitation, water supply, adequate bathing facilities and lavatories, or even sufficiently nutritious dietaries. Descriptions of disabling living conditions and deplorable facilities throughout the history of the POHs are unrelentingly dreary, with the British Columbia and New Brunswick Surveys containing little that was novel except that such descriptions were still appropriate as late as 1927-29. The CCCW surveys, which investigated child welfare conditions in the two provinces, provided Whitton with the opportunity to move into the domestic arena after she had worked strenuously to clean up the juvenile immigration movement and had drawn to the attention of public and professionals alike the inadequacies of the domestic practices.74

The New Brunswick survey, impartially exposing the conditions under which the 885 children in custody in institutions, agencies and almshouses lived, litanized the wretched deficiencies in detail. These included inadequate bathrooms, dirty and malfunctioning toilet facilities, overcrowding, lack of medical examinations, a virtual absence of health records and isolation quarters, community towels and clothing, few individual combs, brushes, or toothbrushes, ragged and filthy washcloths, imbalanced diets, untrained staffs, and lack of healthful exercise and recreation. The Survey report stated that

> All the institutions . . . silently wit-
> ness a constant and wearing financial strain
> which must persistently depress the facili-
> ties that the management knows are essential
> to proper care of their young charges, below
> the minimum level which they would like to
> preserve.75

Not to be outdone by asylums on the mainland, a report for the Newfoundland Methodist Orphanage in the same decade indicated that of forty-two children only four had toothbrushes, thirty-six had unclean heads, and twenty-two had tooth decay. A Committee of Inquiry for the same institution three years previously in 1921 had recommended a weekly bath and supervised daily washing, while deploring the foetid surroundings, the draughts, the dampness, and the insufficient bed covering.76

If the British workhouse dietaries were no worse than those in the POHs, one must stand amazed that any little boy like Oliver Twist could have been inspired to ask for more. It could only have been hunger and not the appetizing food that caused such folly, for institutional children ate as sparingly an unvaried and stodgy menu.

In 1924 a model dietary for children's homes was published by the CCCW. It was "planned to furnish the maximum nourishment for the minimum cost" with a caloric intake ranging between 1248 to 1913 per day. The attempts at variety included navy bean soup, tapioca, stewed tomatoes with bread, lima beans, cornmeal mush with milk, buttered carrots, coleslaw, and cottage cheese. These foods would have provided a banquet for most previous orphanage children. Although the lack of meat, which provided the major means of economy, was noticeable in this model dietary, it was an imaginative contrast with past dietaries which, while agreeing with the second principle of "the minimum cost," all too often implemented this at the expense of the first, "the maximum nourishment."77

For example, the Church of England Home in St. John's boasted of overhead costs per child per diem amounting to a mere eight cents in 1855, but significantly this was only raised another twelve cents almost sixty years later; while in 1917, the Winnipeg Children's Home was boasting of a cost of seventeen and a half cents daily for an average of 152 children, and a reduced mortality rate of two and one-half per cent. In 1925, it reported the cost per meal was approximately seven cents. The Newfoundland home begun to provide its children milk instead of tea when it was given a farm home on Long Pond in 1914 "for outdoor life. . . space and pure air."78

The children spent most days unsatisfied since breakfasts were sparse, suppers were infinitesimal, and the main noon hour meal scarcely satisfying. Matrons were praised if they managed to cut costs and chastened accordingly when they failed to do so. Such actions were not altogether matters of parsimony on the part of the vigilant ladies committees or boards of governors attempting to balance their budgets (which they rarely achieved), but more frequently matters of grinding financial necessity. Many weekly budgets and menus were predicated on regular donations of bread from local bakeries or supplies of meat from butchers. There is evidence that these benevolent acts included donating goods of inferior quality or left-overs, just as donations of second-hand clothing were sometimes offensively useless. In Toronto, last century, the older boys of the Boys' Home took the "market cart" to the market vendors at closing time to have it filled up with donations of left-over food items.79

The congregate nature of poorly funded private asylums, dependent upon the sentimental responses of a fickle philanthropic public committed to many "causes," cast a pall over the child saving ideals they purported to exemplify, and cast doubts on the successful extension of the criteria of protection and segregation, whose very application exaggerated the problems they sought to eradicate. However, it was not unusual for government aided homes to be almost as inadequate, and while it is not within the scope of this study to describe the conditions of many of the industrial schools and detention centres across the country, it cannot be construed that government interest or input caused a radical improvement in conditions. The Halifax Protestant Industrial School, a government aided institution, had no indoor toilet in 1926, and an odorous squalid kitchen, while at the same time, the non-fee paying POH continued a sorrowful history of illness until it was inspected and assisted by the city health department with the support of Dalhousie College in the 1930s, which insisted on blood and schick tests, basic and special dietaries, rest periods for pre-schoolers and vaccinations.80

TRANSFORMING INSTITUTIONAL PATTERNS

The establishment of children's aid society model in Ontario sounded the death knell of the POH as a general purpose children's institution at the same time that the rise of provincial departments for dependent and neglected children marked the first stirrings of professionalism in Canadian child welfare. The Homes that insisted on "doing business as usual" in the face of these legal and occupational shifts found themselves under attack and outside the new streams of professional social service. Those that met the demands of the new model moved to become agencies for the CASs and later to provide specialized services. Professional staff, large injections of government funding, liaison with special hospitals, psychiatric and educational expertise, comfortable furnishings and surroundings, the application of scientific methods of record keeping and patterns of organization - these among other things make it apparent that a major transformation had occurred. The pattern of the preceding century was never to be repeated, for the philanthropic mode of relief and charity with its emphasis on voluntarism had been replaced by the professional mode with its emphasis on accreditation. Sentimental benevolence had paved the way for scientific welfare.

In an almost universal pattern, the congregate form of the orphan asylums went through several stages of transition. First, the Homes either included CAS wards and thus, became in effect, "clearing houses," or they received grants as CAS shelters. Second, they joined charity organization societies that affiliated a variety of philanthropic service agencies, coordinated welfare and charitable services and centralized their budgets into a community chest. Third, still unable to meet overhead costs and facing declining populations as Mothers' Allowances and the Patriotic Fund helped keep families together, some Homes which duplicated facilities for dependent children amalgamated or moved into fostering and adoption. Finally, as the CAS or child welfare departments consolidated their claims to legal wardship which eroded the autonomy of the Homes even as far as fostering and adoptive practices were concerned, many had transformed into specialized facilities by the 1950s.

In effect, the Hamilton Orphan Asylum had always served as a city shelter under agreement with the mayor that children would be admitted for 2s.6d. a week in return for the security of a £20 city council grant per annum and monies for furnishings. Due to the instability such an arrangement incurred in the provision of temporary custody, by 1877 the Hamilton Asylum was shifting from a child caring institution to one that provided care for a more permanent, stable, and fee paying population - aged women. The next decades saw fewer children being admitted. This transformation was a precursor to similar experiences across the nation during the next fifty years. As POHs became more dependent upon grants in order to meet inflationary overhead costs for a declining clientele, they changed from congregate models for ordinary children into specialized facilities - not for adults - but for particular classes of children such as the handicapped or emotionally disturbed.81

One of the most interesting cases of institutional transformation occurred in Kingston whose POH had demonstrated a readiness for structural and philosophical adaptation as early as

1900. Its willingness to adopt new ideas and models was praised in the CCCW Survey of 1931. This POH became the "Sunnyside Centre," a specialized facility for the emotionally disturbed some time after its decreased population led to a shift in policy and the Home turned to fostering arrangements in the 1920s. When the remaining children were moved from its old congregate residence and into the former home of a family that had been involved in its original founding, the 1927 report observed that a "full circle" had been completed in that "the work of the Society is beginning again as it had seventy years ago, in a small residence with a number of children, a matron or superintendent, a garden and a cow." Although this congregate model had evolved out of modest beginnings as did its counterparts elsewhere, and although it became once again a small "Home" for special cases (in the nineteenth century these "special" cases were the carefully selected results of chronic poverty), nevertheless the differences were fundamental.82

By the 1920s, the three major Protestant Homes in Toronto were well underway to changing their mode of child care and adopting the fostering paradigm. The Infants' Home had employed its first social worker in 1919, a year after a reconstruction committee had established a six year plan for the boarding-out of babies, which was at first rejected by management until an epidemic forced the issue. The Home supported a successful booth at the Canadian National Exhibition to advertise and collect names for the placing of children. After this radical shift, a new service of counselling unmarried Protestant mothers and putative fathers was quickly implemented under the auspices of the Department of Public Welfare. After joining the Federation for Community Service, which the POH had joined two years before in 1917, it began to reap the benefits of joint budgeting and fund raising. Feeling the pressures of the economic crisis in the thirties, it seriously discussed amalgamation with the CAS, but the main objection seemed to surround the fact that the Public Health Department would become the supervisory body for boarding homes. Although an increase in professional trained staff and the use of clinical services staved off the dread prospect of such an amalgamation, it finally took place in 1950 when the Home became a receiving centre for child study and personality development with case workers under training consultants.83

Following a survey of Toronto's children's agencies conducted by the Child Welfare League of America in 1921, the POH and Girls' Home moved rapidly towards amalgamation as recommended and five years later, the merger was completed with foster care the prevailing practice. Renamed the Toronto Children's Home, this merger eventually admitted children whose physical condition required special treatment as well as the emotionally disturbed. Until 1950, the Children's Home still received over seventy per cent of its budget from private sources through fees, the community chest, and donations.84

Likewise, a merger occurred in Ottawa between the POH and the Protestant Infants' Home which became the Protestant Children's Village, with the elderly women being finally removed from the POH and placed in the Bronson Home for the Aged. A CCCW survey during the previous year, in 1929, had strongly recommended the amalgamation, although it is doubtful that the advisors would have agreed with the result - a fine edifice on Carling Avenue described as "a model institution" when the age of institutions was well into its demise. The survey had urged fostering. It was not until 1953 that the Children's Village was converted into a residential treatment centre for neglect and abuse cases, and the emotionally disturbed, with fostering for young children. For sixty-three years, the ladies committee had raised funds for the POH by door to door canvassing, and only in 1927 had they resorted to their first fund raising drive. This traditional commitment to the philanthropic mode and the appeal to benevolent sensibilities pervaded the management, and resulted in 1930 in the new and already outmoded institutional arrangements.85

Meanwhile in London, it was not until 1965 that the POH there radically changed its methods of child care by becoming the Merrymount Children's Home, which was supported by the first public appeal three years later. It provided a temporary shelter for families undergoing stress, and lowered the age of admission for children to one and a half years so that siblings would be less likely to be separated.86

324

This Home's loyalty to past ideals and principles is in startling contrast to the Victoria POH, which, because it had never received guardianship rights by statute, boarded-out children at the turn of the century. Even then, it was not until 1909 that the CAS provided the Home with the statutory authority to foster its children. Its seventieth report of 1943 recorded that the Victoria Home at Hillside had forty-four children that year passing through its doors and that it was still maintained by voluntary subscription.87

It was not until 1970 that the Saint John POH moved into providing specialized facilities for the emotionally disturbed as it had intransigently retained the old congregate model despite an amalgamation between it and the Provincial Memorial Home some forty-eight years previously. The Evening Times Globe, 20 May 1970, reported that it still had a population of 122 children, which was to be reduced to no more than forty when it became a residential treatment centre. Indeed, it was only in 1970 that this particular POH closed down its own school and permitted children to attend the public system.88

Even the Methodist Orphanage in Newfoundland, where the move into public welfare programs occurred much later than elsewhere, had undergone reorganization in the 1920s, moving to foster care twenty years later, and then opening its doors to the retarded for a brief two year period in 1954 before it closed down altogether.89

This orphanage, with its strong connections with the Evangelism and Social Service Board of the Methodist Church of Canada, whose involvement in social and settlement work reflected social gospel and progressive philosophy, was more advanced in its ideas in child care than the province generally. In Newfoundland, it was not until 1942 that compulsory schooling was legislated and Mothers' Allowances seven years later. Neither did the systematic coordination of the previous, largely ineffectual, child welfare legislation occur until that decade. Although in 1921 a Child Welfare Association had been established in St. John's in an effort to counteract a fearful rate of infant morality, the

Association's government subsidy was withdrawn in 1934 due to the depression.90

In the west, the Winnipeg Children's Home followed the patterns set by its eastern counterparts. The "terrifying responsibility" of assuming complete control over wardship and adoption was withdrawn under the 1924 Children's Act when the government took over all aspects of wardship, with the result that the protracted tension between the CAS and the Home over this matter was finally settled. The Ladies' Committee was afraid that a "soul-less corporation" was going to churn their children through "a machine without vision or affection for them," and very begrudgingly surrendered "the old heritage of the board [of management]." Once the government assumed full responsibility for the surrender and adoption of all dependent children in the province, there occurred a profound sense of loss, for as it was observed much later, the Board missed "the inspiration of the sight of helpless childhood that went so to the hearts of our women in earlier days." It was noted that in the past, under the mode of sentiment and philanthropy, the ladies had "loved them [the children] only, fed and schooled them, and got them homes as best [we] could." By the late 1930s, the Home had amalgamated as a shelter for the CAS and Child Welfare Department, having joined the community federation in the previous decade, and in 1941, it became a treatment centre for "educable adolescent Protestant girls with accommodation for not more than sixteen." Ten years passed before the requirement of "Protestant" was removed.91

The transformation of the POH in English Canada was aptly described when it had already occurred, and forecast where it had not, in the 1930 superintendent's report of the Kingston POH.

> The Orphan's Home, as a child caring and
> child placing institution and a daughter
> of old time charity, was organized pri-
> marily to meet the needs of childhood;
> today retaining the same idea and spirit,
> it aims to deal with the child on an indi-
> vidual basis, calling to it the specialized
> help of Public Health clinics, schools,
> service clubs, etc. . . . Perhaps one of

326

the greatest factors in developing good
citizens is providing them with a background of happy childhood. This we are
trying to do by surrounding children with
the Christian influences of the normal
Canadian home, where tenderness is tempered
with strength and where the grown ups do not
fail them.92

The first forty years of change in child care
was heralded by the rise of the CAS paradigm, which
emphasized the assumptions about "natural" children
and "natural" homes; however, it took very little
time for boarding-out enthusiasts to recognize, as
did Miss Mason before them, that the ideal was not
so readily attained. The logic of the connection
transformed again during the late 1920s in an
emphasis on family case work, although it was to
take several more decades for the new perspective to
become generally accepted.

Limitations in both the supply and quality of
foster homes led to a general disaffection by the
1930s as to the effectiveness of the fostering
ideal, and these convictions were being replaced by
the new emphasis as to how "natural homes" might
actually be interpreted. A move was afoot to keep
biological families together rather than finding
surrogate family homes in an attempt to lessen the
class of dependent children. As the British
Columbia survey report stressed in 1927, a child's
own family was "the best institution for his
nurture" and "the severing of family ties" was
"ruinous."93

The Montreal Society for the Protection of
Women and Children (MSPCW), one of the first and
most successful to move into family intervention in
the 1920s, supported this view by relating it to
preventive case work, while the Montreal Ladies
Benevolent Society, an affiliate of the MSPWC,
echoed the British Columbia survey of the same year.

We know that a child can be too long in
an institution, grow too accustomed to
being told what he must do and how he must
do it, but there is also the point of view
that is illustrated by the case of one
little girl, who has been bandied about

327

from one home to another until it was
really necessary for her to be placed
where she would feel safe and have some
feelings of permanence.94

Eight years later, the Kingston POH agreed
wholeheartedly with this view and asserted that it
was simply not possible "to cheerfully assume that
there is a free foster home for each neglected
child." It continued:

. . . in fact, the result of this optimism
in past years is often brought home to us
in stories of children so placed, who now,
in manhood, look back on their childhoods
with bitterness.95

It is quite clear that in the history of foster care
in Canada, the weaknesses of the paradigm were
beginning to show within thirty years or so of its
introduction. The cracks were beginning to appear,
and the cleavages, so obvious in the present, were
becoming ominously visible.

Boarding-out and fostering assimilated the four
criteria of the concept of childhood in less blatant
ways than in their institutional manifestation - the
orphan asylum. The natural family, idealized by
rhetoric regarding mother love and the organic
cohesion of a micro-society consisting of surrogate
family members, which initiated the child into good
citizenship and psychological wholeness, was seen as
the most perfect of nurturing agencies, which was
able to provide protection in a spontaneous and
affectionate atmosphere. Carefully selected family
life complemented this protective atmosphere in a
harmonious unit segregated from the contaminations
of imperfect family life. The stress on nurture
rather than apprenticeship into work and family
cooperation rather than economic usefulness assured
the criteria of delayed responsibilities and
psychological dependence.

Dependent children and state wards were to be
in no way viewed as different from normal children
in the bosom of their own families; they were to
live with surrogate siblings, eat at the family
table, learn the lessons of life by emulating
natural models, attend school until the State

permitted them to labor, and they were to leave behind them the psychological and physical deficits of institutional existence and the public nature of their dependence upon charity.

In short, the fostering _ideal_ assured dependent children of a "childhood," although the fostering reality proved to be far more problematic than it promised.

27

28

29

discarding the asylum

31

OPENING OF THE ORPHAN HOME, INNISFAIL, ALBERTA.

32

33

34

335

From Sentiment to Science: Professionalizing Child Rescue   9

> When Miss Whitton's Survey Report brought a gust of bracing air into the heavy atmosphere of B.C. child welfare institutions, it blew in with it new ideas of how best to protect children and with what means. The "means" were experienced people with training in understanding the problems and difficulties of family life, people able to devote all their time and skill in dealing with these difficulties. In a word they were _professional_.
>
> Ann Margaret Angus, 1951

English-Canadian society witnessed a transformation in the several modes of charity and child care from the early decades of the nineteenth century to the mid-twentieth century. Just as binding-out and boarding-out occurred simultaneously with the latter ultimately gaining ground over the institutional basis for the former, and just as institutionalization itself lost its impetus alongside the attractions of CASs and child welfare departments, simultaneous modes of charity organization paralleled each other.

Emerging out of spontaneous and sporadic methods of generalized relief, the most significant shift in child care was the establishment of specialized asylums for the offspring of that class compelled to avail itself of charitable means for its relief. The declining popularity of the orphan asylum, although it had established and legitimized the acceptability of the criteria of childhood for dependent children, coincided with the declining popularity of philanthropy. A new mode of systemized charity organization, based on business principles and a belief in the efficacy of intervention, captured the imagination of the socially concerned. Thus, the philanthropic mode was gradually replaced by the scientific mode of distributing charity to the dependent and assuring the protection of their young. Although the transformation retained characteristics of the previous mode, new forms evolved out of a new view of society, a changed understanding of childhood and family life, and a new conception of the sources of society's ills supported by an ill-founded optimism regarding their eventual remedy.

A further parallel development, whose existence is crucial to the history of childhood in English-Canada if it is understood as a history from child rescue to child welfare under state responsibility, is the major dislocation of sentiment by a profound commitment to the professionalization of child care services. In turn, this professionalization brought with it a changed focus in which the discrete sense of social service exemplified by the founders of the POHs and often the founders of the CAS was replaced by the training, accreditation, and "expertise" represented by a salaried personnel. The new professionals, if they could not absolutely replace the volunteer and the untrained worker were, at the very least, to provide them with leadership and a new set of socially informed theories and assumptions of prevention rather than intervention, new methods of "treating" the problems of child welfare, and a re-examination of the family's needs and responsibilities; in short, they offered an entirely new vision of the social world and an ideology that cleared the way for centralist tendencies in child care under the welfare state.

METHOD OVER MUDDLE

By 1929, the Montreal Ladies Benevolent Society was able to observe that "Efficiency has become the great motto of the world though the real spirit of charitable work remains the same." This claim, of course, was quite erroneous. Efficiency had replaced spontaneity, system had replaced sentiment and method had triumphed over muddle. And in the process, belief in societal transformation had triumphed, resulting in a totally different vision of organizing society. While the new ideology of "progress" turned the philanthropists into fossils, the professionals busied themselves by creating new structures to implement its premises. The philanthropic mode was replaced by varying degrees of state centralism - government intervention in the affairs of its citizens through the provision of services - and, with new scientific notions of cause and effect, reformers sought to invent or discover cures and panaceas for social woes.1

The "real spirit of charitable work" in the Western world had been deeply and irrevocably grounded in ideas of Christian stewardship and the duties of almsgiving as corporate and temporal works of mercy. Even by the nineteenth century, Christian _caritas_, that counsel of perfection regarding personal service and even sacrifice, was being reduced to a mercantile account to be calculated, dissected and socialized. Consequently, the poor were relentlessly categorized not according to actual need, but to who or what was deserving and undeserving. Belief in such categories meant that "discriminate" charity was to be distributed only after scrupulous investigation and assessment of the relative worth of each individual case and after the application of a calculus to determine the comparative degrees of dependency and poverty. By 1900, the coordination of services and the careful balancing of budgets had led to a rudimentary administrative apparatus that paved the way for the paid experts - the first "professionals."2

The development of case work method, which automatically included the already familiar worthy and unworthy categories, tended to restrain any extravagance on the part of agencies in the distribution of funds. Case work implied investigation aligned with counselling; thus, self-help principles were stressed, support could be withdrawn if the recipients' attitudes or conduct were not approved, and a diagnosis of the areas of weakness could be attempted and rectified. At no time did those who enthusiastically embraced the new methods question their right to make such judgments about the lives of other adult members of society nor to intervene in the privacy of the family life of the less fortunate.

Investigation was intended to assure the advocates of scientific methods of three things: first, that the recipient was not an imposter but a genuine object of assistance; second, that his case history would be faithfully recorded and his family be visited by a volunteer; and third, that recidivism be avoided by scrupulous counselling. To supplement these efforts, charities in most major centres in nineteenth century Britain and in twentieth century Canada formed themselves into a central exchange not only to avoid overlapping and duplication by pooling the case histories of recipients for the information of affiliate member agencies, but also to prevent improper solicitation of public monies by issuing certificates of endorsement for the approved charities (usually those already affiliated in the central charity organization society). Thus, "pet schemes" of old philanthropists were to be eliminated and the previous extravagances of benign charity were to be replaced by methods of efficiency and economy.3

James S. Woodsworth best articulated the Canadian changes from old to new charity when he observed in 1911 that "Charity, chief of the virtues, ceases to be even a virtue when wise order is missing from it," and that in order to prevent pauperism and cure poverty "individual sentimentality must make way for enlightened sympathy and cooperative effort." Moreover, in an address on "National Social Efficiency" presented before the Canadian Conference of Charities and Correction, 1917, the President, Dr. P. H. Bryce, optimistically enthused that "if the maximum social efficiency existed, charity as we understand it, would be in practice non-existent." The Social Service League of Victoria believed counselling, visiting, recording, and investigating encouraged thrift and self-respect, and that individual service on the part of charity givers was "more helpful than food" if society wanted to develop "not paupers but good citizens."4

The urge towards scientific charity was not without its critics. The resulting conflict between old and new charity forms cannot be seen simply as

340

another example of historical inevitability with "progressive ideas" replacing outmoded social philosophies. The battle was more complex than such a view suggests, for if the various Charity Organization Societies seemed to be the antecedents of advanced social thought, many of their members, while advocating charity registration or organizations to facilitate economy and efficiency, disapproved of institutions for children not only on grounds of expense but because the custodial care provided for part-orphans or children of families in dire need was seen as encouraging parental irresponsibility. Thus, the Montreal Society for the Protection of Women and Children (MSPWC) in 1914 expressed anxiety lest its sheltering home would encourage parents "to become careless of their children and throw them on the care of the Society."5

As Canada's foremost child welfare expert, Charlotte Whitton's view on the matter in her report for the Manitoba Royal Commission in 1928 is telling:

> . . . the very generosity and philanthropic impulses of prosperous and warmhearted citizens and the respective enthusiasm of unrelated groups, have provided and are still providing institutional accommodation for the care of children, on such a scale, and in some cases with such cases of admission, as to offer a "standing" invitation to needy, indifferent or blameworthy parents, to place their children therein as the easiest and happiest "issue from all their afflictions."6

Whitton's views followed the precedents set by 1916 by A. Percy Paget, Secretary of the Winnipeg Civic Charities Bureau and later involved in the CCCW, who advertised the beneficial results of charity organization by indicating that thirty agencies in the city had affiliated into a confidential exchange which issued certificates to endorse the solicitation of funds.7

Although Newfoundland was not noted for its scientific methods at any organizational level in the first decades of the twentieth century, nonethe-

341

less by 1925, the object of a newly established Charity Organization Bureau in St. John's was "to list and discover . . . those who [were] suitable objects for charitable relief and to repress unseemly and degrading mendacity." The Salvation Army, which refused to relinquish notions of old charity, declined affiliation by concluding that all would become "investigation and no relief" and that to "tabulate poverty" was to add to the sorrows of the poor. It viewed such attitudes about "economy" in charity as penalizing the poor.8

Neither were the new approaches to wise charity always as efficient as they were purported to be, except perhaps, in the case of the Toronto Social Service Commission which guaranteed the ultimate prevention of duplication and overlapping by <u>tabling</u> as many cases which came before it as was decent. The Commission, a city experiment, had been accused of being tactless and overbearing and was replaced by the Federation for Community Service in 1922. In 1913, the Toronto Protestant Orphans Home had not welcomed the Commission's overtures fearing the loss of its autonomy; however, by 1920, social welfare opinion, debts, and declining clientele compelled it to join the voluntary Federation of Charities. Once they registered with Councils of Social Agencies, orphanages were frequently urged to employ social workers or qualified superintendents to update their facilities or to amalgamate their services. The common purse had economic advantages, but certain requirements had to be met in order to partake of these.9

While the Toronto POH and the Winnipeg Children's Home alike were acrimonious in their relations with their respective Associated Charities and preferred voluntaristic, if inefficient, service and paternalism to centralized and professionalized oversight, not all child rescue institutions or agencies were so reluctant. A case in point is the Kingston POH which responded early to organized charity. In the early part of the century, due to two particular ladies on the Board of Management, Miss Muckleston and Miss Chown, it followed the new trends and kept a filing and classification system, up-to-date records, and cooperated more fully with the CAS. It was reported by the British <u>Charity Organization Review</u> that, addressing the Third

Conference on Charities and Correction, Miss Chown in 1900 praised the idea of bringing Kingston's charities together. This occurred some forty years before a positive response could be elicited from the Calgary Wood's Christian Home and a quarter of a century before the Winnipeg Children's Home sought cooperation with the Federated Charities Board, although in 1910 the Affiliated Charities had encouraged membership.10

Nowhere, however, is the influence of charity organization more clearly demonstrated in relation to child rescue in Canada, and reflecting the several layers of shifting forms, attitudes and practices, than in the case of the Montreal Society for the Protection of Women and Children, founded in 1882. Over a period of forty years, many orphanages and child rescue agencies affiliated with it, and from its inception the MSPWC embraced broad social welfare issues as well as a variety of children's services.11

Just as the Kingston POH provides an almost classic case study of the transformation from asylum to specialized facility, MSPWC is the most useful study of a Canadian child rescue society undergoing several modes of change. Although it originated out of the philanthropic impulse that practised traditional modes of child rescue and charity-giving in the last two decades of the nineteenth century, the Society rapidly moved into assimilating, first, a philosophy of scientic charity, and, second, by the 1920s, progressive modes of coordination with various other agencies that employed central fostering and family case work services. Covering almost seven decades, that is, from 1882 to 1950, the MSPWC mirrors the philosophical changes, the organizational and structural transformations, and the flux and flow of practice and attitude in English-Canadian society for this period. It is in effect a microcosm of the shift from sentiment to science.

Organized in 1882 by a committee of philanthropically inclined businessmen, who originally intended to support a Society for the Prevention of Cruelty to Children, the Montreal Society quickly included women in its efforts, recognizing that the arbitrary separation of mother and child was both

343

unsound and unimaginative. The laboring women as a class were identified as equally downtrodden, neglected, and in need of protection from abuse and exploitation as their children. From its beginnings, the MSPWC's interests lay in the area of legal protection for these classes, and its first campaigns were subsequently concerned with factory acts, child labor, parental abuse, street begging and "other degrading occupations," compulsory school laws, and the separation of children from adults after conviction and awaiting trial. Attention was also given to the appointment of a female searcher and matron at the police station for that class of woman which had been customarily "rudely and indelicately treated by the Policemen. . . ." The legal defence of women and children and the separate construction of female washroom facilities in factories and stores also were included under its mandate.12

The MSPWC bypassed the philanthropic mode of "cure" in favour of rehabilitation, for at the very time of its founding, the emphasis on charity organization was becoming popular in the United States, Great Britain, and English-Canada. Within a year of its founding, it had joined the neophyte Protestant Associated Charities of Montreal and enjoyed the advantages of a joint secretary - a "professional" - who was salaried at $400 per annum.13

The modus operandi of the Society was quite distinct from that of the orphan asylum mode, which had been popular several decades before, as it favoured family intervention rather than rescue. The MSPWC observed after its first year of operation that "drunkards had been reformed, and houses made comfortable and many of the children placed in various institutions in the city." Intervention in what was perceived as unsatisfactory family life was not based on the assumptions of the orphan asylum model, which emphasized the rescue and subsequently resocialization of children who were in acute need of protection, subsistence and shelter.14

The Society obtained convictions for underage girls in brothels and youthful newspaper vendors as readily as it did for indecent assault upon children or for "traffickers in girlhood." By 1890, the idea

344

of an industrial school for girls to be supported by the Society had been rejected by the management committee and a preference demonstrated in favor of boarding-out along with a bland caution that parental rights should no longer "be invaded except for grave cause." The problem of insufficient foster homes forced the MSPWC to establish a shelter whose temporary nature was distinct from the old idea of the orphan asylum as a place of permanent refuge (despite those constraints that quickly altered the original assumptions of the asylum). Problem boys, under the care of the Society, were sent to the Belmont Boys' Home in Sweetsburg which, in effect, became the Society's shelter.15

If the MSPWC very early emphasized foster care and the compilation of case histories after individual investigation, it just as rapidly moved into areas of family intervention and reconciliation rather than removal and placement of children in institutions or foster homes. This policy was rapidly transformed again with the introduction of professional staff, who advocated rehabilitation rather than punitive interference in family life. A receiving center for medical, mental, and social diagnosis, was included in the children's shelter, and a child placing agent, who was responsible for visiting and supervising placed children, kept up-to-date records and index systems. By 1921, all of this had occurred.16

The MSPWC had been in the forefront of the campaign for the establishment of a Montreal Council of Social Agencies that quickly affiliated forty charity agencies in the city with coordinated budget and mechanisms and services. At the same time, the Society also assisted in forming the Children's Bureau in 1920 which quickly became the foremost child placing agency for dependent Protestant children in Quebec. The Bureau itself promptly affiliated with the CCCW and Children's Bureau in America. In other words, a pyramid of charity organization and child care services had occurred in Montreal by the 1920s, and the MSPWC had contributed to its formation.

The structure of the Council of Social Agencies were further refined when it became the Welfare Federation of Montreal, among whose affiliates were included the POH, the Infants' Home, the Ladies Benevolent Society Home, the Foundling and Babies Hospital, the day nursery, the Family Welfare Association, several settlement houses, the House of Industry, the YWCA and YMCA, the Sheltering Home, the Royal Victoria Hospital, the Salvation Army and several milk stations.

After 1922, the MSPWC split into providing two separate services, that is, Legal Aid and a Children's Bureau. The Bureau facilitated such mergers as the Women's Directory and the Infants' Home into the Protestant and Foster Home Centre. The Society acted as a clearing house for legal matters concerning other social agencies, and in 1928, Whitton, as Executive Secretary of the CCCW, collaborated with the Montreal Society to secure reciprocal provincial endorsement of maintenance orders. From then on its relationship with the CCCW was secured, and throughout Whitton's tenure a steady correspondence was pursued between the local society and the national body on numerous matters of child and family welfare. The Society eventually took over the concerns of the Montreal Legal Aid Bureau and continued these into the 1950s.

By telescoping the assumptions and policies of the MSPWC, the major shifts from child rescue to child welfare, and from philanthropy to charity organization can be sharply discerned, as can the shift from scientific charity to professionalized social work. In Montreal, by the 1920s, those societies (the Ladies Benevolent Society, the POH, the Infants' Home and the Foundling Hospital), clearly founded on the former philanthropic assumptions, had been assimilated into the formal arrangements of financial federation with the encouragement of the Society. The advantages of coordination and the amalgamation of services and/or facilities were primarily financial, for such cooperative efforts inevitably eroded the former spheres of influence as supervision under professionals narrowed their autonomy, reduced their populations, and compelled them to adapt to changing conditions by embracing appropriate strategies or organization.

By 1920, a pattern had emerged out of the sentiments of the nineteenth century. The ethic of

unpaid service was gradually being replaced by a
growing concern for professional leadership and
cooperative child care services, and child care was
increasingly identified as being inseparable from
family life. These shifts were only one layer in a
subtly multi-tiered system of charity organization
at the church, private, quasi-public, civic and
provincial levels which saw as interrelated all
aspects of welfare and relief including the problems
related to dependent child life. Given the
direction, the acme - that of membership of many
individual and affiliated agencies with a national
agency - seemed logical.17

Although the Child Welfare Division, which had
been established in 1920 within the new Dominion
Department of National Health, might have
coordinated the child care service tier, restricted
concepts of public social welfare and federal/pro-
vincial tensions meant that a quasi-public agency
best reflected Canadian perceptions and attitudes
during the intermediate phase between the two world
wars. This agency proved to be the Canadian Council
on Child Welfare.* Founded in 1920, the CCCW
struggled the next two decades to standardize
efforts across the nation by propagandizing those
centers that were reluctant to come under its aegis
or were anachronistic in their practices. The
guiding genius during the first decades of the CCCW
was Charlotte Whitton, who combined amazing
organizational talents with a strong social
vision.18

THE UBIQUITOUS MISS WHITTON

During the period between 1920 and 1949, it was
impossible to separate either Charlotte Whitton and
Canadian child welfare or the CCCW and professional

---

*The Canadian Council on Child Welfare changed
its name to Canadian Council on Child and Family
Welfare in the late twenties, and to the Canadian
Welfare Council in the thirties. It is now the
Canadian Council on Social Development. For the
purposes of this study we shall refer to it as the
CCCW, its founding name.

child care. Moreover, the CCCW was certainly during the interwar years the lengthened shadow of Charlotte Whitton. There was no place in English-Canada between 1920 and 1949 in which either the presence of Whitton or the CCCW was not felt. No history of social welfare in this country and no history of institutionalized child care for this century can be seen as complete without a careful articulation of Whitton's work during her tenure as the luminary of the CCCW. Her ubiquitous presence in the juvenile immigration debate and in the many social surveys that helped bring about a transformation of institutional patterns has already been observed. Thus, the direction child welfare took in English-Canada and the realities of the experience during the first half of this century are only understandable within a careful consideration of Whitton and the CCCW.19

Apart from her prestigious and powerful position at the helm of the Council, Whitton's contribution to child welfare was felt whenever a child welfare problem arose. Descending on each trouble spot with astonishing vigor, she would ruthlessly dissect it and then either boldly engage in confrontation if necessary, or tactfully arrange a pacification if that course seemed wiser. The Royal Commission of 1928 in Manitoba led to a study of delinquent girls in that province the following year, both of which served her as an apprenticeship for future service as commissioner for child welfare sections of the Ross Commission on Public Welfare in Ontario (1930), the Mothers' Allowances in Nova Scotia (1930), and the Mothers' Pensions Services in British Columbia (1930-31). After sharpening her skills with her experiences with the reorganization of the New Brunswick Boys Industrial School (1929-30) and the Croll Committee on Industrial Schools (1934), Whitton conducted studies for the Ontario Minister of Welfare, including an investigation of girl delinquency in 1943-44.

Besides lecturing in social work at McGill and Toronto, Whitton devoted a great deal of time and effort to raising standards of training and recruitment of social workers and improving the quality of university schools of social work. Moreover, she wrote numerous articles on child welfare for MacLean's and Saturday Night as well as for the press in many provinces, and gave numerous speeches and addresses before conferences on child welfare. R. B. Bennett's Conservative government used Whitton's expertise in conducting social surveys to study problems of relief and unemployment in the west, while her services as a consultant were used by the Liberal Prime Minister, W. L. Mackenzie King, with the National Employment Commission, in 1937.

After a brief sojourn with the Social Service Council, Whitton had left Toronto for Ottawa in 1920 and subsequently became Honorary Secretary for the newly organized CCCW, Executive Secetary in 1926, and finally, Director until 1941. In this position, she defined its policies, implemented its programs and articulated its philosophy; in short, she shaped its direction and structure. When she resigned in 1941, some Canadian child welfare interests could not imagine the Council having a future without its prime mover. Under her vigorous leadership, its functions had expanded from an original mandate to deal with child life problems to include the whole spectrum of social problems, and its tentacles stretched across the nation to embrace scores of private and public agencies in all provinces. During Whitton's tenure, the Council's significance in shaping programs and educating opinion concerning all aspects of child and family life cannot be over-estimated. This development was due in no small measure to her energy and intelligence, political acumen, forthright views on social welfare, and finally, an unswerving certainty as to the correctness of her cause, which first and foremost was the professionalization of child care services.20

The CCCW was the result of a Conference called by the newly formed Dominion Department of Health in October, 1920, which urged that there be a nation-ally based agency that would operate as "a clearing house of child welfare." A quasi-public agency with an annual federal grant, whose original aims included examining aspects of child hygiene, employ-ment, education and recreation, the special care of dependent, delinquent, neglected and defective children and aspects of ethical development, was formed. The dissemination of information on every conceivable topic related to child life as well as development of mother-care kits and child care programs through the affiliation and coordination of social agencies were crucial; mothers and family allowances, child legislation, delinquency, moral reform, drugs and liquor traffic, birth control, immigration, housing, playgrounds, handicapped persons, and divorce all fell under its purview. The Council acted as the moral watchdog over all aspects of child and family life.21

Whitton's zeal at "empire building" coincided with her commitment to professionalization. Every avenue that opened up provided a new opportunity for placing another professional social worker. During Whitton's tenure, the harvest was plentiful but the Canadian labourers were so few that her hand-picked choices had to be carefully situated in key positions. The recurring problem of an under-populated country with a numerically small and self-proclaimed elite resulted in a CCCW "network." Moreover, she attempted to repatriate Canadian social workers who had left the country either to receive their training at the more prestigious American schools of social work had taken up employment in social service work in the United States.22

A close working relationship between the CCCW and the Canadian Association of Social Workers (CASW) assisted in the strategic placement of hand-picked social workers in key positions in provincial and municipal departments or social agencies. Thus, the Council's ability to effect changes in policy and practice was proportional to the people it recommended and helped to place, to the influence it was able to exert over its affiliated membership, and to the prolific educational campaigns it conducted. The Council's careful liaison with members of other influential agencies and organizations kept it informed and politically sensitive. Whitton and the Council insinuated themselves wherever it was expedient and her advice was sought on innumerable occasions from groups, individuals and prestigious social and welfare agencies. Moreover, the nexus of the Council was reinforced and its influence expanded in another way. As editor of both Social Welfare, Canada's leading organ in the area, and Child and Family Welfare, Whitton was able to disseminate both her views and the Council's. Almost without exception, every influential member of the social work network contributed to these journals which also reported the proceedings of annual and special conferences where Whitton and her cohorts met to discuss problems and strategies and to provide each other with moral support and a sense of cohesion.

That an agency originally intended to be a national "clearing house" grew into an organization of wide-ranging impact and national reputation must be attributed primarily to Whitton's vision of the Council's purpose as well as to her personal ambition. As Whitton's ambitions and the Council's growth coincided, they became increasingly recognized as one and the same. Elsie Lawson of the Manitoba Department of Public Welfare commented to Whitton that she could not think of the Council and Charlotte ever being separated "because the structure is of your building." Whitton herself was able to observe without self-consciousness that much national support turned around the Council "because it turns around me."23

What Whitton and the new social workers had in common was a rejection of the old forms of philanthropy and a commitment to the progressive views of social change that insisted less on relief and more on preventive measures as well as the professionalization of welfare work itself. Her many American contacts were established because of common assumptions about the improvability of society. Katharine Lenroot of the United States Children's Bureau, Edith Abbott, Dean of the Chicago School of Social Service, and her remarkable younger sister Grace Abbott, the influential American social worker, were friends as well as colleagues. Many of Whitton's international contacts were made in Geneva where she represented Canadian child welfare at the League of Nations on seven occasions, and in Washington at the White House Conferences on problems of child life.

During Whitton's leadership, the Council urgently sought to implement uniform standards across Canada, while at the same time maintaining the fragile balance between government interest and funding and voluntary participation at the community level. If it was true, as a 1927 CCCW pamphlet maintained, that Canadians seemed "against a broad,

351

public conception and serious national attitude toward many of their social problems," Whitton did much to overcome this indifference. She and a band of sympathetic professionals engaged in a concerted effort to ameliorate the conditions of dependent child life across the country and by relentlessly exposing the dissonance that existed between policy and practice.24

In the fifty year anniversary history of the Vancouver CAS in 1951, Ann Margaret Angus observed that Whitton's 1927 Survey Report "brought a gust of bracing air into the heavy atmosphere of B. C. Welfare Institutions" by introducing professional methods and professional workers. The contemporary records, however, indicate that the gust of fresh air was perceived in many quarters as a gale that battered many volunteers, social workers, and private agencies. The transition from "old" philanthropy to the "new" scientific and organized charity was not as smooth as Angus's narrative suggests. If the criticisms directed at the CAS shelters and practices in the British Columbia Survey were severe, orphanages such as Providence, St. Ann's, Alexandra and the Protestant Orphans Homes fared little better. The British Columbia Survey, however, did spur volunteer agencies to establish a social service exchange and a federated budget organized around principles of family case work and the avoidance of duplication of monies, services, and facilities.25

Although history is concerned with significance of events, such events are shaped by individual actors who gain or lose from them; therefore, no historian, in an honest effort to humanize the task, can afford to lose sight of the pain and ravages that such events cause in the lives of the "losers." In the replacement and displacement of so many non-salaried workers, whose volunteer effort often represented their self-worth and service to the broader community, and who had given a great deal of time and sometimes money to their causes, the professionalizers denigrated these women's finest qualities into middle class matronly busybodism, dismissed their not inconsiderable talents, and dispassionately predicted their demise. Some "lady bountifuls" retired graciously and even heroically; others with weariness, bitterness, and a feeling of irrevocable loss. If Whitton had any scruples about these displacements, her remorseless logic and driving energy over-rode them for she and her fellow professionalizers saw these women as "the apostolic succession of volunteers" whose positions had been sanctified merely by family connection or privilege. Nevertheless, the complacency of ascription was to be replaced by the arrogance of qualification. If the old group had been unsufferable, the new one being firmly committed to the belief that their individual ability was an innate virtue that deserved public recognition and concrete rewards would be no less so. Harsh criticism of child care agencies, government bureaus, and private institutions, might have been more palatable had it not been apparent that the critics had so much to gain in their crusade for professionalization.26

Perhaps the one supreme irony that can be found in all of this is that Whitton herself was obliged to resign from the CASW because she had never "qualified" in social work. Her resignation was doubly ironic given her insistence that qualified people should have the key positions where non-professionals had formerly presided, the amount of effort she had put into the CASW, the development of recruiting and training policies, the inclusion of social work programs in several universities, and finally the prominence she had achieved in the area of social work and child welfare. Yet, in 1934, she had said, "It is an untenable philosophy that insists on social work training as a prerequisite to executive positions in the area in respect to many of the executive and educational posts held in Canadian, United States, and British social work today by persons of brilliant capacities and thorough education of the mind." Moreover, she asked, should the "head of railways be recruited only from the ranks of locomotive engineers?" To Whitton, social work was a crusade, and one that commanded "personalities of verve, energy, and often passion." These comments were undoubtedly autobiographical.27

A CCCW pamphlet, which was probably written by Whitton, stressed that "making the way more comfortable" for dependent children was to be found in boarding home care, subject to sound case work because it was not "in an institution that a child would have to live when he reaches maturity but in a community of which family life is the central unit." Indeed, if there was any one _leitmotiv_ throughout Charlotte Whitton's turbulent career in child welfare, it was that of her total commitment to the "boarding-out" principle of child care and the Ontario CAS model for assuring its success.28

This is not to say, of course, that she either originated the principle or monopolized its promotion; however, she did articulate and formulate it in the CCCW surveys and defended it in communiques, writings, and in addresses before conferences. Moreover, being able to exert considerable influence in reorganizing institutional practices, Whitton exercised her commitment in concrete and discernible ways, that is, through the conduct of a series of painstaking and merciless surveys that she introduced as the Council's main strategy in influencing child care on a national level. During her tenure from 1920 to 1941, she was personally involved in several of these surveys or she delegated her authority and point of view to colleagues either well connected or beholden to her. After she resigned, the Council continued to conduct surveys using the strategies that had been perfected under her leadership; and finally, she was personally involved in her _tour de force_ of child welfare criticism - the Alberta Survey and its aftermath between 1947-49.

The boarding care of dependent children cannot be separated from Whitton's equally strong opposition to child labor, a problem she became immersed in as delegate to International Child Labour Conventions sponsored by the League of Nations between 1926 and 1933. As a Canadian representative she was constantly embarrassed by the fact that disparate Canadian provincial laws caused Canada to be ranked well below so-called "backward" countries in Europe with regard to child labor. Thus, the juvenile immigration movement and similar domestic practices that Whitton condemned in her surveys were identified as part of the child labor question.

Whitton had recognized the advantages of having a national organization that used survey methods after being introduced to their effectiveness in

354

Toronto and Montreal between 1921 and 1923 when C. C. Carstens of the Child Welfare League of America conducted studies in these centres which led to the re-organization of social agencies. She quickly realized that an indigenous agency which contracted its services out would not only contribute substantially to its self-support but would be able to disseminate its policies and philosophy. Certainly she could not have been unaware of the ambitious surveys that had perfected the "scientific" social survey methods in Great Britain, such as Rowntree's study of poverty in York, as well as those conducted in the United States, investigating housing, education, and labor conditions. Nevertheless, it was Whitton, through the instrumentality of the CCCW, that legitimized the social survey method in Canada.29

The surveys themselves concentrated on charity organization, the coordination of child care services, the updating of private philanthropic agencies, social policy planning, child care and protection services, family welfare intervention and case work methods. Between 1927 when the first general social survey was conducted in British Columbia and 1947 when Whitton with a hand-picked survey team applied the same tried and true survey method in Alberta, there had been a score or so of surveys. Three years after the British Columbia experience, Edmonton, Manitoba, Hamilton and Ottawa were surveyed by the Council and by 1934 social welfare and child care conditions in Fredericton, Saskatoon, Calgary, Victoria, Regina, Winnipeg, Kinston, Prince Edward Island, Quebec, Hull, Brandon and Greater Ottawa had all been investigated. Ontario cities such as Brantford, Galt, York, London, and Smith Falls as well as Cornwall County would also come under the Council's purview. Some centres such as Calgary, Edmonton, Ottawa and Saint John were surveyed more than once because the recommendations presented by the survey team in the original report were ignored or only partially implemented.30

The Juvenile Immigration Survey had set much of the organizational theory for the following efforts. While its deemed significance lay in its being the "first definite research work undertaken by the Council," its main purpose was to demonstrate the

Council's skill at conducting a "scientific survey" and to publicize this function. At the same time that the report of the survey was receiving attention in Ottawa from child welfare interests, the Council swiftly embarked on a similar study of conditions in British Columbia and concentrated on the institutionalization of dependent children and their foster care programs to coincide with the focus on the British children. Thus, while drawing attention to fostering, child labor, supervisory safeguards, pre-placement practices through the juvenile immigration survey, Whitton adroitly focused attention on similar problems in the western province. This was a brilliant psychological strategem, for one could hardly pretend that different principles applied to the domestic than to the imported practices of child placement, and those who criticized the one could hardly abstain from criticizing the other. Thus Whitton left the doors wide open for a national spring cleaning of child welfare, the introduction of professionalized services and scientific methods of placement, and the standardization of policy.31

The surveys that quickly followed from the British Columbia and the New Brunswick ones during 1927 and 1928 operated on an identical pattern. First, having established a receptive climate for a reorganization of child welfare arrangements by gaining initial local support, the Council moved into the second stage of using the "survey" method of investigation. The Council itself was contracted to conduct the survey by a local service club or a coordinated effort of several clubs such as the Association of Canadian Clubs and the Women's Canadian Club of Montreal for the juvenile immigration survey, the Kiwanis in New Brunswick, the IODE in Alberta, or the Service Clubs of Vancouver. Third, using information concerning the backgrounds, training, and qualifications of the existing personnel in child welfare agencies elicited during the survey, attempts were made, often successfully, either to replace them with professionals or to create new key positions to be filled by trained social workers. Finally, the Council encouraged a sophisticated press coverage to publicize the findings of the survey and to open the way for change through public pressure. As much as possible, Whitton was personally involved in the conduct of the initial surveys. In cases where this was not possible, she maintained such a barrage of correspondence and advice with her surrogates that the surveys were virtually her own.

As stated in the report of the Ottawa Survey, the organizational theory of the CCCW survey was premised on replacing "the casual appointee indiscriminately chosen from any trade or calling" with a skilled expert who possessed the "analytical attitude of a trained mind." The Ottawa Report of Children's Agencies observed that "no-one would expect a Board of Trade or Chamber of Commerce to function without a paid executive."32

Although most of the professionals belonged to the Canadian Association of Social Workers, Whitton preferred them to be appointed with her approval, as revealed in correspondence with Dr. H. L. Abramson, President of the Saint John Welfare Bureau, when she diverted him from seeking advice from the CASW about a new appointment for the Family Bureau by telling him that the Association "would not suggest anyone for a job that has arisen out of our work without coming to us first." Whitton assurred Abramson that, as she was closely connected to the CASW and to the School of Social Work in Toronto, he should not bypass the Council on the matter.33

It is pertinent to note that in a letter in the Times-Globe in 1930 Mrs. M. H. Lawlor (one of those on the Associated Charities whom Elizabeth King, director of the New Brunswick survey, described as having "outlived their usefulness") had caustically observed that Miss Charlotte Whitton, who had "saddled. . . three expensive imported experts" on the province, ought to pack them back to Ontario from whence they came. Such reaction was not unknown in the west where the new child welfare programs and policies were seen as yet another central Canadian attempt at domination. These suspicions or hostilities were prevalent enough for Whitton to warn one of her workers that the west believed easterners sought appointments merely for the "salary and not the task."34

Nevertheless, she became irate when her recommendations were overlooked as in Manitoba in 1928. When Dr. E. W. Montgomery, Minister of Health

357

and Public Welfare, rejected her suggestions favouring eastern appointments over Manitobans, he implied that her interests were self-serving. In reply, he received a generous dose of Whittonian bombast. However, he rose to the occasion by retorting that her arrogance had been "well defined by Shakespeare - when I open my mouth let no dog bark." Refusing to accept her recommendations for out-of-province workers to lead reorganization of child welfare in his province or a non-Manitoban superintendent for a new girls' home, Dr. Montgomery pointed out that it would be reprehensible in times of chronic unemployment and that Winnipeg social workers resented the incursions of the Council into their domain.35

In British Columbia, Mrs. T. Morward-Clark in her 1928 address had added that women from the east had been "dumped on the Social Service Council" and that now "young CCCW women" who had never "stepped foot on B. C. soil before" had come to criticize "the wild and woolly west" with such "audacity" that they even intended to survey it. In the same year, the Reverend Menzies of the British Columbia Neglected Children's Department was alarmed at the intrusions of "outsiders" and their contempt for westerners while wishing to run social work on the Island. Rejecting "Eastern people" who were attempting to establish an "expensive system," he bluntly said - "Outsiders, Hands off Victoria."36

A further example can be seen in the attitudes of the secretary of the Board of Evangelism and Social Service for the United Church, the Reverend James Mutchmor, who resented Whitton from the time of her involvement in the Manitoba Commission to well into the forties. He objected to what he perceived as her highhanded and singleminded imple-mentation of policies which conformed to her particular view of professionalization, and her inordinate influence in the CASW recruitment and training committee in the thirties. He feared that the new codes of ethics and of professionalization being formulated by the CASW would enable Ontarians to control both the rules of admission into the profession and appointments across the country by monopolizing qualifications and standards. Mutchmor perceived a tendency toward increased eastern influence in child welfare given the predominant Ontarian membership of the Council and the CASW.37

Correspondence between Whitton and Isobel Harvey of the Department of Neglected Children in British Columbia during the thirties, suggests that the Council's criticism of her leadership prior to her resignation was not entirely unfounded. Her tendency to dominate all aspects of child welfare and unwillingness to delegate authority were part of this criticism. Harvey, a close associate of Dr. George Davidson, Director of Social Welfare in British Columbia, wrote of receiving "excited epistles from Charlotte, none of which we can understand," concerning the Dominion plans to bring British Guest Children to Canada for the duration of the war.38

Davidson was a key figure in these plans much to Whitton's annoyance, for she had nominated Robert E. Mills of the Toronto CAS to be chairman of the Children's Overseas Reception Board. Her insistence that the Council should be the agency to coordinate the reception of the British children led Davidson to leave the task to her and return to British Columbia. The antagonism that had generated between them was compounded later when Davidson took over Whitton's position as director of a reorganized Council after her resignation in 1941. His quick rise to become the federal Deputy Minister of Welfare did not improve their relationship. In some ways it can be argued that Davidson's appointment to the Council was an attempt by the board of governors to meet the growing criticism of the western provinces that they were alienated from the decision making processes which guided Canadian welfare practice and which seemed to emanate out of Ontario.

Interestingly, then, Whitton and the Council came to epitomize, in the minds of some Canadians involved in social welfare, the spectre of Ontarian domination which roused deepseated fears about Central Canada as "colonizer" - fears that are all too familiar in other aspects of Canadian history. Whether these perceptions represent objective social reality is not as important as their existence. Such perceptions must be taken into account to understand more fully the confrontation which was to take place in 1947 and 1948 between the Alberta government and Charlotte Whitton.39

Under Whitton's direction, the Council remained a quasi-public agency typical of an intermediate stage of centralization and professionalization between the older one of sentiment and service and a welfare state of intervention and bureaucracy. Its propaganda articulated Whitton's own belief that the active involvement of private and quasi-public agencies provided the humanizing leaven that offset the impersonalism of state welfare. She insisted upon the autonomy of such agencies while cooperating with those necessary state supports such as funding, legislation, city relief, provincial welfare, and government inspection. She feared, however, that when "the State steps in other supporters step aside" and that in the final analysis, state control of child services was "a vicious principle that ultimately means the death of the private agency." Yet this intermediary stage could not remain frozen and suspended between private philanthropy and social welfare. By advocating the coordination of child welfare efforts across the nation and insisting upon uniformity and standardization, it contained the seeds of its own transformation by supporting the principle that the greater the centralization the better the child welfare.40

A strong believer in the principle of subsidiarity, Whitton was convinced that a smaller unit was preferable to the depersonalization of government bureaucracy in handling social problems. The frequency with which Whitton emphasized her belief that wherever "the State steps in other support steps aside" is noteworthy. In child welfare work, she sought to coordinate private agencies and to achieve the maximum cooperation among the private, public, and government sectors as well as the development of voluntary associations of citizens. Uniformly expressing a profound belief in the dignity of personal effort, Whitton cautioned the demise of the voluntary instinct would lend to the dehumanization of services. It is this context that she defended the role of the CAS model in humanizing child care. In many ways the CCCW itself was a concrete example of Whitton's theory turned into practice, and it was only after she retired from its leadership that it began to embrace fundamentally different approaches to child welfare.

Suggesting that the Council represents an intermediary mode of child rescue in Canada is not to argue that residual modes did not co-exist during the transformation, or that they have even yet been absolutely eradicated. Every era is one of transition and during the interwar years residual modes of "old charity" competed with the demands of new charity which the Council typified. For example, in 1928, Mrs. T. Morward-Clark objected strenuously to the arrival of a CCCW survey team in Vancouver. Before an audience of women, she passionately defended the old forms of charity and decried municipal welfare experiments.

All your work has been given freely without even a care fare while these highly paid superintendents ride about in automobiles provided for them by a generous public.41

The speaker in this case was fighting a losing battle, and the story of such confrontation is one of both pathos and self-interest. Groups committed to their benevolent schemes, some with a long history, struggled against the tide of "progress" and subsequently drowned in the transition.

Another source of frustration to the CCCW and its survey investigators was the stubborn resistance offered by certain forms of voluntary charity such as the Roman Catholic Children's Aid Societies in Victoria and Manitoba, the Salvation Army, and even the Orange Order that insisted on founding institutions for children in two western provinces when fostering had become a preferred method of special care. Despite the frustration about the vestiges of old charity that Roman Catholic child care retained, Whitton was circumspect in her relations with these agencies.42

Roman Catholic orphan asylums did not remain untouched by Whitton's advice or the surveys conducted by the CCCW under her vigilant scrutiny; neither did they escape her attentions during the Manitoba Royal Commission of Inquiry in the late twenties. It is an interesting fact that Catholic institutions were treated with more empathy,

361

circumspection and delicacy than were their Protestant counterparts during her surveys of the problems of institutional child care. An explanation for what amounted to a mutual respect is founded on a mixture of possibilities. Perhaps the mother superiors of the institutions surveyed - orphan asylums and monasteries of the Good Shepherd for reformatory girls - recognized instantly another woman of commitment and authority (a laicized version of themselves) just as she quickly recognized similar qualities in them. Second, since the socio-political principles of subsidiarity which framed Catholic social action were quite compatible with her views, the compatability may have tempered her usual tendency toward forthright condemnation of the kind of child care that the sisterhoods represented.

Again, Whitton's personal orthodox Christian convictions and loyalties to a similar confessional faith as well as her intimate connections with the Sisters of St. John the Divine (an Anglican sisterhood who founded the Sherbourne Home in Ottawa) may have enhanced her sympathies for the devotion, sincerity, and care such vocations gave to dependent child life. Moreover, given her connections with Catholic representatives on child welfare organizations and committees, with some of whom she kept close and congenial contact, such as Fr. Joseph Haley of Ottawa as well as W. L. Scott, she chose to tread the fine lines between church-state relations warily. Or, finally, perhaps her Protestant biases prompted her to believe that Protestant organizations were more likely to respond to progressive thought and new modes of welfare than such medieval structures as the Catholic Church or the religious orders with their old methods of discipline and dispensing of charity. Whatever the reasons for it, there was no similar patience or tolerance for the POHs if they clung to outmoded practices of stubbornly resisted modernization and transformation. With them she tended to be consistently candid, critical, and, if the occasion called for it, even ruthless.

It is tautological that social work is a profession that must thrive on the disadvantages of others; indeed, one might suggest that the social worker, tacitly at least, must be in complicity with

362

misfortune to maintain a sense of service accompanied by a rather comfortable socio-economic position. The Council exemplifies this irony. While the Great Depression wrought social and individual havoc with ruthless impartiality, positions for social workers multiplied rapidly, and in 1935 the CCCW altered its name to the Canadian Welfare Council to reflect its "emergence into the whole field of social work and generalized organization in community planning." Thus, while the working classes of Canada bore the most terrible burdens of the economic depression, the professionalism of social welfare and child care steadily gained in status, and middle class social workers steadily gained entry into the domestic affairs of those struggling to overcome economic and social dislocation.43

That Whitton succeeded in building the Council into an agency of some national significance suggests that hers was an influence beyond merely reflecting values and ideas that were already in practice or were emerging. If not originating them, she nevertheless helped to give form to them in rhetoric and practice. Without a doubt, Whitton had acute psychological insight and a political acumen that led to the effective manipulation of emerging views on child welfare. Although never equivocating over the application of the four criteria of the concept of childhood in the lives of dependent children (she regarded it as an undisputed right that all children were entitled to the fullest enjoyment of the criteria as a separate and special class in society), Whitton's inflexibility as to the means of assuring this remained her Achilles heel. While she clung tenaciously to the intermediate mode of welfare organization by insisting on the necessary contribution of private agencies and the efficacy of the CAS model, the new professionals (whom she had helped create) and advocates of the welfare state passed her by.44

Within twenty years, her views had become as fossilized as they had once been dynamic and radical. Their displacement was exacerbated by the destructive experience of the Great Depression, the traumas of wartime, and excitement of postwar reorganization of the social services represented by the British Beveridge Plan and the views of the Canadian Committee for Social Reconstruction. If

363

"cure" had not occurred and if "prevention" were not possible under existing arrangements, then social workers came increasingly to believe that the welfare state was the solution and that only the state could and should organize, fund, and control child welfare programs. Whitton decried these sympathies as illusion and folly but subsequently found herself isolated and out of step with the mainstream of social welfare thought. Even previously loyal colleagues, who had now come of age, were embarrassed by her conservatism.

With the exception of her lectures at the McGill School of Social Work during the 1940s, Whitton's subsidiarist socio-philosophical principles were rarely intellectualized by her. It is only by examining her child welfare policies, the justifications offered in their defence, and her growing alienation from child care philosophies which embraced state welfarism, that can we explicate them. Curiously, there is nothing to suggest that the people who came to embrace state welfare principles were any less committed to bourgeois ethics or the maintenance of private property interests and capitalist socio-economic organization than Whitton; however, their pragmatism induced them to seek the most efficient methods of providing services and of tinkering with structures.45

Whitton was nothing if not consistent in her defence of an "organic" view of community over an "organizational" view of society subjected to massive state intervention. In accord with a belief in a system of social work in solidum (that is, one that emphasized the relationship of mutual rights and duties to order the entire social system), she attributed a personalistic character to the common good that would, in turn, maintain the delicate equilibrium between individual and social interests. Fundamentally, this organic view reflected a metaphysical justification derived from the essentially social and moral nature of the human personality in community and of the working relationship of concrete persons in a concrete society. The organic ordering of society guaranteed the autonomy of personal human existence and maintained specific organizational guarantees for social justice. Whitton believed that a socio-political theory _in solidum_ (or of subsidiarity) was the appropriate leaven to humanize the situation of the dependent child, to maintain the essentially personal interaction necessary to child welfare, to guarantee the individualization of social case work, to protect the integrity of family life, and finally, to minimize bureaucratic trends.46

In 1949, Whitton asserted that the centralization of welfare was a threat to human liberty with the greatest peril of pluralism being the erosion of individual freedom by the operation of large scale social programs. Centralist tendencies, she believed, inevitably paved the way to state welfarism. Although states such as the USSR and Nazi Germany both had started from humane assumptions regarding child welfare, Whitton pointed out that they had ended with the "nationalization of children" by means of ideology and smoothly organized and impersonal state mechanisms. Indeed, her confrontation with the Alberta Social Credit government between 1947 and 1948 during her final child welfare survey can be understood in light of her repugnance for governmental centralization of child care services at the expense of citizen participation.47

Throughout her turbulent career, Whitton had demonstrated an intolerance for those who objected to the expense required to maintain modern child care programs as well as those who were unwilling to change outmoded practices. Her impatience was not unnoticed in her work within the Council itself and thus alienated some of its membership. These temperamental characteristics, as well as her inflexibility and inability to compromise with changed societal demands, eventually culminated in her resignation from the Council. Despite the singleminded and sometimes dubious means that Whitton resorted to in her determination to impose her beliefs, nowhere is the sense of social conscience, pragmatic effort, and humane criticism more apparent in the annals of Canadian child welfare than in the career of Charlotte Whitton and her Council. The Council had become, indeed, the lengthened shadow of the woman and the vehicle for her personal crusade to "make the way more comfortable" for a generation of Canadian dependent children.

REFORMING THE BAD BOYS OF CHILD WELFARE

Two provinces continued into the late forties to be the bane of the CCCW in its efforts to standardize and professionalize child care. Although New Brunswick and Alberta represented the extremes of child welfare philosophy, they succeeded despite quite dissimilar premises of welfare organization to remain remarkably similar in actual practices of dependent child care. Charlotte Whitton, and the Council after her, continued to believe that the root of the problem regarding the boarding-out and institutionalization of dependent children lay in two extremes: the ineptitudes of private philanthropy in conjunction with the rudeness of the poor law system in the Maritime province and the perceived inordinate powers of a centralized system of child and social welfare occurring in the west. Since both systems had one thing in common - their unwillingness to profession-alize child care services - radical reforms were requisite in both regions.

Along with New Brunswick, Alberta had resisted the professionalization of welfare and child care principles at a time when changes were occurring elsewhere. Standing outside the mainstream of changing practice and policy, Alberta and New Brunswick were viewed by Whitton as last bastions of anachronistic child welfare and a standing reproach to the uniformity and standardization which she had worked for twenty years to achieve. In 1944, after the Council had conducted yet another survey of Calgary welfare agencies, the Calgary Herald reported an interview with Whitton in which she "deplored" the Alberta "set up" and observed that, "It [was] regrettable that Alberta should continue to have the lowest standards of any province but New Brunswick in child welfare."48

Although both provinces had largely ignored council survey recommendations, Alberta was in some ways easier to attack than New Brunswick because its systemized government machinery virtually controlled all aspects of child care including the private sector. As New Brunswick had no such centralized control, one could only attack isolated pockets such as Fredericton, Moncton or Saint John one at a time. Steeped in custom and law of several centuries, its ineptness was more nebulous than that of the western province. As the survey report of 1940 observed

> It is a sobering reflection that Section
> XIX of the Elizabethan Poor Law of 1601
> provided "that this Act shall endure no
> longer than the end of the next session
> of Parliament." It would doubtless be as
> surprising to the members of Elizabeth's
> parliament as it is to many Canadians that
> many of the actual provisions of those
> early Poor Laws and many of the social and
> political ideas which lay behind them, had
> endured into the middle of the twentieth
> century, and are embodied in some of the
> social legislation of the province of New
> Brunswick.49

New Brunswick found itself castigated by the CCCW on four occasions. Provincial welfare and child care services were criticized in 1929 and 1949, and services in Moncton and Saint John were specifically examined in 1939 and 1941 respectively. Over two decades the reforms that were implemented following the recommendations of the survey teams ranged from negligible to non-existent. New Brunswick, like an intransigent child, remained impervious to the advice of those who had set themselves up as the watchdogs of Canadian child welfare and as "experts" in new philosophies and practices. The Moncton survey recommendation that a trained worker be used to establish and operate an index system for coordinating community services was rejected on grounds that the "importing of a worker" was extravagant when a local could be quickly trained to operate the new system. Whitton, slighted from being ignored so deliberately after the ambitious 1929 survey, retained her interest in the province after she resigned from the Council.50

The repetitious nature of the criticism in each survey is tedious. Certainly, when Isobel Harvey, Department of Child Welfare in British Columbia, wrote to Whitton in 1943, inquiring about the state of affairs in the Maritime province, Whitton's depressing reply could have described equally the conditions as she had come first to understand them in 1929. Always prone to over-statement, she claimed that children were "herded into alms-houses," that New Brunswick was "the only province of the Dominion where children may be kept together with adults in the ordinary alms-houses," and that even in the 1940s there were more children in the Saint John municipal institution than the CAS shelter. Two score or so children in nine municipal institutions can hardly be described as "herding together" although they were, as claimed, suffering under poor living conditions, with casual school classes in the basement, and unclassified according to race, religion or language. The very presence of such a circumstance tells something about "the whole horrible inadequacy" of child welfare in the province.51

As there was no provision whatsoever until past 1950 for the mentally defective child, many of the children in almshouses were probably in this category although some were attached to their families. The law still provided for a debtor's prison with family members being sent to the municipal house if the breadwinner was found bankrupt and unable to support his family in any other way. The findings of the 1941 Saint John survey noted that as the law stood, public outdoor relief was not available through public agencies; therefore, unless the Family Welfare Association intervened, the position of suffering families was sometimes untenable. The consequence of such alarming laws was that "a pathetic condition of need and suffering [had] developed for those who attempt[ed] to cling to a semblance of a home which a semi-furnished room or meagre shelter typified." As the Family Welfare Association dealt with 125 families a month, when approved standards at the time demanded a load of no more than fifty, assistance could not be guaranteed. The surveys repeatedly commented on the appalling circumstances of the poor in the port city of Saint John.52

The 1949 report observed that, although some reforms had been introduced in the last five years, of 280 people in the municipal houses, twenty-nine of these were children, promiscuously mixing with the defective, alcoholic, bedridden, blind, aged, paraplegic and unwed mothers. Eleven of the children, who were between three and one-half and thirteen years, had been institutionalized for several years. If the physical conditions of the

368

municipal homes recounted in the survey reports were true, the deplorable circumstances described in the opening chapter of this book still pertained, especially with regard to "bedbugs" and the "odour of vermin." In 1949 the commissioners of the poor still retained the power to bind-out apprentices or to adopt-out illegitimate or orphan children. Their ability to bypass the authority of the child welfare officer rested on the fact that legal provision, such as those under the Adoption Act of 1946, did not supercede former pieces of legislation. Whitton's view of New Brunswick, although prone to exaggeration, nevertheless reflected genuine concern over the informality and casualness of the indenture and adoption practices of the municipal houses. As she noted in her correspondence to Isobel Harvey, children were made available for indenture "like litters of pups to be placed anywhere."53

With regard to the overseers of the poor who executed such operations, it was agreed that they scarcely had characteristics that fitted them to the task of caring for the needs of adults, let alone the adoption and placing-of children. In 1948, in a brief presented to the CCCW, William E. Hart of the New Brunswick Association of CASs wrote that as a result of experience with the local overseer of the poor he would "hate to ask him for anything for himself" and that the overseer was a "little man with a brief authority." This comment is reminiscent of Mary Carpenter's 1861 criticism of guardians of pauper children in Bristol that "it would be difficult to select men who [were] less friendly to it and more unqualified by sympathy or aptitude to take part in the work."54

As isolated as the cases might have been, no major alteration to the plight of children in almshouses had occurred and echoes of the following terse remark found in the 1929 report can be found throughout the one of 1949.

In some of the alms-houses utterly unsuitable women inmates, in some cases obviously
feebleminded, were 'hauling' and 'pulling'
at unfortunate little mites, who were in
their immediate charge. Tiny, little,
normal toddlers will hardly realize their
best potentialities at school age if

'gently nurtured' under such conditions.
Nor, so trained and cared for, are they
likely, presenting the appearance and problems they do, to appeal strongly to the
prospective foster or adoptive parent
calling to see them.55

In New Brunswick, it was not so much the numbers of
children placed in such circumstances, but that
there were any at all. The criteria of protection
and segregation were not operative in this case
because they could not be assimilated into an
outmoded poor law system suited for a totally
different time and to previous social norms.

Another class of child to be found in the almshouses were "bad boys" who could not be admitted
into an overcrowded Boys' Industrial School. Housed
in a pre-confederation penitentiary and
intermittently subjected to charges of grave
mismanagement, the School was hardly a salubrious
environment. Some boys in Shediac found themselves
confined to the Women's section of the common jail
for a few days when it was empty and cared for by a
matron whose antecedents were somewhat shady, being
suspected of having gained this unprestigious
position through "undesirable friendliness with the
police."56

In the area of juvenile delinquency, New
Brunswick had not kept pace with changes in
perception or treatment. The 1949 report noted that
the Industrial School records demonstrated an
excessive amount of recidivism, a school program
that allowed only for part-time attendance,
inadequate manual training, and that older boys were
apprenticed and young boys under twelve allowed to
mix with the more hardened type. In that year, the
School's objectives retained terminology that barely
reflected any shift from punitive to rehabilitative
views of childhood in that it sought the committal
of a boy who was "of such incorrigible or vicious
conduct" that he was "beyond the control of his
parents."57

The Juvenile Delinquents Act had been
proclaimed in three cities only - Saint John,
Moncton and Fredericton (although the capital lacked
a court); therefore, juvenile delinquents in all but

370

two centres of the province appeared before the county magistrate as did adults with police officers often laying charges. Subsequently, children found themselves with a "record" that prevented them finding suitable employment afterwards. Not only were social histories and psychological, psychiatric or even medical examinations rare occurrences in most cases, probationary or parole procedures were uncommon. As typified by a 1929 incident, an uninformed attitude toward legislation prevailed. Mr. Scott of the Saint John CAS had committed a child of seven to the Sisters of the Good Shepherd until she was twenty-one. It was only after a complaint from the sisters about the extraordinariness of such a term that Scott's attention was drawn to the fact that he had operated under the provisions of a former 1919 act and not the 1927 revised statutes.58

As with the almshouses, the New Brunswick POH retained guardianship rights with full and complete control and custody even after the Children's Protection and Adoption Acts had been amended and passed in the mid 1940s, and even where parents were alive but the three month fee requirement had not been met. Visitors were permitted access to the children only once a month. Placements or adoptions, which did not have the same legitimacy if they had operated under a court decree, were continued, as was the indenturing of children. There was little investigation of homes or supervision after placement, and the placing of children in American homes was not prohibited until 1949. The Home received boarders at $20 a month (or $15 for two children) with the majority of its population being illegitimate infants. It gave over its "unadoptables" to the CAS. The POHs indiscriminate adoption policies were headlined by the Saint John Evening Times-Globe which proclaimed: "ADOPT-A- BABY-WEEK. . . . CHANCE IN LIFE SOUGHT FOR THESE WAIFS."59

The institutionalizing of children had been condemned in the late twenties with the usual observations regarding regimen, dietaries, health standards, physical conditions and psychological handicaps. Soggy and unpalatable food, lack of quarantine units (or even a working knowledge of the techniques of isolation and asepsis), regimentation at the expense of natural habit formation, a dependence on routine, the physical and moral dangers of unsupervised recreation and group life, and the lack of a sense of property and privacy - all of these constituted the case against the congregate systems of New Brunswick. In 1949, these conditions still pertained and the following important observation was made.

> It reflects the time when institutional care was regarded as the main form of child-care, and continues to provide institutional care and training for almost every type of physically and mentally normal child, at a time in the history of child welfare when institutions are planned more and more for specialized groups of children, who because of physical, mental or emotional problems, cannot be placed in normal family groups: The Protestant Orphans' Home provides care for children, who in our opinion, are not generally appropriately placed in an institution.60

The Wiggins Male Orphan Institution was given but faint praise also when it was noted that its financial endowments meant that it was "the most fortunate - perhaps the only fortunate - social agency in all New Brunswick." Its impressive three tiered structure was disapproved of, and the fact that the Institution operated as a "closed corporation," which actually discouraged any community input, was deplored. This isolated existence from the point of admission until a lad was seventeen years was viewed as incurring a "serious natural loss" to the boy and the comunity alike. The survey report encouraged the Institution to move into a smaller group-home model, for given its financial security, such an experiment would be an example of its kind to the rest of the province.61

Given the criticism of New Brunswick institutions, it is not surprising that the CASs in the province were neither paragons of efficiency nor exemplars of the latest methods of child placing. "Professionals" were few and far between, boarding homes were ill supervised if at all, parental consent for adoptions not required, and case loads heavy. Free foster care had been the custom rather than boarding care until the 1940s. Rarely community and cooperative ventures, CASs often operated under the directives of county councillors or an agent in consultation with one or two members. There were, in 1949, very few active representative organizations and most memberships were apathetic.62

Supervision of placements by the single child welfare officer was quite unsatisfactory as were the records and statistics from his office. Because municipal maintenance payments depended upon wardship, there was a tendency to obtain the money rather than to assess whether the child's situation demanded a transfer of guardianship. Such procedures were in contravention of the CCCW policy that

> . . . the permanent removal of a child from his own family is as radical a treatment as amputation in the practice of medicine, and should only be used as a last resort.63

This 1949 statement merely reinforced the view promulgated twenty years previously that where a home was otherwise decent and wholesome it was

> . . . the consensus of modern social think- ing that if poverty be the sole disrupting force, it is wise and better to remove poverty than breaking up the home.64

Not only was it no longer tenable that child protec- tion meant removal from a poor home, but in New Brunswick the fact that the majority of children were returned at a later date to their homes demonstrated that it had not been necessary in the first place. Yet, as late as 1948, 85.3% of the funds for provincial CASs came from wardship main- tenance payments and only 14.7% from private sources.65

Although the claims of the 1929 New Brunswick report, which had been closely supervised by Whitton, may have seemed extravagant and sensational in some quarters, they were unfortunately confirmed by later Council surveys. Uncovering scores of children "living in distressing circumstances of penury, immorality, viciousness, disease, cruelty and neglect," the first New Brunswick Report groaned under the heavy burden of illustrating the point with stories of boys behind bars, feebleminded fertility, familial transmission of gonorrhea, illiteracy, incest, inbreeding and child battery. It took the Alberta Report some nineteen years later to compete with these depressing details. In relation to the New Brunswick survey, Whitton advised Elizabeth King, the field worker, to "verify all the lurid stories you can," as "it is the only thing to stir New Brunswick." King caught the contagion and wondered how they could "originate some good publicity stunt."66

In Alberta, a series of press articles in the Calgary Herald during May 1947 provided the publicity required for that province. They were called "Children in Iron Cages," and some months later, an article in New Liberty magazine, "Babies for Export," followed the example. Whitton, a shrewd strategist, had perfected the press campaign tactic in New Brunswick where she planned with King that the Survey findings should leak out gradually after "licking the Report into shape." She advised King to "get the province really excited" with photographs and by stating that although she [King] originated from New Brunswick, she had never suspected the conditions that existed in her home province. One day they were to stress the lack of medical treatment for children, another, the "breaking up of families," while the next, examples of "extreme cruelty."67

One of Whitton's consistent criticisms of Alberta's child welfare focused on its tendency to minimize municipal units and encourage the integration of voluntary services under government personnel. Although its 1909 Neglected Children's Act was seen as the most progressive in Canada at the time, subsequent legislation bypassed the municipalities, and dependent children became increasingly included as just another class of "public charge." Whitton saw the Child Welfare Act of 1925 as the culmination of the provincial legislation intended to control all aspects of child care. Neither had she been satisfied with the Western provinces' tendency to under use or to entirely neglect the contribution of the Childrens' Aid Society.68

The centres that responded sympathetically to Council surveys, even if they had not succeeded in placing sympathetic social workers in key positions or creating new machinery and structures, were rarely criticized vigorously by Whitton. Although not models of efficiency, cooperative centres such as Kingston and Ottawa as well as Vancouver, Victoria and Saskatoon in the west, received relatively gentle treatment. The Alberta Health and Welfare Department, however, had consistently declined to affiliate with the Council, to participate actively in the national conferences on child and social welfare, or to appoint Central Canadian experts in key positions once the provincial welfare machinery came into operation. Moreover, the recommendations of the Council surveys of Edmonton in 1929 and 1939, and of Calgary in 1931 and 1944, were ignored by the Alberta Welfare Department. All this led to such an unfortunate impasse between the Department and the Council and a mutual intolerance between it and Dr. Whitton that by 1947, when she was called in by the IODE to conduct another survey of the whole province, the relationship between Whitton and the Department was extremely acrimonious.

Moreover, while Whitton disagreed with a principle of child care that imposed rates upon a municipality for the maintenance of dependent children but which discharged the municipality from any further responsibility for the care and protection of its ward, she simultaneously argued that the development of a system of children's aid societies would overcome the problem of public indifference. Her views on fostering, adoption, and child placement were in opposition to Alberta practices and she protested against the discretionary power vested in the juvenile court to create wards "by indenture or otherwise." The words "or otherwise" permitted an unwise flexibility and vested too much power in the Superintendent's office. Thus, farm placements were still the order of the day although generally not the practice elsewhere. It is not surprising, therefore, that while such practices were still prevalent, government officials continued to reject the principles of "scientific" case method and modern child welfare. Indeed, the comments made by Alberta officials during the forties indicated a public contempt for these principles, and it is noteworthy that Alberta did not have a chapter of the Canadian Association of Social Workers, which suggests a cavalier attitude toward the profession-alization of social services and the necessity of qualifications for social workers.69

Not all centralized child welfare advocates in other provinces were similarly condemned. Manitoba and Saskatchewan both responded positively to the recommendations from Whitton in Manitoba in 1928 and the several surveys conducted in Winnipeg during the thirties, and the Council surveys in Saskatoon and Regina in 1930 and 1931 respectively. In Saskat-chewan, the government in no way obstructed investi-gations and Whitton advised on the appointment of several personnel for charity organization agencies. For example, Lillian Thomson was appointed as director of the Saskatoon Social Service Bureau in 1931 and she kept Whitton informed of proceedings in the province until she left to take up a similar position with the Edmonton Council of Social Agencies. It was Lillian Thomson who constantly alerted Whitton to any child welfare problem in the province between 1940 and 1947. By 1940, Thomson, in correspondence to Whitton, was criticizing Mr. Blaine, the Superintendent of Dependent Children and the Minister of Health, Dr. Cross, and energetically condemning Alberta's participation in the British Overseas Children's scheme.70

Whitton's views of Alberta had become public in 1940 when she criticized its child placement methods as ad hoc in regard to British refugee children before the Coordinating Committee on the Reception of British Children. Besides berating Alberta's handling of the children and lack of CASs to facilitate their humane treatment, Whitton attacked the Alberta Department of Child Welfare. The criticism was publicized by the Lethbridge Herald, 27 September 1940, under the headline "Alberta Should Change System of Handling Children From Old Land." Lillian Thomson had written to Whitton about Mr. Blaine's purported cavalier attitudes regarding the matter. The superintendent of dependent children was reputed to have described the placement of children into homes with similar socio-economic background as "ridiculous" and to have asserted that his department had not time for "scientific child welfare." Whitton saw such a confession from a

376

child welfare official as symptomatic of even more alarming attitudes.71

As the 1944 Calgary survey indicated, criticisms of institutionalized child care were almost identical to those of New Brunswick. This survey condemned the large barracks-like annex for older boys attached to the original building of the Wood's Christian Home as not recognizing the boys' need for privacy or the development of individuality. It conceded, however, that despite its 90 to 100 inmates the Wood's institution had a "natural and homelike" atmosphere that emphasized a family setting. It strongly recommended that the public schools should be used, not only to save money by educating the children at public expense, but to encourage the children to mix more naturally in the community.72

The criticisms of the Catholic Lacombe Home were more candid especially as the sisters not only sheltered 110 children, but also 50 aged or handicapped adults with little distinction between the care required by children and that by handicapped adults. Children in this Home were institutionalized for long periods. Despite the "serenity, orderliness and quiet evidence of discipline" at the Lacombe Home, that stood out in marked contrast with the Wood's children's "easy going, natural relationships," the survey could find no evidence of artificial restraint or repression. The Salvation Army's William Booth Memorial Home with 100 to 110 children was praised on one hand for allowing its children to attend public schools, and admonished on the other when it was noted that the small children "clustered" and "swarmed" around the survey team visitor, obviously craving attention. This suggested some "underlying deficiency in the program developed for pre-school children."73

All three Homes were criticized for remaining child caring institutions and not converting their facilities into treatment centres for special problems and for not adequately preparing their children for life on leaving the institution. Records were inadequate; no coordination existed betwen the three institutions or any other welfare agencies; supervision, placement, and follow-up procedures were deficient; nutrition poor; and older girls continued to be engaged in domestic duties. Moreover, the Family Welfare Bureau, consisting of unqualified staff, had no skilled case workers "capable of diagnosing intimate family problems and bringing the family along through its own processes and initiative as a self evolved solution of its problem." Nevertheless, all the criticisms in all preceding Council reports made either under Whitton's leadership or after her retirement in 1941, would pale beside the blistering report and sensational publicity issued in 1947 during her own study of Alberta Child Care conditions.

In 1946, the IODE Provincial President, Mrs. R. C. ("Daisy") Marshall of the Edmonton Chapter, asked Charlotte Whitton, aided by a hand-picked advisory team, to conduct a study of child welfare in Alberta. By January 1947, when the four month survey commenced, Whitton already had a certain degree of insight into the complaints of non-government child serving and social agencies. Indeed, within a few days after commencing "field work," Whitton felt sufficiently informed to address the Edmonton Council of Social Agencies and the Alberta Educational Council Conference in an attempt to establish a favourable climate of opinion.74

Originally, Whitton had hoped that her survey would be under the auspices of the Social Credit government. Such support would have insured both the requisite cooperation across the province and access to government records. Interviews as early as 1945 with Premier Manning and the Minister of Welfare, Dr. W. W. Cross, had come to nought and they did not agree to assist her project when she interviewed them again in 1947; however, with or without government support, Whitton was determined to expose child welfare conditions and facilitate major reforms in the area.75

Before the IODE published Welfare in Alberta, its final and official report on the results of the study, Whitton's proficiency at gaining press publicity and the advantages of public support had already produced results. Besides provincial press coverage including the "Children in Iron Cages" series, Time magazine featured an outright condemnation of "Alberta's penny-saving welfare system." Moreover, Whitton staged several carefully orchestrated meetings before key provincial service groups throughout the conduct of the study and after to report its conclusions and recommendations.76

The IODE report and the Calgary Herald articles, which freely used Whitton's evidences, uncovered a litany of horror, many unhappily substantiated by the later Commission of Inquiry. Specific charges included the problematic practices of placing dependent and delinquent children in "free" and "work" homes in rural areas. Dr. Cross in 1946 had defended farm placements over Borstal models and industrial schools which he likened to "jail-like incarceration." Farm placements, he said, not only kept boys out of institutions but successfully separated various classes of delinquents from influencing each other which institutionalization could not effectively do. Ordinarily speaking Whitton might have agreed but only if adequate safeguards were operative to avoid exploitation of their labor and the neglect of their schooling which it seems was not the case.77

"The bartering of unborn babies," that is, adoption agreements before birth between mothers and child welfare division, was condemned as were the deplorable physical plants and neglect of infants' "boarding homes," the "dank and evil smelling" detention centres for children awaiting attendance upon the juvenile court, children with "prison pallor," youths over fifteen years being incarcerated in the common jail with adult criminals, and the whipping of boys in the South Side Detention Home in Edmonton. The general charges included matters concerning child welfare organization and government control which was identified as "tainted with authoritarianism" as well as inefficient and frequently negligent and the inadequacies of the Children's Welfare Act which lead to increased centralization of child welfare with the consequent decline of public input through Children's Aid Societies, which had virtually become defunct since the early 1920s in Alberta.78

Section 69 of the Act was particularly criticized for it seemed to ensure "water tight secrecy" through the application of a clause which prohibited the use of any information on child welfare "without the Minister's authorization."

This section effectively muzzled comment from local agencies or divisions within the Department itself which either criticized practices or sought to reform them. The powers of the child welfare branch were seen as inordinate, too bureaucratic and centralized, yet retaining anachronistic practices and attitudes. Finally, despite a centralist model, it was incompetent and "cheap."[79]

Moreover, "unscientific" attitudes toward child welfare policy and practices were said to predominate. Charles Hill, Superintendent of Child Welfare, had inadvertently drawn attention to these attitudes in 1944 and 1945 when he had claimed that "love" and not "science" should rule adoption procedures and that he did not pay much attention to "fads, pet theories and new discoveries about babies." As for scrupulous socio-economic, personality, or psychological matching of adoptive parents with adoptive children, he disclaimed the importance of hereditarian possibilities by stating that "a baby born of a healthy mother has 100% chance of becoming anything." In this case, what might have been construed as a progressive and even humane environmentalist view of childhood was perceived by the Toronto Daily Star, which reported these opinions as retrogressive.[80]

The views of Frank Drayton, Superintendent of Edmonton's Civic Relief and Child Welfare, were similarly reported in the Globe and Mail on 7 January 1948 with headlines of "Edmonton Boss no Love of Education," which distorted beyond recognition the interview he had given. The lack of sympathy, however, might be understood if one recalls the verse of an adoptive parent who had benefitted from the Alberta methods in gaining a baby girl called "Cynthia." The proud father, Geoffrey Gilbert, published a poem in a newspaper in Trail, B. C., which duly noted:

> Don't fool with B. C. - it isn't done
> The place for babies is Edmonton,
> There's Mr. Hill there who is grand,
> He keeps the best babies in all the land,
> I've got a good stock of girls and boys,
> Just look them over and take your choice,
> And he showed her a row of cupboards and racks,
> All filed with babies filed neatly in stacks.[81]

380

Such laudatory comments, however, were ill received as Whitton castigated the Child Welfare Division's unqualified staff, its lack of commitment to professionalizing child care services, its laxity pertaining not only to adoption but also to fostering, and a lack of modern case work methods or family investigation. At a meeting of the Catholic Women's League, she berated the unnecessary breaking up of family life.82

The IODE report and press publicity surrounding it provoked the Social Credit government into calling a Commission of Inquiry in the summer of 1947. Expert witnesses on modern child welfare principles from across the country were called. Whitton was subject to extensive cross-examination as to her motives and views. Briefs to the Commissioners were presented by the Children's Aid Departments of Edmonton and Calgary, as well as the Councils of Social Agencies of these two cities, the Canadian Legion, the Calgary Local Council of Women and the Calgary School Board, and finally the Indian Association of Alberta. The Calgary Children's Aid Department brief was particularly sharp in its criticism of the investigation into "unwed parenthood" and the break up of family units. Single mothers, it noted, "live in constant fear of being unable to pay regularly for the child in a home or an institution and of the authorities, because of such failure, stepping in and taking the child through neglect action." If the Edmonton Council of Social Agencies referred to maladministration, lack of medical examination of dependent children, the anachronistic use of RCMP officers in apprehending children, and the promiscuous mixing of delinquent with neglected juveniles in shelters, then the Calgary Social Agencies complained of neglected girls being committed as delinquent to the Mountview Corrective Home without Court Order. Although this complaint was substantiated by the Commission, it rejected the complaint that Protestant girls were being accommodated on a permanent basis with the Good Shepherd sisters. The report of the Commission of Inquiry also praised institutions such as Wood's Christian Home, Booth Memorial, Providence Crèche, and others which had received criticism in the IODE Report.83

381

The conclusions of the Commission, Report on the Child Welfare Branch, largely vindicated Whitton's work although resisting the maligning of Charles Hill's character and the criticism of centralized child welfare in the province. A centralized model, the Commission insisted, was the one that had been chosen in the west and was, therefore, functional in meeting its needs. The Commission castigated the government's obstructionism and the fact that the Child Welfare Department had officially circulated instructions for its staff not to cooperate in any way with the IODE study. Its findings recommended more citizen participation in child care services and insisted that the expertise of private agencies be used together with a concentrated effort to professionalize personnel and services. Many of the particulars to which the IODE report had drawn attention were also substantiated, and it seems that the claim that Alberta in the forties represented "one of the sorriest areas of human frailty anywhere" was a convincing one.84

The wide ranging recommendations of the Commission included the training of personnel; introduction of family case work; increased public input and cooperation with private agencies; the curtailment of "work" homes; pre-placement inquiry and post-placement supervision; compilation of case histories for government wards; counselling for unwed mothers; and the alteration of adoption procedures. Regarding qualified professionals, the Commission did not go quite as far as Mrs. G. Cameron Parker, director of the IODE study, who concluding that the welfare department staff was "not dishonest, just unqualified," had recommended that they be replaced by members of the Canadian Association of Social Workers. The Welfare Department's staff was, indeed, conspicuously unqualified - as were the staffs of most of the private and public agencies throughout the province - with only three departmental staff members having received any social work training whatsoever and with nine totally untrained inspectors being charged with the oversight of 16,794 cases.85

Despite the general tenor of agreement with Whitton's report, the Commission findings nevertheless made the following pertinent comment:

382

. . . if the language of the Report had
been used more scrupulously towards the
avoidance of overstatement . . . the
matters complained of could have been
more easily dealt with; many statements
were made throughout the Report of such
a nature that one would think or fear
that the intention was to heap discredit
on the officials of the Child Welfare
department.86

If many Albertans were uneasy about the IODE
findings and Whitton's singleminded crusade against
Charles Hill, they were subsequently appalled when
the Social Credit government issued writs against
Whitton, Jack Kent Cooke, publisher of New Liberty
magazine, and Harold Dingman, a writer for the
magazine, on charges of conspiracy to commit
defamatory libel. For example, a retired nurse in
Edmonton pleaded with Manning to withdraw his
charges, while a fundamentalist preacher and
political conservative residing in Gunn, Alberta,
called the action "political bonehead," for
Canadians, he insisted, had "a genuine belief in
Whitton." Protests were lodged from such Calgary
groups as the Women's Canadian Club, the Wesley
Men's Association, the United Nations Society, the
Book Club and the Gyro Club.87

But the government, humiliated by the press
reaction criticizing its policies in child welfare,
saw itself as goaded into the action; whereas
Whitton, astonished at the extreme consquences of
her zeal, described it as a "fantastic persecution."
In short, the case was so indefensible that the
Attorney-General's department abandoned the charges
and declared a stay in proceedings, but not before
Alberta had been vilified from coast to coast.
Whitton had again proved herself to be "the First
Lady" of Canadian Social Work.88

A major exposé that had warranted extensive
investigation by the Commission was what Whitton
described as "a fast and loose adoption traffic,
largely carried on by one official [Hill] and
notorious in Western Canada [which had] crossed the
U. S. A. line in very considerable proportions in
recent years." Whitton had been interested in
cross-border placements for some years, and had

exchanged correspondence with American child welfare agencies in various states to confirm reports of the practice not only in Alberta but also in Quebec and New Brunswick.89

Although accusations of the "bootlegging of babies" across borders were bound to have repercussions, Whitton could not have anticipated their extent. The publication of "Babies for Export" in New Liberty, 27 December 1947, which was based on her findings, provoked a bizarre trial of an unprecedented nature - "conspiracy to commit an indictable offence," that is "defamatory libel." A corporal of the RCMP laid the charges on behalf of the Child Welfare Commission. The opening paragraph of the notorious article illustrates both the literary style and the contempt it intended to generate for Alberta.

> One of the blackest and ugliest chapters in the development of modern governments has been written against the Province of Alberta. It is the unparalleled story of a government trafficking in illegitimate babies, exporting them to foreign homes and the further story of unjustifiable harsh and delinquent care of Alberta's very young and very old. At these extremes of life bureaucracy and tyranny rule.

The subsequent pages became even more extravagant, and compared Alberta's government to Nazi Germany and the USSR. Its pictorial illustrations were graphically exaggerated.90

But what was the truth behind the accusations of "trafficking infants on the blackmarket" from "Guatemala to Alaska?" It must be confessed that despite the verified incidents, other claims such as "twins being created" of two boys born within days of each other of different mothers had been excessive. The Commission Report found that between 1934 when C. B. Hill first took over the position as Child Placing Officer, and 1947, the year of the IODE study, there were 243 cross border placements out of 11,018 total illegitimate births, that is 2%, and not 10% as the article had indicated. Nearly half had been placed in California with United

States citizens, who had been temporary Alberta residents at the time of adoption However, of the others, there were many cases where the preliminary interview had been circumvented, procedures initiated through correspondence, and Mr. Hill acting as their attorney to secure passports.91

In the House of Commons, 28 April 1947, Mr. St. Laurent was questioned by the member from Calgary West regarding such passports, to which he replied that sixty-four had been given in 1946 and eleven in 1947. Although the Commission strongly recommended discontinuance of such practices, it resisted any suggestion of bootlegging, blackmarkets, or trafficking. It insisted that the reports from the adoptive families during the investigation were highly suggestive that the success rate was high and that the child and parents had been matched to mutual satisfaction.92

While neither suggesting that two per cent of babies was no cause for alarm, nor that the practice was not to be discountenanced, it is obvious that the emphasis on this aspect of Alberta child welfare had been blown out of all proportion. The reason, of course, for the emphasis was that whereas juvenile delinquency might provoke only mild interest on the part of the public, a richly embellished exposé of blackmarkets for babies assured the type of righteous indignation that critics of Alberta child welfare felt was necessary to implement reforms. The claims also reflected changing assumptions about the necessity for the standardization of adoption practices across borders, both national and international, a problem which had become more prevalent with the dislocation of juvenile refugee populations after the Second World War. The problem was receiving some attention in the United Nations as well as benefitting from increased awareness of contemporary psychological theories about personality and children's emotional needs. Whitton herself had demonstrated her interest in matters of custody and guardianship of dependent children as early as 1926 when she helped draft the proposals for Ontario's Children of Unmarried Parents and Adoption Act.93

New Brunswick and Alberta were unable to permanently lag behind in professionalizing child welfare and ignore the strident demands of the professionals. It was only a matter of time before they succumbed and conformed, for the territorial and professional imperatives of the trained worker would force open career opportunities in these remaining pockets of social welfare left largely untouched until mid-century.

The custodians of the dependent child in the nineteenth century had created an enabling institution - the orphan asylum as a place of refuge - so that the criteria of dependence, segregation and protection could best be effected, and the two tensions of rescue and restraint could be psychologized. In the twentieth century, those matrons, superintendents, ladies' committees, boards of governors, directors, and the philanthropic public were replaced by the new caretakers of the dependent child who created enabling legislation, "scientific" structures and new bodies of knowledge to transform, expand, and finally incorporate the last criterion of childhood, delayal of responsibilities, into the lives of dependent children. Subsequently, expertise, certification, advanced training, standards of ethics, and welfare bureaucracies, as well as social workers, pediatricians, psychologists, diagnosticians, parole and probation officers, juvenile court judges, and family counsellors, proliferated and became identified with the new "helping professions." The circle was complete with the intervention of the "friendly social worker," whose middle class identification was guaranteed by professionalization and a concomitant life-style. Once professionalized by ever-expanding services, psychologized by socio-cultural norms, legitimized by the consensus of capital and labor, and transmitted by common childhood experiences, the ideology of childhood was entrenched and the asylum recreated in non-physical but far more potent means.

If the orphan asylum had made possible the experiment in extending the first three criteria of the concept of childhood to dependent children, then the professionalizers had aided the state in enforcing the fourth criterion - the delayal of responsibilities - by being the instrument by which the final criteria could be implemented and supervised.

386

35

THE UBIQUITOUS MISS WHITTON

State as Asylum   10

> The conservation of child life is now
> attracting greater attention than ever
> before and it is accepted without
> question that the welfare of the State
> and the welfare of the child are
> inseparable.
>
>   Hon. H. C. Nixon, Provincial Secretary,
>   Ontario, 1921

With the indifference of the early nineteenth
century in sharp contrast to the growing sensitivity
regarding the nature and needs of children that
would occur after the 1860s, the history of child
life in English-Canada has been written as the
triumph of modern views on childhood. The child
health movement, the New Education, and the juvenile
justice system along with the debates over
appropriate means of caring for dependent classes
and the decline of institutionalization, the gradual
acceptance of foster care as the only appropriate
way of providing for dependent children outside
their families, and the growing belief that if the
natural family were the best setting for child
development then it ought to be kept together, were
too easily turned into a progressive story of
enlightenment and social uplift.1

Unfortunately, virtually every student of the
care and treatment of deviant and dependent classes
in modern societies had come to quite opposite
conclusions. If good intentions and new scientific
knowledge have eliminated the most obvious problems,
social critics have identified new and seemingly
unsolvable ones. Consequently, the story in the
previous chapters is neither one of optimism nor
despair, but one of the complexities and surprises
of human intention, institutional structures, and
the tenuous relationships of means to ends.2

Historical interpretation is further complicated by the paradoxical nature of "childhood" as a concept. In addition to the four criteria of dependency, protection, segregation, and delayal of responsibilities previously explicated, the concept also implies rescue and restraint. For those who campaigned to remove children from unprotected or threatening circumstances, rescue meant care and solicitude as manifested in children's protection acts, child labor laws, and compulsory school attendance legislation. At the same time, they worked to restrict the freedom of children and youths through a variety of laws on vagrancy, street trades, public amusements, and curfews, to name only a few. It is this dual nature of child rescue that accounts for the opposite interpretations of its purpose and effects. Supporters of the movement hastened to stress its protective aspects and argue that being forced to receive a social or moral benefit was no real hardship. The critics, however, emphasized such repressive elements as the denial of essential human freedoms. Indeed, some basic parts of the movement, for example, compulsory school attendance legislation, are paradigms of childhood as rescue and restraint.

The paradoxical nature of childhood hardly makes for either a success story or an unmitigated tragedy. While those prone to a whiggish interpretation cannot evade questions of denial of freedom and consideration of persons, or how intervention in the best interests of others can be justified, those who argue a social control interpretation have to consider the circumstances out of which child rescue grew and the alternatives available. Consequently, we have attempted to take into account the contradictions, paradoxes, and dilemmas of childhood, social reform, and state intervention, and to treat the historical actors and the socioeconomic problems they faced as seriously as possible. It is easy enough to see those with different social and moral views as quaint and droll and it is also tempting to pass judgement on historical actors from the safety of hindsight and from the high ground of our "scientific" knowledge. Likewise, it is seductive to view the removal of children from the labor force and from general relief institutions, the establishment of children's institutions, the rise of child welfare agencies, and the advent of the welfare state as signposts in the history of Canadian social progress.

The late beginnings of settlement in British North America meant that in contrast to the more thickly settled parts of the original colonies, the new outposts would retain well into the nineteenth century the characteristics of pioneering societies, that is, much land for settlement and shortage of labor and institutions. The new colonies would also lack either the poor law structure of England or the parish system of Scotland. As death, epidemics, and destitution left their residue in the form of widows and orphans, the ill, the hungry, and the dependent, the first attempts to deal with such cases treated them as a single class of needy requiring assistance from public or private sources.

The early programs of relief instituted in late eighteenth and early nineteenth centuries indiscriminately mixed children and adults as objects of charity. Whether outdoor or indoor relief, the major purpose was to provide the basic minimal care to insure survival. In colonies with limited established resources and considerable opportunity, relief from either public or private sources was seen as a temporary palliative. Although negative attitudes regarding the undeserving poor were widespread, there were no concentrated efforts at reformation under guise of relief despite the concerns with uplift present in the early philanthropic societies of Quebec and Nova Scotia.

The Quebec Society for Promoting Education and Industry Among the Indians and Destitute Settlers in Canada, while mixing the objects of its benevolence, exhibited some specific concern for the children in its schools by advocating a daily dose of labor to prepare then for adulthood. Clearly, the inclusion of children in the provision of general relief merely brought them under a weak form of the criterion of dependence since there were no efforts to segregate them within the institutions, protect them from adult contamination, or to delay their responsibilities. The Quebec Society, in its schooling activities, was a colonial version of the various eighteenth century British institutions founded for the poor, where, if there was much

391

discussion of religious inculcation and discipline and training for industry, little was said about reading and writing.

The early British institutions, whether called schools of industry, charity schools, or houses of industry, rested on a rather simple view of character development, namely, that properly organized institutions, which enforced careful regimens of religious inculcation, literacy instruction, and useful labor, would produce respectable members of the deserving poor. To the limited extent that such institutions for children appeared in British North America, they represented this characteristic belief in the psychological power of order and discipline.3

The establishment of industrial schools and orphan asylums in early nineteenth century Great Britain marked a shift in the sensitivity towards child life. A significant part of that shift was a growing psychological sophistication regarding human development and the nature of dependence. Rather than viewing the institutional regime as a form of social inoculation against the diseases of pauperism, irreligion, and criminality, the proponents of the new socialization and training were concerned with the necessity of guidance and surveillance. Supported by new perceptions of human nature as expounded Rousseau and the early nineteenth century educational theorists, they sought to implement new institutional patterns and educational practices.4

Despite the fact that most early Canadian orphan asylums were founded in response to natural disasters and, consequently, without substantial debate regarding their nature and purpose, the founding and management of these colonial institutions indicate a similar if largely unarticulated transformation. With few exceptions, the POHs soon restricted their clientele to children, and occasionally their mothers, and began to create a protective wall between their charges and the world. Unlike the earlier examples that made no effort to protect or segregate, the orphan asylums were committed to protecting their inmates from the dangers of society generally, and of their families in particular. Such protection was only possible through segregation that strictly controlled the interaction between inmates and the world. By means of regulations regarding admissions and demissions, custody and wardship, and training and placing-out, the POHs were able to create an insulated environment in which to rear <u>their</u> children.

The orphan asylums represented a new view of human development by shifting the emphasis from a shaping or forming metaphor emphasizing institutional regime to a growth or gardening one in which careful guidance and nurture were requisite for proper development of individual potential. The asylum, thus, marked the beginnings of the <u>individualization</u> of rescue in contrast to a reliance on institutional routine to transform a mass of unclassified inmates. Although the lack of staff and scientific knowledge limited the effectiveness of the attempted resocialization, the managers of the POHs sought to inculcate a sense of dependence through psychological control, training, and indoctrination. Consequently, the asylums brought together the criteria of dependence, protection, and segregation, in a modern relationship of psychology and sentiment.5

As incorporated in the new children's homes, the optimism regarding resocialization and a growing sentiment about dependent child life were accompanied by similarly transformed views on the sources and causes of poverty. Unlike earlier beliefs that poverty and the lower orders were providential mandates, the asylum promoters recognized the social origins of unemployment and distress while holding individuals at least partially responsible for the socio-economic misfortunes that befell them. A belief in the plasticity and potential of human nature simply underlined the failures of families and friends and the unsavory character of their class and neighborhoods. To allow children, while inmates, to freely associate with their families, or at the age of demission, to return to their former circumstances, was to risk all the gains achieved by institutionalization. As the concept of "childhood" increasingly became part of middle class ideology in British North America, families failing to ensure the necessary protection, segregation, and dependence of their children were seen as unfit guardians. Despite paeans to the benefits of family life, the asylum promoters routinely disregarded the interests of parents who voluntarily placed their children in the Homes as well as those who had abandoned or neglected them.6

The paradoxes exemplified by the POHs are significant because they were representative of the first signs of modern child life perspectives in the colonies. Although the asylum promoters were never very articulate about their work, an analysis of institutional records lay bare their underlying assumptions and dominant ideas. Despite a basic optimism about human malleability, the POHs generally took in only children of the deserving poor and, thus, avoided the more difficult cases. As much as possible, inmates were to be respectable, that is, legitimate and untouched by disease or psychological problems. Destined naturally for lower class occupations by the training and sociali- zation, and systematically denied the benefits of the fourth criterion - delayed responsibilities, such children were placed out as domestic servants and agricultural laborers as soon as practicable, that is, usually between twelve and fourteen years of age. It needs to be pointed out that children, whether from the Canadian POHs or the British Emigration Societies, were routinely exploited by those Canadian families and households who received them as apprentices or "adopted" children. The temptation to blame only the institutions and societies, or the middle class men and women who ran them is disingenuous in light of general Canadian complicity in this form of child labor.

Just as "incarceration" in the Homes protected the children from contamination by separating them from a disorderly society and the unseeming example of families and friends and helped to establish their dependence and social inferiority, binding-out made possible a continuation of surveillance and control over the children's lives and confirmed their menial status by the very nature of their occupations. In brief, the POHs combined a number of conflicting assumptions that would be resolved as their implications were explicated by critics of institutionalization during the latter half of the nineteenth century.

The mid-nineteenth century debate over the consequence of institutionalization was framed both in economic and developmental terms. Institutionalization, then as now, proved to be an expensive way of caring for children. Although as voluntary institutions the POHs had perennial financial problems, they were generally reluctant to accept public funds or to cooperate with public agencies because such assistance, which never substantially reduced recurring annual deficits, meant the eventual loss of institutional control and the introduction of undesirable kinds of children. Nevertheless, public support did slowly increase, and with it institutions fitfully modified their policies and practices to meet provincial requirements. Even with provincial funding, however, the cost of residential care remained a major obstacle to its expansion, and governmental officials were compelled to consider more economical means of child rescue than the standard children's institution.

The developmental arguments against institutional care usually included the inherent debilitating consequences of an unnatural setting for children, and the difficulties in classifying inmates and preventing the corruption of the innocent and vulnerable by street or delinquent children. While an economic critic might concede the advantages of institutionalization in theory while rejecting it as uneconomical, a developmental critic condemned it as fundamentally flawed and suitable only for such residual cases as the delinquent and defective. Although it is difficult to determine which argument shifted public attitudes and policies, the move away from institutional care certainly accorded with the triumph of childhood as ideology at the end of the nineteenth century.[7]

The shift in child rescue sentiment undermined the POHs on two points - the nature of institutional life and placing-out practices. On the institutional side, only the repressive aspects of the criteria could be provided, that is, separation and protection "from" undesirable conditions and dependence as a preparation for menial occupations. The positive aspects, which required trained staff and financial resources to individualize the care and training of children, were unattainable. Although the placing-out had derived from older forms of apprenticeship and binding-out that had served as a respectable education for ordinary children as well as a means of providing for the destitute and orphaned, by mid-nineteenth century, the practice was now confined to only the latter and, consequently, identified with poverty and impotency.8

The binding-out practices of the POHs incorporated the least desirable characteristics of the early forms in that children and adolescents were "indentured" as domestic or farm labourers under minimal, if any, conditions into uninvestigated and unsupervised situations. Thus, even good placements represented the repressive values of separation and protection from family and friends, surveillance and regulation of the children's personal lives both in and outside the households. Finally, the vague ways in which the Homes described the children bound out suggest that the status of demitted inmates was unclear, problematic, and, more unfortunately, irrelevant to the institutions.

It was, however, on the deficiencies of institutional life that the argument finally turned. The rhetoric of family life meant that the best institution had to be inferior to all respectable working class families because families - unlike the POHs - could provide for the psychological development as well as the occupational training of children. Just as the orphan asylum represented a new view of human development, boarding-out reflected a new sophistication regarding the manner in which values were assimilated and habits formed while at the same time not challenging the social order. The British boarding-out practice under the Poor Law involved the placing of children in working class families - usually outside the particular union - subject to regular visits of H. M. Poor Law Inspectors. A "modeling" theory that asserted the power of respectable family life to socialize, and policies that paid householders to receive such children as family members and not as servants, that tried to narrow the class gap between children and households, and that prohibited more than two boarded-out children to a home in order to inspire individual attention, were used to justify the new practice.

British boarding-out practices stressed the positive aspects of the criteria of childhood, that is, not simply separation from their unsavory families and backgrounds but placement in respectable homes; not separation from moral contamination but association with successful lower class life; not protection from social disorder by incarceration but inculcation of the habits of decency, industry and regularity in stable families; not separation from the world but lodgement in its basic social unit; not protection within a world of children but assimilation within a home that was a functioning socio-economic unit; and not dependency as a preparation for binding-out but as an initiation into respectable family life and regular employment. The new emphasis represented a further refinement of the notion of childhood since the children were no longer placed out as employees but as family members whose upkeep was paid for by the state. When understood in this light, it is easy to see why the challenge of the boarding-out principle was too powerful to be deflected for long. The benefits - real or apparent - of boarding-out simply destroyed the moral and intellectual bases for institutionalization. Moreover, they demonstrated that the two major exponents of the old patterns - the POHs with their institutional and binding-out practices and the British Juvenile Emigration Societies with their apprenticeship schemes - were psychologically and socially flawed forms of child rescue.

Even if the POHs had been able to justify their existence as appropriate shelters for small children, the problems associated with moving from binding to boarding-out were beyond their resources to resolve. Then as now, the costs of identifying, inspecting, and paying for suitable homes were something only governments could undertake.

Theoretically and practically, the child rescue movement had been altered significantly by the boarding-out debate. In addition to the stress on the positive aspects of the criteria, there was also the recognition that children needed to be placed in settings in which they were treated as children and not as employees, and in which they were expected to participate in the natural rounds of family activities. Although major reservations regarding depen-

397

dent children still persisted, particularly, the centrality of their social class for care and placement, boarding-out marked a major refinement and expansion of the concept of childhood.

Advocates of child rescue had attempted first to remove children from the dangers of social disorder, bad families and destitution by establishing orphan asylums for dependent children. Although this was a recognition of the criteria of protection, segregation and dependence, the asylum made manifest their repressive side by attempting to quarantine socially and morally their inmates. Proponents of boarding-out rejected institutionalization for the more "natural" setting of paid home placements under government inspection. Despite a more generous understanding of childhood, the boarding-out supporters agreed with the asylum promoters in the desirability of separating children from their families. The common assumption that the protection of children routinely called for the intervention into poor and working class families showed the limits of even the most progressive of the second generation of child rescuers.

Although the advocates of boarding-out gradually won the day, the asylum continued as a competing, if declining, form of dependent child care well into the twentieth century. Indeed, the layered nature of modern child welfare in Canada is in part a legacy of the successive waves of innovation and intellectual ferment that swept over charity and welfare in North America between 1800 and 1950. It is also a tribute to organizational endurance and intellectual stagnation. While POHs in Ontario came under criticism for their inherent deficiencies by the 1890s, similar Homes were being founded in the new western provinces as late as the 1920s. Consequently, the pattern of child welfare is related to regional as well as temporal considerations.

Despite these provincial variations in child welfare, as boarding-out principles became "official" policy among private and public agencies, those seeking to place children found securing the required number of homes a difficult problem. Although cheaper than institutional care, homes still needed to be investigated prior to placement and regularly inspected or supervised thereafter. Because public authorities were as reluctant to fund boarding-out as they had been to assist the orphan asylums, the decline in institutional care was matched by the placement of children in "free" or "work" homes, euphemisms for the old practice of binding-out. Thus, despite the rhetoric of Canadian child rescuers, paid homes remained the exception rather than the rule into the twentieth century.

Without an equivalent of the British Local Government Board, Canadian aftercare of children in either paid or free homes would remain sporadic and desultory. The establishment of the Toronto Children's Aid Society (CAS) in 1891 represented the first major attempt to coordinate private and public interest in child rescue. Initially, the CAS manifested the same eagerness to separate children from their families as had the first generations of child rescuers; however, gradually it came to represent the view that if a foster family was better than an institution, then a natural family was better than a foster family.

The conclusion that even a flawed natural family was the best setting for its children did not denote any decline in commitment to childhood but rather the increased orderliness and regularity of early twentieth century society, the growing body of legislation protecting the interests of children, and the new scientific knowledge and professional skills that made family intervention desirable and practicable. By linking child and and family welfare, child rescuers opened the door for systematic intervention into lower class life while apparently showing the human face of social welfare. Although the view that children were a means of reforming their families had been voiced by early nineteenth century British philanthropic societies and writers of moral tales for children, the rise of state guardianship under the aegis of the CASs and provincial departments of neglected and dependent children and the passage of the Juvenile Delinquents Act (1908) gave a new legal sanction for family case work. Moreover, as social work moved from volunteers and job-trained staff to professional personnel, new psychological theories bearing on child development and the dynamics of social groups were assimilated into the old traditions of friendly visiting and charity organization practices.9

Ideas of scientific charity and economy were behind the pressures beginning in the 1880s for coordination among voluntary organizations. The establishment of provincial departments and the introduction of government funding for child welfare activities in the early part of this century forced these agencies to organize and staff themselves in order to meet requirements of accountability. Although these demands brought about changes in institutional and agency practices and gradually eroded the autonomy of the private sector, they did not directly affect the relationships between staff and clients as would the new psychological dimension being added to charity work.

The union of case work methods and modern psychological knowledge marked the beginnings of the shift from child rescue to child welfare. Instead of working with children in isolation from their network of experiences and emotional connections, child welfare promoters sought to treat them within their families and communities. Since providential and hereditarian theories of behavior were generally eschewed by child rescuers, children with problems had to be in some degree the products of their environments, which included most significantly their families and neighborhoods. Consequently, the stress on keeping children with their natural families led logically to the need for investigating and counselling families, the compilation of dossiers on other family members, cooperation with other community agencies, and the promotion of social worker as friend _and_ agent of government authority.

Protecting children and ensuring their dependence meant eliminating the conditions within the family and community that were endangering and, more positively, creating the conditions that would insure proper child development.

> If we fail to intervene we cost the state
> much more and with our increasing knowledge
> of human behavior and the increasing facili-
> ties for dealing with family problems our
> successes should become more numerous and

our failures fewer.10

Surveillance and solicitude were still essential ingredients, but they were now deployed differently and more subtly.

As with the earlier shift from repressive to a more positive understanding of protection, segregation, and dependence, manifested in the move from institutional care to boarding-out, the emergence of family case work also demonstrated the growing confidence of child welfare agents in their ability to control human behaviour and change human values. When the Canadian Council on Child Welfare was founded in 1920, it still reflected much of the older child protection perspectives characteristic of the first provincial legislation and the Juvenile Delinquents Act.

> The home rather than the institution, the
> family rather than the relief agency, the
> mothers' allowances instead of palatial
> orphanages, the second chance rather than
> the court, the Family Maintenance Act
> rather than the Criminal Code clauses for
> the family deserter . . . these are the
> social workers' high water barriers
> against the tide of poor homes, careless
> marriages, selfish home life, corrupting
> divorce legislation, and the old age
> stress of instinct against restriction,
> of man and woman against society's
> guarantee to its own survival - the family.11

During the next twenty years, the Council underwent a series of name changes that demonstrated the expanding nature of its work. As it moved from the child-centred focus (Canadian Council on Child Welfare, 1920), to a child-family one (Canadian Council on Child and Family Welfare, 1929), to a broad social welfare perspective (Canadian Welfare Council, 1937), the breadth of intervention and control expanded. At each stage, the concentration on children diminished and the social context became more significant.

The CCCW mounted its prototype social survey with a campaign against the British Juvenile Immigration Movement by exploiting the issues of

401

child protection. Following this initial success, the Council undertook surveys in all provinces and most major cities during the next two decades. Although child welfare remained a major aspect of every survey, none would ever recapture the intensity and single-mindedness of the first. The work of the CCCW demonstrated that the legislation surrounding child welfare was unable to ensure a full childhood for dependent children and the need for a broadly focused concept of child welfare. The limits of legislation protecting women and children and of coordinated services and agencies meant that substantial state intervention was necessary. Only when government provided universal social security and properly funded welfare services would there be adequate conditions for delayed responsibilities for even dependent children.12

Concomitant with the emphasis on retaining children in their natural families, the rise of family case work, and the need for community-based programs - all of which ultimately required massive state funding and control - was the appearance of residual classes of dependent children, who increasingly became the object of state responsibiity and institutional care. Among these categories were the delinquent, the feebleminded, and developmentally handicapped, who had been identified in the nineteenth century as deviant groups in need of special care. Indeed, one of the refinements in child rescue had been the distinction and separation of the neglected and abandoned from the delinquent and the separation of both categories from the mentally and developmentally handicapped.13

The perception of deviance was always tinged with the need to prevent the contamination of "normal" children as well as a concern for more effective treatment. As the literature of the societies demonstrate, early nineteenth century interest in the rehabilitation of juvenile delinquents, which had been one of the contributing factors to the rise of the child rescue movement, had at first conflated ordinary street children with the criminal. Reformers were also concerned over the indiscriminate mixing of children with adults in common gaols and prisons and the use of incarceration as a means of dealing with vagrancy and destitution. The earliest institutions for the reformation of delinquents in North America and Great Britain were organized by private philanthropy and even as late as the 1850s exhibited in their rhetoric an optimism regarding the power of institutionalization and the malleability of human nature that was florid even for child savers.14

Early Canadian training or industrial schools such as those established under the Ontario Industrial Schools Act of 1884 or those in Nova Scotia under church auspices were expressions of private benevolence that gradually came under provincial control. Whereas the cost and perceived deficiencies of institutionalization of normal neglected and dependent children led to boarding-out and eventually foster care, institutional care remained standard treatment for delinquents. Moreover, new models of congregate care, for example, cottage systems, which were intended to eliminate the worst effects of institutionalization, proved even more costly than old institutional forms.

Care of the feebleminded was related in several ways to the control of the criminal. First, a recurrent theme throughout the nineteenth and early twentieth century was the question of mental deficiency with the propensity for criminal behavior as well as with uncontrolled fertility. Consequently, feeblemindedness was seen both as a problem of incompetence that required institutionalization in order to provide the requisite care, and as a threat to the moral and physiological well-being of society. Eugenic theories, which reflected class antipathies as well as virulent religious, racial, and ethnic antagonisms, stressed the threat of unlimited breeding by the weakest members of society while advocating increased fertility among the best. Second, unwed motherhood was deemed by many advocates of child welfare, for example, Charlotte Whitton, as clear proof of mental deficiency. Sexually active girls and women lacked the intelligence, prudence, and moral character associated with normal development. As a result, all statistics on illegitimacy could be understood in two supporting ways: first, since the feebleminded were believed to be immensely fecund, they had to be controlled by incarceration or sterilization in order to reduce illegitimacy.

403

Second, illegitimacy was seen to be prima facie evidence of feeblemindedness. Thus, illegitimacy was both the results of feeblemindedness and the indisputable evidence of its existence.

These two major categories of specialized children, the delinquent and feebleminded, were increasingly segregated at the very time when "normal" dependent children were assimilated into childhood by foster care and family intervention, and the common school. Consequently, these two categories represented the residual elements of institutional child rescue who were doomed either by their anti-social behaviour or their incompetence to control, restraint, and surveillance as opposed to care, rescue, and solicitude.

Due to declining populations, diminishing public support, a withdrawal of professional sympathy, and the rise of a "rival" child care model (the CAS), the POHs found themselves in the curious position of becoming the depositories for the very children - those with social problems and handicaps - that they had formerly refused to admit. Before the rise of the CAS, many physically handicapped and mentally retarded children remained at home or had been placed in public institutions because the POHs would not accept them. Now such children were surrendered to the new quasi-government agencies, the CASs, which in turn finding them "unplaceable," sheltered them temporarily in institutional settings. Subsequently, the POHs and CASs, claiming insufficient staff and funds, lobbied along with many other service and professional groups for the institutionalization of such children under state aegis.

The "normalization" of dependent and institu-tionalization of deviant children destroyed the raison d'être of the children's institutions. Faced with the gradual loss of their clientele and the justification for philanthropic support, the asylums converted to institutions for the care and treatment of new categories of specialized children. Just as the original orphanages had been established in the 1850s in response to the needs of small groups of specialized children - orphaned, abandoned or destitute - some institutions had begun as early as the 1890s to accommodate the demands of emerging

404

provincially supervised systems of child welfare by acting as a temporary shelter first for CAS wards and later children charged under the Juvenile Delinquents Act. As these adjustments and later attempts to economize and rationalize failed to protect declining institutions, some asylums began to transform themselves into new specialized centres for such children as the emotionally disturbed and learning handicapped. By the 1950s, the process of transformation from congregate institutions for ordinary dependent children to specialized professional agencies for small numbers of children was well underway.

By the 1940s, the mainstreaming of most dependent children had reduced greatly institutional populations and created the appearance of a benign concept of childhood. Between appearance and actuality, however, there still yawned the chasm of free homes and inadequate family casework services. Those provinces, such as Alberta, with highly centralized and seemingly efficient departments of child welfare still made massive use of unqualified staff and confidently ignored modern principles of child welfare in adoptions, institutionalization, and foster care. Twenty years of leadership by the CCCW, the modernization of some provincial departments of social welfare under competent professional personnel, and the popularization of ideas about child life, had failed to bring Canadian child welfare to either minimum national standards or a consensus. Gross economic inequalities, enduring historical and political experiences, unique social characteristics, and varying degrees of openness to change, resulted in a crazy quilt of modern, antiquated, and slowly changing agencies and practices.

Despite Charlotte Whitton's energetic leadership of the Canadian Welfare Council in its campaign to reorganize and coordinate old systems of social welfare and to introduce modern social work standards and personnel throughout Canada in the inter-war decades, the limits of a quasi-public national agency to pursuade or pressure private societies and municipal and provincial officials to make changes were evident in the uneven results of the social surveys conducted by the Council. Not unexpectedly, some provinces such as Ontario easily assimilated the new standards, others such as Nova Scotia, Manitoba and British Columbia reflected acceptable if uneasy blends of professionalism and provincial autonomy, and a final group composed of Alberta and New Brunswick so deviated from the new norms that they were the repeated objects of surveys and criticisms.

The different behavior was partially a product of personalities in the cases of Nova Scotia's Ernest Blois and Ontario's J. J. Kelso. In New Brunswick and Prince Edward Island, it arose with having adopted colonial equivalents of the English poor law. In Manitoba and later British Columbia, governments were committed to efficient organization of their services. Alberta and Saskatchewan were driven to centralization by economic and social dislocations. While Ontario enjoyed the distinction of being Canada's more populous and prosperous province, Alberta's social and economic distress was exacerbated by political alienation and sectional antagonisms. During the first decade of the Council, the focus was primarily on coordination and modernization of existing systems and the placement of professional social workers in key positions. The scope of activity, while varied and demanding, had centred on the needs of children and families at risk. Consequently, although the clientele broadened to include more than traditional objects of charity, it remained obvious that the reception of social services carried with it the stigma of economic and social failure. No matter how leaders such as Whitton drew analogies with medicine and engineering, case work treated problems that seemed the results of social or economic incompetence or moral flaws.

Although such areas as mothers allowances and old age pensions might attract provincial or federal interest, and issues such as unwed parents and adoption might finally receive modern legislation, because it was in the interest of administrative efficiency, governments, who increasingly bore the responsibility for funding extended social welfare, could respond as little as they wished to the needs of society's failures. The Great Depression altered many of these attitudes by transforming large segments of respectable Canadian society into the destitute and unemployed. Relief had to be extended in amounts and to new categories previously unknown. As private and municipal agencies came to the end of their resources, provinces too found it difficult to sustain the level of expenditures required for relief.15

The continuing distress of the 1930s compelled both the Bennett and Mackenzie King governments to provide huge grants in support of relief programs. The problems associated with the intervention of the federal government and pauperization of a significant part of Canadian society were clearly influential in altering popular perceptions about the nature and objectives of social welfare. The precipitous issues were the confusion of relief for unemployed employables and for the traditional categories of dependents, and social work's distinction between mere relief and investigation and counselling through case work. At the same time, the Great Depression placed heavy burdens on the always understaffed social work profession as municipal and provincial departments turned to those with training and experience in the organization and administration of social services.16

The unbelievable dislocation of the 1930s had moved social work and social service from the margins of society to the mainstream of public consciousness as part of the general concern for social security. As a profession dealing not merely with society's losers but with the victims of an appalling economic disaster, social workers would later find their value in counselling and aiding the families and dependents of service personnel, and assisting in the maintenance of their morale reaffirmed during the Second World War. Despite the dreadful pressures and distress, the new demand on the profession created a new sense of purpose and relevance that would flower in the 1950s in the confident expansion of social work.

The distress of the 1930s that focused attention on the general issue of "social security," and the dedication and sacrifice of the war years, suggested that the unmet agenda of the 1920s - such as the 1929 discussion of family allowances and other matters before the Select Standing Committee on Industrial and International Relations of the House of Commons - would be addressed.

The appointment of the Royal Commission on Dominion-Provincial Relations in 1937 allowed for the first national consideration of social services in the light of Canada's socio-economic coming-of-age as a major developed nation. The Commission's recommendation for National Adjustment Grants was based on two fundamental principles: respect for and strengthening of provincial autonomy in spheres reserved to them and the need to enable "every province to provide for its people services of average Canadian standards." Although the Conference called in 1941 to consider the implementation of aspects of the recommendations for the Report broke up acrimoniously, wartime conditions provided the opportunity for greater governmental intervention. The mood of optimism of the late war years and the perceived need for substantial reconstruction in the post-war period encouraged governments to appoint committees and task forces, and for individuals and societies to undertake to examine a wide range of social and human needs.17

The questions addressed and recommendations made in the 1940s along with the specific actions undertaken over the next quarter century, would gradually transform Canada into a North American version of a welfare state and radically alter the nature of dependence, especially as it pertained to child life. The 1940s witnessed the completion of the transformation of dependent child life and the final framing of a consensus - now embedded in legislation and social policy - regarding children in Canadian national life. The following decades would be the working out of the logic of the consensus and the surfacing of the contradictions and flaws in it.

Central to the consensus of the 1940s was the tentative beginnings of state welfarism in Canada. To some extent, the work of Sir William Beveridge - his earlier studies as well as the 1943 Social Insurance and Allied Services - inspired Canadian efforts such as the Marsh Report, Charlotte Whitton's The Dawn of Ampler Life and Harry Cassidy's, Social Security and Reconstruction in Canada (1943), the Haegerty Report (1943-44), and the Curtis Report (1944), as well as provincial legislation, for example, The Vivian Act (1944) in Ontario. The creation of the new federal Department of National Health and Welfare followed by the appointment of Dr. George F. Davidson - then Executive Director of the Canadian Welfare Council - as the First Deputy Minister of Welfare and the passage of the Family Allowance Act, all in 1944, signaled a new era of public social services.

The reports, discussions, and legislation of the 1940s represented the tentative outlines of state welfarism in Canada. As elusive and blurred as the outlines were, and as faltering the implementation over the succeeding decades, the forties provided the essential documents and legislation to transform an historically fragmented and governmentally uncoordinated collection of organizations, institutions, and individuals into a confident and optimistic consensus. Once the federal government was committed to such a massive financial intervention as the family allowance, the possibilities for future action - either directly or through cooperative arrangements with the provinces - were greatly enhanced. Moreover, the family allowance was analogous <u>not</u> to social assistance but to public education, <u>and</u> thus, was immediately acceptable to those outside the traditional reach of private and public welfare agencies. The allowance came as a right of citizenship and not charity. The provision of citizen-right benefits legitimated an increase in public assistance services and benefits.18

The various reports on social security and the main protagonists often muddied the waters with their adaptation of British and American ideas and models. Those who bothered to read the reports and the debates in the journals were treated to turgid arguments on "social utilities" and services "in kind" that consistently missed the crucial issue of who received the benefits. Universal medicare, public schooling, and cheap post-secondary education, all of which seem to fit the service in kind model, carry no stigma.

What was clearly lacking in the reports and comment was any powerful philosophical or psychological insight into the issues, and any historical perspective on the development of social welfare in Canada. Information about existing provincial health and social services, the costs of the various proposed programs, and the pertinent sections in the Beveridge Report, were mixed with perennial Canadian concerns about regional, religious, linguistic, cultural, and ethnic differences, and mortared together with arguments from the experiences of Great Britain.19

Despite the failure to articulate clearly what was at stake in the debates, the protagonists did realize that a major shift in Canadian life was in the making. As indicated earlier, the transformation involved the dramatic extension of government provision of citizen-right benefits to all class of Canadians as well as an increase of means test benefits to the traditional recipients of social welfare. The initiation of family allowances in 1945 co-opted the working and middle classes, forced improvements in provincially regulated services such as registration of births, and extended the reach of provincial departments of child welfare due to potential misuse of allowances by parents. In brief, the Family Allowance Act laid the basis for an incipient Canadian welfare state by uniting the interests of the respectable classes with universal government subsidies.20

The controversy of the 1940s really centred on the issue of co-option and not the extension of public assistance services. All would have agreed with Whitton that as "the medium through which civilization itself is transmitted . . . [the child's] well-being becomes the first concern of society." The question was how and under what conditions the well being was to be insured. When George Davidson wrote that the allowances were based on the assumption "that all but an infinitesimal fraction of our Canadian fathers and mothers will do everything possible to use the sources at their disposal to provide properly for the health and well being of their children," and D. H. Stepler cited the _Times_ (London) "that payments in 'kind' simply indicate a distrust of the working-class mother who is the best judge of the needs of her family, and who is called by the Archbishop of Canterbury, 'the real heroine of our phase of civilization,'" we need to decode these statements. Charlotte Whitton apparently understood the drift and offered social utilities and services in kind with the idea of restricting the recipients.21

410

Whether this failure to deal directly with the issue was a conscious effort to suppress debate or a lack of ideological perspective is unclear. The objections generally raised against family allowances were cast in conventional Canadian concerns of federalism, racial/linguistic conflict, and ethnic fertility rates. It is possible to see the "reconstruction" as a cynical attempt of a government-business alliance to co-opt the working and middle classes into accepting a new Canadian capitalist society that was developing. Such an interpretation claims too much for the vision and political insight of those involved and seems to run contrary to the level of discussion both during the depression and the war years.22

The rise of the welfare state marked another shift in focus by locating new recipients of aid within the general public. Such a shift allowed for massive state intervention into more lives because provision of benefits carried with it the presumption of control, and assumed a general dependence of all citizens and the responsibility of the state to protect them. Earlier efforts at protection, as in the case of childhood, had attempted to eliminate specific dangerous conditions such as demonstrated by legislation in the areas of public health, working conditions, and public amusements. The new view, recognizing the limitations of prohibitions, moved to provide social goods. The 1944 Family Allowance Act represented an early attempt to promote directly a social good. The universalization of benefit also had the effect of removing the stigma attached to relief by identifying the conferral of benefits in cash or services as a citizen-right.

As the state became more ordered and dependable and the dangers inherent in public life receded, the drive to separate children and private family life from public life diminished. Since the first beneficiaries of the well-ordered national state were children who were sent to universal common schooling, prohibited the enjoyments of public amusements, and protected from the dangers of employments, infectious diseases, and noxious conditions, families and child rescuers could relax their vigilance as the gap between the criteria of childhood and the social conditions narrowed.

411

The rise of the welfare state was the final element in the creation of childhood as an ideology in modern industrial societies. Initially, the concept had grown out of the lives of the bourgeoisie who combined a new means of socio-economic mobility and legitimacy (schooling), a knowledge of child development, and a sense of privacy, to create what sociologists have customarily described as the traditional family. Childhood required at that historical stage the development of a private affectionate family life and a prolonged period of education within the protective environment of the school. When the first attempts were made to extend the concept to some of the lower orders, that is, dependent children, the method used was an adaption of the private family and school, that is, a child centred institution that acting in loco parentis protected its members from the contamination of society, particularly families and friends.

For ordinary children within their natural families, the establishment of common schooling in the mid-nineteenth century marked a significant extension of the protection, dependence, and segregation criteria. The later legislation regulating employment, health, and public morals, incorporated major elements of the criteria into public policy and behavior. As with institutions such as the POHs, the early legislation attempted to implement repressive aspects of the criteria. Even those laws that provided limited benefits, for example, mothers allowance, stigmatized the recipients as objects of charity. With the establishment of the welfare state, at least two significant changes occurred. First, since most benefits are identified as citizen-rights, there was no shame attached to the enjoyment of them. Consequently the quality of the benefit and its delivery were considerably better than with quasi-charitable social assistance. Second, the extension of family intervention services to include a wide range of desirable programs, for example, psychological counselling, has made them acceptable to the middle classes.

Just as by the end of the nineteenth century the total institution had lost its relevance for care of dependent children, the family and school would lose part of their essential role in defining childhood by the 1950s. Support needed to ensure keeping children within their natural families would be provided by welfare state programs that included social assistance and income maintenance for the needy as well as psychological intervention for the middle classes. Just as childhood criteria were originally encapsulated within specific institutional settings, i.e., family and school, and then partially assimilated socially by protective legislation of the late nineteenth and early twentieth centuries, the welfare state began to assimilate the positive aspects of the criteria. By mid-twentieth century, the state had taken on the basic characteristics of the nineteenth century asylum and, thus, became the modern "most ordered of rescues" for all.

appendix

PRINCIPAL PROTESTANT INSTITUTIONS EXAMINED

AND FOUNDING DATES

Montreal Protestant Orphan Asylum (1822)

Hamilton Ladies Benevolent Society and Orphan Asylum (1848)

Toronto Protestant Orphan Home and Female Aid Society (1851)

Saint John Protestant Orphan Asylum (1854)

St. John's Church of England Widows' and Orphans Asylum (1855)

Toronto Girls' Home and Public Nursery (1856)

Kingston Orphans' Home and Widows' Friend Society (1857)

Halifax Protestant Orphans' Home (1857)

Boys' Home, Toronto (1860)

Ottawa Protestant Orphans' Home (1864)

Saint Paul's Almshouse of Industry for Girls, Halifax (1867)

Montreal Protestant Infants' Home (1870)

Victoria Protestant Orphans' Home (1873)

Women's Refuge and Children's Home and Home for Orphans, Aged and Friendless, London (1874-76)

Halifax Infants' Home (1875)

Protestant Children's Home, Winnipeg (1885)

Methodist Orphanage, St. John's (1888)

Maternity Home, Victoria (1893)

Alexandra Orphanage, Vancouver (1894)

Kingston Infants' Home and Home for Friendless Women (1894)

Protestant Orphans' Home, Prince Edward Island (1907)

Wood's Christian Home (1915)

abbreviations

MLG	Mitchell Library, Glasgow
MTL	Metropolitan Toronto Central Library
MUN	Memorial University of Newfoundland, St. John's
NBM	New Brunswick Museum, Saint John
NCL	National Library of Canada
NLI	National Library of Ireland, Dublin
NPRL	Newfoundland Provincial Reference Library, St. John's
PAA	Provincial Archives of Alberta, Edmonton
PABC	Provincial Archives of British Columbia, Victoria
PAC	Public Archives of Canada, Ottawa
PAM	Provincial Archives of Manitoba, Winnipeg
PANB	Provincial Archives of New Brunswick, Fredericton
PANF	Provincial Archives of Newfoundland, St. John's
PANS	Public Archives of Nova Scotia, Halifax
PAO	Provincial Archives of Ontario, Toronto
PAPEI	Public Archives of Prince Edward Island, Charlottetown
PLBC	Provincial Library of British Columbia, Victoria
PRO	Public Record Office, London
QU	Queen's Univeristy, Kingston
SABR	Saskatchewan Archives Board, Regina
SABS	Saskatchewan Archives Board, Saskatoon
SJCL	Saint John City Library
UCBC	United Church of Canada, British Columbia Conference Archives, Vancouver

UCSJ	United Church of Canada, Newfoundland Conference Archives, St. John's
UNB	University of New Brunswick, Fredericton
UWO	University of Western Ontario, London
VCA	Vancouver City Archives
VPL	Vancouver Public Library
WMI	Wiggins Male Institution, Saint John

notes

[1] CHILDHOOD AS IDEOLOGY

1. Philippe Ariès, Centuries of Childhood: A Social History of Family Life (New York: Alfred A. Knopf, 1962).

2. Anthony M. Platt, The Child Savers: The Invention of Delinquency (Chicago: University of Chicago Press, 1969); Robert M. Mennel, Thorns and Thistles: Juvenile Delinquents in the United States, 1825-1940 (Hanover, N.H.: University Press of New England, 1973); Stephen Schlossman, Love and the American Delinquent: The Theory and Practice of "Progressive" Juvenile Justice, 1825-1920 (Chicago: University of Chicago Press, 1977); and Ellen Ryerson: The Best-Laid Plans: America's Juvenile Court Experiment (New York: Hill and Wang, 1978).

3. Joy Parr, Labouring Children: British Immigrant Apprentices to Canada, 1869-1924 (London: Croom Helm, 1980); Terrence Morrison, "The Child and Urban Social Reform in Late Nineteenth Century Ontario," (Ph.D. dissertation, University of Toronto, 1970); Andrew Jones and Leonard Rutman, In the Children's Aid: J.J. Kelso and Child Welfare in Ontario (Toronto: University of Toronto Press, 1981); and Neil Sutherland, Children in English-Canadian Society: Framing the Twentieth-Century Consensus (Toronto: University of Toronto Press, 1976).

4. See "Humanitarianism or Control? A Symposium on Aspects of Nineteenth-Century Social Reform in Britain and America," Rice University Studies 67 (Winter 1981).

5. R. L. Schnell, "Childhood as Ideology: A Re-Interpretation of the Common School," British Journal of Educational Studies 27 (February 1979): 7-28.

6. Erik H. Erikson, Childhood and Society (2nd. ed.; New York: W. W. Norton, 1963).

7. See, for example, Melford E. Spiro, Children of the Kibbutz: A Study in Child Training and Personality (New York: Schocken Books, 1965); Urie Bronfenbrenner, Two Worlds of Childhood: USA and USSR (New York: Russell Sage Foundation, 1970); and Karen Wald, Children of Che: Childcare and Education in Cuba (Palo Alto: Ramparts Press, 1978).

8. Fifteenth Annual Report (1908).

9. Peter Gay, The Enlightenment: An Interpretation, 2 vols. (New York: Alfred A. Knopf, 1966-69).

10. David J. Rothman, The Discovery of the Asylum: Social Order and Disorder in the New Republic (Boston: Little, Brown, 1971), and Conscience and Convenience: The Asylum and Its Alternatives in Progressive America (Boston: Little, Brown, 1980); Ford K. Brown, The Fathers of the Victorians (London: Cambridge University Press, 1961); Bernard Semmel, The Methodist Revolution (New York: Basic Books, 1973); and Richard Allen, The Social Passion: Religion and Social Reform in Canada, 1914-28 (Toronto: University of Toronto Press, 1973).

11. R. L. Schnell and Patricia T. Rooke, "The Institutional Society: Childhood, Family, and Schooling," in Approaches to Educational History, eds., R. M. Stamp et al. (Winnipeg: Faculty of Education, University of Manitoba, 1981), pp. 113-130 and 158-163.

12. Michael Zuckerman, "Dr. Spock: The Confidence Man," in The Family in History, ed. Charles E. Rosenberg (Philadelphia: University of Pennsylvania Press, 1975), pp. 179-182.

PART 1 - ESTABLISHING THE ASYLUM

[2] POOR RELIEF AND RELIGIOUS BENEVOLENCE IN BRITISH NORTH AMERICA

1. Such descriptions are found in George C. F. Bartley, The Seven Ages of a Village Pauper (London, 1874) and "Pauper's Creches," in A Handybook for Guardians of the Poor (London, 1876).

2. Quoted in a paper read by Major G. F. Ramsay, Chairman, Barton Regis Board of Guardians, 18 March 1898, surveying the evolution of the poor laws, BCA. See also, Judith Fingard, "The Winter's Tale: The Seasonal Customs of Pre-Industrial Poverty in British North America 1815-1860," CHA Historical Papers (Ottawa: CHA, 1974): 65-94; and J. M. Pitsula, "The Treatment of Tramps in Late Nineteenth Century Toronto," CHA Historical Papers (Ottawa: CHA, 1980): 116-132.

3. B. W. Heise, Trends in Public Welfare Administration, pp. 3-6. Charlotte Whitton Papers, MG 30, E256, vol. 37, PAC. (Hereafter cited as WP/37).

4. The most comprehensive treatment of the beginnings of social programs for Ontario is Richard B. Splane, Social Welfare in Ontario 1791-1893 (Toronto: University of Toronto Press, 1965), pp. 65-69.

5. Splane, p. 68.

6. Charlotte Whitton, "The Evolution of Social Government and the Welfare Services in Canada," Pt. III, pp. 3-4, in lectures delivered at the Montreal School of Social Work 1942-47, WP/80, file 3; and Mrs. Marguerita Grant, "Historical Sketches of Hospitals and Almshouses in Halifax, Nova Scotia, 1749-1859," The Nova Scotia Medical Bulletin (May 1937): 250-312.

7. Whitton, p. 6; and Welfare Council of Halifax, The Brief on Nova Scotia Poor Relief Act, April 2, 1957, RG 25, Series C, vol. 9, #8, PANS.

8. "An Act to Regulate and Provide for the Support of the Poor in this Province," Cap. XLIII (XXVI George II, III) A.D.1786, New Brunswick. Almost identical terminology was retained in the Revised Statutes, 1952, Chpt. 221, "Support of the Poor Act," discussed in the Canadian Welfare Council Survey of New Brunswick, 1949, pp. 12 and 63, Canadian Council on Social Development Papers, MG 28, I 10, vol. 135, PAC. (Hereafter cited as CCSD/135.) See also James M. Wahlen, "The Nineteenth Century Almshouse System in Saint John County," Social History 7 (April 1971): 5-27, and Brereton Greenhaus, "Paupers and Poorhouses: The Development of Poor Relief in Early New Brunswick," Social History 1 (April 1968): 103-126.

9. Report of Committee for the Relief of the Poor (1819), MGU.

10.   The Poorhouse Minutes (1864-1889) tell us much about the extent of poverty on the island, PAPEI.   Prince Edward Island, House of Assembly, Journal (1852), p. 48; and discussed by Margaret E. Anstey, director of Saint John CAS, in "Memo: Re-Organization of Child and Family Welfare, Charlottetown," (August 1931), CCSD/19.

11.   Marguerita Grant, pp. 253-254; T. B. Atkins, A History of Halifax City, in Collections of the Nova Scotia Historical Society (1892-94), vol. VIII (Halifax, 1895).   C. E. Saunders, "Social Conditions and Legislation in Nova Scotia," (M.A. thesis, Dalhousie University, 1949), Chapter 3, PANS; K. Williams, "Poor Relief and Medicine in Nova Scotia," Nova Scotia Historical Society, vol. 24, pp. 40-42; and G. E. Hart, "Two Centuries of Child Welfare," RG 25, Series C, vol. 9, #12, pp. 1-2, PANS.

12.   Grant, p. 254; Nova Scotia, Statutes (1823), George IV Cap. III, and Journal (1838), pp. 339-340; and Nova Scotia, Journal of Assembly (1832), pp. 58-59.   Also see, Statutes of Nova Scotia, (1813) George III, Cap. VI; (1813) George III, Cap. VI; (1823) George IV Cap. XXIII; (1823) George IV, Cap. VI; and Saunders, p. 74.

13.   Grant, p. 257.

14.   Nova Scotian, 11 January 1832 and 18 January 1832. The discussion is explicated by Saunders, pp. 100-105.

15.   Nova Scotia, Journal of House of Assembly (1834), Appendix 12; Nova Scotia, Journal of House of Assembly (1828), Appendix C; and Saunders, p. 96.

16.   John Withers, "St. John's Over a Century Ago - As Revealed in the First Volume of the Royal Gazette (1907)"; and H. M. Mosdell, "When Was That? A Chronological Dictionary of Events in Newfoundland Down To and Including the Year 1922," PANF; Barbara Smith, "The Historical Development of Child Welfare Legislation in Newfoundland, 1832-1949," B.S.W. thesis, Memorial University, 1971; and Richard Urquhart, "A Survey of the Newfoundland Government Toward Poor Relief 1860-69," (Dec. 1973); and Stuart R. Godfrey, "Introduction of Social Legislation to Newfoundland," address to the Newfoundland Historical Society, 19 April 1979, p. 4, CNS.

17.   Godfrey, pp. 3-9. A similar Nova Scotia auction of paupers found in "Return of Paupers, Dalhousie and Perot, 1951," RG 25, Series C, vol. 5, PANS.

18. Mosdell, 1846-1861; and Paul O'Neill, The Oldest City: The Story of St. John's, Newfoundland, vol. 1, (Erin, Ontario: Press Porcepic, 1975-76).

19. Quoted in Mosdell for Poor Asylum entry, 1861; James Spratt, Secretary to E. P. Morris, Premier, 22 April 1911, F. A. Hall, Government Engineer to Hon. R. Watson, Colonial Secretary, 15 December 1911; F. A. Hall to Morris, 10 April 1911; and L. Harcourt, Downing Street to Sir Ralph Williams, Governor, Newfoundland, 3 February 1911, file: Poor Asylum (1910-11), PANF; and Reports of governor's speech and House of Assembly's reply are in St. John's Royal Gazette, 4 December 1860 and 12 December 1860; also Journal of Legislative Council, 12 December 1860, and 1861, app. 14, p. 99, and app. 15, pp. 101-3. The Standard and Conception Bay Advertiser (Harbor Grace), 23 May 1860, included a letter from "Humanity" who observed "there is great destitution among the poor people for want of seed potatoes."

20. The Royal Gazette and Newfoundland Advertiser, 24 November 1835 and St. John's Globe, "Old Charitable Societies of St. John's," 20 April 1885.

21. Census of Canada (1870-71), vol. 4, Population of Nova Scotia, Appendix A, pp. 94, 125, 232, and 234.

22. Saunders, pp. 87 and 84; and for the year 1818 in T. B. Atkins, "A History of Halifax City."

23. John Withers, St. John's A Century Ago (1907).

24. In "File: Able Bodied Poor Relief, n.d.," employment in rockbreaking and snow shovelling was stipulated as "condition"; Journal of Assembly (1862), pp. 408-411, about the regulations for the management of the poor house; Journal of Assembly (1860-61), Appendix 14, contains a letter from J. Shea, Commissioner of the Poor, 20 December 1860, insisting on labor in return for relief in the outports. Duties of the Commissioner of Distribution are found in Legislative Council Journal (1861), Appendices 14, p. 99, and 15, pp. 101-3.

25. Journal of Assembly (1863), pp. 1188-1190; and Public Notices from R. Carter, Acting Colonial Secretary, 17 May 1862 and 27 October 1862 with Circular, 26 October 1862, to Poor Commissioners in Outports, Journal of Assembly (1863), pp. 1188-1190.

26. "A Report of the Society for Improving the Condition of the Poor of St. John's from 31 July 1808 to 31 July 1809";

and "A Report of the Society for Improving the Condition of the Poor of St. John's . . . 31 July 1810 to 31 July 1811," PANF.

27.   "Constitution of the Nova Scotia Philanthropic Society, revised Oct. 2, 1837," PANS.

28.   The following pages on the Benevolent Irish Society come from: "Rules and Constitution of the Benevolent Irish Society, 1806, 1807,"; Centenary Volume of the BIS, 1806-1906; Centenary Souvenir Book of the Basilica Cathedral of St. John the Baptist, St. John's (1855-1955); "The Irish Society Half a Century Ago," The Trade Review 15 March 1902, PANF; Account Books, BIS, (1862-1875), MUN; The Patriot and 'Terra' Nova Herald, 28 February 1859, St. John's Public Library; John C. Pippy, "The Benevolent Irish Society," in The Book of Newfoundland, ed. J. R. Smallwood (St. John's: Newfoundland Book Publications, 1937), pp. 171-185 and M. F. Howley, "Ecclesiastical History of Newfoundland" (Belleville, Ontario: MIRA Publishing Company, 1979), p. 228.

29.   Saint John Almshouse, New Brunswick (1853-1963), PANB; and Prince Edward Island, Journal of House of Assembly, (1852), p. 48, PAPEI. It was not until 1854 that specialized facilities were available for Newfoundland's destitute Catholic children when the first Catholic orphanage at the Convent of Mercy opened its doors. By the end of the century Catholic children had several other orphanages including Belvedere and Villa Nova as well as the Mt. Cashel Boys' Industrial school. Howley, pp. 276-277. Also discussed in The Book of Newfoundland, pp. 303-304.

30.   The Second Annual Report of the Central Auxiliary Society for Promoting Education and Industry Among the Indians and Destitute Settlers in Canada, 8 April 1829 (Montreal: 1829), pp. 38-40.

31.   Ibid., pp. 14-16 and 38-39.

32.   Ibid., pp. 35-39.

33.   Splane, p. 76.

34.   In 18th Annual Report of the Ladies' Benevolent Society of Montreal (1851); St. George's Ladies' Benevolent Society Report (1843-1844) of Halifax; and "The Story of the Ladies' Aid Society, 50th Anniversary 15 February 1924," The

Message (March 1924), pp. 6-13, in Bronson Family Papers, MG 28, III 26, vol. 383, file: St. Andrews Kirk, PAC.

35. Edna Potts, "The Dorcas Society (St. John's)," in The Book of Newfoundland, pp. 90-93.

36. Ibid.

37. Report of St. George's District Visiting Society (1853); and Seventh Report of the Halifax Methodist Female Benevolent Society (1823), p. 6, PANS.

38. Reports of Association for Improving the Condition of the Poor in Halifax (1877-79), PANS. According to the Nova Scotian, 28 January 1867, the society was founded in late 1866 in response to the relief work conducted by the Catholic St. Vincent de Paul Society.

39. Discussed by Margaret B. Simey, Charitable Effort in Liverpool in the Nineteenth Century (Liverpool: Liverpool University Press, 1951), pp. 33 and 81-90. J. C. Pringle, Social Work of the London Churches: An Account of the Metropolitan Visiting and Relief Association 1843-1937 (London: Oxford University Press, 1937), discussed the ideas behind charity organization giving due attention to American experiments and reformers such as Samuel Gridley Howe and Charles Loring Brace as well as Chalmers and C. S. Loch who began the Charity Organization Society in Britain.

40. Eleanor F. Rathbone, William Rathbone (London: Macmillan, 1905), p. 128; William Rathbone, Method Versus Muddle In Charitable Work (London: Macmillan, 1867); and Anne Hole, A Ministry to the Poor (London: Henry Young and Sons, 1936).

41. All references to the Halifax Poor Man's Association came from the minutes and annual reports of the PMFS (1820-26), PANS; and George E. Hart, "The Halifax Poor Man's Friend Society: An Early Social Experiment," Canadian Historical Review 34 (June 1953): 109-123. Count Rumford's ideas which were important to the PMFS are found in Collected Works of Count Rumford, ed. Sanford C. Brown, vol. 1: Public Institutions (Cambridge: Harvard University Press, 1970).

42. Public Address, 17 February 1820.

43. New Brunswick, Journal of House of Assembly (1857), p. DLVII.

44. Final Report to the Hon. Commissioner of Public Works on the Completion of the North-East Wing of the Common Gaol at Montreal by Thomas McGinn, Gaoler and Superintendent of Works (Montreal, 1857), pp. 7, 15-16, and 37.

45. Howley, pp. 276-277.

46. Report of Inspector, George L. Sinclair, M.D., of Charities Department Halifax to Warden of Queen's County, N.S., 22 October 1898, Poor House and Farm Journal, Feb. 1885-1907, RG 35 Series King County, Cornwallis Township; Paupers in Poor House (1821): Petition 102 to Lt. Governor Re Poor House and Bridewell; and Proceedings of Committee of House of Refuge, Halifax (1853-57), PANS. The Citizen and Evening Chronicle, 17 March 1883, reported that the Halifax Poor's Asylum now had segregated facilities according to sex.

47. Prisoners' Aid Association of Canada: County Paupers and County Houses of Industry (Toronto: Dudley and Burns, 1894), p. 13.

48. David J. Rothman, Conscience and Convenience: The Asylum and Its Alternatives in Progressive America (Boston: Little, Brown, 1980), p. 106.

49. "Poor Relief," RG 25, Series C, vol. 5, file 1898, PANS. B. Mulcahy, Secretary of the Office of Charities Committee, Poors' Asylum to Hon. Commissioner, Works and Mines, 2 June 1898, Halifax, and "Report of Inspector," G. L. Sinclair to Hon. C. E. Church, Commissioner of Public Works and Mines, in Public Charities, Legislature of Nova Scotia (1900), p. 36, MGU.

50. Ibid., pp. 23 and 43.

51. Ibid., pp. 21 and 32.

52. Ibid., p. 32; and William Hattie, Health Officer "Report on Public Charities, Nova Scotia," (1914), pp. 8, 30 and 50, MGU. The Acadian Recorder, 26 December 1882, reported unabashedly the children of the Halifax Poor's Asylum enjoying their Christmas fare.

53. Toronto House of Industry, 21 August 1837, 2 December 1857, 25 April 1856, and 30 May 1850, in Minute Books (1836-1858), CTA.

54. Information regarding this Orphan House is taken from the following: Report of the State of the Orphan House

428

(1762), RG 2, CO. 217, vol. 18, pp. 216-226; Jonathan Belcher, Governor of Nova Scotia, to Lords of Trade, 3 November 1761, RG 1, Sect. 4, p. 37, PANS. Also discussed in Grant, pp. 250-252; G. E. Hart, "Two Centuries of Child Welfare" (1953), p. 1, RG 25, Series C, vol. 9, #12, PANS; and Saunders, pp. 69-70, and 99.

55. Journal of House of Assembly (1838), pp. 339-340. Also G. B. Atkins, p. 63; Petitions to the Governor Re: Poor House and Bridewell, #31 to Sir John Wentworth, n.d., and #55 M. B. Almon to Sir Rupert D. George, 17 August 1839, RG 1, 411, PANS.

56. Saunders, pp. 75 and 99. Statutes of Nova Scotia (1831), II William IV, Cap. 24, whereby provision was made for the setting aside of land for an orphanage with £600 government allotment for a building to match the people's £1200.

[3] CHILDHOOD SENTIMENT AND SPECIALIZED CHILDREN

1. Pelly Documents (1816-23) MG 2, A 5, PAM.

2. As Michael Katz observed, "industrialization in North America did not create cities as much as interact with well established urban patterns." The People of Hamilton, Canada West: Family and Class in a Mid-Nineteenth-Century City (Cambridge, Mass.: Harvard U.P., 1975), p. 9.

3. Historical Sketch of the Montreal Protestant Orphan Asylum From its Foundation on the 16th February 1822 to the Present Day Compiled from its Minutes and Annual Reports . . . (Montreal, 1860); and the Ladies Benevolent Society 18th AR (Montreal, 1851).

4. The term "snatch" is not uncommon to child saving literature, e.g., the Kingston POH annual meeting referred to its aim as "snatching forlorn and destitute children from misery and degradation," and the Halifax Industrial School, 1st Report (1865), said its aim was "to snatch children from certain ruin."

5. Kathleen Heasman, Evangelicals in Action (London: G. Bles, 1962); Carroll Smith Rosenberg, Religion and the Rise of the American City (Ithaca: Cornell U.P., 1971); Anne M. Boylan, "Evangelical Womanhood in the Nineteenth Century:

The Role of Women in the Sunday Schools," Feminist Studies 4 (October 1978): 62-80.

6. M. G. Jones, The Charity School Movement (London: Frank Cass, 1964); and Philippe Ariès, Centuries of Childhood (New York: Alfred A. Knopf, 1962), pp. 286-314.

7. An Account of the Proceedings of the Acting Governors of the House of Industry (Dublin, 1798); and The State of the Ladies Charity School Lately set up in Baldwin Street, in the city of Bristol, in Teaching Poor Girls to Read and Spin (Bristol, 1756), p. 3.

8. Isaac Watts, An Essay Toward the Encouragement of Charity Schools (London, 1728), pp. 8-9.

9. Society for the Suppression of Beggars (Edinburgh, 1813), pp. 13-14.

10. Andrew Gairdner, A Looking Glass For Rich People and People in Prosperity . . . (Edinburgh, 1728).

11. Rules, Orders, and Regulations . . . the House of Industry . . . in Suffolk (Ipswich, 1759).

12. Rules, Orders and Regulations in the Parish School of Industry in King Street (London, 1792).

13. I. Wood, Some Account of the Shrewsbury House of Industry (Shrewsbury, 1791), pp. 3, 8, and 33.

14. Hints Toward the Formation of a Society for Promoting a Spirit of Independence Among the Poor, 2nd ed. (Bristol, 1812), pp. 16-17; and Plans for the Sunday Schools and Schools of Industry, established in the city of Bath (Bath, 1789).

15. Manchester Juvenile Refuge and School of Industry (Manchester, 1846), pp. 2 and 4.

16. Ibid., pp. 5-6.

17. Alexander Thomson, Industrial Schools (Aberdeen, 1847), pp. 7-8 and 11-16.

18. Ursula R. Q. Henriques, Before the Welfare State (London: Longman, 1979); Derek Fraser, The Evolution of the British Welfare State (London: Macmillan Press, 1973); and Maurice Bruce, The Coming of the Welfare State, 4th ed.,

(London: B. T. Batsford, 1968). For 19th Century discussion of boarding-out versus the congregate system, see Mary Carpenter, "What Shall We Do With Our Pauper Children?" Social Science Association, Dublin, 1861; Reports on the Boarding-Out of Orphans and Deserted Children and Insane belonging to the City Parish, Glasgow (Glasgow, 1872); and Henry F. Aveling, The Boarding Out System (London, 1890).

19. John Cleverley and D. C. Phillips, From Locke to Spock: Influential Models of the Child in Modern Western Thought (Melbourne: Melbourne U.P., 1976); Hugh M. Pollard, Pioneers of Popular Education, 1760-1850 (London: John Murray, 1956) and Harold Silver, The Concept of Popular Education (London: MacGibbon & Kee, 1965).

20. Central Auxiliary Society for Promoting Education and Industry, 2nd AR (Montreal, 1829), p. 40; and A Report of the Society for Improving the Condition of the Poor of St. John's (St. John's, 1804), pp. 5-6.

21. Ontario, Inspector of Asylums, Prisons and Public Charities, 7th AR (1874), p. 59; and 22nd AR (1889), pp. 114-115, PAO.

22. Orphans' Home and Widows' Friend Society [Kingston POH] 1st AR (1859), p. 5, QU; and Ontario, Inspector of Asylums, Prisons and Public Charities, 2nd AR (1868-69), pp. 35 and 82, PAO.

23. Historical Sketch of the Montreal POH.

24. Margaret Freeman Campbell, A Mountain and a City: The Story of Hamilton (Toronto: McClelland & Stewart, 1966), p. 67. The most comprehensive social history on cholera in nineteenth century Canada is Geoffrey Bilson, A Darkened House (Toronto: University of Toronto Press, 1980). Also see the Halifax Herald, 2 August 1893, for a piece on the 1834 epidemic.

25. Historical Sketch of the Montreal POH; and Geoffrey Bilson, p. 46.

26. Church of England Widows' and Orphans' Asylum [St. John's POH], 60th AR (1914) and 1st AR (1855), AASJ; The Observer (Maitland), 4 April 1873; Max G. Baxter, "New Brunswick POH," NBM; and Saint John POH, ARs (1867-1914), SJCL.

27.   The Ladies Benevolent Society began the 1821 Kingston Hospital out of which the house of industry grew. In 1847 and in 1852, the LBS was active in exhorting the city on the necessity of a house of industry to prevent "begging and mendicity." Records of the House of Industry (1814-1916), and Diamond Jubilee (1906), pp. 154-155, and Kerry Abel, "The Kingston House of Industry, 1850-1880," (typewritten), QU.

28.   Toronto City Council Papers, 4 May 1837, MS 385(2); and Baldwin Papers, 11 July 1837, MS 88(1), MTL; and Report of the Trustees of the House of Industry (Toronto, 1853), pp. 5-6. Also see, Stephen A. Speisman, "Munificent Parsons and Municipal Parsimony: Voluntary Versus Public Poor Relief in Nineteenth Century Toronto," Ontario History 64 (1973): 35-50, Joey Noble, "Class-ifying the Poor: Toronto Charities 1850-1880," Studies in Political Economy (Autumn 1979): 109-127, and J. M. Pitsula, "The Treatment of Tramps in Late Nineteenth Century Toronto," CHA Historical Papers (Ottawa: CHA, 1980): 116-132.

29.   Background is recorded in Kingston POH, AR (1882-3); and Kingston POH, AR (1859), pp. 3-4.

30.   Ibid.

31.   Richard Splane, Social Welfare in Ontario 1791-1893 (Toronto: University of Toronto Press, 1965), p. 80.

32.   Toronto Daily Globe, 10 January 1866.

33.   The Orphans' Home and Female Aid Society [Toronto POH] 33rd AR (1884), pp. 8 and 11 (emphasis added), L30, vol. 1, MTL.

34.   Minutes, 28 September 1852, L30 vol. 1 (1851-53) and Special Management Meeting (May 1853), MTL; and Halifax POH, 5th AR (1862), PANS.

35.   Letters and Papers (1854-56) L30, PCH(E); Draft Circular, 9 June 1851 on Preliminary Organization, Letters and Papers, n.d. [1851] L30, PCH(B); and L30, PCH (O), MTL.

36.   Toronto POH, AR (1856), and AR (1854), MTL.

37.   Hervey Institute, 7th AR (Montreal, 1917), p. 22, MGU; and Sermon Preached in St. George's, Montreal, on Behalf of the Ladies Benevolent Society Institution by Reverend William Bond, 9 April 1854, MTL.

38.   St. John's POH, 1st AR (1855), pp. 1-2; and
Records of Ottawa POH, MG 28, I 37, vols. 1-9, PAC, and
"One Hundred Years 1864-1964:   The Protestant Children's
Village, Ottawa" (Canadian Welfare Council, 1964).

39.   Isobel   McComb   Brighty,   "The   Diamond   Jubilee
History of the Protestant Home of St. Catherines, 1874-1934,"
PAO; and Emma A. Currie Papers, MG 27, II F5, vol. 3, file:
WCTU,   Women's   Suffrage   and   POH,   PAC.   Also   see   the
Records of the Protestant Home for Orphans, Aged and
Friendless;   Protestant   Orphans'   Home;   Women's   Christian
Association; Caroline L. Conron, Merrymount Children's Home
(1874-1974):   A Century In Retrospect; and Margaret Johnson,
Women's Christian Association: The First One Hundred Years
(1874-1974), UWO.   Minutes 1 December 1874 and Protestant
Home for Aged and Friendless, 1st AR (1874), UWO.

40.   All information regarding the Hamilton Aged Women's
Home is found in annual reports, minutes (vols. 1-6), and the
reports of the Hamilton Orphan Asylum and Ladies Benevolent
Society, HPL.

41.   Caroline L. Conron, pp. 23 and 30-31 and Margaret
Johnson, pp. 2-3.

42.   Report of the Trustees of the House of Industry
(Toronto, 1857) p. 8.   MTL; and Toronto House of Industry,
28 November 1844, Minute Book, August 1838-November 10,
1847, CTA.

43.   Philanthropy: Care of Our Destitute and Criminal
Population (Montreal, 1857).   A Ragged School, also known as
the "Emigrant City School," in Saint John, did not offer meals
but it gave free tuition to the "barefooted, ragged urchins of
the city."   Morning Freeman (Saint John), 3 February 1866,
and Account by Mrs. Eliza Donkin Freeman in Scott, S. Morley
(Collector)   CB   Documents,   NBM.   Halifax   Industrial   and
Ragged Schools, 1st AR (1865), p. 6, PANS.

44.   Halifax POH, 2nd AR (1859), p. 3; and Halifax POH,
8th AR (1865), pp. 3-4, PANS.

45.   Philanthropy, pp. 10 and 20-25.

46.   Halifax Industrial School, 1st Report (1865), p. 13.
This aspect has been discussed by Patricia T. Rooke, "The
'Child-Institutionalized' in Canada, Britain and the U.S.A.:   A
Trans-Atlantic Perspective, Journal of Educational Thought 11
(August 1977):   156-171.

47.   Leeds Ragged and Industrial School, 5th AR (Leeds, 1865), pp. 11-12.

48.   Mary Carpenter, Day and Industrial Schools For Children Beyond the Reach of School Boards (Bristol, 1875), pp. 4-12.

49.   Carpenter, p. 5.

50.   In Ontario, payment-by-results was used in 1876-82. Charles E. Phillips, The Development of Education in Canada (Toronto: W. J. Gage, 1957), p. 513.

51.   Toronto Boys' Home, 2nd AR (1861), pp. 5-6 and 7; and 9th AR (1869), pp. 10 and 12, MTL.

52.   Kingston POH, 14th AR (1871-2), QU. In 1865 a similar analogy was made in the First Report of the Halifax Industrial School, p. 15. "But some may say will not this interfere with the liberty of the subject? the reply is, the justification of such a measure is simply its necessity. No one says, 'my neighbour is drowning, but I shall duly interfere with his freedom of action if I jump overboard and drag him out.'"

53.   Halifax Protestant Industrial School, 2nd AR (1865-66), p. 3; and the Halifax Industrial and Ragged School, 1st AR (1865), p. 8, PANS.

54.   Journal of House of Assembly (1857), pp. DLVII-DLVIII; and New Brunswick Department of Health, Industrial Home Annual Reports (1920-48), NBM.

55.   St. Paul's Almhouse of Industry for Girls, Reports (1868-1895), PANS. For discussions of delinquency, see the following: Barbara M. Brenzel, "Better Protestant than Prostitute: A Social Portrait of a Nineteenth Century Reform School for Girls," Interchange 6 (1975): 11-22; Susan E. Houston, "Victorian Origins of Juvenile Delinquency: A Canadian Experience," History of Education Quarterly 12 (Fall 1972): 254-280; and J. G. Gillis, "The Evolution of Childhood Delinquency in England 1890-1914," Past and Present (May 1975): 96-126.

56.   Saint John Haven and Rescue Work, Reports (1887-1893), NBM.

57.   Halifax Poor Man's Friend Society, 2nd AR (1821), p. 29; and Halifax Protestant Industrial School, AR (1865-66),

p. 4, PANS. The climbing boys are discussed in Journal of House of Assembly (1844), Appendix 25, pp. 45-47 and 53; Morning Chronicle, 18 July 1867; Presbyterian Witness, 1 February 1862; Christian Messenger, 28 May 1862 and 21 October 1863; and Morning Journal, 6 June 1862.

58. Halifax Industrial and Ragged School, 1st AR (1865), pp. 5, 10 and 14; 2nd AR (1866), p. 8; and Halifax Society for the Prevention of Cruelty to Animals, Reports, PANS.

59. 3rd AR (1867), pp. 4 and 8, PANS.

60. Ibid., p. 8.

61. 10th AR (1875), p. 5, PANS.

62. Ontario, Inspector of Asylums, Prisons and Public Charities, 18th AR (1885), p. 106; and 17th AR (1884), p. 126, PAO.

63. Idem, 6th AR (1866), pp. 179 and 180-181; and Report of the Reformatory Prison, Penetanguishene, for 1865, p. 96, PAO.

64. The Newfoundland POH is quoted by the St. John's Daily Mail, 15 February 1862.

[4] THE CHARITY GIVERS AND THE "CHILD-INSTITUTIONALIZED"

1. Sermon Preached in St. George's Church, Montreal, 9th April 1854, on Behalf of the Ladies Benevolent Institution by Reverend William Bond (Montreal, 1854), p. 16. Bond's interest in missionary and educational matters was a natural consequence of his work as a missionary with the Colonial and Continental Church Society and as superintendent of the Montreal Model and Training School. Records of the Colonial and Continental Church Society, MG 17, B 4, PAC. In ecclesiastical terms, most non-Anglican missionaries did not fare as well in the colonies. Patricia T. Rooke, "The 'New Mechanic' in Slave Society: Socio-Psychological Motivations and Evangelical Missionaries in the British West Indies," Journal of Religious History 11 (June 1980): 77-94.

2. Geoffrey Bilson, A Darkened House (Toronto: University of Toronto Press, 1981), p. 45.

3. Members of the Chown family appear throughout the records of both the House of Industry, Collection 604, and the Orphans' Home and Widows' Friend Society, Collection 94, QU. Indeed, the home which was purchased to become a specialized residential centre for children called "Sunnyside" in the late twenties, had been the property of Mrs. G. Y. Chown. Men such as Reverend Stephen Lett, who was energetically involved in the affairs of the House of Industry and the Toronto POH, served both general and children's asylums. Toronto House of Industry, 18 May 1858, Minute Book, August 1838-November 10, 1847, CTA.

4. The following discuss various aspects of female social reform: T. R. Morrison, "Their Proper Sphere: Feminism, The Family and Child-Centred Social Reform in Ontario, 1875-1900," Ontario History 68 (March 1976): 45-74; Anne M. Boylon, "Evangelical Womanhood in the Nineteenth Century: The Role of Women in Sunday Schools," Feminist Studies 4 (October 1978): 62-80; Anthony Platt, The Child Savers (Chicago: University of Chicago Press, 1969); Clare L. McCausland, Children of Circumstance (Chicago: Chicago Child Care Society, 1976); Wendy Mitchinson, "The YWCA and Reform in the Nineteenth Century" Social History 12 (November 1979): 368-384; John T. Cumbler, "The Politics of Charity: Gender and Class in the Nineteenth Century Charity Policy," Journal of Social History (Fall 1980): 99-111; and F. K. Prochaska, Women and Philanthropy in Nineteenth-Century England (Oxford: Oxford U.P., 1980).

5. Margaret Johnson, The First One Hundred Years 1874-1974, (London, Ont.: Women's Christian Association, 1974), p. 2, UWO; and Report of St. Paul's Almshouse of Industry for Girls (1868), p. 4, PANS.

6. Orphans' Home and Female Aid Society, Toronto, "Preamble," vol. 1 (1851-53), L30, MTL; for the description of the gender structures of American advocacy organizations for poor women see Cumbler, p. 105; and Geoffrey Bilson, pp. 45-46.

7. Maria Thorburn, "The Orphans' Home of the City of Ottawa: Sketch of the First Forty Years 1864-1904," in One Hundred Years, 1864-1964 (Ottawa: Canadian Welfare Council, 1964), p. 6.

8. One Hundred Years, 1864-1964, p. 50.

9.   ARs for 1877, 1879, 1945 and 1951, and Correspondence in SCIC, boxes, 1 and 4, files 18 and 22, Toronto Infants' Home and Infirmary (1876-1950), CTA.

10.   The Anglican influences caused considerable friction at various times in both institutions and in Toronto the support of the Orange Lodge particularly led to unfortunate instances.   See Bishop Cridge Papers, vol. 4, file 2:   "POH 1873-1906," PABC; and Minutes for 1855, 1866 and 1899 of Toronto POH, L30, MTL.

11.   Kingston POH, 14th AR (1871), QU.

12.   Toronto POH, Minutes, 15 July 1851 and 31 October 1851, vol. 1 (1851-53), L30, MTL; Maria Thorburn, pp. 4-11 and Ottawa POH, vol. 1 (1865-69), MG 28, I 37, PAC; and Daily Mail, 16 February 1865.

13.   The Colonist, 23 June 1893, gives a brief history on the occasion of placing the corner stone for the new POH. Also see "A Short History," 70th AR (1942), p. 3; and the correspondence between Dean Cridge and Reverend Jenns, 23 September 1873 and 24 September 1873, in Cridge Papers, PABC.

14.   David Rothman, The Discovery of the Asylum (Boston: Little Brown, 1971), pp. 30-56.   Also see James S. Zainaldin and Peter L. Tyon, "Asylum and Society: An Approach to Industrial Change," Journal of Social History 13 (Fall 1979):   23-48, and Christopher Lasch, "Origins of the Asylum," The World of Nations (New York: Alfred A. Knopf, 1973), pp. 3-17.

15.   As late as 1971, R. M. Bird and M. W. Bucovetsky concluded that "annual charitable giving in Canada . . . amount[ed] to about 8/10th of one percent of G.N.P. or $35 per capita.   These figures may be compared with the 1971 U.S. figures of about 2% of G.N.P. and $103 per capita." Canadian Tax Reform and Private Philanthropy, Canadian Tax Papers, 58 (Toronto: Canadian Tax Foundation, 1976), p. 15.

16.   Ottawa POH, Minute, 30 March 1868, vol. 1 (1865-69), MG 28, I 37, PAC; and Toronto Infants' Home, AR (1888), CTA.

17.   Winnipeg Children's Home, Minutes, 8 November 1920 and 27 January 1922, MG 10, B 24, PAM; and Winnipeg Children's Home mentioned these drills, Scrap Book, newspaper cutting, n.d.; while a report of a Kingston public meeting, 18

April 1870, describes the style of the recitations and songs in this vein.

18.   Kingston POH, ARs (1880-81 and 1881-82); "Twenty-Second Annual Convention of the M.W. Grand Lodge of B. C., Laying Corner Stone of B. C. Protestant Orphans' Home," 24 June 1893, PABC; and Toronto POH, "The Orphans' Prayer," MTL.

19.   St. John's Church of England Widows' and Orphans' Asylum, AR (1882), p. 11, AASJ.

20.   An appeal for "increased zeal and liberality to keep the funds from sinking into a languishing state" was made at the Annual Meeting of the Kingston POH, 19 April 1869, QU; Winnipeg Children's Home, Minute, 11 May 1910, PAM; and Minute, 5 February 1876, cited in Caroline L. Conron, Merrymount Children's Home 1874-1974, p. 18, UWO.

21.   Minutes, January 22, 23 and 27, 1875; and 31 December 1875 and 13 January 1876, cited in Conron, pp. 10-11 and 12-13.

22.   Kingston POH, 14th AR (1871), QU.

23.   This Home was also opened for public inspection each afternoon.   Toronto Girls' Home, Amended Rules, 26 October 1900, vol. 3 (1899-1901), MTL.

24.   Victoria POH, 23rd AR (1896), p. 7, PABC.

25.   Ottawa POH, Minute, 30 October 1865, vol. 1, PAC; and Geoffrey Bilson, pp. 45-46.

26.   Ottawa POH, Minute, 28 October 1867, vol. 1, PAC.

27.   W. Peter Ward, "Unwed Motherhood in Nineteenth Century English Canada," CHA Historical Papers (Ottawa: CHA, 1981) pp. 34-56.

28.   Transactions of the National Association For the Promotion of Social Science, Bristol Meeting, 1869 (London, 1870), pp. 206-209 and 212-213.

29.   Ibid., p. 209.

30.   Excerpt from AR (1887) of Children's Home of Winnipeg in RG 5 G 2, box 4, file 40; and Christian Women's Union, Greenway Papers, MG 13E file 12013, PAM.

31. Johnson, <u>The First One Hundred Years 1874-1974</u>, p. 2.

32. Halifax Infants' Home, Minute, 7 July 1884, PANS.

33. Seventy-sixth Annual Meeting, 6 December 1921, in Home of the Friendless and Infants' Home (newspaper clippings), HPL; and Toronto Infants' Home, <u>ARs</u> for 1878, 1879, 1887, and 1925, SCl-C, box 1, CTA.

34. Toronto Infants' Home, Minutes 3 March 1885 and 4 March 1879, <u>Executive Minutes</u> (1875-1951), SCl, box 1A; <u>ARs</u> for 1877, 1881, and 1882; and Minute 23 April 1876, <u>Board of Managers Minutes</u> (1875-1884) file 1 SCl, box 1A, CTA.

35. Halifax Infants' Home, Minutes, 16 February 1875 and 2 March 1875, PANS.

36. Toronto Infants' Home, Minute, 3 January 1882, <u>Executive Minutes</u> (1875-1951); and Minute, 2 August 1881, <u>Board of Managers Minutes</u>, CTA.

37. Toronto Infants' Home, Minute, 16 February 1885, <u>Executive Minutes</u> (1875-1951), CTA.

38. Toronto Infants' Home, <u>50th AR</u> (1925); Annual Meeting, 25 October 1886, <u>AR</u> (1886), and Minute, 27 May 1886, <u>Executive Minutes</u> (1875-1951), CTA.

39. Cooke vs Et. Al. Kingston Infants' Home in "Child Welfare: Legal Citations (1923-34)," MG 28, I 10, vol. 45, PAC.

40. Toronto Infants' Home, <u>ARs</u> for 1879, 1882, 1886, and 1887 and <u>50th AR</u> (1925), CTA.

41. Halifax Infants' Home, Minutes, 7 September 1875 and 5 March 1877; Report for October, 1875; and Report of the Fifteenth Annual Meeting, in <u>The Herald</u>, 3 February 1890, PANS.

42. Toronto Infants' Home, <u>ARs</u> for 1903 and 1907. Subsequent acts in respect to baby farming are An Act to Make Further Provision Respecting Boarding Houses and the Protection of Infant Children, 1897, amended 1898, and the Ontario Maternity Boarding House Act of 1914.

43. The Friendly Home for Young Women, Montreal, <u>ARs</u> (1903), pp. 5-6, and (1918), pp. 6-7, MGU; Toronto Infants'

Home, AR (1885), CTA; and "Deputation to Members of the Legislature of Manitoba, 4/2/1890," in Greenway Papers, MG 13E, file 12013, PAM.

44. Toronto Infants' Home, ARs for 1878 and 1879, CTA.

45. "Deputation . . . 4/2/1890"; and Winnipeg Children's Home, Minute, 3 August 1911, Book 1 (1905-21), PAM.

46. Protestant Infants' Home, Montreal, AR (1879-80), pp. 6-7; and Montreal Female Home Society, AR (1872), pp. 18-19, MGU.

47. One Hundred Years 1864-1964: Ottawa Children's Village, pp. 44-46. Although historical studies of developmental and mental handicap are rare, considerable attention has been given to the issues in recent years. For example, see Seymour B. Sarason and John Doris, Educational Handicap, Public Policy and Social History (New York: The Free Press, 1979); and Wolf Wolfensberger, The Origins and Nature of Our Institutional Models (Syracuse: Human Policy Press, 1975).

48. Winnipeg Children's Home, 24th AR (1909); Scrap Book Newspaper cutting, n.d., and Visitors' Reports (April 1909), PAM.

49. Winnipeg Children's Home, Minute, 5 April 1911, Book 1 (1905-21), PAM.

50. BC Survey (1927), CCSD/43, file 208, PAC.

51. Philip S. Carpenter, On Some Causes of the Excessive Mortality of Children in the City of Montreal in 1869 (Montreal, 1869), pp. 18-21; and Montreal Sanitary Association, 3rd AR, 6 April 1869, MGU.

52. Carpenter, pp. 21 and 17.

53. Carpenter, pp. 15-17. This Foundling Home's record pales when compared with the mortality rate of a similar institution in Paris (although population and time, that is the previous century, explains the difference). With 83% mortality for infants and 16-17% for other classes of abandoned children in 1772-78, it could be said that

> We know everything about the attempts to keep
> them alive, feed and educate them, and we know
> all about the terrible mortality rate that

transformed the Foundling Home into an abyss
that swallowed up the greater part of the
children sheltered within its walls.

Claude Delasselle, "Abandoned Children in Eighteenth Century
Paris," in Deviants and the Abandoned in French Society
(Baltimore: The Johns Hopkins University, 1978), pp. 47 and
56.

54. The Lancet information is in Toronto Infants' Home,
AR (1879), p. 7, CTA. Montreal Infants' Home, 9th AR
(1879), MGU.

55. Poor House and Farm Journal (Feb. 1885 - Nov.
1907), RG 35, Series King County, Cornwallis, PANS; the
Halifax Evening Express, 27 March 1875, reports infant deaths
in the Halifax Poor's Asylum; and Saint John Almshouse
(1853-1964), PANB.

56. Nova Scotia Home for Coloured Children was
incorporated in 1915, MG 20, vol. 750, PANS.

57. Halifax Infants' Home, Minutes, 4 February 1873, 28
January 1875, and March and April 1875, First Minute Book
(12 January 1875 to 1890), PANS; and Toronto Infants' Home,
Minute, Nov. 1886, Executive Minutes (1875-1951), CTA.

58. Superintendent's Report, 28 April 1896, RG 25,
Series C, vol. 4, PANS.

59. Halifax Poor's Asylum, Record Book, 7 March 1843,
PANS; and Toronto House of Industry, Minute, 11 May 1841,
Board of Management (1836-58), CTA.

60. Veronica Strong-Boag, The Parliament of Women:
The National Council of Women of Canada, 1893-1929 (Ottawa:
National Museums of Canada, 1976).

61. Rush Welter, Popular Education and Democratic
Thought in America (New York: Columbia U.P., 1962); and
Harold Silver, The Concept of Popular Education (London:
MacGibbon & Kee, 1965).

62. W. H. Hattie, "Report of Inspector of Humane
Institutions 1913," p. 9, in Reports on Public Charities,
Halifax, box 1, MGU.

[5] IN SERVICE OF THEIR BETTERS: CUSTODY, RESOCIALIZATION AND BINDING-OUT

1.   Aspects of Canadian children's institutions are examined in Patricia T. Rooke and R. L. Schnell, "Childhood and Charity in Nineteenth Century British North America," Histoire sociale/Social History 15 (May 1982): 157-179, and "The Rise and Decline of British North American Orphans' Homes as Woman's Domain, 1850-1930," Atlantis 7 (Spring 1982): 21-35.

2.   Erving Goffman, Asylums (Garden City, N.Y.: Anchor Books, 1961), pp. 12-13.

3.   The principal Protestant children's institutions (with founding dates) are listed in the Appendix 1; and Goffman, p. 13.

4.   This shift is examined in Patricia T. Rooke and R. L. Schnell, "Child Welfare in English Canada, 1920-1948," Social Service Review 55 (September 1981): 484-506.

5.   Kingston Protestant Orphans' Home, Minute 9 June 1857, QU.

6.   Kingston POH, Minutes, 9 June 1857, 9 November 1858, 10 March 1863; London POH, Minute, 19 December 1892, and Caroline L. Conron, Merrymount Children's Home: A Century in Retrospect (London, Ontario: 1974), p. 28, UWO; and London POH, Minute, 31 December 1883, and Conron, p. 24.

7.   Kingston POH, AR (1871-2); and Hamilton Orphan Asylum Registry, Minutes, 21 July 1853 and 5 December 1853, HPL; Kingston POH, AR (1871-2); and Records of Methodist Orphange, UCSJ.

8.   Widows' and Orphans' Asylum, AR (1855), AASJ; records of Home for 1851-55, the Orphans' Home and Female Aid Society, MTL; and Toronto Girls' Home, Minutes, vol. 9R, MTL; and Hamilton Orphan Asylum, Registry, Minutes, 21 November 1853 and 30 April 1855, HPL.

9.   Kingston POH, AR (1859).

10.   Report of New Brunswick Survey (1949), p. 109, CCSD/135, PAC. Almost identical terminology is found in the Prince Edward Island POH, AR (1931), p. 3, PAPEI.

11. The Hamilton Orphan Asylum (HOA), which received an annual grant from the city council, was forced to accept children committed by the mayor on the payment of 2/6 per week. Hamilton Aged Women's Home (HAWH), Minute, 27 June 1848, and Annual Meeting, 8 June 1849, HPL.

12. See R. Christie, 14th AR of the Houses of Refuge and Orphan and Magdalen Asylum . . . Ontario (1883), and in House of Industry, Minute, 17 July 1855, CTA.

13. Constitution of the Orphan Home and Widows' Friend Society of Kingston, Incorporated 1862, 25 Vict. Ch. 97; and Kingston POH, Minutes, 13 October 1857 and 10 April 1860, and 11 November 1862. Also HAWH Minute, January 1881.

14. "The BC POH, Victoria," p. 1, British Columbia Survey (1927), CCSD/43, file 201; and Report of New Brunswick Survey (1949), p. 109, PAC.

15. Kingston POH, Minutes, 10 April 1860 and 13 November 1860. Neither can it be overlooked, however, that the founders of POHs were committed to the principle that something even nominally paid for was valued more than something received for nothing.

16. Kingston POH, Minutes, 12 July 1859, 9 August 1859, and 12 November 1861; Toronto POH, Minute, 26 February 1867, L 30, vol. 1; and Winnipeg Children's Home, Visitors' Reports (November 1904), p. 6, and box #9, (n.d.), PAM.

17. Winnipeg Children's Home, Minutes, 6 June 1921 and 25 September 1912, and Visitors' Reports (Jan. 1913); and box #7 (1906-08), PAM.

18. Toronto POH, Minute 27 January 1874, vol. 1; and Hamilton OA, Registry Minutes, 31 January 1854 and 29 September 1869; and Winnipeg Children's Home, Minute, 6 December 1894.

19. L. M. Montgomery, Anne of Green Gables (Toronto: Ryerson Press, 1907), p. 8. Although the Hamilton OA agreed that eleven was a suitable age for apprenticeship, it frequently bound out much younger children. 12th AR (1858).

20. Montreal POH, AR (1873), p. 6, MGU; and Toronto Girls' Home, AR (1894), pp. 8-9, and AR (1896), p. 4, vol. 3 (1899-1901), MTL.

443

21. This rule was reaffirmed in the Constitution and Rules of Admission, Methodist Orphange, 18 December 1927, UCSJ.

22. Winnipeg Children's Home, Visitors' Reports (May 1905), p. 22.

23. Toronto Girls' Home, Minute, 12 November 1895, vol. 1 (1891-1896).

24. Toronto Girls' Home, Minute, 7 March 1893, and AR (1896), p. 41, and AR (1897), p. 9; and Minutes, 2 April 1895, 22 October 1895, 4 April 1896, and 5 May 1896.

25. Ottawa POH, Minute, 28 October 1867, MG 28, I 37, vol. 1 (1865-69), PAC.

26. See Patricia T. Rooke, and R. L. Schnell, "The 'King's Children' in English Canada: A Psychohistorical Study of Abandonment, Rejection and Colonial Response (1869-1930)," Journal of Psychohistory 8 (Spring 1981): 387-420.

27. Michael Anderson's argument that nineteenth century British working class life was dominated by a calculative orientation which saw relationships in terms of exchange that would enhance the mutual attainment of personal goals seems to be no less applicable to the Canadian situation. Michael Anderson, Family Structure in Nineteenth Century Lancashire (Cambridge: Cambridge University Press, 1971); and Michael Katz, "Essay Review," Journal of Social History 7 (1973): 86-92.

28. N. Murray, The Experience of an Old Country Pedlar Among the Montreal Servant Girls and Their Mistresses (Montreal: N. Murray, 1887), p. 15.

29. Report of Methodist Orphanage, January-February 1912, UCSJ.

30. Report of Methodist Orphanage, 30 April 1928.

31. Toronto Girls' Home, AR (1894), pp. 8-9.

32. Toronto Girls' Home, AR (1892), p. 9.

33. Winnipeg Children's Home, Minutes, April 1910, June 1910, 5 October 1910, 3 November 1910, October 1912, 17 April 1912 and November 1912.

34. Sometimes the visits of former inmates signified not institutional loyalty but the need for companionship. Hamilton OA, Minute, 9 March 1903.

35. Michael Rutter, Maternal Deprivation Reassessed (Harmondsworth: Penguin, 1972), pp. 47-49, 50-53, 71-72, 100-106, and 110-119.

36. Helm Stierlin, Separating Parents and Adolescents (New York: Quadrangle/New York Times Book Co., 1974), pp. 37 and 67.

37. Rutter, pp. 71-72, 100-101, and 119.

38. Rutter, p. 48; and London POH, Minute, 28 April 1876, and Conron, p. 19.

39. Kingston POH, Minutes, 11 December 1866 and 14 December 1866; Ottawa POH, 28 August 1871; and Winnipeg Children's Home, 2 July 1908, all record exceptionally strong feelings on the matter. Although the Hamilton OA regularly allowed its inmates to attend the local Sunday School, it also soon rid itself of any significant numbers of children.

40. Kingston POH, Minute, 14 December 1866.

41. Ottawa POH, Minutes, 29 July 1868 and 26 May 1873, record the matron's request to the ladies' committee that she might be able to take the children for a walk outside the grounds now and again. Also see Minutes, 24 February 1896 and 30 March 1896.

42. Kingston POH, Minute, 8 October 1857.

43. Widows' and Orphans' Asylum, AR (1860-61).

44. Kingston POH, Minutes, 10 September 1866 and 11 September 1866 and AR (1899-1900); Minutes 30 August 1866, 18 May 1867, and 27 June 1868; and Midland District School Society, Minutes, 23 June 1870, 13 May 1881, 14 November 1881, 8 October 1886, 29 January 1930, and 24 July 1962, Coll. 52, QU. Also see Reverend J. D. Mullins, Our Beginnings: Being a Short Sketch of the History of the Colonial and Continental School Society (London: CCSS, 1923), p. 8; and the ARs (1824-1861), Minutes, Proceedings, and Correspondence of the Colonial and Continental Church Society, MG 17, B 14, PAC. The Saint John POH is discussed in the Observer (Maitland), 5 April 1973, and the Report of

the New Brunswick Task Force on Social Development, vol. 1 (Sept. 1971), p. 6, SJPL.

45. "The Act Incorporating the Governors and Wiggins Male Institution," 10 June 1867, pp. 5-6, 7-8; "An Act in Addition to an Act Entitled . . .," 1 April 1884, pp. 13-14; and "An Act in Addition . . .," 21 April 1894, p. 23, NBM. Also Daily Telegraph, 16 March 1874, and Wiggins Home, Minute Book (1 June 1891 - 28 January 1901), WMI.

46. Saint John POH, AR (1867), p. 3, NBM.

47. One Hundred Years, 1864-1964: Protestant Children's Village, (Ottawa, 1964), p. 42; and Ottawa POH, Minute, 26 April 1869.

48. Toronto Girls' Home, Minute, 3 March 1881.

49. London POH, Minute, 1 October 1906, and Conron, p. 33; and Hamilton OA Registry, vol. 2.

50. F. N. Stapleford, "Child Immigration," Typescript copy for Christian Guardian (n.d.), CCSD/26.

51. Toronto Girls' Home, Minutes, 3 November 1891 and 1 December 1891.

52. Manitoba Free Press, 15 November 1919, cutting in Scrap Book, Winnipeg Children's Home.

53. Winnipeg Children's Home, Minute, 2 July 1908.

54. Hamilton OA, Minute, 26 June 1854; Widows' and Orphans' Asylum, AR (1874), p. 19; and Knowles Home for Boys, Minute, 12 November 1907, MG 10, B7, PAM.

55. Halifax POH, AR (1858), p. 5; (1859), p. 3 and (1860), p. 4; and AR (1862), p. 2, PANS.

56. Victoria POH, AR (1886), PABC; and Toronto Girls' Home, Minute, 9 October 1900, vol. 3 (1899-1901). The Toronto rules were changed at the 26 October 1900 meeting. In the AR (1893), it was noted that the girls were taught by the matron, Mrs. Bright, "to respect manual labour, to assist in the household work . . ., [with] good manners, habits of cleanliness and helpfulness as part of their training," p. 6, and AR (1896), p. 6.

57. Kingston POH, AR (1874-75), pp. 3-4; and AR (1876-77), pp. 4-5.

58. Widows' and Orphans' Asylum, AR (1916), p. 13.

59. Toronto POH, AR (1869), p. 6.

60. Wiggins Home, Minutes, 31 July 1893 and 30 October 1893, Minute Book (1 June 1891 - 28 January 1901).

61. Daily Examiner (Charlottetown), 25 July 1883, PAPEI.

62. Poor House and Farm Journal, Minute, 15 February 1845, RG 35, King County Cornwallis Township; Minute, 19 November 1855; and "List of Apprentices Bound Out From 1/1/1832 to 1847," HVP 79 (1847), PANS.

63. A classic statement of the honorable nature of apprenticeship is contained in Edmund S. Morgan, The Puritan Family, rev. ed. (New York: Harper Torchbooks, 1966).

64. Hubbard Papers, 14 February 1814, Shelf 28, LD3 859579, NBM.

65. Forrester Family, 17 August 1837, NBM.

66. Delesdernier Family, 5 June 1815; and Forrester Family, 17 August 1837, NBM.

67. Toronto POH, Minute, 28 November 1893. On various occasions Mrs. M. R. Van Koughnet had served since 1856 as a first or second directoress and in 1899 was named honorary president.

68. London POH, Minute, 2 March 1888, and Conron, p. 26.

69. Victoria POH, AR (1886); and Toronto POH, Minute, 27 April 1897.

70. Toronto POH AR (1854) and Minute, 26 March 1856.

71. Toronto Girls' Home, AR (1892), pp. 7-9; AR (1894), p. 8; AR (1895), pp. 41-43; AR (1896), p. 41; AR (1897), p. 9; and AR (1899), p. 44.

72. Kingston POH, Minute, 8 March 1870 and Annual Meeting, 19 April 1869; Minute, 8 December 1865; and Minute, 8 March 1870.

73. Winnipeg Children's Home, Minute, 3 October 1895; and Minute, 3 October 1894.

74. Hamilton OA, Minute, 28 October 1901.

75. Kingston POH, Minute, 10 July 1866; and Minute, 12 November 1861.

76. Toronto Boys' Home, AR (1891), p. 6; Ottawa POH, Minute, 31 August 1874; and London POH, Minute, 3 June 1901, and Conron, p. 32.

77. Toronto Boys' Home, AR (1883), p. 5.

78. Halifax POH, AR (1872); Widows' and Orphans' Asylum, 59th AR; and Hamilton Orphan Asylum, Minute, 9 November 1891.

79. Winnipeg Children's Home, Visitors' Reports (December 1905), p. 40.

80. Charles Loring Brace, The Dangerous Classes of New York and Twenty Years' Work Among Them (New York: Wynkoop and Hallenbeck, 1872), pp. 44-45. Also see Miriam Z. Langsam, Children West: A History of the Placing-Out System of the New York Children's Aid Society, 1853-1890 (Madison: State Historical Society of Wisconsin, 1964).

81. Widows' and Orphans' Asylum, AR (1890-91), p. 16; and Hamilton OA Annual Meeting, 5 February 1857.

82. Brace, pp. 328-329.

83. Patricia T. Rooke and R. L. Schnell, "Child Welfare in English Canada, 1920-1948," Social Service Review 55 (September 1981): 484-506.

PART 2 - TRANSFORMING THE ASYLUM

[6] BOARDING OUT AND CHILD EMIGRATION:
THE BRITISH BACKGROUND

448

1. For recent studies, see Neil Sutherland, Children in English Canadian Society (Toronto: University of Toronto Press, 1976); Joy Parr, Labouring Children (London: Croom Helm, 1980); Kenneth Bagnell, The Little Immigrants (Toronto: Macmillan of Canada, 1980); Gillian Wagner, Barnardo (London: Weidenfeld and Nicolson, 1979); Phyllis Harrison, The Home Children (Winnipeg: Watson & Dwyer, 1979); and Wesley B. Turner, "Miss Rye's Children and the Ontario Press, 1875," Ontario History 68 (September 1976): 169-203. Also, by the authors, "Imperial Philanthropy and Colonial Response: British Juvenile Emigration to Canada 1869-1930," The Historian (in press) and "The King's Children in English-Canada: A Psychohistorical Study of Abandonment, Rejection and Canadian Response to British Juvenile Immigrants 1869-1930," Journal of Psychohistory 8 (Spring 1981): 387-420.

2. Toronto Boys' Home, 9th AR, p. 5, MTL. For Quentin Hogg's activity in Shaftesbury's Ragged Schools see his grandson's comments, Quentin M. Hogg, Shaftesbury A New Assessment, Nineteenth Shaftesbury Lecture (London: Shaftesbury Society, 1957) and David Williamson, Lord Shaftesbury's Legacy (London: Hodder and Stoughton, 1924), p. 55. Joseph Talbot to R. B. Sullivan, 14 March 1835, MS 385(11) Toronto City Council Papers (April 1834 - February 1837), PAO. Minute 18 May 1858, House of Industry, Board Minutes (1836-1858) CTA.

3. Since the literature on boarding out is massive, the following are only illustrative: Rev. William Pitt Trevelyan, Some Results of Boarding Out of Poor Law Children (London, 1903); John Skelton, The Boarding Out of Pauper Children in Scotland (London, 1876); Robert Anderson, Reports on the Boarding Out of Orphans and Deserted Children . . . Belonging to the City Parish of Glasgow (Glasgow, 1872); Mary Carpenter, What Shall We Do With Our Pauper Children? (Bristol, 1861); M. H. Mason, Classification of Girls and Boys in Workhouses (London, 1884); Report . . . on the Boarding Out of Pauper Children (Dublin, 1876); Henry F. Aveling, The Boarding Out System . . . for Poor Law Guardians (London, 1890); Reports on the Boarding-Out of Orphans and Children and Insane Belonging to the City Parish, Glasgow (Glasgow, 1872), MLG; and Report of a Drawing-Room Conference on Boarding-Out Pauper Children (London, 1876), NLI.

For another colonial experience with institutionalization and the problems of "emptying the barracks," see Brian Dickey, No Charity There: A Short History of Social Welfare

449

in Australia (Melbourne: Thomas Nelson, 1980), pp. 57-64 and 80-87.

The reports of H. M. Inspectors, including H. G. Bowyer (1866-67), E. C. Tufnell (1863-1871) and (1885-1887), Messrs. W. E. Knollys and Mount (1875), Miss Mason (1886), and Mrs. Nassau Senior (1873-1874), who debated the issue are in MH 32/19, PRO.

4.   Children's Home and Training School for Christian Workers, AR (1885-1886) (London, 1886), p. 14.

5.   Walter Monnington and Frederick L. Lampard, Our London Poor Law Schools (London, 1898), p. 184; and Mary Carpenter, p. 14.

6.   Carpenter quoting Mrs. Senior, p.4. Critics of poor law relief spoke incessantly of professional beggars.

7.   George C. T. Bartley, The Seven Ages of a Village Pauper (London, 1874) and "Effects of Charities Illustrated," reprinted from COR, 1880 (London, 1880), pp. 11-17. The summary of private and public charity is given in "Effects of Charities Illustrated," p. 15.

8.   George Bartley, A Handbook for Guardians of the Poor (London, 1876), p. 114. Woodhouse is quoted in Bartley, p. 116. Tufnell's 1867 Report observed that the large district schools encouraged a dislike for dependence on the rates, Inspectors Reports, MH 32/19, PRO.

9.   Edward Carleton Tufnell, Observations on the Report of Mrs. Senior to the LGB as to the Effect on Girls of the System of Education at Poor Law Schools (London, 1875), p. 5.   Also discussed in Carpenter, p. 13; John Skelton, pp. 82-83; and Tufnell to Poor Law Commissioner, 21 May 1838 and 10 May 1845, in Inspectors Reports (1838-1840, and 1841-1846), MH 32/70-71, PRO.

10.   Skelton, pp. 82-83; Carpenter quoting Senior, p. 5; Carpenter, A Letter on the Charges of the Bristol Guardians to the Editors of the Bristol Daily Post (Bristol, 1861), quoting Cumin, p. 14; F. C. Clayton, "On the Education of Pauper Children in Cottage Homes," p. 16, read before the Midland Poor Law Conference, 1883, BCL; and R. M. Noordin, Through A Workhouse Window (London, 1929), pp. 106-109.

11.   T. G. MacNamara, Children Under the Poor Law: A Report to the President of the LGB (HMS, 1908); Report of a

Drawing-Room Conference, pp. 20-26, but especially p. 23; The Boarding Out System: Further Practical Experiences (London, 1882), p. 1; and Trevelyan, especially pp. 30-38. Robert Anderson, Reports on the Boarding Out, said much the same when he referred to "a training calculated to fit them for that sphere of life which they are likely to occupy" according to the arrangements of the "Sovereign of the Universe." P. 5.

12. Bartley, pp. 109-111 and 118-120; Tufnell is quoted by Bartley, p. 115.

13. Conference on Poor Law Administration held at New Castle-Upon-Tyne, August 4-5, 1874 (London, 1874), p. 9.

14. "Some Aspects of the Problem of Charity," in A. C. Piguo, The Heart of the Empire (London: T. Fisher Unwin, 1909), pp. 238-240, and Report of the Proceedings of the Third International Congress for the Welfare and Protection of Children, London, 15-18 July 1902 (London: P. S. King & Son, 1902), p. 61; and Henry F. Aveling p. 13.

15. Correspondence to Colonial Office include Memos from Henry Rogers, H. M. Inspector of Industrial Schools, 17 January 1889; J. G. C. Parson, Clerk of Salford School Board, 12 December 1888 and 10 January 1889; Memo re Vaughan to Home Secretary, Oct. 1888; Parsons to Secretary of State, 19 September 1885; Rev. G. W. Saffenreuter to Colonel Inglis, HMI, 10 July 1885 and 19 August 1885; and Parsons to Inglis, 13 August 1885, HO 45/9635 A28889; and Rev. L. Burke, St. Catherine's, Sheffield, to Secretary of LGB, 7 June 1883, to Home Secretary, 26 July 1883, and 27 February 1884 to Sheffield School Board, 12 November 1883; Inglis to Under-Secretary, 9 August 1883; and Rogers to Home Secretary, 28 December 1883, HO 45/9635 A29551. Also see Items 1-5, "Provision for Young Children in Industrial Schools," 16 May 1902 and 9 June 1902; "Emigration of Young Children," 25 November 1902; and "Special Accommodation," 19 December 1902, HO 45/10240 B37686, PRO. The Harvest: An Organ of Catholic Works published by Salford Catholic Protection and Rescue Society No. 61 (October 1892): 2 and 72, MCL.

16. Richard F. Clarke, Our Waifs and Strays (G. B.: Catholic Truth Society, 1889), pp. 6-8; and Liverpool Sheltering Home, Minutes, 12 March 1874 and 7 March 1876, in Minute Book #1 (11 July 1873 - 4 April 1911), LCL. In 1925 this Home, due to straitened circumstances, amalgamated with Barnardo's.

17.   Canon   Bennett,   "Father   Nugent: Nobody's
Children," The Cathedral Record (June 1948):120-123; "Save
the Boy," CR (November 1948): 255-260; and "The Catholic
Emigration Association," CR (August 1949): 208-211, LCL.
Reports of Birmingham Diocescan Rescue Society and Homes for
Homeless and Friendless Catholic Children (1902-1913); William
Canon Berry, "The Problem of Lost Catholic Children" (1912);
and The Fold, organ of the Birmingham Diocescan Rescue
Society (1903-1907), BCL.

18.   "Liverpool Catholic Children's Protection Society" in
Father Berry's Homes for Friendless Children (Liverpool,
1922), BL.

19.   Children's Emigration Homes, 2nd AR (1875), p. 3,
BCL.

20.   Sir Walter C. Trevelyan, Addresses from Bands of
Hope Conference, Friday June 5, 1857 (Bristol, 1857), p. 33.

21.   Ibid.

22.   Children's Friend Society, 4th AR (London, 1834),
pp. 7-19; Report of the General Committee of Managers of CFS
(London, 1839); and A Statement of Facts Showing the Claims
of the CFS to Public Support (Hackney Wick, 1838), pp. 4-5,
and 8. The statement of the "grand disideratum" is found in
Sentiment of the Views and Reports of the Society for the
Suppression of Juvenile Vagrancy Upon the Plan that proved
so successful in Holland, by providing Agricultural Employment
for Destitute Children of the Metropolis (London, 1830), pp.
3-5.

23.   Anderson, Reports of the Boarding Out of Orphans
and Deserted Children, pp. 4-5.

24.   Carpenter, What Shall We Do With Our Pauper
Children?, pp. 5 and 15; and Anderson, p. 5.

25.   Wilhelmina Hall, Boarding Out, As a Method of
Pauper Education and a Check on Hereditary Pauperism
(London, 1887), p. 17; and T. J. MacNamara, Children Under
the Poor Law, p. 19.

26.   MacNamara, pp. 4-20; and Charles Loch, "Charity
and Its Problems," Organized Help, #34, 15 October 1901,
(Glasgow COS 1896-1923), pp. 439-445, MLG.

27. Miss M. H. Mason (1886-1893), "General Reports," 15 February 1884 and 3 February 1886 in Boarding Out Inspectors, MH 32/92, PRO.

28. Mason, "General Report," 25 April 1892.

29. Mason, "General Report," 3 January 1889; and Hannah E. Harrison (1909-1939), "General Report," 21 April 1909, HO 45/17842, PRO. J. Skelton, The Boarding Out of Pauper Children, agreed that money was a major inducement, pp. 60-62.

30. Doyle to LGB, 23 January 1874, and Doyle to Rt. Hon. G. Sclater-Booth, President LGB, 14 May 1877, MH 32/30/49184/72, PRO; and Tufnell, Observations on a Report of Mrs. Senior, citing the Assistant Commissioners' inquiry into the conditions of children and women in Agriculture, p. 22.

31. Mason, "General Report," 15 February 1884 and 25 April 1892.

32. Quoted in Trevelyan, p. 84.

33. Children's Emigration Homes, 10th AR (1883), pp. 9-10, BCL. Emphasis added.

34. George K. Behlmer, Child Abuse and Moral Reform in England, 1870-1908 (Stanford: Stanford University Press, 1982); and J. S. Hurt, Elementary Schooling and the Working Classes, 1860-1918 (London: Routledge & Kegan Paul, 1979).

35. Benevolent Society of Ireland for Establishment of Poor Colonies (Dublin, 1829), pp. 1-3; and Statement of the Views and Reports of the Society . . . Destitute Children of the Metropolis (London, 1830), BL; and Society for the Permanent Support of Orphan and Destitute Children by Means of Apprenticeship in the Colonies (London, 1831), GLL.

36. A. F. Young and E. T. Ashton, British Social Work in the Nineteenth Century (London: Routledge & Kegan Paul, 1956), pp. 134-141. An early history of fostering through poor law organization is provided by Sir George Nicholls, A History of the English Poor Law, rev. ed., 3 vols. (1854; reprint ed., New York: Augustus M. Kelley, 1967), and A History of the Scotch Poor Law in Connexion with the Condition of the People (London: John Murray, 1856).

37. A Statement of Facts Showing the Claims of the CFS to Public Support (1838); and Park Row Industrial School, Report (1875), BCA.

38. Georgina Battiscombe, Shaftesbury: A Biography of the Seventh Earl 1801-1885 (London: Constable, 1974), pp. 205-206; G. F. A. Best, Shaftesbury (London: B. T. Batsford, 1964), pp. 115-117; and Edwin Hodder, The Life and Work of the Seventh Earl of Shaftesbury, KG, 3 vols. (London: Cassell & Co., 1886), 2: 414; and Barnardo Report (1885-86), chapter 2, pp. 12-19, PAC.

39. Different views on the subject of obtaining parental consent are found in the following: "The Emigration of Children, 2 February 1888," Proceedings of the Liverpool School Board, indicated that the Board requested it, LCL; whereas the Times 20 May 1892, inferred that it was not always obtained. The Local Government Board, "Scheme for Emigrating Children to Canada From Industrial Schools, 5 December 1885," said it was difficult to obtain, HO 45 9672 A 46505b, PRO. The Manchester and Salford Boys and Girls Refuge, 21st AR (1891), remarked that "We Hope the Custody of Children Act of 1891 will explode the old fashioned theory of parental rights and control," MCL.

40. Parr, "Family Strategy and Philanthropic Abduction," in Labouring Children, pp. 62-81.

41. Miss Florence Penrose Phelp, "Emigration to Canada of Poor Law Children," paper before the Northern District Poor Law Conference, July 1903, pp. 208-209 and 233, NLC.

42. "The State and Parental Control," COR (April 1887): 139-145.

43. Great Britain, Parliamentary Papers, vol. 39 (1911) (Reports, vol. 32), "First Report of Standing Committee on Boy Labour in Post Office," Cd. 5504, p. 203; vol. 33 (1913) (Reports, vol. 19), "Report of the Departmental Committee on the Hours and Conditions of Employment of Van Boys and Warehouse Boys," Cd. 6886, p. 463; vol. 33 (1912-13) (Reports, vol. 19), "Evidence Taken before the Departmental Committee on the . . . Employment of Van Boys and Warehouse Boys," Cd. 6887, p. 495. Also see vol. 44 (1914) (Reports, vol. 34), "Fourth Report of Standing Committee on Boy Labour in Post Office," Cd. 7556, p. 871.

44. Birkdale Farm School, ARs (1886-1911), Liverpool Catholic Reformatory Association, vol. 4, LCL; and R. S.

Forman, Warden of Passmore Edwards Settlement, "Juvenile Emigration," COR 33 (January - June 1913), p. 259.

45. Joseph Forster, Stay and Starve (London, 1884), pp. 7 and 16; "A Canadian Sheaf: An Outline of the Boys' and Girls' Refuge at Strangeways (1906)," p. 18, (Immigration Branch Records), RG 76, vol. 30, file 674, pt. 3, PAC; George Bogue Smart, "A Visit to G. B. and Ireland (1906)," NLC; and "Out of the Depths: Life and Hope for the Slum Child in Canada," The Fold 4 (July 1904): 70-75, BCL.

46. Forster is quoted in Miss Florence Phelp, "Emigration to Canada," p. 233; and Gutter Children's Homes (Middlemore), 6th AR, p. 5, BCL.

47. Millie and Ann were brought over by Charlotte Alexander, Charlotte Alexander Papers, (1885-1893), MG 29, C 58, vol. 1, PAC.

48. National Children's Home, AR (1894-95), p. 38, BCL. The previous report noted the prejudice among large bodies of people in Canada that did not judge an immigrant boy "as a Canadian boy would be. If unhappily, one of them should be charged with any public offence, the case is reported and commented on in the newspapers much more eagerly and extensively than if the young criminal were native born." P. 37.

49. Charlotte Alexander Papers, vol. 3; and Further Letters Furnished to the Department of Agriculture in Rebuttal of Mr. Doyle's Report, by Maria Rye (1875), NLC.

50. Captain Palliser, Regina, to the Governor-General, the Marquis of Landsdowne, 15 March 1886, SABS; The Children's Farm Association (1907), NLC, and RG 76, vol. 323, file 312973; Conference of Guardians at Mansion House (1905) and Extract from a Report of the Paddington Guardians, 20 July 1904, Items 31 and 32, and the Times, 31 January 1905, HO 45/9676 A47-79, PRO; and William Reed Lewis, Letter to Mrs. E. Close, Elaborating the Canadian Portion of her Scheme (1904), NLC.

51. Chapter 10, "Off to Canada," pp. 105-6, in W. Y. Fullerton, J. W. C. Fegan: A Tribute (London & Edinburgh: Marshall, Morgan and Scott, 1930), and press notice from The Westminster Gazette, "A Dominion Homestead in the Heart of Kent," RG 76, vol. 59, pt. 2, PAC.

52. Denis Crane, John Bull's Surplus Children (London: Horace Marshall and Son, 1915), p. 13.

53. Gutter Children's Home, 1st AR (1872-73), pp. 3-4, BCL.

54. Liverpool Catholic Reformatory Association, 27th AR (1889), LCL.

[7] BRITISH CHILDREN FOR RURAL AND DOMESTIC
SERVICE: THE CANADIAN RESPONSE

1. See H. G. M. Johnston, British Emigration Policy 1815-30: Shovelling Out Paupers (Oxford: Clarendon Press, 1972); and Edward Gibbon Wakefield, A View of the Art of Colonization (London: John W. Parker, 1894), p. 145.

2. The mini-biographies collected by Harrison in The Home Children show the reluctance until recently of ex-home children to make public their origins. For discussions of the results of the hostile reception and the shame of abandonment see the authors' "The 'King's Children' in English Canada: A Psychohistorical Study of Abandonment, Rejection and Canadian Response to British Juvenile Immigrants 1864-1930," Journal of Psychohistory 8 (Spring 1981): 387-420, and "Imperial Philanthropy and Colonial Response: British Juvenile Emigration to Canada 1869-1930," The Historian (in press).

3. Select Committee on Immigration and Colonization, "First Report," Journal of the House of Commons, (1875); and also the "Fifth Report," RG 76, vol. 121, file 23624, PAC; Report to President of Local Government Board by Andrew Doyle (1875), NLC. Evidence that few in proportion to the total movement of British children originally came out under the poor laws is found in Journal of the House of Commons, "Final Report," Standing Committee on Agriculture and Colonization, 1895; D. J. O'Donaghue to Clifford Sifton, 21 March 1897 and reply, RG 76, vol. 121, file 23624, PAC.

4. Doug Whyte, "The Evolution of Federal Juvenile Immigration Policy 1894-1920" paper prepared for History Department, Carleton University, (January 23, 1978), surveys this aspect of the movement; and Gwynth Joy Parr, "The Home Children" (Ph.D. dissertation, Yale University, 1977), pp. 61-67.

5. "Dr. Barnardo's Industrial Farm, Russell, Manitoba," The Colonist 2 (1896-97): 125-128, and The Emigrant 2 (June 1887): 54, describes this experiment which ceased to operate by 1907, PAM; and Att. "G" 867 (1898) re: John Sergeant and 1272 (1901) re: George Watt - Barnardo Boys, SABS.

6. Report of the Commissioners Appointed to Enquire into the Prison and Reformatory System of Ontario (Toronto, 1891); and Parr, Labouring Children: British Immigrant Apprentices to Canada, 1869-1924 (London: Croom Helm, 1980), pp. 53-54.

7. Superintendent of Dependent and Neglected Children, Ontario, 5th AR (1897), Appendix, pp. 31-32; O'Donaghue to Sifton, 21 March 1897; and L. Pereira to O'Donaghue, 7 August 1897, RG 76, vol. 121, file 23623, PAC.

8. Parr, Labouring Children, pp. 54-55; and Rooke and Schnell, "Childhood and Charity in Nineteenth Century British North America," Histoire Sociale/Social History 15 (May 1982): 157-179.

9. O'Donaghue to R. W. Scott, 25 July 1896; and Toronto Trades and Labour Council, "Extract from the Report of Legislative Committee," 6 December 1895; A. B. Owen, Barnardo Agent, Toronto, to Pereira, 19 January 1896; and O'Donaghue to Minister of the Interior, 3 March 1896, RG 76, vol. 121, file 23624, PAC. To demonstrate the continuity of this curious reversal of justice whereby the victim bore the burden of blame, many years later Mr. Reynolds, Superintendent of Neglected Children in Saskatchewan, noted in 1923 that a boy who had been found dead after extended neglect "must have been very docile or he would not have stood for the things he did." Presumably feeblemindedness was insinuated in this sententious comment. "Extract from Conference Proceedings of the Canadian Council on Child Welfare" (September 1923), p. 4, CCSD/6, PAC.

10. Manitoba Free Press, 22 November 1893. The Russell Farm Investigation is found in RG 76, vol. 94, file 10216, PAC.

11. National Council of Women, MG 28, I 25, vol. 105, file NCW, June 1895 - March 1896; and file NCW, April 1896 - May 1896, PAC.

12. Ibid., file NCW, January 1897 - June 1897; and Rosa L. Shaw, Proud Heritage (Toronto: Ryerson Press, 1957), p. 14. For continued, if sporadic interest, see "Withdrawn

resolution from Toronto Local Council of Women," 16 March 1910; Emily Cummings, Corresponding Secretary NCW, to Local Council of Women, 18 February 1913; and Mrs. Soma Leathers to Executive Committee, NCW, October 1915, 74.1, box 7/195, PAA.

13.   P. H. Shelton to C. Whitton, 4 July 1928, CCSD/5, file 33, PAC.

14.   Superintendent of Neglected and Dependent Children of Ontario, 2nd AR, (1895), Appendix, pp. 30-35; 5th AR (1897), Appendix, p. 4; and Manitoba, 60 Victoria 1897, ch. 1; Quebec, 62 Victoria 1899, ch. 47; and Nova Scotia, Revised Statutes, 1900, ch. 118.

15.   Parr, "Home Children," pp. 115-116.

16.   The Empire Settlement Act (1922) put the age of unaccompanied juvenile emigration from fourteen years to seventeen years for girls and nineteen years for boys although some under twelve could proceed under "A special scheme arranged by the Child Emigration Society." RG 78, vol. 68, file 3115, pt. 19, PAC. See also G. F. Plant, Overseas Settlement: Migration from the United Kingdom to the Dominions (London: Oxford University Press, 1951), for child and juvenile emigration schemes placed in a broader context.

17.   See press articles by the authors responding to a series of exposés of existing child welfare and fostering conditions in Ontario and Alberta: "So What's New in Alberta Child Welfare?" Calgary Herald 28 August 1980; "Alberta Continues 'Sorry Record' of Foster Care," CH 28 October 1981; and "The CAS: Starved For Money, Ignored by Public." The Globe and Mail, 3 December 1981.

18.   MG 29, C58, vol. 1, file Z, PAC.

19.   "Further Letters Furnished to the Department of Agriculture in Rebuttal of Mr. Doyle's Report, by Maria Rye" (1875), pp. 24-25.

20.   MG 29 C 58, vol. 3; and Press Cutting, "Child Immigration," by Eleanor Stuart, Simmonds, Ontario, 10 July 1930, CCSD/6, file 33, PAC.

21.   Harrison, pp. 135-137, 196, 175 and 86.

22.   RG 76, vol. 68, file 3115, pt. 15.

23. Ibid., vol. 67, file 3115, pt. 11; and vol. 62, file 2869, PAC.

24. Liverpool Sheltering Home, 5th AR, in Minute Book I (11 July 1873 - 4 April 1911), LCL. The first specific "Adoption" Acts were passed in British Columbia in 1920, Ontario, 1921, Saskatchewan, 1922, and Quebec, 1925. "Technically, adoption in the sense of the transfer of parental rights and liabilities was unknown under English common law until 1928." George K. Behlmer, Child Abuse and Moral Reform in England, 1870-1908 (Stanford: Stanford University Press, 1982), p. 17n. Early American interest is discussed in Jamel S. Zanaldin, "The Emergence of Modern American Law: Child Custody, Adoption, and the Courts, 1796-1851," Family Northwestern University Law Review 73 (1979): 1038-1089.

25. "Canadian Conference on Child Welfare Proceedings (1925)," pp. 65-66; and "Conference . . . of Lambeth Guardians: Emigration of Poor Law Children, 29 June 1903," NLC.

26. Emily Bayley, Lady Superintendent of Western Home to Smart, 9 October 1902, RG 76, vol. 78, file 6648, pt. 1., PAC

27. J. Obed Smith to Scott, 3 December 1904, RG 76, vol. 100, file 13204, pt. 2; Harrison, p. 188; and RG 76, vol. 62, file 2869.

28. All references to J. Sterling King come from RG 76, vol. 62, file 2869, pt. 1 and vol. 63.

29. Parr, pp. 123-141. Gail H. Corbett enthuses that her Barnardo Children in Canada" are children building a better world for themselves and their descendants. It is the materialization of the hope that Canada promised to those who would journey" (Peterborough, Ontario: Woodland Publishing, 1981), "Preface."

30. Parr, pp. 158-161.

31. Parr, chapter 5, and especially pp. 85, 108-109, and 115-116.

32. The work of the Canadian Council of Immigration of Women for Household Service in the 1920s is merely a later example of the function of servant-keeping in a colonial society.

459

33. MacGill to Margaret Bondfield, in "An Analysis of a Report of the British Delegation on Child Immigration Submitted by the Executive Committee of the CCCW (1924)," pp. 10-11, CCSD/26. Walters, 23 October 1916, Great Britain, Parliamentary Papers, vol. 8 (1917-18) (Reports, vol. 5), Dominions Royal Commission, "Minutes of Evidence taken in the Central and Western Provinces," Part I, Cd. 8458, pp. 319-321.

34. The Canadian Post, 18 April 1884. To balance such sentiment were the even earlier comments that the "children from the street" were "not wanted here." John Walters to the Colonial Office, 12 July 1875, RG 76, vol. 65, file 3115, pt. 1.

35. "Social Welfare Charity Cases: Committee of the Executive Canadian Council of Immigration of Women," CCSD/7, file 56 (1929), and National Council of Women, "Problems of the Feebleminded," MG 28, I 25, vol. 60, (1899-1907), PAC; "Official Report of a Conference on Care of Mental Defectives," 18 June 1920, Mg X-162, and Toronto Mental Hygiene Committee, "Problem of Feeblemindedness in Toronto" (1921), MTL; Canadian National Committee for Mental Hygiene (1918), items 4073 (The Globe, 27 January 1919), 4079 and 40950 ("The Defective Immigrant"), Second Annual Meeting, Vancouver, 22 June 1920, SABS. Also see the First Quarterly Meeting of Edmonton Local Council of Women, 29 June 1908, where Mrs. Murphy cited the case of "Margaret Jukes," 74.1/190-197, box 7, PAA; and Meeting of the NCW Executive Committee, 16 January 1907, MG 28, I25, vol. 106, where Canada's Juke, "Margaret" is cited with six generations adding 900 imbeciles, idiots, drunkards, prostitutes and paupers to the nation's dependent population.

36. John Cleverley and D. C. Phillips, From Locke to Spock (Melbourne: Melbourne University Press, 1976).

37. See for example, Ivy Pinchbeck and Margaret Hewitt, Children in English Society, vol. 2: From The Eighteenth Century to the Children Act 1948 (London: Routledge & Kegan Paul 1973); Susan E. Houston, "Victorian Origins of Juvenile Delinquency: A Canadian Experience," in Education and Social Change, ed. Paul H. Mattingly and Michael B. Katz (New York: New York University Press, 1975), pp. 83-109.

38. R. L. Dugdale, "The Jukes": A Study of Crime, Pauperism, Disease and Heredity (5th ed.; New York: G. P. Putnam's Sons, 1895); and Henry Herbert Goddard, The Kallikak Family (New York: The Macmillan Co., 1931).

39. See, for example, Kenneth M. Ludmerer, Genetics and American Society (Baltimore: Johns Hopkins University Press, 1972), and Mark H. Haller, Eugenics (New Brunswick, NJ: Rutgers University Press, 1963).

40. The Orphans' Homes of Scotland, AR (1897), p. 48, MLG.

41. Barnardo's, AR (1907), pp. 27-32, AR (1885), p. 14, and AR (1907), pp. 27-32; and James S. Woodsworth, Strangers Within Our Gates (Toronto: Methodist Mission, 1909), pp. 51-58, and 59-72. Woodsworth represented the "progressive" elements of Canadian social reform. See Kenneth McNaught, A Prophet in Politics (Toronto: University of Toronto Press, 1959) and Richard Allen, The Social Passion (Toronto: University of Toronto Press, 1973).

42. The paper used material from Ontario Department of Agriculture, Bulletin LIII, (June 1895), RG 76, vol. 119, file 22877; and House of Commons, Standing Committee on Agriculture and Colonization, Final Report, 1897, RG 76, vol. 121, file 23624, PAC.

43. Superintendent of Dependent and Neglected Children, Ontario, 5th AR, Appendix, "Special Report on Immigration of British Children" (1897). Similar appendices are included in 1895, 1898, and 1903 reports. F. C. Blair to Col. O'Kelly, 14 November 1929, to Walker, 8 November 1929, and to Innis, 12 February 1930, RG 76, vol. 271, file 768363, pt. I. For Blair's subsequent role in preventing the admission of European Jews (including children) into Canada, see Irving Abella and Harold Troper, None is Too Many (Toronto: Lester & Orpen Dennys, 1982).

44. Charity Organization Review/Reporter (April, 1887): 139-145; Palladium of Labour, 1 November 1884 and 16 August 1884; Pereira to Rye, 24 April 1894, and Rye to Pereira, 26 April 1894, RG 76, vol. 94, file 10216; and The Toiler, 10 July 1903, and 28 October 1904.

45. Two examples of prejudicial medical "inspection" occurred at Halifax in February 1907 and March 1910, RG 76, vol. 32, file 724, pt. 3. In 1920 a boy was subject to "indignities" when it was later discovered he was probably only nervous, timid, not talkative, and had a broad Scots brogue which characteristics were sufficient for him to be rejected as a "mental defective." W. Douglas to Smart, 16 April 1920, and Smart to Little, 17 April 1920, RG 76, vol. 46, file 1381, pt. 2.

46. Superintendent of Dependent and Neglected Children, Ontario, 5th AR (1897), Appendix, pp. 31-32. As a result of these attitudes, cases of abuse or exploitation -- many not involving British children at all -- were publicized as if they were. For example, Winnipeg Tribune, 14 September 1923, and Ottawa Citizen, 18 October 1923, cited cases of cruelty to "Home" children who were not "Home" children; John Bull, 3 November 1923, "Appalling Child Slavery," was a sensational version; The National Society of Prevention of Cruelty to Children, London, wrote to the Prime Minister, W. L. MacKenzie King, 27 February 1924, about Charles Bulpitt and John Payne which was all out of proportion to the facts of the cases, RG 76, vol. 67, file 3115, pt. 2.

47. Donald Messenger to J. A. Kirk, 10 February 1898, and J. V. Lantulum to Smart, 15 November 1904, RG 76, vol. 99, file 13204, pt. 1; and Charlotte Alexander Papers, vol. 3, PAC. For references to "immoral habits," "wicked and evil tendencies," and "bad passion," see RG 76, vol. 63, file 2869, pt. 4; and vol 68, file 3115, pt. 15. Also see, Rooke and Schnell "The King's Children" for a full discussion of the labelling of immigrant children and adolescents.

48. Donald Messenger to J. A. Kirk, 10 February 1898 and J. V. Lantulum to Smart, 15 November 1904, RG 76, vol. 99, file 13204, pt. 1.

49. Some examples of child saving literature include: Lady Hobart, Hon. Sec. to East London Family Emigration Fund, Help for the Helpless: London's Bitter Cry Hushed in Canada (London, 1884); William Mitchell, Rescue the Children or Twelve Years Dealing with Neglected Girls and Boys (London, 1886); M.A. Spielman, H. M. I. of Reformatory and Industrial Schools, The Romance of Child Reclamation (London, 1920); Within Our Gates, The Spurgeon Orphanage Quarterly (March 1894); Rev. Marshall George Vine, Warden of Redhill Reformatory, In Loco Parentis (London, 1905); Delving and Diving: Or Voices from the Slums of Salford and Manchester (1881-82); Homeless, the organ of the Fr. Berry's Home for Friendless Children, Liverpool; Loving and Serving and Hiving Off, of Fegan's Homes; Church Army Blue Book: The Reports of the CA Among the Criminal, Outcast, Careless and Distressed (1908-1909); and Gutter Children's homes [Middlemore, Birmingham], ARs (1872-1926).

50. W. Morgan, "The Arabs of the City: Or a Plea For Brotherhood With the Outcast," an address before the YMCA, Birmingham, 29 November 1863, p. 7, BCL

51. Carpenter, p. 4.

52. Edward Carleton Tufnell, Observations on the Report of Mrs. Senior, p. 11; The Emigrant, vol. 2, no. 2 (June 1887): 54; and Church of England Waifs and Strays Society, "Inspection of Union Children," HO 45/9676, PRO.

53. RG 76, vol. 65, file 3115, pt. 2.

54. Items 37, 38, and 46, (1910-13), HO 45/9676 A47079. The Reformatory Act (1866), the New Elementary Education Act (1876), and the Prevention of Cruelty and Protection of Children Act, 1889 dealt with destitute and morally endangered children. The "Cornwall" - Attacks on Boys, and "The Clio," HO 45/10413 B21202 and B19615; the Clyde Industrial Training Ship, the "Cumberland," 15th - 18th ARs (1874-87), MLG; The "Formidable" - Bristol Training Ship for Homeless and Destitute Boys (1879), BCA; the Society of the Industrial Training Ship, "Clio," 15th AR (1891-94), MCL; and Inspection of Immigrant Children (1900-02), RG 76, vol. 231, file 128477; and Annie Macpherson, The Little London Arabs (London, 1870), p. 11.

55. "Tom Moore Opposes Child Immigration," United Farmers' (1926-46), B2 IX 332, SABS.

56. Juvenile Immigration Report No. 2 (Ottawa: CCCW, 1925), p. 6; Whitton to James W. Woodsworth, M. P., House of Commons, 24 April 1924; Miss J. M. Kniseley, Head Worker, Toronto General Hospital to Whitton, 27 February 1924; Claude Winters to J. J. Kelso, 7 November 1925; Winters to Jane Wisdom, 7 November 1925; Wisdom to Whitton, 31 November 1925, CCSD/26, file 137. Whitton and the CCCW are discussed by the authors in "Child Welfare in English Canada 1920-48," Social Service Review 55 (September 1981): 484-506.

57. "Mental Deficiency as a Child Welfare Problem" [circa. 1921], WP/19. Also see "Immigration of British Women Workers to Canada," Social Welfare, (October 1, 1918): 18-19.

58. "Canada's Child Immigrants" (Toronto: SSCC, 1925), pp. 16, 33, and 38, PAO; and Whitton to G. Pott, 16 August 1928, CCSD/6, file 33.

59. Kelso to Whitton, 23 July 1923, CCSD/26; and file: "Institutions and Immigration Homes 1924-25," CCSD/45. Kelso's faux-pas at the juvenile immigration conference of 1924 is found in CCSD/26, file 137.

463

60. "Apology by Professor MacPhee to Dr. Barnardo's Homes (1925)," CCSD/45.

61. The following are only some examples: the Social Service Council of Canada, "Canada's Child Immigrants," TA (1925) 63, PAO; D. J. Dunn, M.D., Medical Inspector, Edmonton Public School Board to Whitton, 13 January 1925, MG I 10, vol. 26 (1924-25), Immigration file 137, PAM; G. K. Clarke, Professor of Psychiatry, University of Toronto, "The Prevalence of V. D. in Canada" (Ottawa, 1918), and Carrie M. Derick, "The Feebleminded, Dec. 1918," Montreal Local Council of Women, MG 28 I 164, vol. 7; Conference on Request of CCCW, 23 October 1928 - McPhee's Survey, CCSD/7, files 33 (1928-30) and 56 [Social Welfare Charity Cases, Minutes of the Executive Committee of the Canadian Council of Immigration of Women (1929)]; P. D. Macpherson, Department of Psychology, University of Toronto, to Mrs. Thorburn, 15 March 1929, vol. 6, file 33; Salvation Army (1908-15), RG 76, vol 494, file 768363, pt. 1; Resolution from Council of Social Service of the Church of England in Canada, 24 January 1923, vol. 67, file 3115, pt. 11; Smart to Blair, 13 March 1928, and Whitton to Blair, 13 March 28, CCSD/12 (1929); Blair to Smart, 31 January 1927, RG 76, vol. 68, file 3115, pt. 15; J. M. Kniseley, Toronto General Hospital, to Whitton, 3 November 1925, Whitton to Professor Kemp, University of Toronto, 11 November 1925; and Kemp to Whitton, 14 November 1925, CCSD/45, PAC.

62. Whitton to Pott, 16 August 1928, CCSD/6, file 33.

63. James Webb to G. Bogue Smart, 6 February 1924, RG 76, vol. 67, file 3115, pt. 11.

64. Doug Whyte, p. 24, quoting Order-in-Council P.C. 1190, 29 May 1920.

65. Denis Crane, John Bull's Surplus Children: A Plea for Giving Them a Fairer Chance (London: Horace Marshall & Son, 1915), p. 13. Also see Thomas E. Sedgwick, Lads for Empire, (London: P. S. King & Son, 1914).

66. See Sutherland, Children in English-Canadian Society.

67. See Rooke and Schnell, "'Making the Way More Comfortable': Charlotte Whitton's Child Welfare Career, 1920-48," Journal of Canadian Studies (Winter 1983).

68. The Orphans' Homes of Scotland, AR (1897), p. 73, MLG.

69. "An Analysis of a Report . . . (1924)," pp. 22-23; and "Resolution" (about provincial authority to legislate on juvenile immigration) from Judge Helen MacGill and Magistrate Emily F. Murphy, 13 September 1923, representing the Canadian Association of Child Protection Officers, RG 76, vol. 67, file 3115, pt. 11.

70. "An Analysis of a Report," p. 6; "Extract from Conference Proceedings, CCCW, Winnipeg" (September 1923), p. 3, CCSD/26. A. P. Paget, Director of Child Welfare, Manitoba, would present the same view at the 1925 CCCW Conference. "The Juvenile Immigrant," in Child Placing (Ottawa: CCCW, 1925), pp. 12-14.

71. See Andrew Jones and Leonard Rutman, In The Children's Aid: J. J. Kelso and Child Welfare in Ontario. (Toronto: University of Toronto Press, 1981), pp. 91-96, and Toronto CAS, AR (1896), pp. 24-25, in SCI-C, box 3, CASOT, CTA.

72. The Orphans' Homes of Scotland, AR (1897), p. 93, MLG.

73. W. F. Nickle to Miss Kate Dixon, 15 August 1924, CCSD/26; and "Summary of Present Day Problems Worthy of the Council's Considerations (n.d.) [probably 1924-25] WP/95.

74. McGregor to Whitton, 15 June 1927, CCSD/6, file 33. BICA records are found in RG 76, vol. 102, file 16120, pts. 1-4; vol. 68, file 3115, pts. 15-19; vol. 103, file 16120, pt. 5; and Minute Books (1920-41), MG 28 I 62, PAC. Also see Minutes of Oversea Settlement Committee, 17 July 1928, HO 57/72 file 1828, PRO; and "Report of the OSC for the Period 1 January 1930 to 31 March 1931," vol. 16, (1930-31) (Reports, vol. 7), Great Britain, Parliamentary Papers, Cmd. 3882, p. 426.

75. The labor elements were at least more consistent on this point than the middle class elements. Anti-child labor laws were supported by them for reasons often distinct from childhood sentiment. Thus, the Hamilton Palladium of Labour observed on 16 May 1885 that "the labour of young children is the greatest enemy that working men ought to fear. If a man puts his child to work when the child is of school age he puts his child's labour in direct competition with his own," and on 3 July 1886, child labor "wrongs children" and "the grown

465

people who work in the same shop with it." Just the same, the irony of the following views cannot escape even a die-hard labor supporter. On 10 July 1903 The Labour Journal condemned the Home Children as doing injury to the country because they were "the lowest scum of the slums," and then on 4 September 1903 printed a piece on "Working Children," which in relation to the British Children's Act claims that, "it took 30 years of heroic sacrifice and continuous parliamentary struggle . . . to restore the right of childhood to children of England's working class."

76. Blair to Egan, 11 July 1926, RG 76, vol. 65, file 3115, pt. 14; Hobday to McGregor, 21 November 1927, CCSD/6, file 33. Similar statements are in Claude Winters (Superintendent of Fairknowe home) to Whitton, 29 January 1926, and Smart to Egan, 15 November 1924, commenting on the 1924-26 Children's Acts in Manitoba, Alberta, and Nova Scotia, which included sections on immigrant children. Smart, federal inspector of British Children, agreed that if a child was allowed entry into Canada he had "the right to settle where he wishes, without being enrolled as a ward of that province." RG 76, vol. 67, file 3115, pt. 12.

77. Ottawa CAS, ARs (1902-1904), and Toronto CAS, AR (1912), MG 30 C97, vol. 25, PAC.

78. In YWCA, MG 28 I 198, vol. 14, file (1928-29), PAC. (Also see a report of the IODE National Meeting on Immigration held in June 1928, requesting the "best quality" and "a better class of British women" as domestics, ibid.); and COR 2 (January - December 1886): 108. Subsequently we are not surprised that a Toronto Globe's editorial, "Importation of Waifs," 10 January 1894, commenting on the murder of a Mrs. Martin by a boy said to be an "emigrant waif," recommended that to prevent any replication of this unfortunate event the public must do everything possible "to assist farmers and others in obtaining Canadian boys and girls as household helps."

79. St. Patrick's was refused funding by the Saskatchewan government and therefore sought aid from Britain. Item 16099, Motherwell Papers, M 12-2, VI; Miscellaneous 8 January 1909 - 10 June 1917, Bradshaw Papers, A 35 I; and Prince Albert Times 4 March 1908, SABS.

80. "Canadian Conference on Child Welfare (1925)," p. 60.

81. This concern is well documented in Rosa Shaw, Proud Heritage: A History of the NCW of Canada (Toronto: Ryerson Press, 1957), pp. 11-36; and Veronica Strong-Boag, The Parliament of Women: The National Council of Women of Canada, 1893-1929 (Ottawa: National Museum of Canada, 1976).

82. Examples include the London LCW Resolutions (1917) in MG 28 I 25, PAM; Ottawa LCW, Minute Books 1894-1920, MG 28 I 32 and Montreal LCW, MG 28, I 164, vol. 7, PAC; Regina LCW Minutes, RG 136, SABR; Marion R. Earl, "A History of the LCW of Kingston 1894-1974," in Coll. 31, QU; and "An Analysis of the Report . . . (1924)," p. 3.

83. Shaw, pp. 18 and 22, 12-13, and 29-30. The Prairie provinces were anxious to receive juvenile immigrants for domestic and agricultural service. Even before World War I, Colin Campbell, Premier of Manitoba, and F. J. Billiarde, the provincial Superintendent of Delinquent and Neglected Children, had instituted a plan for emigration using the services of the Church of England Waifs and Strays Society, the Quarrier homes, some Poor Law unions, the Salvation Army, the Barnardo Homes, and the Church Army. In "Poor Law Children," HO 45/9992 A46505 (October 1909), PRO.

84. "Conference of Canadian Council of Immigration of Women for Household Service, 13-15th Jan. 1920," Item 40019, Marten Papers M4, I 90, SABS.

85. Brockville CAS alone provides us with abundant examples of this attitude. For example, Mr. Trail to D. Couper, Kingston, 18 March 1913, tells him as there are no girls over school age he should apply to Mr. Grierson, Superintendent of Fairknowe Home, Brockville, who will "supply you." Fairknowe was a distributing and receiving home for the Quarrier Orphanages. On 18 April 1913, Lydia McCoy, who being over fourteen years would not be "of much use to you," was being held for an applicant. Letterbook, 24 January 1913 - 19 March 1914, MS 506, PAO.

86. Correspondence around the Elizabeth Rye Home is preoccupied with the mental and moral propensities of the girls there, RG 76, vol. 253, file 193596, (1925-30). Other examples include the records of the NCW, MG 28, I 25, vols. 66-68 and 107-108, PAC; Winnipeg Local Council, MG 10, C 45, PAM; Montreal Local Council of Women, MG 28, I 164, vols. 4 and 7 (see especially Carrie Derick, "Is the Mentally Defective a Problem in Preventative Medicine?" AR [1915-16], pp. 10-14; "Report of Committee on Mental Defect, 1918-20," AR

[1918-19], pp. 25-29; and "An Historical Sketch 1893-1910"); Ottawa Local Council of Women, Minute, 11 March 1915, MG 28, I 32, vol. 6, PAC; and Edmonton Local Council of Women, Minutes 7 April 1911 - 1915, 74.1/190-197, box 7, PAA.

87. The Gazette, 28 September 1925, in File: Child Employment 1923-25, CCSD/8.

88. Gillian Wagner's perceptive biography on Barnardo illustrates this success and response to it.

89. McGregor to Blair, 15 June 1927, and Blair to Egan, 11 July 1924, RG 76, vol. 65, file 3115, pt. 14.

90. Doug Whyte cites Sutherland, Parr and Morrison regarding Canadian groups developing alongside British Child Welfare groups and subsequently reaching "their level of proficiency and eventually pass[ing] them." P. 25.

91. The Alberta situation is discussed fully by the authors in "Charlotte Whitton Meets 'The Last Best West': The Politics of Alberta Child Welfare, 1929-49," Prairie Forum 6 (Fall 1981): 143-162; and "Charlotte Whitton and the 'Babies for Export' Controversy," Alberta History 30 (Winter 1982): 11-16.

92. Whitton to Moore, 15 December 1926, CCSD/8, file 38.

93. "Child Labour," Echoes (March 1924) in MF 28, I 10, vol. 8, file 38, PAC. See also Major J. P. Cowles, Provincial School Attendance Officer, "The Juvenile Employment System of Ontario," (Ottawa: CCCW, 1923).

94. See CCSD/2, files: League of Nations, 1925-1935.

95. MacGill, "The Child in Employment" before the Canadian Conference on Child Welfare (1925), pp. 34-45. MacGill noted that due to a lack of fundamental principles the result in Canada had been that legislation was adopted "holus-bolus" - "sometimes in contradiction to other provincial laws of the same province, indicating a haphazard snatching at the removal of some grievance publicly aired or demanded publicly." P. 38.

96. Memo re: "Barnardo Girls" from Whitton and CCCW, 1 February 1926; Whitton to G. F. Plant, 1 February 1926; Plant to Whitton, 17 February 1926 (in which he encloses a

copy of Professor MacPhee's apology about his wrong figures)
DO 57/22 (1926), file 1729, PRO.

97. In CCSD/6, file 33 (1928).

[8] BOARDING OUT IN CANADA: THE DE-INSTITUTIONALIZATION OF DEPENDENT CHILDREN

1. Toronto CAS, 7th AR (1898), p. 14, SCIC, box 1, CASOT, CTA.

2. See, for example, Neil Sutherland, Children in English-Canadian Society (Toronto: University of Toronto Press, 1976); and T. R. Morrison, "'Their Proper Sphere': Feminism, the Family, and Child-Centered Social Reform in Ontario," Ontario History 68 (March /June 1976): 45-64 and 65-74.

3. Wood's Christian Home (1915-74), GAA; and "Twenty-Five Years of Guarding Canada's Greatest Asset: The Benevolent Society's Home for Protestant Children, 1923-48," SABR.

4. Leo Kanner, A History of the Care and Study of the Mentally Retarded (Springfield, Ill.: Charles C. Thomas, 1964).

5. The evidence for this statement is so profuse the authors think it wiser not to start with it; however, see the relevant notes from Chapter Six as some indication of the extent of the discourse in Canada.

6. Michel Foucault, The History of Sexuality, vol. 1 (New York: Vintage Books, 1980). Also see, Elinor Shaffer, review of The History of Sexuality, in Women: Sex and Sexuality, ed. Catherine R. Stimpson and Ethel Spector Person (Chicago: University of Chicago Press, 1980), pp. 299-307.

7. Foucault, pp. 53-54.

8. P. H. Bryce, "Address of the President on National Social Efficiency," Canadian Conference of Correction and Charities, 16th AR (1917), p. 37.

9. The Children's Aid and Humane Society, Stratford, County of Perth and Town of St. Mary's, AR (1918), p. 4.

10. F. R. Clarke, Montreal CAS, to Scott, 22 July 1910 and 8 November 1910, MG 30 C 27, vol. 1, file 1, PAC.

11. Ottawa CAS, AR (1901); Hamilton CAS, AR (1908), p. 4; and Belleville CAS, AR (1911) p. 14.

12. Owen Sound CAS, AR (1900).

13. Secretary to Lathans, 7 February 1913, Letterbook 24 January 1913 - 19 March 1914, Brockville CAS (1894-1945) MS 506, PAO

14. See Rooke and Schnell, "Child Welfare in English Canada 1920-1948," Social Service Review 55 (September 1981): 484-506; and "Charlotte Whitton Meets 'The Last Best West': The Politics of Child Welfare," Prairie Forum 6 (Fall 1981): 143-162.

15. E. W. Montgomery to Whitton, 27 March 1928, "Child Welfare in Manitoba," pt. 2 (1928), CCSD/29, file 147; "Report of the Royal Commission, Child Welfare Division of the Department of Health and Public Welfare, Manitoba (1928)," WP/20. In Scrapbook, Winnipeg CH, MG 10, B24, PAM.

16. Confidential Memo Re Personnel of Child Welfare Division, Manitoba (1925), p. 2, WP/19.

17. "Report of the Royal Commission . . . 1928," p. 38; and Whitton to CCCW, 3 July 1928, and to McGregor 1 July 1928, McGregor to Whitton, 22 July 1928, "Child Welfare in Manitoba" pt. 2, CCSD/29, file 147. Also see Welfare Supervision Board, Public Welfare Division, files 30, 32, and 33, which discuss the Manitoba CAS and Child Welfare situation after the survey, RG 5, G 2, box 3, PAM. The St. Adelard CAS was particularly dissected.

18. Ethel MacLachlan, "History of Government and Departments: Neglected Children," Public Service Monthly (December 1917), SABR. Also see Gertrude S. Telford, "The First Child Welfare Conferences in Saskatchewan," Saskatchewan History 14 (Spring 1951): 57-61 and "Memorandum Re Certain Child Welfare Problems" presented to Hon. Dr. J. T. M. Anderson, Premier of Saskatchewan from Whitton, 20 January 1930, CCSD/26, file 133.

19. Toronto CAS, AR (1912), SCIC, box 3, CASOT, CTA.

20. Association of Ontario Children's Aid Societies, Minute Book #2 (1919-24), PAO.

21. Reports of the BC Child Welfare Survey on CAS of Vancouver (1927), pp. 2-3; Victoria CAS (1927), pp. 1-8; and Catholic Mass Meeting, 31 May 1927, pp. 1-4, CCSD/43, file 208. Also see additional items on the CASs of Vancouver and Victoria in Miscellaneous Child Welfare Correspondence (unprocessed) 1920-41, PABC.

The Roman Catholic CAS in Vancouver fared little better. The Child Welfare Survey (1927), pp. 12, 16, 45 and especially pp. 75-79, WP/36. Also see Vancouver Children's Aid Society, ARs (1901-1913), PL; Ann Margaret Angus, Children's Aid Society of Vancouver (1901-51), PABC; Helen Gregory MacGill, The Story of Vancouver Social Service (Vancouver: City Hall, 1943), pp. 3 and 72-78; J. C. McNelly, Chairman, BC Survey Committee, to Mrs. C. H. Thorburn, President CCCW, 21 June 1927, RG 5, G2, box 1, file 14, PAM; and correspondence (1926-29), WP/18, files 4 and 5.

22. All details on the Victoria CAS are taken from the following: W. G. Wilson, History of the CAS in Victoria; Victoria CAS ARs (1919-40); Victoria CAS, Daily Journal, vol. 11; and CAS, Minutes (1902-31), vols. 1-10, in MSS.431, PABC. Also see "A Year's Experiment in Private Home Care - The Victoria CAS," Child and Family Welfare, 10 (March 1935): 35-36; and "Child Welfare in BC (1932)," CCSD/28, file 139.

23. A History of the CAS and Department of Dependent Children in Nova Scotia is found in Ernest Blois's outgoing report in Department of Dependent Children, AR (1947), PANS.

24. "Interim Report: Community Welfare Agencies in Fredericton, N.B. (1930)," Kierstead Papers (Correspondence 1919-38), case 6, box 1, UNB.

25. "New Brunswick Child Welfare Survey Report (1928-29)," WP/36; Correspondence surrounding survey in CCSD/19 and CCSD/37, file 167; Moncton Survey (1939), CCCD/132; Saint John Survey (1941), WP/4 and CCSD/132 and 134; New Brunswick Survey (1949), WP/4, CCSD/134 and 135, and "Report of the NB Task Force on Social Development" (1971), SJCL.

26. "The Children's Aid Societies in PEI Survey (1929)," and correspondence surrounding re-organization of Child and

471

Family Welfare, Charlottetown (1931-32), CCSD/19, files 13 and 18.

27. See CAS, PEI Minutes (Sept. 1909 - Nov. 1925), PAPEI.

28. Ottawa Survey of Social Agencies (1929), CCSD/28, file 143.

29. Williams to Whitton, 22 April 1929, CCSD/28, file 143.

30. Fr. Madden of the CAS of the Church of the Holy Rosary to Scott, 28 October 1909; Scott to Madden 16 November 1909; Madden to Scott, 9 November 1909; Scott to Hon. A. B. Ayleworth, Minister of Justice, 24 November 1909; Scott to Kelso, 11 May 1910, MG 30, C27, vol. 1, file 1.

31. Rev. F. X. Brunet to Scott, 11 March 1911, and Scott to Brunet, 22 May 1911, MG 30, C27, file 4.

32. For example, Scott to Whitton, 10 April 1928, wanted CCCW to investigate CAS inspection procedures as he said inspection of foster homes was only conducted once a year by a government official, MG 30, C27, vol. 13, file 47.

33. Minutes, 19 April 1923, box 13, SCIA CASOT, CTA; Whitton on "R. E." p. 2, WP/5, file: Sept. 1947; and Dickie to Kelso, 23 February 1916, Kelso to Dickie, 25 February 1916; Kelso to Millman, 22 March 1916; MG 30, C97, vol. 1 and Kelso to Mayor of Toronto, 19 March 1915, vol. 4.

34. Minutes, 19 February 1920, 20 January 1921, 16 February 1921 and 19 May 1921, box 13, SCIA, CASOT, CTA.

35. Robert E. Mills, Utilization of Provincial Legislation in Connection With Child Placing (CCCW, 1925), pp. 3-5, VPL.

36. Ibid., p. 5; and file: Hamilton CAS Survey (1929-30), CCSD/45.

37. Toronto CAS, ARs (1924 and 1928), box 3 SCIC, CASOT, CTA.

38. Philosophy of Child Care and Organizational Concepts, file 23, SCIB, CASOT, CTA.

39. In "Child Placing" (CCCW, 1925), p. 7. Kelso said this about "natural homes" in a pamphlet, Child Saving (n.d.), MG 30, C97, vol. 4.

40. P. 54.

41. See <u>Twenty-First Report of the Evangelism and Social Service Board of the Methodist Church (1922-23)</u>, pp. 49-52, SABS; and <u>Report of Girls' Cottage Industrial School, Sweetsburg, P. Q.</u>, pp. 186-189, in "Welfare Work in Montreal (1923)," MG 18, I 129, vol. 10, PAC.

42. File CAS Ontario Notes and Activities (1906-1929), MG 30, C97, vol. 4; and Scott to Kelso, 31 October 1912; Kelso to Scott, 1 November 1912; Scott to Kelso, 22 November 1912, MG 30, C27, vol. 2, PAC. See, also, Jones and Rutman, pp. 1-47; MG 30 C97, vols. 1, 4, 6, and 8.

43. The variety and personal quality of Kelso's early efforts were representative of the older form of child rescue, which combined sentiment, personal service, and religious commitment. Jo Manton, <u>Mary Carpenter and the Children of the Streets</u> (London: Heinemann, 1976).

44. "Can Slums Be Abolished or Must We Continue to Pay the Penalty?" (Toronto, 1910), pp. 17-20, MG 30, C97, vol. 1, PAC. Helen Reid is quoted in, "Victoria Report (1932)," CCSD/28, file 139.

45. Kelso to Whitton, 10 March 1934, CCSD/38, file 79.

46. In "Autobiographical Files (1864-1935)," MG 30, C97, vol. 1, PAC.

47. Negative comments are found in the following: Scott to Snowden 23 April 1928, MG 30, C27, vol. 13, file 47; Scott to Editor, <u>Juvenile Court Record</u> (Chicago, n.d.), vol. 1, files 1-4; exchange between Scott and Kelso, 9 July 1909, vol. 5; Scott to R. Chadwick, Superintendent of Dependent Children, Alberta, 1 April 1912; Miller to Scott, 18 November 1912; Scott to Kelso, 22 November 1912; and Wright to Scott, 19 May 1924, vol. 2. Also Dymond to Whitton, 26 December 1923, CCSD/26; Margaret E. Anstey to Whitton, 17 July 1930, CCSD/39; and Whitton to MacLachlan, 11 November 1922, CCSD/25. Kelso's Statement in "Notebook: Charity and Child Saving (1907-31)," MG 30, C97, vol. 8, PAC.

48. Typescript (n.d.) but probably 1934, MG 30, C97, vol. 18.

49. Kelso to Scott 9 June 1922, Scott to Kelso, 8 June 1922; and Scott to Kelso, 13 June 1922, MG 30, C27, vol. 2.

50. Kelso to Scott (1922), MG 30, C27, vol. 3.

51. "Report and Recommendations Regarding the Establishment of a Children's Department or Bureau at Ottawa by R. H. Murray, Secretary, NSSPC, and Ernest Blois, Superintendent of Department for Neglected and Dependent Children (1913)," PANS; and Blois to Mrs. William Dennis, Halifax, 26 April 1918, in Papers of Mrs. Minnie (Colin) Campbell (1862-1952), MG 14, C6, file: Child Welfare, PAM.

52. Jane Wisdom to Whitton, 19 November 1940, CCSD/134, file 600.

53. Whitton to O. D. Skelton, Under-Secretary for External Affairs, 2 January 1933, CCSD/2, file 15: League of Nations, 1934. Also see, "Revised Memo Re: The Placement of Children in Family Homes," p. 9, CCSD/67, file: Child Placement 1935-37.

54. Ibid., pp. 4-5.

55. "To the Inter-Organization Group on Child Welfare," 31 March 1930, CCSD/38, file 167; The Royal Commission on Public Welfare Report (1930), especially pp. 49-57, VPL; and Minute, 8 January 1931, Association of CASs of Ontario, PAO. Also see editorial, "Extravagence Charged Against CAS," Social Welfare 9 (November 1926).

56. In pt. IX, "Child Welfare Organizations, Province of Manitoba (1928)," RG 5, G2 box 2, PAM.

57. Br. Barnabas, Housing and Care of the Dependent Child (CCCW, 1924), p. 3; and Fourth Conference of Canadian Child Welfare, (Winnipeg, 1923), pp. 48-49.

58. Ibid., p. 48; and Br. Barnabas, p. 10.

59. "First Principles of Social Work," (1909), MG 30, C27, vol. 6; and also see "Child Saving: Impressions of the National Conference of Charities and Correction, Nashville, May 1894," in which he quoted Dr. Gregg of the Chicago CAS, vol. 4, PAC.

60. Typescript on Orphan Children (n.d.), MG 30, C27, vol. 18.

61. Toronto POH, AR (1866); and Report of Children's Bureau, pp 44-57, in "Welfare Work in Montreal" (1927), MG 28, I 129, vol. 10, PAC.

62. Toronto POH, <u>ARs</u> (1866-71).

63. <u>Protestant Children's Village: One Hundred Years 1864-1964</u>; Kingston POH, Minute, 13 January 1863; and Winnipeg Children's Home, "Visitors' Reports" (January, May, August and November 1905 and April 1906), pp. 13, 22, 32, 39, and 48; and Widows' and Orphans' Asylum, <u>AR</u> (1860), AASJ.

64. Methodist Orphanage, <u>AR</u> (1912), UCSJ; Toronto Boys' Home, <u>37th AR</u> (1897), pp. 11-15; and Toronto POH, Minutes, 8 April 1909 and 13 March 1917.

65. Toronto POH, <u>AR</u> (1871) and Minute, 29 May 1860, MTL; Saint John POH <u>AR</u> (1887), p. 5, AASJ; and Kingston POH, Minute, 10 July 1860, QU.

66. See Kingston POH, <u>ARs</u> (1896 and 1899-1900).

67. Winnipeg Children's Home, Minutes, April 1912, June 1913, 20 February 1919, and August 1919, PAM.

68. Ottawa POH, Minutes, 22 February 1896 and 30 March 1896, MG 28, I37, vol. 3, PAC. Catholic orphanages expressed similar resentment about CASs "dumping" children. For example, Fr. Brueck of St. Patrick's Orphanage, Prince Albert, Saskatchewan, commented that "The city of Prince Albert has a 'dead CAS,' she has no shelter for neglected children simply because the orphanage fills the want and the city has always made use of the orphanage . . . and has dumped children without compensation and we took them to show gratitude for the favour of a tax rebate." Rev. W. Brueck to Mayor Morton, 31 July 1913; and also, City Clerk to City Assessor, in Prince Albert Municipality City Clerk Roll 249, SABS.

69. Kingston, POH, <u>AR</u> (1925).

70. Halifax Protestant Industrial School <u>ARs</u> (1919 and 1916), PANS.

71. Charlottetown CAS, <u>AR</u> (1909), and PEI Survey (1929), CCSD/19, file 80; and London Infants' Home, The Women's Refuge and Children's Home Records, UWO.

72. Winnipeg Children's Home, Minutes, 10 April 1912, and 5 July 1923.

73. Ann Margaret Angus, Fiftieth Anniversary of CAS, Vancouver (1901-51).

74. WP/13 and 18, and CCSD/19, 37 and 39.

75. NB Survey Report, pp. 81-192.

76. Methodist Orphanage, Minute, 1 March 1924, and Committee of Enquiry Report (1921), UCSJ.

77. Br. Barnabas, "Housing and Care of the Dependent Child: A Model Dietary, Appendix A." (CCCW, 1924).

78. "Diamond Jubilee (1914)"; and Welfare Supervision Board, RG5/G2, box 11, file 138, PAM.

79. Toronto POH, Minute, 8 April 1909.

80. Halifax Protestant Industrial School, AR (1926); and Halifax POH, ARs, PANS. Such conditions were common in the Ontario Industrial Schools in 1891, 1916 and 1927. Industrial Schools Association (1884-1934), MU 1409, series B, box 2, file 7 and MU 1410, box 3, file 16, PAO.

81. Letter, City Council to Marshall, 27 June 1848 in Minutes, Hamilton Aged Women's Home, vol. 1, HPL.

82. Kingston Survey (1931), CCSD/45; Kingston POH, AR (1927); and Proceedings of the Third Regional Conference (1948-49), p. 23, Association of CASs of Ontario, box 10, PAO.

83. Toronto Infants' Home, 50th AR (1925).

84. File: Toronto Children's Home (1947), WP/81.

85. Protestant Children's Village, p. 50.

86. Caroline L. Conron, Merrymount Children's Home (1874-1974): A Century in Retrospect (London, 1974), p. 43, UWO.

87. Victoria POH, ARs (1905, 1908, and 1943), PABC.

88. Max G. Baxter, General Superintendent, "New Brunswick POH, Saint John," 5 March 1965, NBM.

89. Methodist Orphanage, ARs (March 18, 1931 to June 12, 1944), UCSJ; and "A Century of Service Ended," The Clerical Caller (June 1979): 19.

90. Charity Organization Bureau (1925-1932), GN 2/5, file 424B, PANF.

91. "Historical Sketch," in Winnipeg Children's Home AR (1935), pp. 13-15, PAM.

92. Kingston, POH, AR (1930), QU.

93. BC Survey Report (1927), p. 13, WP/36.

94. Montreal Ladies Benevolent Society, 112th AR, p. 69, in "Welfare Work in Montreal (1927)," MG 28, I 129, vol. 10, PAC.

95. Kingston, POH, AR (1935), QU.

PART 3 - DISCARDING THE ASYLUM

[9] FROM SENTIMENT TO SCIENCE:
PROFESSIONALIZING CHILD RESCUE

1. Montreal Ladies Benevolent Society in "Welfare Work in Montreal (1927)," 112th AR, p. 69, MG 28 I 129, vol. 10, PAC. All comments on the Montreal Society for the Protection of Women and Children (MSPWC) are under this call number.

2. Roman Catholic views on charity reflected their medieval origins, which consequently explain the quaint nature of their institutions and social services by the twentieth century. William J. Kerby, The Social Mission of Charity (Washington, D.C.: Catholic University of America Press, 1944). For different perspectives on the practical charity and religious motive, see W. K. Jordan, Philanthropy in England, 1480-1660 (London: George Allen & Unwin, 1959); and Natalie Zemon Davis, "Poor Relief, Humanism, and Heresy," Society and Culture in Early Modern France (Stanford: Stanford U.P., 1975).

3. The origins of casework method is usually attributed to the parochial visiting systems. The method was first used in the United States. J. C. Pringle, Social Work in London Churches: An Account of the Metropolitan Visiting and Relief

Association, 1843-1937 (London: Oxford University Press, 1937), pp. 166-67.

4. James S. Woodsworth, My Neighbor: A Study of City Conditions and a Plea for Social Service (Toronto: Missionary Society of the Methodist Church, 1911), pp. 284 and 288-90; Dr. Peter H. Bryce, "National Social Efficiency," in 16th AR of the Canadian Conference on Charities and Correction (1917), MGU; and AR of the Social Service League (1923-24), vol. 18, PABC.

5. MSPWC, Minute, 11 March 1914, Minute Book (Dec. 10, 1913 - Nov. 13, 1918), vol. 3.

6. Charlotte Whitton, "Child Welfare Organizations," MG 28, I 10, vol. 29, file 147, pt. 9, p. 8, PAM.

7. Civic Charities Bureau, 2nd Report (January 10, 1916); Crawford Papers (1903-16), box 1, item 352; and Paget to W. J. Stanbridge, 14 December 1917, box 4, RG5/G2, Welfare Supervision Board, PAM.

8. Charity Organization Bureau, St. John's (1925-32), GN/2/5, file 424B, PANF.

9. Mrs. Ruth Massey Tovell of the Toronto Big Sisters Association described the commission to Mrs. Selley of the Girls' Home as "a chloroform chamber" where all proposals involving public expenditure were "put painlessly to death regardless of the merits of the case." 7 January 1921 in L30 PCH (J), MTL.

10. Winnipeg Children's Home, Minutes, February and June 1913, April 1914, March 1915, June and July 1924, July 1925 and October 1928, MG 10, B24, PAM; and Toronto Girls' Home, Minutes, vol. 7 (M) (1917-24), vol. 3, (1899-1901), and Minute, 29 April 1919, vol. 5 (M) (1909-19), MTL; Kingston Orphans' Home and Widows' Friend Society (1857-1946), Coll. 94, QU; and "Notes on Social Work Abroad," COR (May 1901): 268; and Wood's Christian Home, BJN894, GAA; Winnipeg Children's Home, MG 10, B24, and Federated Budget Board (1928), RG5/62, box 4, file 39, PAM.

11. MSPWC, vols. 1-5.

12. Society for the Protection of Women and Children: A History of Seventy-Five Years' Operations in the Service of the Community (Montreal: Legal Aid Bureau, 1956), pp. 8-9,

PLC; and <u>Annual Meetings</u>, 23 January 1885, 29 January 1886 and 28 January 1887.

13. MSPWC, Minute, 10 December 1883, vol. 1.

14. MSPWC, Minute 27 September 1883.

15. <u>Society for the Protection of Women and Children</u>, pp. 10-11; Minutes, 20 May 1884, 12 March 1889, 24 June 1890, and 13 May 1880; and <u>Annual Meeting</u>, 12 February 1889.

16. For a similar discussion of institutional transformation in the United States, see Jamil S. Zainaldin and Peter L. Tyor, "Asylum and Society: An Approach to Industrial Change," <u>Journal of Social History</u> 13 (Fall 1979): 23-47.

17. Woodsworth typified this belief by preferring voluntary participation in charity organization while insisting that "justice is substituted for charity" only when facilitated by paid social work expertise in leadership roles. "The Canadian Welfare League" (1916), SABR.

18. R. H. Murray and Ernest H. Blois, "Report . . . Regarding the Establishment of a Children's Department or Bureau at Ottawa" (n.d.), PANS; "Federal Child Welfare Bureau, 1916-18," in Campbell Papers, Child Welfare, MG 14, C6, PAM; Billiarde to Scott, 1 November 1916 and 30 November 1916, MG 30, C27, vol. 5, PAC; and F. J. Billiarde, <u>A Brief in Favour of the Establishment of a Canadian Child Welfare Bureau</u> (Winnipeg, March 1918), Hugh Dobson Papers, UCBC. Also see Tamara Haraven's discussion of the CCCW in "An Ambiguous Alliance: Some Aspects of American Influences on Canadian Social Welfare," <u>Social History</u> 3 (April 1969): 82-98.

19. See the following articles on Whitton's career by the authors: "'Making the Way More Comfortable': Charlotte Whitton's Child Welfare Career," <u>Journal of Canadian Studies</u> 17 (Winter 1983); and "'An Idiot's Flowerbed': A Study of Charlotte Whitton's Feminist Thought, 1941-50," <u>International Journal of Women's Studies</u> 5 (January/February 1982): 29-46.

20. Elsie Lawson, Department of Public Welfare, Manitoba to Whitton, 1941, WP/18.

21. Canadian Welfare Council, <u>17th AR</u> (1937); and the statement in the Scott Papers that "The CWC is designed to serve as a nation-wide clearing house in social welfare in the Dominion. It seeks to provide a medium through which the

interested private citizens and the organized social agencies, whether under private or public auspices, can explore and discuss social problems of common concern," MG 30, C27, vol. 14, file 51, PAC.

22. Haraven, pp. 92-94.

23. Lawson to Whitton, 16 May 1939 and Whitton to Davidson, 26 April 1939, WP/18.

24. "Canada and the World's Child Welfare Work (1927)," p. 8, MGU.

25. Ann Margaret Angus, Children's Aid Society of Vancouver, B.C., 1901-1951; Rooke and Schnell, "Child Welfare in Canada" and "The Rise and Decline of Protestant Orphans' Homes and Woman's Domain, 1850-1930," Atlantis 7 (Spring 1982): 21-35; and BC Survey Report, pp. 36-38 and 75-91, and Correspondence, file 20B, WP/34; and CCSD/28.

26. Social Service League/Commission, PABC; and C. J. McNeely, Chairman, BC Survey Committee, to Mrs. Thorburn, President CCCW, 21 June 1927, box 1, file 14, and "The Vancouver Council of Social Agencies," box 13, file 164, RG5/G2, PAM; BC Survey, WP/36 and 18; and "Child Welfare in B. C. (1932)," CCSD/28, file 139.

27. Whitton to Heise, 30 March 1937, discusses her membership, and CASW (1927), file 150, CCSD/30, covers her involvement in recruitment and training; Whitton, "Memorandum," 6 March 1934, WP/18; and "The Social Worker Pleads for Faith (1935)," WP/19.

28. "Private Home Care for Children in Need" (CCCW, 1930), p. 5, PLBC.

29. For a short discussion of the social survey in Great Britain, see Mark Abrams, Social Surveys and Social Action (London: William Heinemann, 1951). An interesting case study of the social survey in early 20th Century America is given in John F. McClymer, War and Welfare: Social Engineering in America, 1890-1925 (Westport, CT: Greenwood Press, 1980).

30. In chronological order, the surveys included: British Columbia (1927); New Brunswick (1929); Fredericton and Saskatoon (1930); Calgary, Victoria, Regina, Winnipeg, Ottawa, Kingston, Quebec, Prince Edward Island, and Brandon (1931-32); Winnipeg and York (1934); Cornwall and Greater

Ottawa (1935); Hamilton (1936); Saskatoon, Hamilton, London, and Smith Falls (1937); Winnipeg, Galt, and Hull (1938); Edmonton and Moncton (1939); Glace Bay (1940); Saint John and Kingston (1941); Winnipeg (1942); Calgary and Brantford (1944-45); Alberta (1947); Hamilton, Moose Jaw, and Saskatoon (1948); and New Brunswick (1949). For costs, see "List of Surveys" (1940), CCSD/132. The following volumes contain reports and correspondence regarding the surveys: CCSD/18-19, 21, 28-29, 43 and 132-136, and WP/1-2, 4, 21, and 36.

31. Canadian Welfare News 2 (November 15, 1926).

32. Ottawa Survey, CCSD/28, file 143, pp. 6, 3 and 23. The CCCW conducted further Greater Ottawa Surveys in 1932 and 1935 (CCSD/28 and WP/21).

33. Whitton to Abramson, 1931, NB Survey, CCSD/38, file 167.

34. Times-Globe, 29 October 1930; King to Whitton, 23 March 1929; and Whitton to King, 26 March 1929; CCSD/19; and Whitton to Dorothy King, 6 October 1931, WP/6, file 5.

35. Montgomery to Whitton, 10 October 1930; Whitton to Montgomery, 13 October 1930 and 23 May 1930, MG 28, I 10, vol. 29, file 147; also "Confidential Memo Re Personnel, Department of Public Welfare, Manitoba (1928)," MG 28, I 10, vol. 19; and "Report of the Royal Commission of Child Welfare Division, Manitoba (1928)," RG5/G2, box 2, PAM.

36. Lion's Gate Gazette, 17 March 1928, in Social Service League, vol. 18; and Rev. Menzies, Department of Neglected Children, to A. C. Bayley, 16 March 1928, file: CAS (Vancouver) and Assorted Papers, PABC.

37. Hugh Dobson to Mutchmor, Secretary, of the Winnipeg Welfare Supervision Board, 20 July 1933, RG5/G2, box 12, and Mutchmor to CASW, 20 February 1931, box 1, PAM. While Secretary to the Board of Evangelism, Mutchmor's relations with Whitton remained cool, WP/4 (January-March and April-June, 1942).

38. Harvey to Davidson, 29 April 1940 and 6 December 1939, and Whitton to Harvey correspondence in "Overseas Children" (1939-40), unprocessed, Child Welfare materials, PABC.

39. See "Charlotte Whitton Meets 'The Last Best West.'"

40. See "Aid to Dependent Mothers and Children in Canada: Social Policy Behind Legislation" (1931), CCSD/2; and "Report of a Committee Appointed by the Government to Investigate the Finances of BC," pp. 36-39, 12 July 1932, RG5/G2, file 9, PAM. Also see correspondence to Mr. Usher Miller, 20 March 1930, CCSD/38, file 167. Whitton's social philosophy has been elaborated by the authors in "Women as Social Reformers: Charlotte Whitton," a paper presented at the Fourth Bi-Annual Conference on Social Policy, Carleton University, April 1981.

41. Lion's Gate Gazette (Vancouver), 17 March 1928.

42. The Orange Home, Manitoba, was incorporated in 1921 and the Indian Head Home, Saskatchewan, in 1923, RG5/G2, box 10, file 124, PAM, and the Orange Benevolent Society, "Twenty-Five Years of Guarding Canada's Greatest Asset," 1948, SABR. Alfred A. Sinnott, Archbishop of Winnipeg, had insisted that Catholic institutions were preferable to boarding children, Sinnott to W. A. Weston, CAS, 3 March 1931. Whitton subsequently sent Weston copies of "Introduction to Social Work" by Father O'Grady, editor of Catholic Charities Review and professor of sociology at Catholic University of America, and of "Foster Homes Versus Institutional Care" by Mother Austina, St. Mary's Home, Nova Scotia, MG 28, I 10, vol. 29, file 147, PAM. Holland refers to similar problems in correspondence to Whitton, 13 July 1933, WP/18.

43. "Canadian Calvacade (1935)," WP/2, p. 1.

44. In support of her social views, Whitton was able to reconcile some rather strange government-CWC relationships. Patricia T. Rooke and R. L. Schnell, "R. B. Bennett Privatizes Child Welfare: The Elimination of the Dominion Child Welfare Division, 1932-1937," typescript (Calgary, Alta., 1983).

45. The ideas and activities of such "new light" social welfare advocates as Harry M. Cassidy, George F. Davidson, and Leonard C. Marsh place them clearly in the Progressive tradition of North American politics. For a discussion of the Liberal Establishment's ability to assimilate such ideas, see J. T. Granatstein, "Public Welfare and Party Benefit," Canada's War: The Politics of the MacKenzie King Government, 1939-1945 (Toronto: Oxford U.P., 1975), pp. 249-293; and The Ottawa Men: The Civil Service Mandarins, 1935-1957 (Toronto: Oxford U.P., 1982), pp. 134-168.

46. For traditional Roman Catholic social thought, see Joseph N. Moody, ed., Church and Society: Catholic Social and Political Thought and Movements, 1789-1950 (New York: Arts, 1953).

47. "Threat to Liberty Clearly Seen in Central Welfare Control," Saturday Night, 12 April 1949.

48. Calgary Herald, 18 February 1944.

49. CCSD/135, p. 12.

50. See New Brunswick (1929), WP/36 and CCSD/36-38, and 19; Saint John (1941), WP/4 and CCSD/132 and 134; New Brunswick (1948), CCSD/136; and New Brunswick (1949), CCSD/135, and RA 360/136, SJCL; Moncton (1939), CCSD/132 and 134; and CCSD/132, pp. 27-29.

51. Whitton to Harvey, 27 March 1943, WP/4, file (Correspondence January-August 1943).

52. CCSD/132, pp. 10-11, and Moncton Survey (1939), CCSD/132, pp. 27-30, PAC.

53. CCSD/135, p. 62; and Whitton to Harvey, 27 March 1943, WP/4.

54. William E. Hart, "A Brief Concerning Child Welfare in New Brunswick (1948)," CCSD/135; and Mary Carpenter, "What Shall We Do With Our Pauper Children?" p. 6 and "A Letter Re the Charges of the Bristol Guardians to the Editors of the Bristol Daily Post and the Western Daily Post," 10 October 1861 (Bristol, 1861), p. 20.

55. WP/36, pp. 183-184.

56. Moncton Survey (1939), CCSD/132, and Whitton to Harvey, 27 March 1943. Also see CCSD/36, pp. 174-176, and CCSD/136, pp. 126-129.

57. CCSD/135, pp. 126-127.

58. CCSD/135, p. 117; and Whitton to A. M. Belding, Saint John, 12 March 1929, CCSD/37.

59. CCSD/135, pp. 108-111.

60. WP/36, pp. 163-165.

61. WP/36, p. 171.

62. CCSD/135, pp. 95-104; and WP/36, pp. 22 and
151-161.

63. CCSD/135, p. 100.

64. WP/36, p. 47.

65. CCSD/135, p. 103.

66. Whitton to King 7 November 1928 and 14 November
1928, and King to Whitton 9 November 1928, CCSD/37.

67. Whitton to King, 7 November 1928 and 14 November
1928, CCSD/37.

68. Whitton, "Alberta's Confused Welfare Picture (1948),
WP/34; and Rebecca Coulter, "Alberta's Department of
Neglected Children, 1904-1929: A Case Study in Child
Saving," (M.Ed. Thesis, University of Alberta, 1977), and
"'Not to Punish But to Reform': Juvenile Delinquency and
Children's Protection Act in Alberta, 1909-1929," in Studies in
Childhood History: A Canadian Perspective, ed. Patricia T.
Rooke and R. L . Schnell (Calgary: Detselig Enterprises,
1982), pp. 157-184.

69. Whitton to Children's Service Society, Utah, 27
March 1947, WP/21; and also in Commission of Inquiry Report,
3 December 1948, pp. 19-21, WP/34.

70. Thomson to Whitton, 28 June 1940 and 5 September
1940, WP/18. Thomson was brought to Saskatoon in 1931 from
New York Settlement Work on Whitton's recommendation,
CCSD/26.

71. WP/18 and WP/21.

72. "Survey of Private Community Welfare Services in
the City of Calgary (1944)," pp. 111-112, CCSD/132.

73. Ibid., pp. 103-106; and p. 121.

74. The Alberta School Trustee (March 1947): 23-26.
'Daisy' Marshall and Whitton had been friends through their
mutual involvement in the IODE. Whitton was a favored
daughter of the organization. Whitton to Marshall, 8 November
1946 and also 16 April 1945 and 11 December 1945, and
Marshall to Whitton 2 May 1945 and 26 September 1945, WP/31.

75.   Manning to Whitton, 10 March 1945, and Whitton to Manning 26 March 1945, WP/4; and correspondence in Premiers' Papers, file 1378, PAA.   Also, interviews with Cross and Manning, 15 January 1947, and 23 January 1947, WP/32, and Whitton to Marshall, 11 December 1945 and 16 April 1945, and Marshall to Whitton, 2 May 1945, WP/31.

76.   "Determined Woman," Time (4 August 1947):   17.

77.   Manning to Rev. Canon F. E. Smith, Peace River, 3 September 1946, Premiers' Papers, file 1296, PAA.

78.   "Children in Iron Cages," and Calgary Herald, 22, 23, 24, and 26 April 1947.   The IODE published A Report on a Report (1949) which discussed the charges contained in the 1947 report.   Calgary Herald, 31 December 1948, discussed the Commission findings and the IODE Report, while on 12 January 1948 Drayton's view on the whipping of boys had been recorded.   Whitton called the trial "a fantastic persecution" in a letter to Rev. Frank Morley, Grace Presbyterian Church, Calgary, 14 February 1948, WP/31.

79.   See "Survey in Alberta," by W. R. Clarke in Regina Leader Post, 6 June 1947, who referred to Alberta's "high minded authoritarianism."

80.   "Let Love Not Science Rule Adoption," 9 December 1944; "Adoption of 12,000 Babies," 18 September 1945; and "Let the Child Know the Facts," 11 December 1944, Toronto Daily Star.

81.   "For and About Cynthia," WP/32.

82.   Calgary Herald, 26 April 1947.

83.   See, Report on the Child Welfare Branch, 3 December 1948; and "Autocratic Handling of Children in Alberta," WP/34; Welfare in Alberta (IODE, 1947) was later revised to become A Report on a Report (IODE: 1949), WP/32.

84.   Correspondence surrounding the briefs and Commission are in WP/37.

85.   Albertan, 13 December 1948, and "Memorandum" (1948), WP/32.

86.   Report on the Child Welfare Branch, p. 35.

87. Kennedy to Manning, 22 January 1948, and Adams to Manning, 23 January 1948, Premiers' Papers, file 1716; and also see the correspondence in file 1378, PAA.

88. The Albertan, 29 January 1947.

89. Whitton to Child Welfare Division, Montana, 13 January 1947, WP/31.

90. "Babies for Export," p. 6. For her defence, Whitton wrote several careful and informative research papers: "Legislation . . . and Other Measures Relative to Children in the USSR," "Comparison of Centralized Bureaucracy in Child Protection and Care in Alberta with Nazi Germany and the USSR," and "Provisions on Guardianship . . . in Pre-Nazi and Nazi Germany" (February-March, Ottawa, 1948), WP/32. For charges of authoritarianism, centralism, and bureaucratization, see the editorial pages of the Winnipeg Free Press in August 1947, which were subsequently reprinted as "Welfare in Alberta," Winnipeg Free Press, Pamphlet no. 17, WP/37; W. R. Clarke, "Survey in Alberta," Regina Leader Post, 6 June 1947. The Report on Child Welfare Branch rejected her claims regarding excessive bureaucratization, pp. 41-42. Whitton To Dr. Janet Clark, College of Women, University of Rochester, 27 February 1948, said that the government was "tainted with authoritarianism," WP/31.

91. Report on the Child Welfare Branch, pp. 34-35.

92. Canada, Debates of the House of Commons, 28 April 1947. Emotions aroused by Whitton's survey are still evident today as indicated by a letter from Mr. Hugh Peck in response to the article in Alberta History. Despite his sincere defense of Charles Hill, Mr. Peck's description of his experience in adopting a child through Hill's office simply confirmed Whitton's accusation regarding the lack of scientific professional adoption practices in the province. Hugh Peck to Schnell and Rooke, 22 March 1982.

[10] STATE AS ASYLUM

1. J. Donald Wilson, "Historiographical perspectives on Canadian Educational History: A Review Essay," Journal of Educational Thought 11 (April 1977): 49-63; and J. Stewart Hardy, "A Review of Selected Materials in the Educational History of Western Canada: Opportunities for Further Study," ibid. 14 (August 1980): 64-79.

2. See, for example, Andrew T. Scull Museums of Madness (New York: St. Martin's Press, 1979); and Michael B. Katz, Class, Bureaucracy, and Schools (New York: Frederick A. Praeger, 1971).

3. M. G. Jones, The Charity School Movement (London: Frank Cass, 1964); and Carl F. Kaestle, ed., Joseph Lancaster and the Monitorial School Movement (New York: Teachers College Press, 1973).

4. Ernst Cassirer, The Question of Jean-Jacques Rousseau (Bloomington: Indiana University Press, 1963); John F. C. Harrison, ed., Utopianism and Education (New York: Teachers College Press, 1968).

5. David J. Rothman, Conscience and Convenience (Boston: Little, Brown, 1980), places the individualization of treatment in the United States in the Progressive Era.

6. The best discussion of the "well-ordered asylum" is David J. Rothman, The Discovery of the Asylum.

7. See, for example, Lloyd deMause, "The Evolution of Childhood," History of Childhood Quarterly 1 (Spring 1974): 503-575; Michael B. Katz and Ian E. Davey, "Youth and Early Industrialization in a Canadian City," in Turning Points, ed. John Demos and Sarane Spence Boocock (Chicago: University of Chicago Press, 1978), pp. 581-591; and R. L. Schnell, "Childhood as Ideology," British Journal of Educational Studies 27 (February 1979): 7-28.

8. For a discussion of apprenticeship as education, see H. I. Manou, A History of Education in Antiquity (New York: Sheed & Ward, 1956).

9. Roy Lubove, The Professional Altruist (Cambridge: Harvard U.P., 1965); and Kathleen Woodroofe, From Charity to Social Work (Toronto: University of Toronto Press, 1971).

10. "Aid to Dependent Mothers and Children in Canada: Social Policy Behind our Legislation" (1931), p. 14, CCSD/2.

11. Charlotte Whitton, "Progress Report," Canadian Conference on Child Welfare, 1925, p. 61.

12. Robert M. Stamp, "Canadian High Schools in the 1920s and 1930s: The Social Challenge to the Academic Tradition," in CHA Historical Papers (Ottawa: CHA, 1978), pp. 76-93.

13. Harvey G. Simmons, From Asylum to Welfare (Downsview, Ontario: National Institute on Mental Retardation, 1982).

14. See, for example, Mary Carpenter, Reformatory Schools (London: C. Gilpin, 1851).

15. H. Blair Neatby, The Politics of Chaos: Canada in the Thirties (Toronto: University of Toronto Press, 1972).

16. James Struthers, "A Profession in Crisis: Charlotte Whitton and Canadian Social Work in the 1930s," Canadian Historial Review 62 (June 1981): 169-185.

17. Report of the Royal Commission on Dominion-Provincial Relations (Ottawa: King's Printer 1940), II: 125.

18. Dennis Guest, The Emergence of Social Security in Canada (Vancouver: University of British Columbia Press, 1980).

19. Charlotte Whitton, "Health Services for the Canadian People," The Bulletin, No. 115 (June 15, 1944): 2-12.

20. George F. Davidson, "Family Allowances: An Instalment on Social Security," Part II, Welfare (September 1944): 10; and "Family Allowances," Part III, Welfare (October 1944): 15-17.

21. "The Challenge of Relief Control" (March 1934), WP/19; Davidson, "Family Allowances," Part II, p. 10; and Dorothy H. Stepler, "Family Allowances for Canada?" Behind the Headlines 3 (1943): 5-6.

22. C. E. Silcox, The Revenge of the Cradles (Toronto: The Ryerson Press, 1945).

index

Rutter, Michael, 155

St. Antoine's Home, 198
St. Catherine's Orphan Home, 85
St. George's Home, 198, 259
Saint John Haven and Rescue Work, 95
Saint John POH, 160, 161, 165, 325, 371
St. John's Child Welfare Association, 325
St. John's POH, 74, 78, 99 110-111, 142, 159, 166, 175, 312, 320
St. Joseph's Home (B.C.), 259
St. Joseph's Orphanage, 144
St. Patrick's Orphan Asylum (Ottawa), 144
St. Patrick's Orphanage (Halifax), 259
St. Patrick's Orphanage (Prince Albert), 259
St. Paul's Almshouse of Industry, 94, 95, 103
St. Vincent's Orphanage, 291, 317
Salvation Army, 226, 250, 264
Sargison, Mrs. G.A., 105
Schnell, R.L., 8
School training, 48, 159-161, 164-177, 392-393; and childhood, 16, 20, 58, 67, 75-76, 90. See also Orphan schools; Schools of industry
Schools of industry, 42, 48-49, 67, 74
Scientific charity, 50-53, 56, 178, 264, 273, 321-322, 337-341, 346, 352, 361, 386, 399-400. See also Social welfare; Social work; Professionalization; Charity organization
Scott, W.L., 4, 7, 292-293, 300, 302-303. See also juvenile delinquents
Sedgewick, Reverend, W.H., 13-14

Senior, Mrs. Nassau, 194, 206, 207, 246
Serial contamination, 118, 120-122, 159, 310-314, 317-318, 321. See also Epidemics
Sherbourne Home, 362
Smart, G. Bogue, 215, 231, 250, 255
Social Service Council of Canada (SSCC), 248, 294, 349
Social work, 253-254, 263-264, 268-269, 288, 327, 362-363, 375, 399-401, 405-406. See also Scientific charity; Social welfare; Professionalization; Child welfare
Society for Promoting Education and Industry Among the Indians and Destitute Settlers in Canada, 48, 74, 391
South, Mr., 292-293
State welfare, 408-413. See also Social welfare; Child welfare
Stierlin, John, 156-157
Sunnyside Centre, 323. See also Kingston POH
Surveys, Alberta, 374-385; British Columbia, 352-353; New Brunswick, 366-374. See also CCCW; Whitton, Charlotte
Sutherland, Neil, 4, 7

Thomson, Lillian, 376
Thorburn, Mrs. Charles, 262, 264
Thorburn, Mrs. Maria, 104-105
Toronto Boys' Home, 86, 87, 92, 175, 185-186, 187, 259, 313, 320
Toronto Girls' Home, 86, 87, 113, 149-150, 152-154, 162-163, 165-166, 172, 324
Toronto House of Industry, 36, 61, 78-81, 130, 144, 186
Toronto Industrial Farm, 36
Toronto Infants' Home and Infirmary, 106, 108, 117-118, 120-124, 126, 129, 323
Toronto Orphan Asylum, 61, 74, 81-83, 87, 104, 106, 110, 142,

the authors

PATRICIA ROOKE

Patricia Rooke received a Ph.D. from the University of Alberta and has published major articles on West Indian slavery and missionary education in such journals as Caribbean Quarterly, Caribbean Studies, the Journal of Religious History and Baptist Quarterly. Her original training was in teacher education at Melbourne Teachers' College, Australia. In 1978 she moved into the teaching and research of childhood history and has published extensively in this area. She is presently researching with R. L. Schnell a biography called "What the Devil Can't Do a Woman Can: Charlotte Whitton's Social Welfare Career." Editor of the Journal of Educational Thought since 1981, she is currently editing a special issue, "Women's Studies and Higher Education." She is visiting and assistant professor at the University of Calgary and has an honorary appointment with the University of Alberta.

R. L. SCHNELL

R. L. Schnell received a Ph.D. from the University of Michigan published as a monograph, National Activist Student Organizations in American Higher Education 1905-44. He taught in the history and education departments of the University of Detroit before taking up an appointment with the University of Calgary in 1964. He is Professor and Head of the Department of Educational Policy and Administrative Studies at the University of Calgary. He teaches childhood history to education students and has published extensively in journals such as British Journal of Educational Studies, Paedagogica Historica, Canadian Review of American Studies, Psychological Reports and the Irish Journal of Education. Co-authored articles have been published on Canadian childhood in Social History, The Historian, the Journal of Canadian Studies and the Journal of Psychohistory. With his wife, Patricia Rooke, he is currently researching a biography on Charlotte Whitton.

497